CHEAP BIBLES

This study of the publishing programme of the British and Foreign Bible Society between 1804 and 1864, based on correspondence and other archival records, demonstrates that the Society's demand for Bibles, generated by the development of Bible distribution as a popular evangelical crusade, placed significant pressure on the contemporary book trades. Earlier historians have regarded the BFBS solely as a religious phenomenon, but this is to ignore the way the Society refused to engage in theological debate and expended most of its funds on Bible manufacture: it was simultaneously a publisher and a Victorian social institution.

The book is of interest to historians of the book publishing and printing trades, of nineteenth-century Christian institutions and missionary enterprises, and of nineteenth-century society in general.

CAMBRIDGE STUDIES IN
PUBLISHING AND PRINTING HISTORY

GENERAL EDITORS

Terry Belanger and David McKitterick

TITLES PUBLISHED

*The Provincial Book Trade in
Eighteenth-Century England*
by John Feather
Lewis Carroll and the House of Macmillan
edited by Morton N. Cohen & Anita Gandolfo
The Correspondence of Robert Dodsley 1733–1764
edited by James E. Tierney
Book Production and Publication in Britain 1375–1475
edited by Jeremy Griffiths and Derek Pearsall
*Before Copyright: the French Book-Privilege
System 1486–1526*
by Elizabeth Armstrong
The Making of Johnson's Dictionary, 1746–1773
by Allen Reddick
*Cheap Bibles: nineteenth-century publishing and
the British and Foreign Bible Society*
by Leslie Howsam

TITLES FORTHCOMING

*The Commercialization of the Book in
Britain 1745–1814*
by James Raven

CHEAP BIBLES

NINETEENTH-CENTURY PUBLISHING AND THE BRITISH AND FOREIGN BIBLE SOCIETY

LESLIE HOWSAM

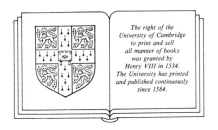

The right of the
University of Cambridge
to print and sell
all manner of books
was granted by
Henry VIII in 1534.
The University has printed
and published continuously
since 1584.

CAMBRIDGE UNIVERSITY PRESS

CAMBRIDGE

NEW YORK   PORT CHESTER

MELBOURNE   SYDNEY

Published by the Press Syndicate of the Unviersity of Cambridge
The Pitt Building, Trumpington Street, Cambridge CB2 1RP
40 West 20th Street, New York, NY 10011, USA
10 Stamford Road, Oakleigh, Melbourne 3166, Australia

First published 1991

Printed in Great Britain at the University Press, Cambridge

British Library cataloguing in publication data
Howsam, Leslie
Cheap Bibles – (Cambridge Studies in Publishing and Printing History.)
1. Bible societies. British and Foreign Bible Society, history
I. Title
220.0601

Library of Congress cataloguing in publication data
Howsam, Leslie.
Cheap Bibles: nineteenth-century publishing and the British and Foreign
Bible Society/Leslie Howsam.
p.   cm. – (Cambridge studies in publishing and printing history)
Includes bibliographical references and index.
ISBN 0 521 39339 6 (hardback)
1. British and Foreign Bible Society.
2. Bible – Publication and distribution – Great Britain.
3. Publishers and publishing – Great Britain – History – 19th century.
I. Title.   II. Series.
BV2370.B8H69   1991
070.5'0941'09034 – dc20   90-21900 CIP

ISBN 0 521 39339 6 hardback

CE

To Neil

The Devil trembles when he sees
Bibles sold as cheaply as these.

                              Popular couplet

Bibles are never *cheap*, so long
            as they could be sold *cheaper*.
                    Congregational Magazine (1833)

CONTENTS

ILLUSTRATIONS

TABLES

PREFACE

'Light postage, quick transit, cheap Bibles and cheap Periodicals, for the Millions of England!' John Campbell's list of popular necessities evokes the atmosphere of early-Victorian times with disconcerting precision: all of the items but one are familiar components of our image of the period. These years – he was writing in 1845 – were the age of the penny post, of popular journalism, and above all of the railway.[1] But the equal importance of cheap Bibles to the early Victorians has faded from memory. That nineteenth-century Britain was deeply attached to its Bible as the source-book of Protestant Christianity is well known; the text did not, however, enter the minds and hearts of its readers without the mediation of publishers and printers. The nature of Bibles as physical artifacts, and the social and political forces affecting their circulation, constitute a neglected chapter of nineteenth-century history. This book deals with the most important aspect of that subject, the history of the British and Foreign Bible Society as a publisher.[2]

Founded in 1804, the British and Foreign Bible Society eschewed doctrinal issues as much as possible, and concentrated its energies on publishing books. The cheap Bible, its best seller and indeed the only title on its list, in numerous formats and a multitude of languages, was the Society's *raison d'être* and its product. The BFBS believed that no barrier – of language, of cost or of supply – should stand between readers and the means of salvation. They were convinced that individuals could be changed, and social and political systems thereby transformed, by offering scriptures for sale to the literate in their own language. The ideal of the cheap Bible became a commonplace in the Victorian years, and Bible Society subscribers supported an ambitious project of translating and distributing scriptures to heathens and catholics abroad, as well as to Britons of all social classes. This was the 'simple object' that many hoped would transform the world. Instead, over a period of about sixty years, the programme transformed the contemporary printing and binding trades, and institutionalized the Bible Society as a fact of Victorian life.

This publishing venture was inspired and informed by the revival of 'serious' or 'vital religion' that invaded and transformed nineteenth-century British churches and homes, and eventually the national public morality.

Evangelical logic was simple: since the scriptures held the key to salvation, it was up to serious Christians to make them widely available, in English and translated into foreign languages, at affordable prices, in appropriate formats. Such was the duty of human agency: the Bible text would do the rest. And while Protestant Christians agreed on the divinity of the scriptures, they disagreed passionately on questions of interpretation. So it was that while religious impulses motivated the Society and its members, the potentially divisive discourse of doctrine and denomination was rigorously excluded from its day-to-day operation.

The popular evangelicalism of the Bible Society idea meant that rather poor people, as well as middling and very rich ones, were involved, not merely as consumers but as distributors of books. The structure was decentralized, with local Auxiliaries established in large and small towns, and subsidiary 'Associations' in both rural and urban neighbourhoods. Their purpose was to provide Bibles in English for the poor and working-class people of Britain, by means of soliciting and then collecting subscription payments for Bibles and New Testaments. There was considerable interest in the political significance of these local societies, particularly during the early years of the Society, which coincided with a period of working-class unrest and fears that a parallel of the French revolution might occur in Britain. Moreover these local bodies were almost always organized and operated by women, so that ideas about appropriate behaviour for middle-class 'ladies' were being challenged at the same time as the poor were being offered cheap Bibles in place of economic or political advantages.

The cheapness of cheap Bibles was relative. Wealthy subscribers bespoke for the objects of their charity a very austere product, the calf-bound Bible printed on cheap paper. The cover, and sometimes the pages, of this kind of book bore the so-called charity brand: 'sold at a loss for schools and the poor'. For themselves, subscribers preferred the attractive roan-bound, gilt-edged product of the book trades: what John Sutherland calls 'that attractive Victorian thing, "a cheap luxury"'.[3]

As publisher of these desirable products, the BFBS was involved with the printers, typefounders, papermakers and bookbinders of London and the provinces. When the project began in 1804, the book trades could not keep up with the demand: there was not enough paper, printing was too slow, and too often books were bound volume by volume, not in whole editions. All this changed by the mid-nineteenth century, and the Bible Society was an important impetus for the transformation of the book trades: the development of stereotype, of machine printing and papermaking, and of mechanized processes at the binding shop. But because the Society was also a social entity, few of these changes were allowed to pass without comment, and the moral aspects of, for example, sweated labour at the bookbinders were considered to be within the purview of any member of the organization.

Preface

The British and Foreign Bible Society was part of the fabric of nineteenth-century culture. The Society was an institution, like visiting cards and chaperonage, or like the printed *Parliamentary Debates*, and Blackwood's in Edinburgh – both publishing projects founded with the Society in 1804. Like Sunday Schools and charity bazaars, it was taken for granted.[4] This state of affairs, I believe, resulted from the way the Society handled the commercial and cultural relations of publishing. The Society was a voluntary organization, whose mission was the process by which books were financed, produced and distributed in Britain and abroad. Its project was organized around Bibles as books, as artifacts constructed of ink and paper, leather and glue, by skilled tradespeople and published in a commercial market-place. And it is the books, with the records of their production, that remain as documentary evidence. In this sense, the present book is an exercise in the history of the book, or historical bibliography, the subject that D. F. McKenzie calls the sociology of texts.

Bibliography is the study of books as physical objects, and much can be learned from close examination and comparison of their design, typography, paper and binding. Furthermore, as McKenzie has reminded us, the physical object is also a cultural object. In his Panizzi lectures at the British Library in 1985 (published there in 1986) McKenzie spoke of 'the full range of social realities which the medium of print had to serve, from receipt blanks to bibles'. He added that the notion of books as social entities 'also directs us to consider the human motives and interactions which texts involve at every stage of their production, transmission and consumption. It alerts us to the roles of institutions, and their own complex structures, in affecting the forms of social discourse, past and present.'[5] The present study concerns the human motives that inspired the evangelical enthusiasts of the British and Foreign Bible Society to publish Bibles for the whole world, and the interactions that ensued when their project became part of the fabric of social discourse. And as an artifact of late twentieth-century interdisciplinary scholarship and publishing practice, it is evidence of our culture's renewed interest in the history of the book in society.

SOURCES AND ACKNOWLEDGEMENTS

The materials for a study of the Bible Society as publisher are to be found in the Society's own archives, scrupulously preserved through the years and now deposited in the keeping of the Cambridge University Library. I was introduced to these archives by Michael Collie, whose talent for discovering repositories of manuscript material and rewarding subjects for research is legendary. He helped me to think about how the publishing records, hitherto unresearched, could be used to illuminate the history of books and, both as teacher and as colleague, initiated me into the study of books as historical objects. Even before visiting the archives I benefited from the advice and generous assistance of Kathleen Cann, the Society's former archivist. Both in London and in Cambridge, as well as by post, she tirelessly tracked down the documents she knew I would like to see. I also thank Alan Jesson, the Society's Librarian at Cambridge, for his help, especially with illustrations, and I acknowledge the generosity of the Society itself for making its records open to researchers. A brochure on the collection is offered to the public as No. 15 of the Cambridge University Library's *Guide to Reader Services*.

Because printers' records are notoriously scarce, the existence and easy accessibility of the archives of the Cambridge University Press have been especially useful. I acknowledge the help of E. S. Leedham-Green, and thank the Syndics of the Cambridge University Library, the Syndics of the University Press, and the Keeper of the University Archives for permission to use them. Many (although not all) of these records have been published on microfilm by Chadwyck-Healey Ltd. The staff of the Manuscript Room and the Anderson Room of the University Library have been uniformly helpful. For material from the Ranyard collection I acknowledge the assistance of the Corporation of London, Greater London Record Office. St Bride's Printing Library provided me with copies of the *Bookbinders' Circular*.

This project began in 1983 at York University in Toronto, with research for a PhD dissertation in the Graduate Programme in History, under the supervision of Albert Tucker. I am grateful for his guidance and for that of Nicholas Rogers and Ian Gentles. J. M. Robson, University Professor in the University of Toronto, has generously supported from the beginning my investigation of the history of the book as an interdisciplinary subject in Victorian studies. The dissertation was entitled 'The Bible Transaction: A

xvi

Publishing History of the British and Foreign Bible Society, 1804–1864', and defended in 1988. My doctoral work was supported by the Social Sciences and Humanities Research Council of Canada, in a Doctoral Fellowship for 1986–7 (number 452-86-0630), and by the Ontario Graduate Scholarship program, in 1985–6 and 1987–8. I received a Research Fellowship in 1986 from the Bibliographical Society of America, which permitted an extended research trip to Cambridge during that summer. Since then the project has expanded to incorporate additional material, notably the printing in London of foreign-language Bibles and their distribution by a global network of missionaries. The business of resuming the research and expanding the scope of the project for publication in the series Cambridge Studies in Publishing and Printing History would not have been possible without the advice and support of David McKitterick. I am also most grateful for the counsel of Michael Black.

Neil Campbell and Jessica Kamphorst have provided the encouragement and support that only a family can, and I can't think of any way they could have done it better.

ABBREVIATIONS

BFBS	British and Foreign Bible Society
Canton	William Canton, *A History of the British and Foreign Bible Society.* 5 vols. London: John Murray, 1904–10
CB	BFBS Archives. Correspondence Book
DepMin	BFBS Archives. Minutes of Depository Subcommittee
FCIn	BFBS Archives. Foreign Correspondence Incoming
FCOut	BFBS Archives. Foreign Correspondence Outgoing
GenMin	BFBS Archives. Minutes of the General Committee
HCIn	BFBS Archives. Home Correspondence Incoming
HCOut	BFBS Archives. Home Correspondence Outgoing
Historical Catalogue	A. S. Herbert, *Historical Catalogue of Printed Editions of the English Bible 1525–1961. Revised and expanded from the Edition of T. H. Darlow and H. F. Moule, 1903* (London and New York: BFBS and ABS, 1968) and T. H. Darlow and H. F. Moule *Historical Catalogue of the Printed Editions of Holy Scripture in the Library of the British and Foreign Bible Society* vol. 2 *Polyglots and Languages other than English* (London: BFBS, 1903–11).
RTS	Religious Tract Society
SPCK	Society for Promoting Christian Knowledge
SubMin	BFBS Archives. Minutes of Subcommittees

1 · SAINTS IN PUBLISHING

I𝗇 𝗍𝗁𝖾 𝖺𝗎𝖽𝗂𝖾𝗇𝖼𝖾 𝖼𝗁𝖺𝗆𝖻𝖾𝗋 𝖺𝗍 𝗐𝗂𝗇𝖽𝗌𝗈𝗋 𝖼𝖺𝗌𝗍𝗅𝖾, the young Queen Victoria is making a formal presentation. She offers 'the Secret of England's Greatness' to the black man, perhaps an African prince, who kneels at her feet. He reaches up to accept her gift, a Bible. Both monarchs are magnificently dressed; so is the book, a quarto edition, thick and heavy, bound in fine leather and embellished with metal clasps. Prince Albert, Viscount Palmerston, Lord John Russell and a lady-in-waiting look on. The artist was T. Jones Barker: his work, painted about 1861 and now hanging in the National Portrait Gallery, is an icon of the cultural imperialism of the Victorian age. A gracious monarch offers the hope of salvation, accompanied by the promise of economic and political advancement. At the same time a moral rationale is suggested for Britain's pre-eminence in world trade and commerce. This painting (reproduced in figure 1) captures in a powerful way the 'Victorian cult of the Bible',[1] the popular obsession with scripture translation, with Bible format, and with the political potentialities inherent in the charitable distribution of scriptural texts.

It is not too fanciful to recast the Barker painting in terms of the social reality, rather than the Royal fiction. In place of the Queen might stand the large number of her subjects who were members of local Bible Societies, collecting funds for scriptures to be translated and distributed worldwide. The recipient has a double identity. He represents first the foreign heathen, slave and free, who were deemed to stand in need of immediate salvation. But the Society's objects were British as well as Foreign: the 'secret' is also conveyed to the English working class. The anonymous lady-in-waiting is a reminder that 'British ladies' were significantly involved in the great project. The Prince Consort and politicians, standing discreetly in the background, may be put in place of the Secretaries and officers of the Bible Society's London headquarters, the 'men at Earl Street' who managed both foreign and domestic Bible distribution. And the luxurious book becomes the plain, strongly bound cheap Bible circulated by the British and Foreign Bible Society.

The painting is a compelling example of the iconography of Bibles,[2] but by no means a reliable guide to the past. It portrays the Bible transaction in terms of a gift, not a purchase, and as a unique occurrence, not a continuous

Figure 1 Queen Victoria presenting a Bible in the
Audience Chamber at Windsor, by T. Jones Barker *c.*
1861.

process: the relationship between giver and receiver is static, condescending, *de haut en bas*. But a static, merely charitable, Bible Society might well have failed. The BFBS 'secret' was its dynamic character. The London Committee recruited individuals experienced in commercial transactions of many kinds, as well as politicians, lawyers and diplomats. As new groups of professionals emerged and became a force in the larger society they were brought into the Bible Society. And in local Auxiliaries, large numbers of ordinary middle-class members – 37,500 by 1832–created a way to involve the English poor in their own salvation, and even to make them pay for it, by inviting their participation in the mission to 'biblicize' the heathen.[3]

The dynamic nature of the BFBS can best be characterized as a 'Bible transaction', a complex set of relations that were commercial, personal, philanthropic and cultural. The transaction was inescapably commercial, based upon the purchase and resale of printed books. But its importance was characterized by contemporaries in terms that transcended the cash nexus. The Bible transaction was conceived as a personal relation, too, involving face-to-face encounters between people. Despite the commercial aspect, it was also philanthropic, because charitable funds underwrote the low retail prices that were charged to the Society's customers. Finally it was a cultural transaction, a medium through which the virtues of Protestant Christianity, as interpreted among the more prosperous classes of the British Isles, could be conveyed to less fortunate individuals, whether they lived at home in poverty or infidelity, or abroad in heathenism, or under the 'yoke of Rome'. This notion became identified as a mark of the British national character. Prevalent from the very beginning of the Society, the idea continued at least to mid-century. A pamphleteer of 1810 compared Britain to Napoleonic France:

What a glorious sight! – Great Britain standing in the attitude of presenting the Bible to all the world – contrasted with the tyrant of the continent wielding his bloody sword. – I confess I derive more hope of salvation to my country from Britannia in this posture, than from Britannia in her posture of *defence*, with her trident in her hand, and surrounded by fleets and armies. Let Britons only study, and practise, and circulate the Bible, and we have nothing to fear.[4]

The men and women of the British and Foreign Bible Society chose to direct their formidable energies towards the circulation of the Bible, in the expectation that study and practice would automatically follow.

The Bible Society, officially founded on 7 March 1804, was dedicated to the circulation of the scriptures, in foreign languages as well as in English, to readers who would otherwise have gone without. The founders of the BFBS were a committee of the Religious Tract Society, who first met on 7 December 1802 in the business premises of Joseph Hardcastle at Old Swan Stairs, on the north side of London Bridge. The Religious Tract Society (founded 1799) existed to produce attractive and improving reading materials for the newly literate working-class reader.[5] At the meeting, according to Bible Society legend, the Reverend Thomas Charles of Bala spoke about his experience in Wales, and told an affecting story. A little girl called Mary Jones wanted to have her own Bible in the Welsh language. Even when she saved the price of the book from her meagre earnings, and walked a great distance to make her purchase, there was no copy to be had. The story is said to have so strongly moved the Tract Society Secretary, Joseph Hughes, that he exclaimed: 'Surely a Society might be formed for the purpose; and if for Wales, why not also for the Empire and the world?'[6] Joseph Hughes was to become one of the first Secretaries of the BFBS, the Welsh edition was the first publishing project of the new Society, and a whole generation of children in evangelical households were told the story of Mary Jones and her Bible.[7]

Both the Bible Society and the earlier Tract Society were evangelical organizations, the projects of a group of people who believed passionately in the values of the New Testament and desired to disseminate those values very widely indeed. These were the politicians and philanthropists popularly called the 'Clapham saints', after the London suburb where many of them

3

lived.[8] Under the leadership of people like William Wilberforce, the influential Member of Parliament who spearheaded the movement for the abolition of slavery, and the Thornton family of wealthy merchants who set records for philanthropic generosity, Clapham evangelicals organized and managed their campaigns for moral reform, the missionary societies and the Bible and Tract Societies which provided missionaries with the materials for conversion. Living in the aftermath of the Wesleyan revival of the eighteenth century, the leaders of this second historical stage of evangelicalism were 'pastors and organizers', who set for themselves the task 'to guide awakened and conscience-stricken people in the path of righteousness and to organize their resources for more efficient service to God and Man'.[9] Boyd Hilton, in *The Age of Atonement*, demonstrates in a powerful way how the doctrine of atonement for sins, national as well as personal, dominated the political and commercial lives of evangelicals, shaping their attitudes to social policy. Their charity was munificent, but it was doled out according to theories of expiation and regeneration. As Donna Andrew observes, 'the philanthropists of this period [the late eighteenth and early nineteenth centuries] seemed determined to use charity as an instrument of national regeneration'.[10] No plan seemed to them more appropriate for their purpose than the distribution of inexpensive editions of the scriptures. In the language of Barker's painting, the Bible was 'the secret of England's greatness', and its far-flung circulation would make up for the sins of England's past.

At RTS meetings through the winter of 1803, the Bible Society idea was developed and important patronage secured. William Wilberforce was present at one gathering, and wrote in his diary 'A few of us met together at Mr Hardcastle's counting house ... on so dark a morning that we discussed by candle-light, while we resolved upon the establishment of the Bible Society.'[11] Joseph Hardcastle and his partner Joseph Reyner, cotton importers and shippers, were involved, along with William Alers Hankey, and Samuel Mills, who later drafted the constitution. Three future staff members of the Society were among the founders: Joseph Hughes and C. F. A. Steinkopf, both ordained ministers, were to become Secretaries, and Joseph Tarn would take over the paper work as Assistant Secretary. These people were motivated by dissatisfaction with the Bible publishing service provided by the Society for Promoting Christian Knowledge. An exclusively Anglican organization untouched by the evangelical revival, the SPCK had been the customary source of Bibles for Anglicans, especially clergymen seeking copies of the scriptures for their charges. But a small edition of cheap Bibles in Welsh had been exhausted very quickly, and the SPCK saw no reason to rush any more into print. The Tract Society evangelicals, with their impatient energy, were unwilling to wait, and they were quite prepared to inaugurate an alternative source of supply. The new Society would soon be widely viewed as the chief rival of the SPCK, with the older Society symbolizing the values of the Anglican Establishment. An important early criticism of the BFBS on this ground was that of Herbert Marsh, Lady Margaret Professor of Divinity at Cambridge, who campaigned in pamphlet and pulpit against the new Society, but finally had to admit defeat in 1813, saying that 'when an institution is supported with all the fervour of religious enthusiasm ... an attempt to oppose it, is like attempting to oppose a torrent of burning lava that issues from Etna or Vesuvius'.[12]

The most significant decision of the founders, and the reason for Marsh's opposition, was their policy of including in the organization Dissenters from the Church of England, as well as members of the Anglican Establishment. Roger Martin, author of *Evangelicals United*, characterizes the trend as 'pan-evangelicalism', and shows how difficult it was for the Bible Society and others to achieve co-operation in the tense political atmosphere of the early nineteenth century. Dissenters were increasingly impatient with the limitations on their potential roles in politics and business. In 1811, for example, Lord Sidmouth presented a bill in Parliament to restrict nonconformist itinerant preaching, but it was defeated by a coalition of nonconformists and evangelical Anglican MPs, a circumstance that raised again the eighteenth-century cry of 'the Church in danger'. High-Church Anglicans like Herbert Marsh believed that concessions to dissent constituted a threat to the privileges of Establishment. In 1815 and 1816 the pastoral charges of the Bishops of Lincoln, Chester, Carlisle and Ely all included opposition to the BFBS.[13] But for evangelical Anglicans, other concerns took priority. In Geoffrey Best's words, they 'sat loose to existing institutions and conventions in church and state'.[14] The last thing they wanted to see limited by denominational squabbles was the dissemination of the word of God.

The Society was officially instituted at a public meeting in the London Tavern, Bishopsgate on 7 March 1804, with Granville Sharp in the chair. In the course of the meeting officers were elected and the laws making up the Society's constitution were agreed. The President and Treasurer headed a working Committee and its professional and clerical staff. John Shore, Lord Teignmouth, who served as President from 1804 to 1834, often said that his position with the BFBS meant more to him than his Governor-Generalship of India. He was no figurehead, even writing the annual *Reports* of the Society for the first few years.[15] Teignmouth was succeeded by Lord Bexley (the former Nicholas Vansittart) until 1851, and then by Anthony Ashley Cooper, Lord Ashley, who became Lord Shaftesbury shortly after his succession. The Presidents chaired annual meetings and many Committee meetings, and spoke for the Society when approaches were made to the government of the day. The Treasurers received and disbursed the funds of the Society, under the direction of the Subcommittee of Finance. Henry Thornton, who held this position until he died in 1815, was an authority on matters of finance, and lent his expertise to the Bible Society. In politics he was elected MP for

Southwark in 1792 and supported Catholic emancipation. He wrote an important work on paper currency, and was an active member of the great banking house, Down, Thornton and Free. He was succeeded in 1815 by his nephew, John Thornton, who was to hold several senior Government offices in the course of a distinguished career.

From the beginning, the public response to the formation of a Society with the exclusive object of printing and distributing Bibles was very positive. Joseph Hughes wrote and published a prospectus for the proposed organization, and announcements were placed in metropolitan and provincial newspapers. One early letter advised, 'I have sent you by the bearer ... £2 6s 6d the produce of some Rings earrings & other Jewels, sent me by some Female Friends who stripped themselves of them when they heard of your society for printing the Bible into all Languages, & have devoted them to the Lord. You may intimate it on the cover of the Evangelical Magazine.'[16] More conventional donations and subscriptions arrived, and it became clear that the Bible Society idea had touched a chord.

The 'fundamental principle' of the new Society was the distribution of the scriptures, *without note or comment*, a rule which the founders hoped would avoid doctrinal disputes by organizing Christians around their common acceptance of the canonical books of the Bible. Prefaces and explanatory notes, interpreting the text according to the doctrines of particular creeds or of individual theologians, were explicitly forbidden. The second basic rule was 'that the translation of the Scripture established by Public Authority, be the only one in the English language to be accepted by the Society'.[17] These deceptively simple principles were not unproblematic. The Book of Common Prayer, for example, was regarded as a legitimate set of notes designated by Parliament to foster interpretation of the scriptures. Even more contentious were the marginal notes traditionally appended to English-language scriptures by the authorized printers at the Universities of Cambridge and Oxford and by the King's Printer in London. These notes cross-referenced Old and New Testament events and linked up prophecies with their fulfilment; they had been part of the conventional notion of the Bible in Britain since 1762, but no one claimed they were canonical.[18] And the second rule, ensuring that only the Authorized or King James version would be permitted for domestic circulation, landed the new Society squarely in the lap of the three Presses permitted to print that version. Nor did these rules prevent controversy over versions in other languages: translators felt the need to explain concepts like 'lamb' that were unfamiliar to readers in countries without sheep. But as we shall see, when they began to try to translate 'baptism', with foreign words that meant, specifically, immersion or not, they were thrown into theological dispute.

The 'fundamental principle' of distribution without note or comment was based upon the premise that the BFBS was not a religious society. As Luke

Howard, the Quaker chemist and meteorologist said, 'It is a society for furnishing the means of religion, but not a religious society.'[19] This was a crucial distinction. Denominational differences made it impossible for Dissenters and Anglicans to combine together in their religious characters to distribute the scriptures. The publication of notes and comments would have raised disagreements over interpretation. So the members met as lay persons, agreeing to disagree about doctrine. It was a distinction between content and process: the scriptures themselves were religious, of course, but the process of distribution had to be a commercial one, stripped of all religious trappings, if squabbles over doctrine were to be avoided.

Some critics, particularly Church of England stalwarts, found the notion of unsectarian distribution outrageous. It undermined the idea of one national church, established by royal and Parliamentary authority. One prolific High-Church critic of the Bible Society was Thomas Sykes, who styled himself 'A Country Clergyman'. Sykes believed that:

It is to be expected, that each member of your heterogeneous society, will draw his portion of books for the promotion of his particular opinion: for it is easily seen, that a Bible given away by a Papist, will be productive of popery. The Socinian will make his Bible speak, and spread Socinianism: while the Calvinist, the Baptist, and the Quaker, will teach the opinions peculiar to their sects. Supply these men with Bibles, (I speak as a true Churchman) and you supply them with arms against yourself.

But John Owen, by then the Anglican Secretary of the Society, responded, identifying himself as a Sub-Urban Clergyman:

The line of business is, with few exceptions, as direct at the Bible Committee as it is at Lloyd's; and there is as little reason to expect the peculiar tenets of Calvin or Socinius to enter into a debate for dispersing an edition of the Scriptures, as there would be if the same men were met to underwrite a policy of insurance.[20]

The tension between spiritual ends and commercial means, embedded in the constitution because of contemporary political realities, was to shape the policies of the Bible Society throughout the nineteenth century.

The Society was administered not by a single executive director but by three Secretaries, all ordained ministers. They were highly competent executives who guided the organization through the diplomatic difficulties of sectarian politics. Because of those difficulties there had to be one for the Church of England, one for Dissent, and a Foreign Secretary. It was their task, under the direction of the Committee, to manage a burgeoning publishing business, to remind the Society's subscribers of the fundamental principle of unsectarian distribution without note or comment, and to manage the public image of an organization that distributed Bibles, aggressively and worldwide, but was nevertheless not a religious society. Their primary responsibility was to handle the foreign and domestic correspondence of the Society. They attended all Committee meetings and many gatherings of Subcommittees. The Secretaries travelled for the Society, the Churchman and Dissenter within Great Britain attending local Auxiliary meetings and fostering the creation of new Auxiliaries, the Foreign Secretary abroad, forming a liaison with the Continental Bible Societies. Travel by coach and horseback was rigorous enough at home: abroad in wartime it was dangerous, potentially fatal. But as we shall see, the Secretaries made light of the physical and political strains entailed by their work. For each of them, it was a mission. In fact, for many years they were not paid for their work for the BFBS.

The Secretaries at the outset were John Owen, Joseph Hughes, and Carl Friedrich Adolph Steinkopf. These three were fancifully described in an 1892 memoir as 'the head, and heart, and lungs of the Bible Society ... the eloquent Owen, the sagacious Hughes, the gentle and John-like Steinkopf'.[21] Owen came to the Society from his rectory of Paglesham in Essex. He served as Church of England Secretary through the difficult early years, and wrote the first history of the BFBS, at its tenth anniversary. He was described in Stoughton's *Religion in England* as 'a fervid, indefatigable man, with a pen almost too fluent ... the prince of platform speakers; a warm and steady friend'. Owen not only contributed several pamphlets to the controversies of the first two decades of the Society, but performed a valuable service by gathering and binding the contributions to both sides of these debates, producing a now very rare collection of pamphlets.[22]

Owen died in 1822 and was replaced by Andrew Brandram, whose recruitment marked the beginning of salaries (£300 per year each) for the Secretaries. He was characterized by Stoughton as 'a clergyman of robust constitution and character, of commanding presence, frank in manners, and full of platform power'. George Borrow, in his book *The Romany Rye*, has a character describe Brandram as 'a big, burly parson, with the face of a lion, the voice of a buffalo, and a fist like a sledge-hammer'. Stoughton added later that

To eminence in learning, he conjoined a masculine mind, an uncompromising spirit, active habits, strong affections, and devoted piety. I think I see him now, with the appearance of a country gentleman, portly in figure, honest in countenance, with a loose coat, a large hat, a thick neckcloth, and a bag of papers in his hands, entering a committee room before the commencement of a meeting, with an open hand to return friendly grasps, given by friends waiting for his arrival.[23]

The personality and business style of this highly competent executive, vividly sketched by his admirers, becomes evident in the pages below.

The first Dissenting Secretary was the 'sagacious' Joseph Hughes, who ministered to a Baptist congregation at Battersea. He was Secretary of both the Bible Society and the Religious Tract Society for over thirty years, until his death in 1835. Hughes was educated at Aberdeen University; he tutored at the Baptist College in Bristol, then moved to Battersea where he was friendly with Clapham evangelicals. The Rev. George Browne, minister of the Independent congregation at Clapham, succeeded Hughes. Stoughton noticed that it was the Dissenter Browne who resembled a dignitary of the Church. Unlike his colleague Andrew Brandram, Browne was 'careful in dress, polished in manner, gentle in disposition', and Stoughton continued, he was 'a good man, a diligent worker, respected by everybody'.[24]

C. F. A. Steinkopf came from Württemberg in South Germany to London in 1801 as pastor to the German Lutheran Church in the London district of the Savoy. At the foundation of the BFBS he was twenty-eight years old, 'handsome, winning, eloquent, and eager to enter into the furtherance of every religious enterprise'.[25] He travelled widely for the Society, even while England was at war on the European continent. Born in Ludwigsburg in Germany and educated at the Evangelical Theological Seminary at Tübingen, Steinkopf was in 1795 appointed Secretary of the German Christian Society in Basle, Deutsche Christentumsgesellschaft, which was a network of German-speaking religious and pietistic societies stretching across Germany and Switzerland into Denmark.[26] For a time simultaneously Foreign Secretary of the BFBS, the London Missionary Society and the RTS, Steinkopf remained involved with the Society until he died in 1859, though he resigned his office in 1826.[27] No one replaced Steinkopf as Foreign Secretary. By the 1830s, matters of editing and translation were of crucial importance while contact with European societies was greatly diminished. Four years after Steinkopf's retirement the BFBS engaged an Editorial Superintendent, William Greenfield, to supervise the production of translated texts. Greenfield died almost immediately and in 1831 the redoubtable Joseph Jowett, rector of Silk Willoughby in Lincolnshire, took his place. A relative of Benjamin Jowett of Balliol College in Oxford, Jowett was a competent scholar. Brandram said this of his colleague: 'He is one of the best advisors. His judgment is sound, and he has admirable tact in expressing himself clearly on difficult subjects.'[28]

At the beginning, the Secretaries were assisted by only two staff, a clerk and a collector/accountant. The responsibility for the great mass of business correspondence, and the handling of relationships with suppliers of publishing services, fell upon Joseph Tarn, the Assistant Secretary. He was a Calvinistic Methodist, who had been a member of the Tract Society committee that formed the Bible Society. Tarn had to resign a situation in Ironmongers' Hall, where he had worked for Thomas Pellatt, a solicitor who was an active member of the Committee. From 1804 until his death in 1837 Tarn was Assistant Secretary. He became Accountant also in 1810, because – as we shall see – the first accountant, Thomas Smith, had to be sacked. A letter from Tarn to the Committee on this occasion shows how his work escalated during the first years. Tarn told the Committee that the dual arrangement would be sensible as a good deal of money passed through his hands already. The new system, however, required that his primary office of Assistant

Secretary be rearranged. In 1804, he wrote, it had been 'a pleasant occupation of leisure hours'; by 1807 the job had extended to consume an average of two hours per day. During 1809 it occupied more time than the business of his office in the City. He had to hire another person to copy letters and minutes into the record books. Committee meetings were so busy that he could not write proper minutes, but had merely to enter items briefly, then 'sit down later with the letters & frame them so as to embrace the substance of the correspondence'. Tarn estimated that the work was equal to the superintendence of a large mercantile concern.[29]

The increasing complexity that the Secretaries and their staff had to handle may be charted in their dealings with their first Collector/Accountant, Thomas Smith, a merchant of Little Moorfields. His position must have seemed straightforward in the early days: he had only to receive the subscriptions of wealthy supporters, enter the amount in his book, and turn the cash over to the Society's Treasurer. He also kept the stock of Bibles on his own premises, and sent them out to subscribers. For this he received a commission of 5 per cent. But even before Auxiliary societies and Bible Associations began to burgeon, the mere bulk of the transactions became overwhelming. The minutes of the Subcommittee of Auditors tell the tale, interspersed with increasingly harried letters from Smith to Tarn: 'I am again in the vortex of perplexity in the want of English *Brevier Testaments* and *Welsh Bibles*. Can you help me?' Before long Smith was feeling aggrieved. He said he was willing to accommodate the Committee because of their mission, but that 'otherwise, considering their recent conduct, after having most ardently devoted my self to their cause, I have reason enough to have terminated my vassalage abruptly months ago'.[30]

The Subcommittee tried to relieve the pressure on their staff by arranging that Leonard Benton Seeley become their official bookseller. Smith complained that 'The present arrangements with the Bookseller, believe me, I am thankful for, but the manner in which it has been done, would have disgraced the character of worldly men, acting upon worldly principles to accomplish a worldly project.'[31] Smith may have been over-sensitive to an imagined slight. But his criticism may also be regarded as early evidence of the pragmatic attitude taken by the Committee to many of the 'worldly' aspects of their business decisions. In any event almost a year went by before Smith's employment was terminated. It was decided to separate the offices of Collector and Accountant 'in order that one may be a check on the other'.[32] The minutes of the Subcommittee for 5 July 1810 record that 'Mr Smith attended; &, having thrown down two parcels, which appeared to contain books & papers … & [having stated] that he considered the auditors had personal animosity to him, he should withdraw … Mr Smith then immediately withdrew, in a state of great perturbation.' The accounts were found in disarray. A few days later William Blair reported that Smith had been found by his apothecary 'in a state of insensibility, arising from a high degree of nervous affection'. Blair later reported that Smith's quarrel was with Mr Davies, chairman of the Subcommittee of Auditors. This was presumably James Davies, who was a member of the BFBS Committee in 1808. The Committee decided that the explanation was unjustifiable and they could not take cognizance of it.[33] The 'Subcommittee relative to Mr Smith's business' included some of the most prominent members of the Society: the scholarly Methodist divine Adam Clarke, the leather merchant Samuel Mills, Dr William Blair, the law publisher Joseph Butterworth, Granville Sharp, Robert Howard, and the cotton shipper Joseph Reyner. Also on the Subcommittee was Anthony Wagner who had served on the General Committee from the foundation, and who in 1810 became Collector.[34] In August 1810, Smith was prevailed upon to resign, but the case continued to reverberate. It was finally sent to referees, who discovered over £100 unaccounted for, but nevertheless found 'nothing to impeach the integrity of Mr Smith' and ruled that he was to receive funds due to him.[35]

The unfortunate Smith was probably no more surprised than his superiors to find himself the collector for such a wealthy organization. The annual *Report* for 1811 showed a balance of £33,092 11s 1d. William Wilberforce himself had never expected the Society's income to exceed £10,000 annually.[36] The Smith affair shows the Society moving away from the awkward and amateurish style characteristic of some voluntary organizations, and towards a set of sophisticated and businesslike arrangements. It is also the first signal that Committee members were prepared to act decisively, even ruthlessly, to promote their ends. They reported Smith's breakdown in the minutes, but they took their case against him to arbitration and tried to get a ruling to avoid paying him.

By 1810 the BFBS had become a substantial concern. They were fortunate to have in Joseph Tarn an officer who shared the ideological vision of the founders, while also possessing the administrative and clerical skills required to put their plans into practice. Tarn, who served the Society until his death in 1837, seems to have received little recognition for his diplomacy and efficiency although he was undoubtedly a very powerful person behind the scenes. It is clear from minutes and correspondence that however competent and capable the staff, they were expected frequently to refer to the Committee for decisions, and to keep that body informed in detail about events. Especially in the case of any controversy or dispute, Tarn and the Secretaries deferred to their thirty-six directors.

Almost from the beginning there were plenty of disputes for the Society to settle. Its business proceedings were frustrated by doctrinal and political conflicts. Throughout the 1820s and 1830s, the politics of Bible distribution constituted a seismic test for the various religious and political upheavals of the period. The Society's history of conflict may be set into the context of events in the larger society: Peterloo, the repeal of the Test and Corporation Acts, Catholic Emancipation, the reform agitation and the 1832 Reform Bill, the Poor Law Amendment Act, the factory agitation, and early manifestations of Chartism. Industrialization and urban development were transforming the relations between employer and employee, and between the government and the governed. At the same time, the position of the Church of England was being threatened from without by disestablishment agitation and from within by the Tractarian movement. Dissent was becoming more aggressive and political, so that pan-evangelical co-operation was difficult.

The first controversy to upset the BFBS concerned the Welsh edition that had been the Society's immediate *raison d'être*. Thomas Charles, whose visit from Bala had initiated enthusiasm in London for the Bible-publishing project, was chosen to prepare the text. He used the 1799 edition, published by the University of Oxford for the SPCK, planning to correct nothing more contentious than spelling. Even before publication, however, the book was characterized as inaccurate and potentially heretical by Anglicans committed to the SPCK. Prominent members and supporters were sharply critical of Charles's editorial approach and eventually caused the copy text to be changed to the Welsh Bible of 1752. More important, the affair generated a storm of criticism for the fledgling Bible Society, based upon rumours that the editor was not confining himself to orthography, but taking undue liberties with the text itself.[37]

There was trouble in 1811 over the formation of Auxiliaries at Colchester and especially at Cambridge. In both places, High-Church opponents rallied themselves to oppose the idea of the Bible Society at public meetings. A group of Cambridge undergraduates, inspired by Charles Simeon, initiated the movement for a public meeting in the town. But the academic and ecclesiastical politics of Cambridge combined to make any evangelical activity difficult. There followed much careful planning, behind-the-scenes manipulation, and considerable anxiety on the part of Simeon, Wilberforce and Isaac Milner, the Master of Queens' College. The local Auxiliary was initiated at a triumphant public meeting attended by over one thousand people, including the requisite number of bishops, noblemen and professors. With each such public confirmation of the Society's success, opponents like Herbert Marsh renewed their invectives against the Society.[38]

There was a constant flow of pamphlets and sermons, many of them opposing the BFBS for putting the Church and the nation in danger. Arch-conservatives regarded the mere setting up of an organizational structure as an invitation to subversive radicalism. The 'Country Clergyman' warned: 'The monster Jacobinism has insinuated its poison ... into almost every species of society in Europe ... this destructive principle [exists not] only in clubs and lodges, and spouting societies. This serpent ... is now in a remarkable manner, and with much aggravation of malice and impudence, detected lurking behind the cross', and added, 'you cannot answer for the *real* object of any association, but by being able to answer for the *real* principles and pursuits of its individual members'.[39] To extravagant claims of this kind, the Society's spokespersons replied that their motives were benevolent, and that increasing numbers of subscribers, loyal and law-abiding citizens, shared their enthusiasm.

The Apocrypha affair, in the early 1820s, was the most severe controversy to split the Society. It deprived the BFBS of its links with Scotland and with the European societies, and gave a force to subsequent Protestant criticisms that the Society was too sympathetic to Roman Catholicism. The following description is only a brief summary of a complex controversy; in Roger Martin's *Evangelicals United* the chapter-title on the subject of 'Schism' is no exaggeration.

The Apocryphal books, included in the Septuagint and Vulgate versions of the Old Testament, had been separated from Lutheran and Anglican editions of the scriptures, being printed as a separate section in their Bibles, apart from the canonical books. Such was the arrangement for the English Authorized Version of 1611. On the other hand the Council of Trent had declared these books to be integral to the scriptures for Roman Catholics, in whose Bibles it was part of the Old Testament, while the Calvinist and Puritan tradition, including that of Presbyterian Scotland, excluded the Apocrypha from their Bibles altogether. The situation was further complicated in the early nineteenth century by Lutheran churches' insistence that the Apocrypha be included in their Bibles.[40] There had been no discussion about canonicity when the Society's 'fundamental principles' were established, but when Steinkopf toured Europe in 1812 he realized that if the BFBS was to circulate Bibles on the Continent, they must be somewhat flexible about the Apocrypha. Although the Society's own translations and versions would be circulated without it, they would have to countenance a policy on the part of European societies, supported by BFBS funds, of including the controversial books. This would meet the requirements of both his Lutheran colleagues and of the Roman Catholics into whose hands he hoped to put the scriptures unsullied by notes. But to most British Dissenters, particularly Scottish Presbyterians, the books were not part of the inspired canon and should never be circulated, or subsidized in any way, by the BFBS. On 7 June 1813 the Committee resolved 'that the manner of printing the Holy Scripture by the Foreign societies, be left to their discretion, provided they be printed without note or comment'. As Martin says, this was 'tactfully phrased', not directly mentioning Apocryphal Bibles at all. Nor was the decision publicized, a policy which led to criticism.[41]

An anti-Apocrypha party began to form. Robert Haldane, with William Thorpe, began in 1821 a public campaign against the 'contamination' with the books of the Apocrypha of Bibles paid for by funds raised in Britain.

Haldane, an influential writer and philanthropist, spent £70,000 between 1798 and 1810 on religion in Scotland. He and his brother James Alexander Haldane were leaders of the branch of evangelicals known as the 'Recordites' because of their involvement with the *Record* newspaper. Thorpe was an Irish clergyman, formerly chaplain at the Lock Hospital in London.[42] They refused to accept proposed compromises, such as the limitation of BFBS funds to publication of the canonical books only, and held out for a total withdrawal of support from any society circulating the Apocrypha.

There were both pro- and anti-Apocrypha members of the Committee, but the majority was of the liberal party. While they were quite willing to impose Protestant Christian values, they were more sensitive to cultural differences than were critics like Robert Haldane, who could not accept that the Society should cater to a European preference for Bibles bound with the Apocrypha. To the majority of members of the Committee the choice between Apocryphal Bibles and no European activity at all was clear. Their policy, in contrast to the extremism of the Recordites, was of the pragmatic 'thin edge of the wedge' variety. The Committee and Secretaries were politically astute. Officially their policy was to keep hands off, to let 'friends of the Society . . . in their individual capacity . . . come forward in its defense'. Being interpreted this meant that an anonymous pamphlet supporting the BFBS official position was written by the Rev. Joseph Jowett, who would later become editorial superintendent. Another pamphlet was published by John Radley, who did not mention to the public that he was a member of the Society's Committee.[43]

The Apocrypha controversy reached its peak in the spring of 1826. The Committee's final concession to its opponents was a decision that no BFBS funds were to pay for printing any Apocryphal books anywhere, and in order to ensure that this policy was carried out all books published by the Society were to be issued bound. However they refused to meet Haldane's demand that contact be severed with Societies in Europe that circulated the undesirable books at their own expense. As a result, the two largest Scottish Auxiliaries, Edinburgh and Glasgow, seceded, followed by thirty-eight more of the forty-eight Scottish Auxiliaries and a few in England. The remaining members closed ranks, but the loss was severe, in financial as well as organizational terms. The tables in the appendix show that subscriptions and donations dropped substantially in the mid-1820s.

Aside from the financial blow, the affair had shattered the naïve optimism of those who hoped the BFBS constitution could bypass political and doctrinal differences. The young Marianne Thornton, keeping her diary at Clapham on the fringe of the conflicts, reflected:

We all thought that the Bible Society was so simple in its form and its object that none of the frailties of mortality could touch it, and that, whereas in all other Societies there might be some chance of jarring discords, this alone was secure from all the conflicts which belong to human undertakings: but it was conducted by men, and so there must be imperfections, and the only possible rock on which they could split, the Apocrypha, has crashed them to pieces.[44]

Not quite. The Society was to flourish throughout the nineteenth century, and is still active in the last decade of the twentieth. But the controversies of the early years reinforced the founders' intention that the mandate be interpreted very narrowly, in terms of printing and bookbinding only. No doubt the survival also owed something to the fact that its early Committee included a nucleus of able and influential individuals, experienced in thinking in terms of profit and loss, and of sound policy for international trade. And in Owen and Brandram, Hughes and Browne, Steinkopf and Jowett, the Society had strong executives.

The Apocrypha controversy had some important effects on the publishing programme of the Bible Society. It placed a special emphasis upon the policy of issuing bound books, not books in sheets. Bible Society Secretary and historian George Browne spoke later of the tradition of the Apocrypha as 'an adjunct of the Inspired Scriptures, and a part of the *Book* called the Bible'. This nice distinction in bibliography (the Bible as scripture versus the Bible as book) was lost on the anti-Apocrypha party. As a matter of fact they scorned it:

Let us . . . suppose [an apocryphal Bible] . . . laid on the table of our Committee-room. On taking it up, it is found to contain the Apocryphal books, as well as the Holy Scriptures; nay, to have the former intermixed with the latter, in such a manner as that the story of Bel and the Dragon appears as one of the chapters of Daniel's prophecy. A member of the Society, on observing this, remarks, 'here is a violation of one of our fundamental laws'. 'Oh no', replies the Committee, turning to one side of a leaf which contains the word of God, 'We paid for *this*', but, turning to the other side, in which the Apocrypha appears, 'some other person, we know not who, paid for *that*'.[45]

Nor was the Apocrypha affair the last controversy. In June 1827 the *Quarterly Review* published an article (attributed by the *Wellesley Index* to Edward Edwards) that heaped scorn on the Society's many translations. Edwards suggested that donations were generated by publicity about the large number of translations available and in preparation. But these Bibles were the work of missionaries who did not know the original Latin and Greek, and who were none too familiar with the vernacular languages. He charged, essentially, that the translations were from the English Authorized Version into a pidgin variety of the new language. William Roberts published a pamphlet in reply, scotching some of the more flagrant charges and pointing out that the souls of the heathen could not wait for one of their number to become qualified in the classics.[46] But the charge that the BFBS was unscholarly, philistine and potentially heretical was to be revived in various controversies over 'Versions'.[47] Even the text of English editions came under attack for typographical and textual errors, as we shall see in chapter 3.

In 1831 there was another schism. This time it was not Dissenters but orthodox Anglicans who opposed their leaders' interpretation of the rules. Concerned about the reportedly large number of Unitarians who were BFBS members, they proposed a test of 'real Protestant Christianity', i.e. belief in the Trinity. The test, which opponents called 'a modern Act of Uniformity', would take the form of opening committee meetings with prayer. A statement signed by the majority of the Committee argued the anti-test case: if prayers were to be offered at meetings, who would offer them, and how? 'One petitioner will be distrusted as not evangelical; a second as not spiritual; a third as not educated; a fourth as not discreet; and a fifth as not harmonious with his brethren.' There was a very stormy public meeting at the newly opened Exeter Hall on 4 May 1831. The failure of the pro-test party to amend the BFBS constitution resulted in the formation of a Trinitarian Bible Society as well as an additional spate of pamphlets and journalism.[48]

The 'Baptizo' controversy, in the late 1830s, pitted Baptists against others in a dispute over how one key word was to be translated in versions prepared by the Serampore missionaries in India. The Baptist missionaries in Bengal had translated the words for 'baptism' in restrictive terms signifying immersion, terms which were not acceptable to the BFBS Auxiliary in Calcutta. The Committee eventually resolved that it would continue to support the translation 'provided the Greek terms relating to Baptism were rendered either according to the principle adopted by the translators of the English Authorized Version, by a word derived from the original, or by such terms as might be considered unobjectionable by the other denominations of Christians composing the Bible Society'. The problem was sidestepped, as it had been in Britain in 1611, by inserting into the translation an ambiguous word open to more than one doctrinal interpretation. Again there was a schism, and a Baptist 'Bible Translation Society' broke away from the parent body.[49]

Resolution of the test controversy had not laid to rest the issue of prayer at meetings. Controversy about this question serves to illuminate the Society's paradoxical nature, circulating the scriptures as a mere publisher, not a religious body. Local Auxiliaries and Associations that transgressed the by-law forbidding prayer were chastised from headquarters. Bible Society officers who had lived through the Apocrypha and test controversies were well aware of the pitfalls of extemporaneous public prayer, whereas fervent and pious but politically unsophisticated evangelicals had great difficulty in understanding the rule. They said so, at length, and wondered aloud how the Bible Society, of all organizations in the world, could possibly stop people from praying. There were efforts to get around the problem by motions that meetings should be opened by a reading of that well-known passage from Matthew 6:9–13, which begins 'Our Father which art in heaven.' One anonymous correspondent suggested that a board be mounted at the entrance to the Committee room, requesting each member to make a '*secret* prayer for DIVINE Blessings on the British and Foreign Bible Society ... Thus would all the effect of universal prayer be obtained – without one Member's depending on the formulary of another.'[50] In 1848 the Secretaries and Committee fought off a determined campaign. At the Anniversary meeting in that year, wrote Andrew Brandram, 'We were apprehensive of an attempt being made to carry the question of prayer by a coup de main – but dreadful as it would have been, my mind was made up that it was a point of duty to resist the introduction of such a topic of division. However those fears were happily groundless.' Unfortunately for Brandram and his allies the issue was forced in 1858, and by 1867 J. P. Hewlett could state: 'There cannot be the shadow of a doubt but that, without altering a single letter of our constitution, the all but universal practice of opening our meetings with oral prayer has virtually revolutionized the Society.' However desirable the increased pious tone may have been, Hewlett noted that as a result 'the Society must suffer in regard to funds, to numbers, and to mere worldly respectability'.[51]

There was always criticism. A gentleman who attended meetings in Derbyshire in 1842 reported to headquarters that 'In one instance a friend of the Trinitarian Bible Society; in a second, a supporter of the views known under the name of Tractarian; & in a third a body of Socinians, opposed our meetings. There was never a "better abused" society in being.'[52] It is the high calibre of abuse that alerts us to the importance of the British and Foreign Bible Society as a contemporary social institution. Many of the Society's critics cared so much about Bible distribution that they formed new societies to carry on the transaction within their doctrinal restrictions. The establishment of competing Societies is in itself important evidence that the idea of distributing cheap Bibles had become institutionalized in Victorian culture.

The paradoxical position of the BFBS, of conducting its project without comment at the centre of swirling controversy, required absolute commitment, tremendous energy and sophisticated management skills on the part of the directing Committee. The first Committee of twenty-four was elected at the March 1804 founding meeting. An impressive list of Vice-Presidents was also presented. These were honorary officers, largely bishops and noblemen, chosen because their support would help the Bible Society's political and social position. But they were not active in the management of the organization. The Committee, on the other hand, would have to be diplomats, businessmen, linguists, animators and innovators. An analysis of the composition of this Committee is important to an understanding of how the Society worked, as well as to a better comprehension of the personnel of evangelicalism in general.

Matthew Arnold, in *Culture and Anarchy* (1869), portrayed the evangelicals among his contemporaries as mere narrow-minded philistines, rigid and earnest. Doreen Rosman, in her *Evangelicals and Culture*, has suggested that this image was not altogether accurate. Especially the generation before 1833, she argues, were quite interested and involved in art and literature. 'Biographies and group histories clearly prove that not all evangelicals and not all evangelical groups can be tarnished [*sic*] with the same anti-intellectualist, philistine brush.'[53] Similarly the research documented below suggests a subtler perception of the BFBS Committee. It was made up of cultured, sophisticated individuals, who were also keen and innovative businessmen. They were responsive to the market for the Bibles they had decided to circulate, and to the society in which they were operating.

Because the BFBS Committee was one of the most common centres of evangelical energy and activity in the nineteenth century, a study of its composition should help us to understand the social impact of evangelicalism. The question is important to modern social and cultural history. 'Between 1780 and 1850', to quote Harold Perkin, 'the English ceased to be one of the most aggressive, brutal, rowdy, outspoken, riotous, cruel and bloodthirsty nations in the world and became one of the most inhibited, polite, orderly, tender-minded, prudish and hypocritical.'[54] Social historians ask if the evangelicals associated with Wilberforce and the Clapham Sect were responsible for this dramatic shift in popular morality, or if the similarity between their programme and the results was merely a coincidence, masking other economic and political causes. One historian who adhered firmly to the former view was Ford K. Brown, author of *Fathers of the Victorians*. Brown regarded evangelical societies as the Trojan horse of domestic social reform. Of the BFBS he claimed that 'If every one of the 4,252,000 Bibles issued by 1825 had been printed in the language of the Esquimaux and piled upon the frozen tundra the Bible Society would still have been next to Abolition the most powerful agency of Evangelical reform.'[55] And E. P. Thompson, documenting the effects of economic and cultural change in *The Making of the English Working Class*, argued passionately that this making consisted largely in the oppression of working-class people by capitalists and evangelicals, as well as in their own heroic and defensive culture. Thompson's was a harsher restatement of Elie Halévy's thesis that Methodism prevented revolution, the notion that Methodism and its allies in the evangelical movement crushed a creative and spontaneous society that was 'the most distinguished popular culture England has ever known'.[56]

We shall see that these explanations are based more upon the programme of evangelicalism than on its practice. As for Brown's view of the insignificance of missionary translations, the history of the Bible Society reveals an elite group of evangelicals who were deeply committed to their foreign project. Popular support took them by surprise, and proved very difficult to manage in the early years. But popular support did not effect the cultural transformation described by Perkin, Thompson, Halévy and others. Certainly some BFBS worthies hoped their project would help to civilize and pacify the radical poor, and made very smug statements about the social efficacy of the Bible transaction. It seems, however, much more likely that the experience of Bible Societies, like that of Sunday Schools and other evangelical institutions, was accepted in a matter-of-fact, everyday, and unpolitical way by poor people, who were glad to have a Bible around the house. There is no evidence that working people as a class were induced by the process of BFBS organization to acquiesce in the values of the Establishment. The evidence points instead to the importance of evangelical energy and commitment in the making and marketing of books.[57]

The contribution of the 'saints' to the history of publishing may be approached by a study of the social composition of the directing Committee. This investigation provides a foundation for an understanding of their evangelicalism on the one hand, and their business qualifications on the other. With this in place it is possible to speak of the Bible Society as publisher with a clear idea of who, in a collective sense, that publisher was, and how the complexities of the Bible transaction were to be managed. Who, then, were the evangelical leaders of the British and Foreign Bible Society? The Clapham 'saints' are well documented: many have been the subject of reverential Victorian biographies, and a few of more rigorous historical studies. But they have been described primarily in terms of piety, as if prominent lay people had no other interests than their religious or philanthropic existence. Meanwhile other men and women, equally committed to and actively involved in movements for evangelical reform, have remained obscure. While Wilberforce, Granville Sharp and Zachary Macaulay were involved at the foundation, it was people like the undertaker Edward Norton Thornton and the leather merchant Samuel Mills who controlled the Society in the first half of the nineteenth century.

The pages and tables below present the results of an investigation of the lives of those who sat on the Bible Society's Committee between 1804 and 1864. Recruitment, initially, drew upon the friends, colleagues and acquaintances of members and Secretaries. Within this loose network of social connection, the only formal criterion for selection was religious denomination. The controversial premises of the Society's constitution – interdenominational participation in the distribution of scriptures published without note or comment – were encoded in the very composition of the General Committee. It was made up of equal numbers of Anglicans and Dissenters, with a smaller but significant number of members who were foreign church members residing in London. All of them were lay people, and none was a woman. Provincial men were excluded, unless they could be in London for a long season. There remained a very large number of London males who were influenced by the movement of evangelicalism. Which of them were invited to participate in directing the project of Bible distribution? The study begins with 300 names printed in the annual *Reports* of the Society and their annexed lists of subscribers. In most cases it has been possible to attach addresses and

Figure 2   First Bible House, 10 Earl Street, London, 1816–69.

occupations to these names, and sometimes age, marital status and connec-tions within the evangelical community.[58] This kind of study is collective biography, or prosopography, which has been defined as 'the investigation of the common background characteristics of a group of actors in history by means of a collective study of their lives'.[59] The evidence offered here of the lives of Bible Society Committee members is partial, involving only birth and death, place of residence, education, occupation, religion and sometimes experience of office. But even this preliminary sketch enables us to under-stand something of the ordinary people who became involved with the Society.

The interdenominational balance was maintained by a rule that, for each year's Committee of thirty-six members, fifteen were to be churchmen, fifteen Dissenters and six members of foreign churches.[60] Both the Dissenting and Anglican members of the early Committees were painfully aware of the contemporary hostility to Dissenting involvement in a popular cause. Although as John Owen remarked in his pamphlet, *A Sub-Urban Clergyman*, 'the politico-religious strife which subsisted between our ancestors and theirs [Dissenters] is not a sacred inheritance', it was a fact of political life until mid-century. In terms of the management of the Society, Owen stated that the dissenting founders 'avoided every thing which could be construed into an exhibition of themselves ... Resigning the foreground of the Society to [Anglicans] they contentedly occupied less conspicuous stations.'[61] This reticence was necessary in view of the 'church-in-danger' fears of High Anglicans, who were concerned that they would be outvoted in the BFBS by 'coal-heaving ministers, bird-catching ministers, Baptist ministers of all trades, those of the Roman Catholic communion, together with the green-aproned female ministers of the friends'.[62] The correspondence files are full of requests to supply a churchman to speak at an annual meeting, or regretting that the entire committee of a local Auxiliary happened to be made up of Dissenters. The first three Presidents were Anglican noblemen, and many of the honorary officers were bishops. The dissenting members represented a wide range of the non-Anglican denominations in Britain, several members of the Society of Friends, Methodists and Baptists in about equal numbers, and a few Independents.[63] More surprising was the one Committee member listed as Roman Catholic. He was James Meyer, a merchant of Leadenhall Street who was involved in several evangelical societies.[64]

The six foreign members of the Committee may have been inserted in the Society's constitution for political reasons, to ensure that neither Anglicans nor Dissenters could claim the other was in control.[65] Many of them were foreign business people, representing their firm, or their country as consul, in London. Presumably they were business acquaintances, whom established Committee members knew, or hoped, would share their concern about distribution of the scriptures. Some of these members were very active. The

Swedish consul Charles Tottie served for ten years, and was succeeded by William Tottie and by Charles Tottie jun. Others were quite eminent, such as Baron Ernest [*sic*] von Bunsen, the 'well-loved' Prussian minister in England from 1841 to 1854, who married an Englishwoman.[66] Most of the European names and addresses were Germanic or Scandinavian, while few were Huguenots or Dutch Protestants. The designation 'foreign' also included a few Americans, such as the merchant banker and philanthropist George Peabody who served only on the Committee of 1853–4. Others were the Russia merchants W. Ropes and William Hooper Ropes.[67] It appears, however, that in some years it was difficult to find six foreign members to serve on the Committee. In 1807, for example, both George Meyer and Christopher Sundius had been designated 'ineligible' because of poor attendance, but both were elected.[68] Some foreign names appear in the printed lists misspelled (Edelmann, Edlmann), without Christian names (Grutzow), or with foreign addresses (Baron von Strandman of St Petersburg, or James van der Smissen of Altona), indicating a low level of involvement for these members, who would perhaps not have been chosen if they had been designated Dissenters or Anglicans. Nevertheless, in spite of cultural differences and organizational difficulties, the foreign contingent offered the Bible Society's Committee a sound basis for the implementation of their plan. For European projects, at least, there was expertise at hand. As we shall see, the community of foreigners in London extended to reliable translators, editors and printers who could be entrusted with work that the English-speaking members of the Committee were not qualified to oversee.

The criterion of age reveals that most members joined the Committee during the active years of middle life. The average age was forty-three, while the youngest member, John Thornton, joined at twenty-two and the eldest, Granville Sharp, at sixty-nine. Of the older ones, many were still actively engaged in business, while others followed the pattern noticed by Leonore Davidoff and Catherine Hall in their study of middle-class evangelicals: early retirement from the business or professional enterprise, in order to take up a philanthropic career.[69] Examples of this latter pattern include the Quaker Richard Phillips, a retired conveyancer, and John Bockett. An obituary published in the 1871 *Bible Society Monthly Reporter* suggests that Bockett retired from business for reasons of conscience: 'Having from conscientious scruples given up a lucrative business which he thought to be detrimental to the best interests of his fellow-creatures, and in doing so sacrificed a large amount of property rather than perpetuate an evil of appalling magnitude', he devoted a long life to good causes, including twenty-eight years of involvement with the BFBS, serving as Treasurer and Trustee.

The Committee's members during these sixty years were occupied mostly in commerce, trade and law; they were prosperous and successful individuals, who learned about the publishing business by doing it, undertaking to print

Table 1. *Occupations and denominations of Committee members*

	Number	%	C. of E. %	Dissent %	Foreign %	Unknown %
Commercial						
merchant	42	14.0	5.7	5.6	45.5	2.6
textile	15	5.0	3.8	7.8	3.0	5.3
transport, etc.	10	3.3	0.0	6.7	3.0	5.3
food and drink	10	3.3	2.8	3.3	6.1	0.0
book trade	6	2.0	1.9	3.3	0.0	2.6
luxury	5	1.7	0.0	0.0	7.6	0.0
leather	7	2.3	3.8	2.2	0.0	2.6
other	13	4.3	3.8	7.8	1.5	2.6
	108	35.9	21.8	36.7	66.7	21.0
Professional						
law	27	9.0	14.2	8.9	1.5	7.9
medicine	7	2.3	1.9	3.3	3.0	0.0
military	11	3.7	9.4	0.0	0.0	2.6
	45	15.0	25.5	12.2	4.5	10.5
Financial						
banker	11	3.7	5.7	4.4	0.0	2.6
broker	10	3.3	2.8	3.3	3.0	5.3
other	5	1.7	2.8	2.2	0.0	0.0
	26	8.7	11.3	9.9	3.0	7.9
Gentlemen	14	4.7	3.8	7.8	0.0	7.9
Political						
M.P.	11	3.7	8.5	2.2	0.0	0.0
civil servant	2	.7	.9	0.0	1.5	0.0
	13	4.4	9.4	2.2	1.5	0.0
Intellectual						
scientific	3	1.0	.9	2.2	0.0	0.0
literary	3	1.0	2.8	0.0	0.0	0.0
educational	3	1.0	0.0	2.2	1.5	0.0
other	2	.7	0.0	1.1	1.5	0.0
	11	3.7	3.7	5.5	3.0	0.0
Occupation unknown	83	27.7	24.5	25.6	21.2	52.6
Grand total	300	100.0	100.0	100.0	100.0	100.0

and distribute cheap Bibles wherever they would be received. Table 1 shows how the Committee's composition can be broken down in terms of occupational titles, cross-referenced by denomination. Most members – over one third of the Committee – worked in commercial pursuits. The merchants were engaged in the Russia trade and other global ventures. These were wealthy and powerful people, directors of banks and insurance companies, of shipping lines and of brokerage houses. As might be expected, foreign members were overrepresented among the merchants. Presumably it was congenial as well as a source of useful business and social connections for foreign merchants residing in England to take seats on the BFBS Committee. Some of the members might be called 'professional foreigners'. These were the eight consuls – Danish, Prussian and others – who served the BFBS while also representing the commercial interests of their homelands.

Not surprisingly, many of these business people were in the textile trades: woollen- and linen-drapers, Swiss muslin warehousemen and cotton importers and shippers. The great Thames ports were the source of members concerned with packing, warehousing and transportation. There were a few brewers and distillers, and others in the food and drink business. The numbers in the book trade are significantly small, when it is remembered that the BFBS was a publisher. Almost as many members were in the luxury trades of jewellery and fur. Four foreign members were provided by a single family of furriers, the Polands of Oxford Street. One other trade was that of Edward Norton Thornton, an undertaker of Southwark borough, who began in 1809 a term of thirty-nine years. Although he was no relation to the wealthy family of the same name, from which came the Society's first two Treasurers, Thornton was no mere tradesman. Many of his letters in the Bible Society's archives concern the translation of the scriptures into Ethiopic, and he had a friend at Oxford with whom he corresponded on this difficult technical and political issue. Thornton's case points up the danger of drawing quick conclusions from occupational designations. He and his family prospered; they left Southwark and later joined their evangelical colleagues at Clapham as neighbours. These Thorntons too were obviously a well-connected evangelical family. Edward's daughter Caroline married Josiah Iles Wathen, a solicitor who served on the Committee until his father-in-law died in 1848.[70]

But the Committee was not solidly commercial. Fifteen per cent of its total membership between 1804 and 1864 were men associated with the professions: law, medicine and the armed forces. Law was the next most common occupation after commerce, and solicitors, barristers, proctors and notaries offered their professional expertise and practical services in addition to their contributions to the general deliberations of the Committee. From an early date each annual *Report* included a convenient form by which a legacy to the Society could be written into anyone's will. Bequests became a steady source of income, the practical details of which were handled by members experienced as solicitors. The so-called Professional Members of the Committee, the barristers, got together informally to discuss potential litigation over a bequest.[71] The Society's honorary solicitor was John Poynder, who was solicitor to the Bridewell and Bethlehem Hospitals as well as a theological writer.

Other professions contributed both indirectly and directly to the needs of the Society. One medical man was William Blair, a Fellow of the Royal College of Surgeons who lived in Bloomsbury. But it was Blair's avocations, more than his medical skill, that proved useful. An ardent bibliophile and connoisseur of foreign Bibles, he provided the editors and printers with rare copies used in the preparation of several of the earliest BFBS editions. As for career soldiers, when Major Charles Franklin Head, who had been in India, was nominated in 1840 he wrote: 'should it be thought any local knowledge of colonies or Foreign Countries I may happen to possess can be made available to the valuable and great purposes of yr Society by my being in the Committee I would be happy to give my best services'.[72] The other principal profession, the clergy, was prohibited by the Society's constitution from belonging to the Committee and hence forms no part of the statistics discussed here. But clergymen and dissenting ministers were always permitted to attend Committee meetings, and they undoubtedly exerted an influence. If the unofficial participation of clergymen were taken into consideration, professional members would count even more heavily.

Twenty-six members of the Committee during the whole sixty-year period were financiers: bankers, brokers – of stock and insurance – and others. Thomas Boddington and William Shrubsole, both of whom served during the earliest years of the Society, were Directors of the Bank of England. Boddington also sat on the board of the London Dock Company. Another financier a few years later, in 1814, was James William Freshfield, solicitor to the Bank of England, to the East and West India Dock Company and the Globe Insurance Company. The BFBS benefited from their expert advice when it came to investing its surplus funds. By the time of the third annual *Report* in 1806 the Society had purchased exchequer bills for £6,343 and Three Per Cent Consolidated Bank Annuities at £4,103. Interest income increased steadily, providing 1 to 2 per cent of revenues over the years.

Although the Committee was primarily composed of active business and professional people, there was a small component of leisured gentlemen. Of all the identifying labels in contemporary directories, 'gentleman' is the most ambiguous. Gentlemen, by definition, do not have occupations and the title is certainly less precise than other occupational categories like 'merchant' or 'consul'. These fourteen members are listed at their suburban addresses, as gentry of the district. No doubt a few were scions of genuine landed families, but in view of the fact that a high proportion of those identified were

Dissenters, it seems likely that in many cases these 'gentry' were active or retired businessmen, with experience of commercial premises in the City. Another problematic category among the careers of Committee members is 'political'. Two members were civil servants, and one in municipal politics. The latter, Michael Gibbs, was a member of the livery company of Fishmongers who became Alderman and then Lord Mayor of London in 1843. He served the Society for forty years. Eleven members of Committee were primarily occupied as Members of Parliament during their time with the Society, and seven others, merchants and lawyers, were elected to Parliament at some point in their careers. Many of the members, then, either circulated in the corridors of power themselves, or were acquainted with those who did so.

The category of 'intellectual' occupations includes scientists, professional writers, teachers, artists and one architect. These groups are of particular interest when we remember that the organization was engaged in translation and publishing, and that it was so frequently criticized on grounds of scholarship and accuracy. Although there were one or two translators (notably Christopher Sundius) the Society did not press its Committee members into service as scholars. Nevertheless their sophistication and breadth of experience undoubtedly helped them to deal with the political side of the Bible transaction. The intellectuals included pamphleteer-scholars like Granville Sharp and scientists like Luke Howard the meteorologist. Sharp laid the groundwork for the Society's Library by donating his collection of Bibles. During the 1820s Howard was consulted about how the Society's papermakers could be instructed to improve the quality of their product, and he submitted a very thorough technical report. Two more intellectuals were William Allen and Josiah Forster, both Quakers, who served in the thirties and forties. The former was a chemist, while the latter had been a distinguished schoolmaster.

Many of the lawyers and professionals were also sophisticated scholars. John Poynder, for example, was a solicitor but also a pamphleteer. He opposed the East India Company's policy of tolerating Eastern religions while forbidding Christian missionaries to preach, and wrote several books and articles about his opinions. The merchants were mostly involved in foreign trade, and knew the customs and sometimes the languages of Europe and Asia. The preponderance of Russia merchants, especially on the early Committees, may correlate with the Society's special interest in that part of the world. And Russia merchants had a tradition of involvement in philanthropy. John Thornton (d. 1790) had distributed Russian Bibles as part of his personal programme of charity long before his son Henry and grandson John became Treasurers of the BFBS.[73] Some sort of foreign association, whether in terms of citizenship, of business or of travel, can be ascribed to ninety-two of the 300 members. Sometimes the Committee's foreign connections made the BFBS project possible. In 1811 Joseph Tarn, the Assistant Secretary, was sending books to Palermo. He wrote to the Rt. Hon. Lord Amherst that Hugh Campbell Mair 'a very respectable Merchant (late a member of our Committee) is on the eve of departure for Sicily'. Mair undertook to negotiate the disposal of a shipment of Italian Testaments.[74] Nor were these remarkable individuals unacquainted with the production of literature. A search through the British Library catalogue indicates that sixty-eight (23 per cent) are listed there, mostly as authors of books and pamphlets on a wide variety of topics, a few as the subjects of memoirs or biographies. They knew about books as authors, however, not as publishers or printers: as we have seen, only six members were in occupations that might be even remotely connected with the book trades, and no evidence has been found of Committee members profiting from their connection to obtain contracts for paper, printing or bookbinding.

In terms of denomination it is no surprise that the politicians were almost exclusively Anglican, since few Dissenters sat in Parliament. However, the financiers were about evenly divided between the two groups. The merchants, whose business brought them to London, were most likely to be members of foreign churches, while persons in other trades were predominantly Dissenters.

Although the social-class composition of the Committee cannot be determined with significant precision, it is clear in a common-sense way that almost all the members were middle class: part of the prosperous emerging nineteenth-century bourgeoisie. There were only eight members who were titled, one English earl (Charles Crawford), five English baronets, and two European aristocrats. At the other end of the social scale, although some members were working tradesmen, none can be designated as a labourer. Much of the historical significance of the Committee lies in the fact that it was a middle-class phenomenon. In view of the overwhelming evidence that the British aristocracy continued to hold significant political and social power after the Reform Bill of 1832 and indeed throughout the century, the BFBS directorate may be seen as one of the institutions where the newer wealth of middle-class London was empowered to practise and exhibit its piety and respectability.[75]

Much of the business was not transacted at the weekly meetings of the full Committee, but in Subcommittees – for printing and general purposes, for conducting the business of the Society's funds, for preparing papers for publication and for superintending the depository, examining its accounts and purchasing printing paper (this last group was responsible for keeping up an adequate stock of Bibles and Testaments). Other Subcommittees superintended the Library, promoted and assisted Auxiliary societies, and audited the accounts (this Subcommittee consisted of four members of the Committee and four other subscribers). Two more undertook the tasks of selecting and

Table 2. *Subcommittee participation by denomination*

	Number	Print %	Audit %
Church	70	43.5	52.6
Dissent	61	43.5	40.8
Foreign	14	13.0	6.6

arranging the appendix to the annual *Report* (the list of subscribers' names and donations), where inaccuracy could provoke irritation, and superintending the arrangements of the annual meeting, where considerations of social precedence had to be observed at the same time as business was effectively discharged. Another way to understand the distribution of power among members of the Committee is to analyse their participation in Subcommittees. Subcommittee participation varied dramatically with denomination (see table 2). On the hard-working and practical Printing and General Purposes Subcommittee, the proportions of Anglicans, Dissenters and foreign church members almost exactly paralleled that of the General Committee. But the Audit Subcommittee, whose members were charged with keeping track of the funds, was mostly Anglican, a reminder of Owen's remark that Dissenters were content to sit back and let their Established-Church colleagues take positions of authority.

The Subcommittee responsible for printing and general purposes was at the centre of the Society's operations, ordering stocks of books from printers, and maintaining a roster of approved bookbinders to whom work could be parcelled out. The Secretaries almost always attended the meetings of this Subcommittee, and several ordained ministers unofficially attached to the Committee were also regulars. The most notable of these was Adam Clarke, a prominent Methodist divine and a scholar of Oriental languages. Clarke's work for the BFBS was the reason why he was permitted by the Methodists to stay permanently in London. With a single significant exception, there is no statistical correlation between an occupation in the book trade and membership on the Committee that ordered printing and binding services. Indeed the Subcommittee was characterized by inexperience with the customs of printers and binders. They turned this *naïveté* to advantage by implementing innovative methods, and frequently annoyed craftsmen and university officials by their irreverent approach to established tradition. The one Subcommittee member with publishing experience was Joseph Butterworth the law bookseller. His knowledge of paper, printing and binding surfaces again and again in the minutes of a Subcommittee he served from 1804 to 1826.

While not all members served as long as Butterworth, duration of service on the BFBS Committee was encouraged, and rapid turnover frowned upon. Attendance was taken seriously, and the Committee was constituted to penalize mere nominal participation. At the annual election, the nine members who had attended least frequently each year were dropped from the list of eligible nominees. When members travelled abroad on Committee business they were credited with having attended meetings. Vacancies were filled to make up the denominational balance, so that each April the Secretaries calculated attendances and announced how many places there were to fill in each category. Some members served for astoundingly long periods, the maximum being Josiah Forster's forty-two years. Many others served for a year and left. Some participated sporadically over a long span of years. One of these was Christopher Sundius, a foreign member, who served for nine of the twenty-four years from 1804 to 1827. He was a translator and notary as well as a ship and insurance broker.

As we shall see, the Society changed dramatically in the course of the first half-century of its existence. Some interesting distinctions appear when the criteria are sorted according to the date when a member joined the Committee. Designation of those whose term of service commenced between 1804 and 1824 as members of the 'early' Committee shows that they were most likely to be people accustomed to wielding economic clout in the market-place, or political power in domestic and foreign affairs. Table 3 shows that the highest percentages of merchants and of politicians served during the early years. But what table 3 does not disclose is that, between 1824 and 1844, there was a shift in the nature of evangelicalism itself, as a significant cohort of its 'early men' died during the early thirties. The phrase is the BFBS chronicler William Canton's: 'A natural line of cleavage separates the year 1833-4 from the remainder of the first half century, and may be said to close the era of the Early Men.' This group included most of the names associated with the Clapham 'saints': Wilberforce, Adam Clarke, the two Secretaries John Owen and Joseph Hughes, James Stephen and Zachary Macaulay, and Lord Teignmouth. According to Doreen Rosman, 'there was widespread recognition both within and without evangelical circles that the movement was changing and that a generation was passing'. The 'early men' were replaced by younger people whose religious and social agendas were somewhat different. Boyd Hilton detects a shift from moderate to extreme evangelicalism in these years. And in his book on revivalism, *Holding the Fort,* John Kent speaks of 'the rise between 1830 and 1850 of a "new evangelicalism", lay in spirit, urban in concern, disaffected from the ministry, indifferent to denominational frontiers, expressing its distrust of traditional religious institutions by the formation of new ones, which were kept out of the control of the clergy as far as possible'.[76] Within the BFBS, a confidential pamphlet produced in 1867 by the Rev. J. P. Hewlett addressed the concern that the Society was

Table 3. *Occupations and dates of entry of Committee members*

	Number	%	Early 1804–24 %	Middle 1825–44 %	Late 1845–64 %
Commercial					
merchant	42	14.0	17.3	10.0	12.4
textile	15	5.0	6.0	2.9	5.2
transport, etc.	10	3.3	6.0	1.4	1.0
food and drink	10	3.3	5.3	0.0	3.1
book trade	6	2.0	1.5	2.9	2.1
luxury	5	1.7	1.5	4.3	0.0
leather	7	2.3	4.5	0.0	1.0
other	13	4.3	3.8	5.7	4.1
	108	35.9	45.9	27.2	28.9
Professional					
law	27	9.0	9.8	7.1	9.3
medicine	7	2.3	.8	7.1	1.0
military	11	3.7	0.0	1.4	10.3
	45	15.0	10.6	15.6	20.6
Financial					
banker	11	3.7	3.8	4.3	3.1
broker	10	3.3	3.8	2.9	3.1
other	5	1.7	1.5	1.4	2.1
	26	8.7	9.1	8.6	8.3
Gentlemen	14	4.7	.8	12.9	4.1
Political					
M.P.	11	3.7	4.5	2.9	3.1
civil servant	2	.7	.8	0.0	1.0
	13	4.4	5.3	2.9	4.1
Intellectual					
scientific	3	1.0	1.5	1.4	0.0
literary	3	1.0	2.3	0.0	0.0
educational	3	1.0	0.8	1.4	1.0
other	2	.7	0.0	0.0	2.1
	11	3.7	4.6	2.8	3.1
Occupation unknown	83	27.7	24.1	30.0	30.9
Grand total	300	100.0	100.0	100.0	100.0

becoming marked by 'the decidedly religious element'.[77] How did it happen that an organization which began by insisting on being 'not a religious Society' was troubled sixty years later by a 'decidedly religious element'? The answer lies in the changing nature of the phenomenon of evangelicalism.

Many of the first BFBS officers were associated with the Clapham Sect, leaders of the movements for the abolition of slavery and the suppression of vice. People at Clapham used their high social positions to press Parliament and the society at large for the changes they desired. The first Committee included several of the names associated with Clapham: Granville Sharp, William Wilberforce, John Thornton and Charles Grant; the first President was Lord Teignmouth, former Governor-General of India and, like the others, a Clapham evangelical.[78] The BFBS was the largest of the 'eight great societies' that were inspired and organized by evangelical enthusiasm.[79]

As time went on, the influence of the Clapham 'saints' diminished. But even at the beginning, not every person associated officially with the Bible Society was a committed proponent of the ideals of vital religion and social propriety that are traditionally ascribed to Clapham evangelicalism. There were other reasons to accept an office. Both the national body and local Auxiliaries, particularly in the early years when aristocratic patronage was a mark of respectability, quite explicitly courted 'the drinking squire, the swearing lord, and the man who has taken the chair in the hope of increasing his votes at the next election'.[80] In addition to the working officers and the Committee and staff, the Society had a long list of Vice-Presidents and Honorary Life Members. In 1807 the President, Lord Teignmouth, had to caution the 'Subcommittee for Obtaining Patronage' not to send a circular letter to a list of noblemen, asking them to accept Vice-Presidencies. Teignmouth advised that such requests be made 'in a more private manner, to prevent the unpleasant circumstances of an *official* application being in any instance rejected'.[81] Most of those who accepted the invitation served in a purely formal capacity, but the honour was not always appreciated. Lord Orford, invited to become a patron of the Norwich Auxiliary, wrote to the chairman:

Sir, – I am surprised and annoyed by the contents of your letter, surprised, because my well-known character should have exempted me from such an application, and annoyed, because it obliges me to have even this communication with *you*.

I have long been addicted to the gaming table – I have lately taken to the turf, – I fear I frequently blaspheme – but I *have never distributed religious tracts*. All this was well known to you and your Society; notwithstanding which, you think me a fit person for your President. God forgive your hypocrisy. I would rather live in the land of sinners than with *such Saints*.[82]

Not all aristocrats were so 'honourable' and Presidencies and Vice-Presidencies were routinely filled by upper-class men who participated only at public functions. Hypocrisy of this kind was not what Wilberforce had in mind when he wrote his *Practical View*, urging the upper classes to take a serious view of Christianity. But the regular Committee members and staff of the Society learned early that public approval could be courted at low cost by offering such honorary positions.

The Lord Orfords were not, however, invited to join working Committees of the Bible Society. Rather, it was Committees who invited them to serve in honorary positions. It is possible, therefore, to use the collective biography of the Society's Committee membership to make some limited remarks about the nature of nineteenth-century evangelicalism. The evangelicals have always been associated with Cambridge University and with the London residential community of Clapham.[83] Of the very few members who attended university, thirteen were at Cambridge, while only five attended Oxford. Similarly the *Alumni Cantabrigienses* yields the names of sixteen who sent sons to Cambridge. Many of the latter were merchants and others who represented 'Foreign Churches' on the Committee. But university education was not a characteristic of the BFBS Committee. It was clergy evangelicalism, more than the lay variety, that found such a hospitable home at Cambridge. Another indication of evangelical status was residence at Clapham. Thirty-five Committee members lived there: by far the largest group in any one community, but a small minority of the total number.[84] It seems that while Cambridge and Clapham held their own as evangelical strongholds, they were by no means the only sources for the personnel of 'enthusiasm'. Few members had any formal higher education, and even fewer were fortunate enough to live in the fastness of Clapham.

It is difficult and dangerous to generalize beyond these narrowly quantifiable attributes of the 'saints' and their colleagues. For every landed gentleman, there was an artist or a scientist. Some of the MPs were Whigs, while others were Tories. In the 1840s there were Committee members both pro- and anti-Corn Law. And so on. The occupational diversity found among this cohort of three hundred individuals, especially when cross-indexed with their denominational differences, suggests that the Society did not long remain as it was planned by the Clapham evangelicals of the Religious Tract Society. As our perception of the Society moves away from the elite level of Clapham evangelicals, and towards the people who were inspired by their leadership, we begin to discover a great deal about evangelical occupations, wealth, and family connections, at the popular level. Ernest L. Howse concluded his overview of evangelical achievements with the observation that 'it can be appreciated that their tiny group left a real impression on world history'. There is no question that the Clapham sect influenced the political decisions to abolish slavery and to evangelize India. The argument here is that the group that affected world history was not so tiny, that while the Clapham elite may have inspired popular evangelicalism, they did not dominate its activities.

In summary, the members of the BFBS Committee were sincerely religious, or they did not last long. But they were also tough-minded business people, with extensive connections in London, the provinces and Europe. Far from being stereotypically rigid and narrow in outlook, they were innovators and risk-takers, prepared to think in terms of a global enterprise, and able to manage one when it began to develop. And they were busy men. George Borrow once told a Spanish politician that the Committee members were 'by no means of [a] turbulent and outrageous disposition; ... they were for the most part staid, quiet gentlemen, who attended to their own affairs, and a little, and but a little to the promulgation of Christ's Gospel'.[85]

For the BFBS to survive as an ecumenical organization during the years of controversy, the Committee and the Secretaries had to affirm frequently its theological neutrality and non-proselytizing character, and exclude the Society from the main trends of theological discussion. Distribution of the scriptures without note or comment: the BFBS survived schism and social upheaval by a rigid and pragmatic interpretation of that fundamental principle. The 'men at Earl Street' were committed evangelicals, not the hypocrites their critics believed. But they were also men of the world – confident, convinced of their own merit, protected by a privileged social position and reinforced by sustaining alliances. They were ambitious people, absolutely convinced that the means as well as the objectives of their project were sound. Perhaps because of this certainty, they interpreted their theology more pragmatically than did many of their supporters. The Society lost subscribers over its determination to circulate Apocryphal Bibles in Europe, and again when it refused to purge itself of Unitarians. But nothing was allowed to interrupt its production cycle: translating, printing, distributing and raising money to support further translations and editions.

The Committee were lawyers, merchants, tradesmen and so forth, inspired and empowered by evangelical ideals. It was their ability and collective expertise, not their piety, that got cheap books printed and bound by the thousand. This expertise included not only their knowledge of London business, professional and political circles, but also their experience of holding the Society together in the face of controversy. Members of the Committee, the officers and the Secretaries, were unconditionally committed to the project of circulating the scriptures globally, cheaply, in adequate translations, without note or comment, and without the addition of the Apocrypha or the problem of prayer. As we shall see in their dealings with privileged Presses, with trade printers, and with craft bookbinders, they approached their mission as a business, in a pragmatic way. They used innovative processes and technology, and highly cost-conscious business methods to implement their evangelical purpose.

But before considering the Committee in its relations with the book trade, it is necessary to examine the popular side of the Bible transaction. An unexpected demand developed for the books the Committee published, when a subaltern class of religious enthusiasts formed voluntary organizations called Auxiliaries to reduce the high cost of participating in the BFBS 'noble object'. The concept of distribution abroad inspired these people to disperse the scriptures to the poor in their own communities, and the popularity of local distribution in turn generated more funds for the foreign project. And the 'biblicization' of the British poor led to a new round of criticism and controversy for the Committee and Secretaries to handle.

2 · A BIBLE TRANSACTION, 1804–1840

In dickens's novel *Little Dorrit*, Arthur Clennam remembers about his childhood Sundays that 'his mother, stern of face and unrelenting of heart, would sit all day behind a bible – bound like her own construction of it in the hardest, barest, and straitest boards, with one dinted ornament on the cover like the drag of a chain, and a wrathful sprinkling of red upon the edges of the leaves'.[1] When Dickens cast Mrs Clennam's austerity, rigidity, dogmatism and narrow piety in an image evoking the physical form of a Bible, many of his contemporary readers would have remembered the local British and Foreign Bible Society of their childhood. Thousands of people like Mrs Clennam not only read the Society's Bibles themselves, they bespoke such books in large numbers to circulate to their working-class neighbours in the hope of effecting conversion, edification and even political restraint.

Because of their demand, the Committee and Secretaries of the British and Foreign Bible Society required books from their printers in unprecedented quantities: Bibles and New Testaments in the Authorized Version of King James, for circulation at home. The enormous demand for cheap Bibles came from the women and men who formed Auxiliary Bible Societies at the level of towns and villages. While the founders had been inspired by the dearth of scriptures in Wales to extend their project abroad ('If for Wales, why not for the world?'), people in local Bible Auxiliaries found that the international project motivated them to domestic distribution. Many middle-class people seized upon the idea of reaching out to their poor neighbours with printed copies of the scriptures, while simultaneously contributing to the salvation of heathen, pagan and Roman Catholic souls abroad. They did not ignore the foreign field, but their mission was to save souls among the heathen by indirection, by first 'biblicizing' the British poor.

One result of this movement appears in the Society's financial statements: the mass-production and marketing of cheap Bibles for the domestic market produced sufficient revenue to finance the publication of books for distribution abroad. When it became very popular for women and men all over Britain to sell cheap Bibles and Testaments to the poor in their local communities, the Society became increasingly wealthy. The result was the publication of dozens of translations in foreign languages, and the dispatch of agents to Europe and around the world. These achievements resulted directly from the demand created for cheap Bibles and Testaments for the poor in Britain.

The huge demand of local Bible Societies can be characterized as a function of popular evangelicalism. Leonore Davidoff and Catherine Hall, among other social historians, have shown how the beliefs of the circle at Clapham came to affect the behaviour of a whole generation of middle-class men and women. 'The evangelical struggle for English hearts and minds was conducted not through the political meeting, the ballot box or the hustings, but through the sermon, the tract, the Sunday school, the auxiliary society and the philanthropic visit.'[2] In Dissenting congregations, as in the Church of England, the impulse to 'vital religion' stirred men and women to social action which they believed was necessary, both for their own salvation and for that of the people they were trying to help. For example, a clergyman wrote from Chester that the Bible was 'alas ... scarcely known in those counties I am most acquainted with – a real ignorance, a perverse blindness, and an astonishing indolence prevails'.[3]

Not everyone saw the situation this way. Indeed, one way to measure the influence of evangelical religion is to observe how it horrified those people who opposed it. As one clergyman put it, 'Among the many chimerical projects, in which the spirit of modern adventure delights to indulge its vanity, and boast of success, the most insufferable to every thinking mind, are those which are undertaken in sacred subjects.' Another, Robert Forby, published in the *Norwich Mercury* of 1814 a letter to his Bishop, where he complained of

certain religionists, abounding in the Bible Society, swarming in every corner of the land, and indefatigable in their endeavours to proselyte the lowest orders of the people ... Under the name of *experiences*, (a name dreadfully pregnant with delusion in its current use,) they claim without scruple ... express and sensible interpositions of heaven in their favour, in the most ordinary occurrences of daily life. From their *journals*, their *sermons*, and smaller *tracts*, one would suppose that they not only believed the age of miracles returned, but that miracles are become infinitely more abundant, and are wrought on far less important occasions, than those which the most credulous and enthusiastic of the early christian writers have ventured to record.

A third writer, J. E. Jackson, was equally severe in 1822. The impulse of vital religion, or enthusiasm, he felt, was all-pervasive,

in the Anniversary and the Committee Meeting – in the city and village – in advertisements in the newspapers, and in placards on the walls. It crosses you in your walks, with troops of female associates; it is the theme of your social parties, and of your domestic circles. It ascends your pulpits, and *canvasses* for charity at your doors.[4]

'It' was evangelical enthusiasm, the animating energy that the Committee shared with its followers, but also struggled to control.

Jackson was not alone in his unease with the notion of 'troops of female associates'. There was concern at Earl Street that the fragile nonsectarian constitution of the Society might be undermined by the actions of well-meaning and undiplomatic supporters, especially of women. The delicate politics of interdenominational co-operation, as interpreted by London's business and professional elite, were invaded by the enthusiasm of people of both sexes, anxious to roll up their collective sleeves and start receiving subscriptions, immediately and in large numbers. The Committee gradually adapted its business methods to a geographically dispersed, decentralized organization. As we shall see in chapter 5, methods of distribution were developed that would cater as much as possible to the demand, while also maintaining some control over the transaction.

The concept of a national organization of voluntary auxiliaries was not part of the original idea of the Bible Society, nor did it form any part of the 'fundamental principle'. It seems likely that the founders visualized the Bible transaction primarily in terms of languages other than English, and in terms of free distribution. Wales, as the first area to be supplied, was not of course a foreign country, but it nonetheless seemed foreign, Celtic and remote to the London gentlemen whose charitable impulses were aroused by Mary Jones's tragic story. The first translation to be published, the gospel of St John in the Mohawk language for the native peoples of Upper Canada, no doubt conformed to their notion of what a Bible Society ought to be doing.[5]

An early suggestion from a Birmingham clergyman, that local societies be formed to which poor people could subscribe for Bibles by instalment payments of one penny or so per week, was deferred for later consideration. At an RTS meeting of 28 December 1802, the object of the new society was defined as being:

To promote the circulation of the Holy Scriptures in foreign Countries and in those parts of the British Dominions for which adequate provision is not yet made, it being understood that no English translations of the Scriptures will be gratuitously circulated by the Society in Great Britain.[6]

The founders apparently did not consider the British working class either as a source of funds or as a market for scriptures: like potential readers abroad, the British poor were thought of in terms of need, not of commercial opportunity. And that need was not to be catered to by an overgenerous policy.

On the other hand the British upper and middle classes were regarded as a source of both funds and information. Soon after the founding meeting in April 1804, the Secretaries and officers initiated a correspondence with sympathetic clergymen and also began to travel throughout Britain, seeking to determine what the need was and to begin fund-raising. They expected subscriptions, donations, legacies and collections from the well-off religious community.[7] Translation and printing had to be paid for, and the means by which individuals could support the project was the time-honoured one of voluntary societies, the subscription.[8] Individuals could ally themselves with the Bible Society by subscribing one guinea annually.

Bible Society subscriptions occupied an ambiguous zone overlapping both membership fees and payments for books. In the contemporary book trade, subscription was a very common way for publishers to finance the initial costs of books published for the wealthier part of their market. A prospectus was circulated, and interested readers paid for their copies before they were printed, sometimes before they were written.[9] The resulting books were delivered in sheets or gatherings, and the purchaser arranged for binding to suit his own library. But management models were undergoing innovation and change, in the printing and bookbinding trades as in philanthropic societies. Michael Sadleir, the bibliographer of nineteenth-century novels, notes that

not until the teens of the century was the very genus publisher a more than exceptional phenomenon ... There persisted, in fact, at once demand and machinery for a publishing function which involved merely the cost of printing and announcing, and the arrangement for despatch. But side by side with the old was springing up the new; and the desire to cater for the wider reading public brought big development in new book societies and lending libraries, whose demand for immediate *bound* supplies brought into sudden existence a new form of middleman.[10]

Sadleir is speaking of the publishers of novels. Like them, the BFBS Committee was a go-between, and its demand for bound books, in quantity, to supply a variety of classes of readers, paralleled that of others who were developing the 'genus publisher'. The BFBS had a further reason for issuing bound Bibles only: not only did its public require books ready-to-read, but the Apocrypha controversy demonstrated the danger that noncanonical books could be bound up with the approved text.

The Committee, however, did not act like other publishers when it came to distribution. They developed their own models for book distribution – first the subscription system, then Auxiliaries and Associations, and later, in the eighteen-fifties, colportage. An early suggestion that booksellers be allowed to sell for the Society was answered that 'any connexion with the Trade at large for the purpose proposed, would prove injurious to the interests of the Society'.[11] The initial distribution of Bibles within Britain shows the Committee feeling their way through inexperience. As we shall see, this was also the approach to printing and to binding. But unlike the generic arrangements made in production and packaging, they seem to have understood that the product had to be conveyed to purchasers in a specialized way if it was to be valued as something other than a market-place commodity. In their minds, the BFBS Bible was qualitatively different from Bibles sold in shops, even if it looked identical. It embodied not only its text, but the whole notion of world-wide evangelism. And – more prosaically – an arrangement with the book trade would have increased the price of Bibles by whatever percentage resulted from adding a commission.

The annual guinea not only conferred membership in the organization, but entitled one to subscriber's privilege, the right to purchase Bibles at substantial discounts. The books were kept in the premises of the Depositary, who doled them out to subscribers. Prices had been established on the basis of production cost, with 5 per cent 'poundage' added to pay for handling. But subscribers were offered reduced prices at 20 per cent lower. 'At the *reduced* prices, as specified in the Society's Catalogue, each Annual Subscriber of One Guinea has the privilege of purchasing Bibles and Testaments, within the year, to the amount of Five Guineas: and in like proportion for every additional Guinea subscribed.'[12] That is, a subscriber's initial payment (21 shillings) would cover the discount (20 per cent of up to 105 shillings) and the Society would recover the full cost price of all books sold, whether by subscribers or otherwise. But the funds would not then be available for other purposes, and the costs of administration and especially of the foreign project were heavy.

In any case the subscription method of marketing cheap Bibles had its limitations. What, for example, was a 5-guinea subscriber to do with the books allowed him? Supply them to his dependants, if he was a country gentleman; but not many commercial and professional people like the members of the early Committee enjoyed a direct relation with those whom they wished to convert. The alienation between the classes was a function of industrialization that disturbed evangelicals and their contemporaries. The evangelical solution was to create connections where none existed, visiting the poor to preach, exhort, and provide both physical and spiritual nourishment. The Bible Society's innovation was to make the new connection a commercial one, to build networks of social relations on a retail basis. Their recognition and acceptance of the fact of urbanization is noteworthy. The Committee and Secretaries must have been among the first people in England to deal in a practical way with the increasing population and resulting social distances. But they were matter-of-fact about it. Not long after the founding meeting in 1804, people began to think about providing cheap Bibles by selling them door-to-door and keeping detailed written records. In this context the subscribers' allowance was an unwieldy and inefficient method of handling the problem of distribution.

The Committee's modest efforts to attract support were quickly supplanted by the enthusiasm of Auxiliary Societies, local groups formed to collect subscriptions at a lower rate than the parent Society's guinea-a-year. It was not the 'saints' of the Clapham Sect who first hit upon the idea of popular support for the Society. It was ordinary evangelicals, obscure individuals living in industrial towns distant from London, people altogether without influence over Church or Parliament. What they had to contribute was time and money, both of which could be used more effectively if they were well organized.

The Reading and Nottingham Societies, both founded in 1809, are

Figure 3   Charles Stokes Dudley (1780–1862).

regarded as the first two official Auxiliaries of the parent Society.[13] There had been some earlier approximations: as early as July 1805 there appeared in London 'an association for the purpose of contributing to the fund' of the BFBS, based on an initial donation of between 2 and 7 shillings, and a monthly subscription of 6d to 1s. The members took turns acting as collectors.[14] A similar movement began in Birmingham in April 1806, initiating the plan of dividing the town into districts, with collectors appointed for each. The London plan, however, made no allowance for promoting local activity, while the Birmingham arrangements were strictly short term. 'But', as Charles Stokes Dudley exulted, 'it was reserved for the town of *Reading* to give, to Great Britain and the world, the primary example of a regular "Auxiliary Bible Society".'[15] This was five years after the founding of the parent Society. The Reading Auxiliary's constitution was modelled directly after that of the BFBS. That is, the Auxiliary was to be directed by an interdenominational Committee and two Secretaries, Anglican and dissenting.

The sociology of Auxiliary formation merits more extensive study than is possible here. The official histories of the Society insist that the Auxiliaries appeared spontaneously. Canton had to admit that 'it was not to resourceful prevision, to ingenious and effective organisation, to eloquent advocacy on the part of the founders, that the marvellous growth of the institution was due'.[16] This belief was probably correct, in the sense that the London Secretaries did not go out to organize local bodies. But they did advertise widely in provincial newspapers and correspond with sympathetic clergymen and ministers. And when interest appeared the Committee was quick to respond and to promote it. The Committee minutes of 4 April 1808 recommend 'the formation of Societies in large towns ... in imitation of those at Birmingham & Glasgow'.[17] The Birmingham group had been meeting for two years, but the Glasgow Society had been formed only a few months earlier. By the 17th, at a meeting of the Subcommittee for augmenting the funds of the Society, it was resolved that the minutes of another new Auxiliary be advertised in several periodicals and in the morning and evening papers.

Much of the initiative for Auxiliaries and Associations must be attributed to Charles Stokes Dudley. The powerful rhetoric of this remarkable animator not only supplied the energy for founding most of the local Auxiliary Societies, it also survives, in his correspondence, to narrate and document the remarkable events he inspired. William Canton called him 'a shrewd, far-seeing, indefatigable man, with a wonderful faculty of management, and a quiet confidence that the surest way of getting a thing was to insist on having it'.[18] The organizer of Ladies' Bible Societies was much influenced by his mother, Mary Dudley (née Stokes) of Bristol, who was a minister in the Society of Friends. Her son Charles was born in 1780 in Ireland, and left that country in 1798 with his mother and siblings, to escape the effects of the rebellion. Dudley began his career in England as a merchant in Bristol, where he met Southey and Coleridge. He moved to London in 1807 and became involved with BFBS activity in the borough of Southwark, south of the Thames. Here he expanded upon the Birmingham plan of subdividing a populous region into manageable districts. Dudley was a member of the Committee of the parent Society in 1815, but by that time was already promoting his Southwark system of district subdivision throughout the country. A bankruptcy in 1819 caused him to resign from this volunteer work, but as soon as his affairs were in order, he reappeared as a paid Agent of the Society. He published a book in 1821, *An Analysis of the System of the Bible Society*.[19] At about this time he dispensed with his Quaker heritage and began to attend the Church of England. He travelled widely as the first District Secretary, an estimated 300,000 miles to address nearly 8,000 public meetings and establish nearly 1,500 local Auxiliaries, Branches and Associations. Dudley retired in 1857 and died in 1862. A memorial by George T. Edwards remembered 'his striking personality, his genial presence, his eloquent voice and graphic descriptive powers, his quiet Irish humour, his self-denying labours, his simple godliness and blameless life'.[20]

Edwards claimed that after 1834, 'when the new Poor Law system was being established in the country, hints for its orderly working were taken from "Dudley's Analysis"'. It seems that Dudley's pragmatic attitudes to proselytizing and organization shared some assumptions with the attitudes of utilitarian reformers. Edwin Chadwick and other followers of Jeremy Bentham were subdividing the country in an effort to rationalize and reduce the cost of relieving the distress of the poor. Dudley, too, thought in systematic terms about social problems and was willing to override traditional barriers to achieve his goal of widespread scripture distribution. But unlike the irreligious Benthamites, he always identified divine intervention in his schemes.

Dudley's handiwork may be seen in the social geography of local Bible Societies. The first task for people coming together to start an Auxiliary was to divide their 'town and neighbourhood' into districts. The ambiguous, unofficial category of 'districts' overrode the boundaries of county and parish. Dudley believed that a county was usually too large an area for convenient organization, and a parish too small. In any case the county was contaminated by its association with local government, and the parish by the associated Anglican clergy and congregation. The process of organizing across denominational lines to collect subscriptions, he believed, should not be impeded by the petty, perhaps antagonistic authority of local worthies. If there was a territory that was too large for a district, yet too small to combine several districts in an Auxiliary, a Branch Bible Society was formed there. By 1811 fifty-two Auxiliaries had formed in England, and in 1812 another sixty-three started, bringing the total since 1809 to 115. The next year there were thirty-one more, then sixteen in 1814, nine in 1815 and six in 1816, so that there were 177 Auxiliary Societies by that date. The growth in Scotland was equally impressive, with forty-seven Auxiliaries by 1816. Within ten years of the first Auxiliaries, they were to be found in almost all the English and Scottish counties.[21] Over twenty years before the Poor Law Unions, Bible Society Auxiliaries were drawing new and practical geographical boundary lines, where traditional ones proved awkward to administer.

There was some confusion about the financial relationship between Auxiliaries and the parent Society in the early years of rapid and unexpected growth. Most individuals paid their subscriptions to local Societies, which were supposed to sell the Bibles they distributed at the full cost price. Some Auxiliaries wished to make books available to worthy recipients at the reduced prices, a practice that was discouraged at the London headquarters. For example in 1811 the Rotherham and Vicinity Auxiliary Bible Society in the West Riding of Yorkshire wished to purchase Bibles and Testaments at the reduced prices, up to the total amount of their collective subscriptions. This was refused, 'as it would be ruinous to the Society to make such allowances'.[22] Reduced prices for subscribers were meant only for people who subscribed on an individual basis directly to the BFBS, a very small percentage of the total membership. Auxiliaries made very generous corporate donations to London, but had they been allowed to sell Bibles below the cost prices, the Society would have lost money on the English editions, and have been no further ahead on the foreign account.

In 1812 C. S. Dudley and the Quaker solicitor Richard Phillips developed a set of rules for handling the important relationship between local societies and London. Auxiliaries dispatched virtually all their receipts to the parent Society for management. Half the funds were assigned – as 'Free Contributions' – to the general purposes of the Society. The balance was placed in a 'moiety account' to pay for Bibles and Testaments at the cost prices, not the reduced prices permitted to subscribers, for local distribution. Cost prices were determined by compiling the expenses of printing and binding, with a small percentage added for handling. The books acquired by an Auxiliary or Branch Bible Society from Earl Street were kept in a local depository. Thus was established the economics of the Bible transaction: only half the funds collected locally were assigned to meet local need. Of every shilling collected by an Auxiliary, sixpence went for translation and publication for distribution abroad. In his *Analysis* Dudley modestly attributes to Phillips the honour of having systematized the operations of the local Societies. 'The tree was indeed planted; but he saw the necessity of watching its growth, of training its branches, and of giving a right direction to that vigor which might otherwise run into wild and unprofitable luxuriance.'[23] In fact the two worked together, and when Dudley came on the paid staff of the Society he surpassed Phillips's efforts.

Dudley was an ardent animator. In 1811, in his own London borough of

Southwark, he personally visited over 2,000 families, over half of which he found 'destitute of the holy scriptures'. He organized a system whereby the area was divided into twelve subdistricts, which were then worked by volunteer collectors.[24] Dudley also travelled widely to set up local Societies, staying with local people who had expressed interest, holding public meetings to generate local enthusiasm, and then sitting down afterwards with the core of a committee to give them practical guidelines for their forthcoming work. He wrote lengthy reports to headquarters, some of which were copied almost verbatim into annual *Reports* and the *Monthly Extracts of Correspondence*, while others were private and confidential. But like any travelling agent who speaks on behalf of his superiors, Dudley expected support from headquarters. He wrote from Birmingham in April 1827 to complain about their neglect:

Pray how would you *feel*, & what would you *say*, if you had been absent from Earl St more than *a month* without receiving a line from any of the Officers? Just ponder on this question for half an hour while you are demolishing your Beef Steak next Tuesday, & then I believe you *will* gratify me with a good Budget of news.[25]

Dudley's letter was answered three days later, not a slow response when coach journeys took many days and there was not yet a Penny Post. Dudley's own letters sometimes failed to provide detailed 'intelligence' quickly enough to suit the anxious Committee and Secretaries waiting in London for news.

Dudley's employers, the Committee and Secretaries, were eager to promote the idea of Auxiliaries, but they also wanted to control it. From the beginning there were fears that local evangelical enthusiasm would endanger the precarious partnership between Anglicans and Dissenters. Although the parent Society could not control an Auxiliary's disposal of its own property, they cautioned against free gifts of books, and pressed the 'fundamental principle', reminding their supporters that 'without note or comment' meant no preaching either at the subscriber's door or at public meetings. Not all members obeyed, and there was a fierce attack in pamphlets by writers like Richard Lloyd, who inveighed against such indignities as approaches to the servants of clergymen. It was insulting, he argued, even to imply that a clergyman might have failed to supply his dependants with books. Society supporters replied that rudeness to the master was preferable to eternal damnation for his servants. Other critics were offended by the brashly public nature of the Society's activities. Thomas Sykes, the self-styled 'Country Clergyman', referred to

the frolicksome excursion they [Associations] have made, and the Easter gambols they played off amongst us. But I imagine you did not foresee that they would leave London, and ramble here and there in a disorderly way ... At length this celebrated company has stept forth into the provinces, and, with much pomp and circumstance, has exhibited itself to the wondering eyes of us country-folks. We have seen its stately march, and its imposing appearance; its mighty list of subscribers, thrust upon our notice like the labels of Lucky Turner's Lottery Cart.[26]

Meanwhile H. H. Norris, Rector of Hackney, raised more extreme concerns. The system of district subdivision, he claimed, was not merely undignified, but potentially subversive. He regarded penny-a-week subscriptions as modelled after a dangerous precedent 'the most *recent* exemplification of which will be found in the financial system of the United Irishmen [who]... were only Plagiarists of the English Puritans'. In other places he compared the arrangements to those of the German Illuminati. It is instructive to recognize that some people, in the years of the French wars, believed that local Bible-subscription Societies might be revolutionary cells. Norris was not the only one. R. B. Fisher, the Vicar of Basildon in Essex, wrote to admonish a fellow-clergyman in Hackney about the system of conducting associations there, which included frequent public meetings and addresses on the value and importance of the scriptures. He asked 'what security can you give the friends of the Society, that it will not be the instrument of inculcating errors? What security can you give the Government, that it will not be perverted to political purposes?'[27] The Committee had to deal with the reality behind Norris's criticisms. There is no evidence that anyone was shielding behind district committees to plot treason. But the zeal of dissenting members, who preached to and prayed with the recipients of Society Bibles, was regarded by some Anglican supporters as tantamount to sedition.

Still the enthusiasm of popular evangelicalism had to be managed: there was no question of stopping it. Apart from any other considerations, it was too profitable. The people in Nottingham had explicitly requested that their initial collection of £223 be divided equally between the BFBS and the supply of poor people locally. As we have seen, this sort of arrangement became general, and the financial benefits to headquarters were immediately obvious. Half of each Auxiliary's funds went into the accounts of the parent Society, to pay the expenses of foreign Agents, to purchase or print foreign-language scriptures, and to fund salaries and administration. Canton speaks of the 'golden dawn which was breaking on the prospects of the Society'.[28] The annual 'Cash Accounts' printed in annual *Reports* and abstracted in the appendix, show that only a small fraction of BFBS wealth was produced by subscriptions (about 2 per cent) and other traditional sources, such as legacies. On the other hand by 1812 over 60 per cent of the Society's funds was coming from Auxiliaries, first from the half of their subscriptions devoted to the foreign purposes of the Society, and second from 'free contributions' gathered from members who wished to contribute but not to receive Bibles.

The Auxiliary contributions were especially startling in the first twenty years. They rose from nil between 1805 and 1809, to £5,942 in 1810, £24,813 in 1812, £55,099 in 1813 and a maximum of £61,848 in 1815. The figures remained in the £55,000 range until 1822 when they dropped abruptly, to £15,622. This change reflects the unease of the Scottish Auxiliaries over circulation of the Apocrypha. Eighteen twenty-one was the year of Dudley's

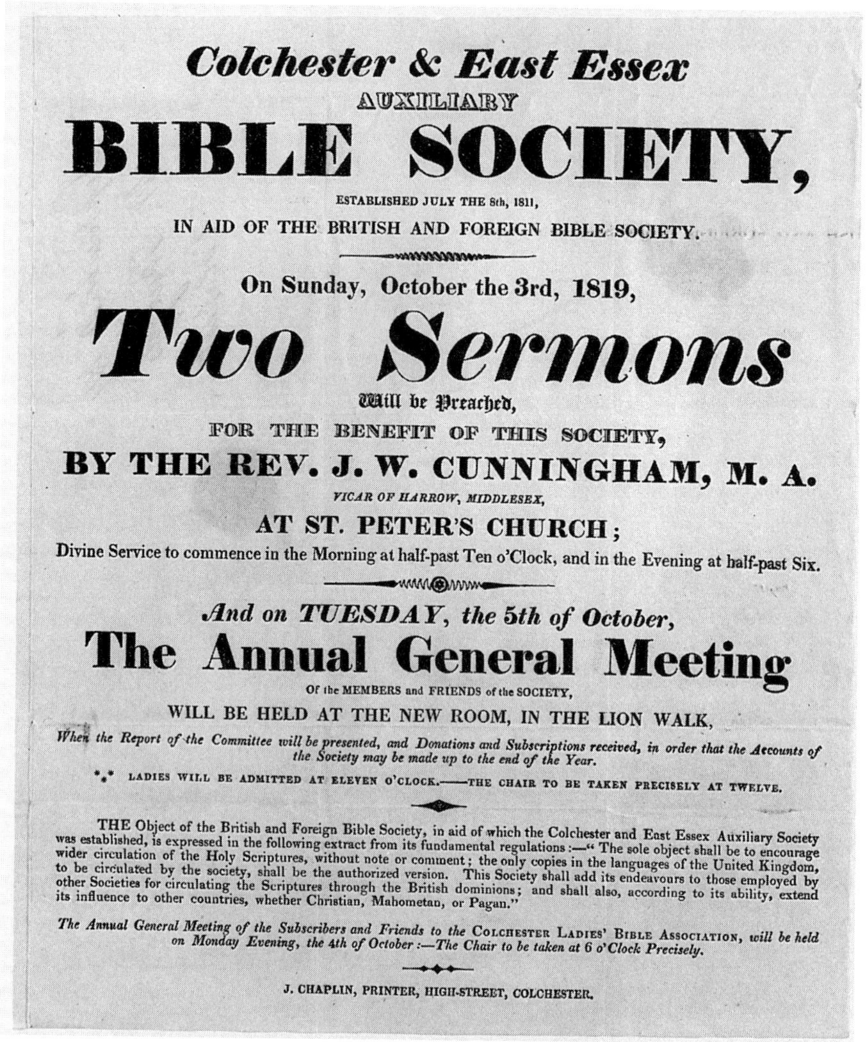

Colchester & East Essex

AUXILIARY

BIBLE SOCIETY,

ESTABLISHED JULY THE 8th, 1811,

IN AID OF THE BRITISH AND FOREIGN BIBLE SOCIETY.

On Sunday, October the 3rd, 1819,

Two Sermons

Will be Preached,

FOR THE BENEFIT OF THIS SOCIETY,

BY THE REV. J. W. CUNNINGHAM, M. A.

VICAR OF HARROW, MIDDLESEX,

AT ST. PETER'S CHURCH;

Divine Service to commence in the Morning at half-past Ten o'Clock, and in the Evening at half-past Six.

And on TUESDAY, the 5th of October,

The Annual General Meeting

Of the MEMBERS and FRIENDS of the SOCIETY,

WILL BE HELD AT THE NEW ROOM, IN THE LION WALK,

When the Report of the Committee will be presented, and Donations and Subscriptions received, in order that the Accounts of the Society may be made up to the end of the Year.

⁂ LADIES WILL BE ADMITTED AT ELEVEN O'CLOCK.——THE CHAIR TO BE TAKEN PRECISELY AT TWELVE.

THE Object of the British and Foreign Bible Society, in aid of which the Colchester and East Essex Auxiliary Society was established, is expressed in the following extract from its fundamental regulations:—"The sole object shall be to encourage wider circulation of the Holy Scriptures, without note or comment; the only copies in the languages of the United Kingdom, to be circulated by the society, shall be the authorized version. This Society shall add its endeavours to those employed by other Societies for circulating the Scriptures through the British dominions; and shall also, according to its ability, extend its influence to other countries, whether Christian, Mahometan, or Pagan."

The Annual General Meeting of the Subscribers and Friends to the COLCHESTER LADIES' BIBLE ASSOCIATION, *will be held on Monday Evening, the 4th of October:—The Chair to be taken at 6 o'Clock Precisely.*

J. CHAPLIN, PRINTER, HIGH-STREET, COLCHESTER.

Figure 4 Broadside promoting the Bible Society in Colchester and east Essex, 1819.

financial crisis, which meant that he was unavailable to perform his miracles of organization. And in the wider world, there was great economic distress in the wake of the Napoleonic wars. By 1830, however, the contributions of Auxiliary Societies were back in the range of £30,000, where they remained until the 1850s.

These massive receipts were offset somewhat by the cost of managing the

Auxiliaries and Associations. Dudley was the only agent until 1828, at a salary of £300. To his travel expenses the Committee had to add the cost of travel for the clergymen who volunteered to represent the Society at annual meetings. In addition there were publications designed to excite and maintain interest in the activities of the Society – annual *Reports*, a one-page description of the BFBS called the *Brief View*, and other publications. In the appendix these costs are described as 'Promotion', since they represent the costs of promoting or marketing the Society's message within Britain. The most important of these, published from 1817, was the *Monthly Extracts of Correspondence*. Forty thousand copies were circulating by 1821 when Dudley published his *Analysis*. He claimed that he had 'often ... beheld the mechanic or the peasant seated, after the labours of the day, in the midst of his family, listening with eager interest, as his wife or child read this announcement of *"good news from a far country"'*. Moreover, it was most desirable 'that *this* is added to the list of periodical antidotes to the poison of infidelity and sedition'.[29] Later renamed the *Monthly Reporter*, this publication was part of the cost of promoting the Bible Society within Great Britain. It also served to inform or remind Auxiliary members of policies established at headquarters, thus offsetting some of the dangers that evangelical enthusiasm would result in betrayals of the 'fundamental principle'.

The rhetoric of the Bible Society maintained that Auxiliaries were independent organizations, whose relationship to the parent Society was freely chosen on both sides.[30] In fact there was a constant tension between the autonomy of Auxiliaries and the authority of the central office. C. S. Dudley believed that just as working-class families would benefit morally from being in debt for copies of the scriptures, so also the relations of Auxiliaries with the parent Society should be characterized by debt. He wrote to Joseph Tarn in 1815, 'speaking candidly ... to make thee master of a secret', about the importance of participation in the larger transaction to members of the Association at Southwark:

For more than 2 years my endeavours have been directed to one point, an Infusion into an Assoc of the important Truth, that *they also form a part, & contribute to the success, of the Parent Soc[iet]y* & the knowledge of our *never* buying a Bible has been a principal Charm, & has acted as a potent spell on our Associations, which are making a rapid progress in their exertions to aid the *foreign* objects of the Society. Take away this Stimulus, by buying a single Bible, & we sink! ... The first *purchase* will be a signal for my resignation as a Secretary, for I cannot remain when the spring of action is broken.

He went on to discuss the Southwark Auxiliary's debt to the parent Society, and promised, 'you *shall* be paid off ... but we cannot, dare not, will not, *buy*. If you refuse to supply us with more on *tick*, till we pay you off, we cannot help it, but I should advise you not to try so dangerous an experiment, which would, probably, extinguish our faith.' Dudley, with his usual magniloquence, was making explicit the process he was working to encourage, which might be called the institutionalization of the Bible transaction in British culture. Local auxiliary members had to feel themselves a part of the decisions made by the Committee at Earl Street. Even more than publication of the *Monthly Extracts* and other promotional materials, the extension of credit to their Auxiliaries helped to generate this sense of involvement. Or as Dudley put it, 'the pressure is felt throughout the whole, and no spring in this moral machinery is overloaded'.[31]

Auxiliaries, however, were only the beginning of the Society's money-spinner. Although they were supposed to inquire into the scarcity of Bibles in their districts, Auxiliaries were expected to appeal directly only to 'the higher and more wealthy classes of the community'. The proper way to put scriptures into the hands of the poor was by indirection, through the medium of the Bible Association.

Again, Dudley's operation at Southwark provided the model. The geographical area of an Auxiliary (based on generally accepted boundaries) was subdivided into districts. The district boundaries were sometimes, but not necessarily, those of a parish. Each had its own Bible Association, complete with secretaries, officers and committee, replicating the structure of the London Committee and of the parent Auxiliary. Conservative critics of the Bible Society like H. H. Norris regarded this arrangement as tantamount to subversion. But Dudley spoke often of the efficient division of labour, comparing the virtues of his system to those of agricultural enclosure:

[The Southwark Auxiliary] beheld the whole of their extensive district divided and enclosed; the boundaries of each allotment defined; the mode of cultivation agreed on, and practically pursued: – above all, they beheld competent and voluntary husbandmen resident on the soil and acquainted with its nature; and they rejoiced in the anticipation of that day, when the *'wilderness and the solitary place* should *be glad for them, and the desert* should *rejoice and blossom as the rose'*.[32]

To compare Dudley's and Norris's view of Bible Associations is to understand the contemporary debate over appropriate ways to deal with poverty and infidelity on the part of working-class people. People like Norris, with revolutionary precedents in mind, feared the potential for working-class unrest. In the years of Luddite machine-breaking and the Cato Street conspiracy, this sort of view was not uncommon. But Dudley was an optimist, and he favoured intervention. Having come to terms with the increased population and the anonymity of urban communities, he looked for new ways efficiently to manage the relief of poverty and the provision of the scriptures.

The first Bible Association appeared at High Wycombe, Buckinghamshire in 1811, but in the same year the 'system' really got under way in the south London borough of Southwark, after Dudley's survey convinced him that working-class people were more generous than he had supposed. 'It was in these visits', he told his readers, 'he first conceived it *possible* to realise the most glowing visions of philanthropy; – to direct the rays of mercy on the obscure abodes of poverty; and, when they had illuminated the narrow walls, and cheered the awakened inmate, to reflect them back on distant and benighted lands.' Henry Thornton attended the founding meeting of the Southwark Auxiliary late in 1811 and spoke of those 'visits to the poor, which seem to connect them with their superiors, and to produce a feeling of mutual regard and general philanthropy'. The new Auxiliary Society established twelve subordinate Bible Associations, and the committee was divided into twelve District committees. They offered to organizers 'a supply of ... minor publications' advising how best to manage the Bible transaction at the neighbourhood level.[33]

Although it was the spiritual effects of Associations that Dudley and his colleagues were most interested in, they were almost equally enthusiastic about the potential social benefits. These may be summed up in the words of the 13th *Report* of May 1817, 'the very principle of those Associations is calculated to operate as a monitory and restraining influence on the members of them'. When he published the *Analysis*, Dudley put it this way:

The poor, taught by the visits of the collectors how they may acquire a Bible at a sacrifice that is scarcely felt even by the most indigent, gladly embrace the opportunity. Gratified by the regular weekly calls of their superiors, they endeavour to render their humble abodes more cleanly and attractive: – the effort is noticed with approbation, and comparative comfort and order are enjoyed. The husband and the father no longer spends his evenings from his family; – he begins to taste the pleasures of home; and to consider whether his weekly earnings may not be more profitably expended than in sensual and degrading pursuits. The expected Bible is at length obtained, – the perusal of it confirms the *habits* recently acquired, and they gradually attain the force of *principles*. He finds he is able to lay by a portion of his weekly gains; and cheerfully devotes the first-fruits of his increase to that cause which he has found to be a blessing. The visits of the collectors are consequently continued regularly, their advice is solicited, and the SAVINGS' BANK is recommended as a secure depository for the newly-formed basis of future independence. Here is the natural progress of the system.[34]

As time went on and Associations proliferated, every achievement could be interpreted as vindication of their existence, and every setback as evidence that further organization was required. In 1817 the local Auxiliary at Dudley (near Birmingham) reported that 'the diffusion of pernicious publications, although attempted, has made no progress in this neighbourhood'. In the opinion of the writers, the Bible's precepts constituted 'the best basis of social order, and the best security against the poison of infidelity, or the seeds of anarchy and schism'.[35]

Bible Associations would not only prevent working-class unrest, drunkenness and other kinds of disorder, but they were immensely profitable. Joseph Tarn, in a letter to the impecunious Wakefield Auxiliary, admonished the Secretary to direct his attention 'to another Class of persons who are among the warmest and most efficient Friends of the Institution. I mean the poor, whose wishes and energies are brought extensively into action where Bible Associations are established and the wants of the Poor ascertained by the regular and punctual weekly visits of the Collectors.'[36] The Secretaries and officers of the parent Society found themselves writing panegyrics to their working-class Associations, and recognizing that not only did these organizational offshoots virtually handle distribution in Britain, but that they were largely funding the operation abroad. The 1815 Report admitted that 'these humble Associations leave, by their natural operation, a larger disposable fund at the service of the Parent Society, and accomplish so much of its work as relates to the supply of the inferior orders of the people, without occasioning it trouble or expense'. This 'natural operation' was of course the carefully planned system established by Dudley and Phillips to involve even the poorest subscriber in the foreign project of the Society.

There were cries from the critics of the BFBS, that the system of Auxiliaries and Associations constituted a tax on the poor. The BFBS position was defended by the Rev. Thomas Chalmers, in *The Influence of Bible Societies on the Temporal Necessities of the Poor* (London, 1814), who argued that 'the institution of a Bible Society gives you the whole benefit of such a tax without its odiousness'. The supposed moral effects on poor people's behaviour justified the twinges of evangelical consciences, and served as ammunition against critics who preferred to give the poor bread, rather than encourage them to subscribe for Bibles.[37]

The fact that Bibles were sold, and not given away, was vitally important to the Society. It made the transaction a commercial one, not a philanthropic occasion. In this concept the Secretaries and Agents, and the Committee, were no doubt influenced by contemporary concerns about the degenerating effects of charity upon the poor. To charge a small price for a cheap Bible, even to the poorest customer, would avert the danger that philanthropy might cause moral decay. It seems unlikely that working-class subscribers understood or cared about the subtle distinctions between the portion of the book they received that was paid for by voluntary donations and the part that they paid for out of their own pockets. But they almost always had to pay something. In Dudley's opinion, which was shared by the Committee, 'a *gratuitous* distribution could not satisfy the minds of those who wished to counteract the degrading influence of Pauperism, to check the progress of Infidelity, and to extend the empire of Religion and Morality'.[38]

The Committee could not forbid its subscribers or Auxiliary leaders to make free gifts of Bibles, but such gifts were hedged around with warnings. At the inaugural meeting, 7 March 1804, the sixth resolution had stated that 'Each member shall be entitled ... to purchase Bibles & Testaments for the purpose of gratuitous distribution, at the Society's prices, which shall be as low as possible, but no English Bibles or Testaments shall be *given away* in Great Britain by the *Society itself*.'[39] But even cheap distribution raised suspicions. A Cornwall surgeon wrote in 1809 for a quantity of books beyond his privilege, to sell 'throughout the Country at the prices they would be charged to him, he sinking the expense of Carriage, in which case he would make it publicly and generally known that such Books were on sale'. A cautious Committee resolved to tell him they were 'fearful that the measure ... may induce some persons to take an improper advantage of the terms on which [the books] are issued by the Society'.[40] Both the reputation of the Society and financial considerations suggested that the Auxiliary-Association system was preferable to individual agency and direct subscription. Local members, in their role as agents of the parent Society, would make sure that no book be purchased at a price lower than cost, unless circumstances warranted a temporary relaxation of the regulations.

The Bible transaction necessitated careful management on the part of the London Committee. It was essential that the charitable aspect of the transaction be recognized and appreciated by the poor, even while they enjoyed the benefits of setting aside funds from week to week to pay for the privilege. The Committee issued constant reminders to their subscribers and Auxiliaries about how Bibles for Britain were to be interpreted. Cheap Bibles, in the words of C. S. Dudley, were 'a *moral sinking-fund* ... which operates powerfully towards the liquidation of [pauperism]'.[41] Much of the social history of Britain written in recent years has been devoted to the critical examination of claims – like those of Dudley and others – that philanthropies like the Bible Society simply changed people's lives, stopped them drinking and set them to work and to respectable leisure-time pursuits.[42] Dudley told his readers what happened to the poor at Auxiliary annual meetings: 'Having never before heard a similar appeal to their feelings and their judgment, the effect is decisive.'

The object, pure and simple in its nature, is comprehended, while its value and importance are felt: and the conviction that even *their* limited support may be rendered conducive to the promotion of the glorious design, and *their* services availing in the extension of its benefits, produces a moral effect to which they had hitherto been strangers.[43]

This is a classic example of the rhetoric of what has been called 'social control', the notion that working-class people were subtly coerced into offering '*their* limited support' to a whole range of causes including Sunday Schools and temperance as well as Bible distribution. Built into this notion is the assumption that such support, although given under pressure, caused a decline in antisocial activities like bread riots and political radicalism. And a further important assumption is that participation in a project like the Bible Society's meant to the poor the same thing that it meant to those who believed in its moral efficacy.

In this context, it is important to know in what way poor people were 'members' of Bible Associations, and to what extent, if any, they were involved in the direction of these organizations. As we have seen, some evidence implies that the members of the Associations were working-class people. Dudley was happy to claim it, while Norris was afraid that malcontents were using meetings sanctioned by their social superiors to foment insurrection. Further research, based on a close study of one or more communities with active Bible Associations (and extant records), will be necessary before the question can be answered with precision. However the answer seems to be that subscription – that slippery concept – for a two-shilling Bible was interpreted to mean participation in the larger transaction. Writing from Norwich in 1813, John Joseph Gurney told Tarn that he could not give the Committee a 'defined account' of the Associations in his district: 'We have a large one at Norwich & almost all our Branch Societies are surrounded with them – but we have not ascertained what is their real nature & whether they will have any continuance after the poor are supplied with Bibles. I rather fear not.'[44] Reports during the ensuing years are a narrative of revival and re-revival of moribund Bible Associations, and the supply and re-supply of neighbourhoods whose impoverished residents were characterized by mobility as much as by piety. F. M. L. Thompson observed that of the 'actual results' of groups with social controlling motives, 'it seems that the intended recipients picked out what they wanted from the facilities on offer, and rejected the moral or authoritarian message'.[45] Poor people, like wealthy ones, had all sorts of reasons for wanting to have a Bible in the house. The Bible Society's scheme of Associations supplied them on easy terms.

The great mass of Dudley's letters, as well as official documents of the Society and other sources, stress the value of involving the poor in the project. But most ordinary working documents, like Gurney's letter, imply that the people running Associations were of the middle class: it is only when rhetorical attention is directly and specifically focused on the value of Associations that poor people are said to be members. This is clear in the construction of Dudley's *Analysis*, a manual of instruction on the practical conduct of Associations. The book divides the subject into chapters on 'Bible Associations conducted by gentlemen', and the same by ladies. In the end, the question of working-class participation in the Bible transaction dissolves in the light of a much more useful one about gender.

Women's participation in the Bible transaction must have seemed a perverse notion to the Committee, officers and Secretaries of the early years. They had gone to a good deal of trouble to define their methods in terms of business and commerce, so that the 'fundamental principle' of the Society forbade anyone circulating scriptures on its behalf to comment upon them. Luke Howard had proclaimed that the BFBS was 'not a religious society'. But middle-class women were permitted by contemporary custom only a very narrow role in public life, a role that eschewed contact with the sordidness of business, and was defined largely in terms of organized religious activity.[46]

Women – middle-class ladies – however, came to participate very actively in the Bible transaction. They did this by turning the transaction inside out, by ignoring or re-interpreting the 'fundamental principle'. Soliciting subscriptions from poor and working-class neighbours became a respectable, because religious, occupation. This is not to claim that women participated fully or equally with men in the Bible transaction. They did not attend annual meetings at Exeter Hall until 1834, or join the parent Society's Committee until 1945. Even in local organizations, they were excluded from the direction of Auxiliaries and from the public platform at annual meetings. But their energetic door-to-door collecting was nevertheless the foundation of the Society's fortune.

The Bible Association, rather than being a vehicle for working-class participation in the British and Foreign Bible Society, was in fact the place where female involvement was sanctioned and encouraged. It took the form of collecting subscriptions from poor people for cheap Bibles, visiting to solicit the original commitment and first payment and then returning for the balance at the traditional rate of a penny a week, until the book was paid for. Bible Associations run by 'ladies' appeared simultaneously with their male counterparts (initially in Westminster, in 1811). But the Ladies' Associations were enormously more successful and widespread than those of gentlemen. Dudley, applying Southwark principles and drafting appropriate by-laws, had them organized to his own satisfaction and that of the Committee by 1817.[47] Funds collected from subscribers and accounted for by the women's committee were passed on to the (men's) Auxiliary for transmission to London. Women were not supposed to appear on public platforms, although there may have been some exceptions to this rule.

Thus it was that Bible Associations were largely run by women, in an age when the 'delicacy and retirement which are among the greatest graces of female character' were being established as important signifiers of middle-class status. These were the years when the ideology of separate spheres for men and women – his the public world of business and commerce, hers the private one of home and family – were being established. But as Frank Prochaska has shown, women inspired by evangelicalism insisted on involving themselves in philanthropic activities like bazaars, even at the expense of their 'modesty'.[48] And other middle-class women formed or supported pressure groups that sought to change government policy on issues from the abolition of slavery to that of the Corn Law.[49] Women in the Bible Society, perhaps even more than those who organized bazaars, were engaging in quasi-commercial transactions. There was no objection to their visiting the poor. In fact the injunction not to comment or preach on the scriptures could be interpreted as a vote for feminine retirement. But the money collected had to be accounted for and used to purchase books; furthermore some of these books were distributed at public meetings, not merely handed to recipients across the doorstep. These facts made Bible Society activity different from the merely charitable type of evangelical visiting.[50] By being active in Bible distribution, women began subtly to undermine the distinction between their proper role and that of their husbands and brothers. For example, communications from working-class districts had to be collected and interpreted by women, fed back to the gentlemen in their local Auxiliary, and then transmitted to Earl Street.

The notion of proper modesty, however, was strong enough to make correspondence from women members to Bible Society headquarters very rare, and the number of such documents in the archives is consequently distressingly small. Much more common are men's commentaries on the virtue of Ladies' Associations. A sample of these is a remarkable effusion from Robert Steven, a London leather merchant who was active on the BFBS Committee and other evangelical charities, notably the London Society for Superseding the Use of Climbing Boys. Steven wrote to Joseph Tarn in October 1818 announcing 'the formation of four new Ladies Bible Associations, viz. Ross, Hereford, Leominster & Bromyard'. He went on:

What an interesting & important part of our plan are Bible Associations! Without them, the B & F B S might indeed like some of the vast Rivers on the Western Continent, rolling on in her majestic course have become a Sea before She reached the Ocean, & carrying on her bosom the inestimable treasure of the Scriptures to foreign lands. But our own country would not have reaped all the benefit, many would have perished for lack of these living waters, which the Society was providing amply for the wants of nations on the other side of the Globe. But by the formation of Bible Associations, these living Streams have fertilized & refreshed our villages & Hamlets, have been conveyed along our lanes & alleys, into the cellars & garrets of the most destitute. And could the enemies of Bib. Asso'ns, especially of Ladies B. A. but see one tenth of the moral benefit resulting from the weekly visits of the Ladies at the Cottages of the poor they would cease to oppose – they would become their warmest advocates.[51]

Robert Steven's watery metaphors and touching optimism represent an idealization of women's participation in the project of Bible distribution. The reality was somewhat more contentious.

Liverpool may be taken as an example of a community with an active Ladies' Association. Burgeoning with industry and commerce, poverty and slums, the city was ripe for evangelical missionizing. According to a historian of Liverpool charity, 'almost the only machinery by which an outsider might penetrate Darkest Liverpool, was that of the religious mission. To women in particular these organizations provided that moral and physical chaperonage without which they might never have effected their first steps into the world outside their home.'[52] The Bible transaction was a very popular philanthropy in Liverpool. The Auxiliary had been established in 1811, but by 1817 its Committee was lamenting 'the great inefficiency of Gentlemen, in a plan professing to embrace the distribution of the Bible, through every part of a numerous, poor, and ever-varying population', and the gentlemen were smugly certain that lady collectors would soon 'abundantly supply *their* lack of service'.

The Ladies' Auxiliary Bible Society began in March 1817 with a treasurer, two secretaries and a committee of twenty-four, as well as about sixty volunteer collectors. But according to Dudley their first few months were badly planned:

> No provision was made for exciting and perpetuating that feeling, which gives to every individual engaged in the work, an interest in its success; – the local districts were too extensive, and many parts of them were, consequently, unvisited; – the mode of gratuitous supply was carried to a mischievous excess; – but, above all, no measures were devised for awakening, in the labouring classes of the community, the benevolent principle.

Dudley arrived in December to reorganize the Ladies' Auxiliary on 'more correct principles'. Liverpool had a larger population than other areas he had organized, so that he set up ten districts with a Ladies' Association in each. The officers and secretaries of all these would constitute 'The Ladies' Branch of the Liverpool Auxiliary Society' which in turn would communicate with the gentlemen of the Auxiliary proper. A year later, he was able to calculate that 20,000 visits had resulted in 10,000 subscriptions, the sale of over 3,000 Bibles and Testaments, and over £500 for the 'general object of the Parent Institution'.[53]

However, in Liverpool there were no Associations run by gentlemen, although the local Society was a popular and respectable philanthropy. When Dudley attended the Liverpool Auxiliary annual meeting in April 1818, the Town Hall was 'inadequate to the accommodation of the numerous Company, [so] they assembled in the Music Hall'. In the absence of Lord Stanley the chair was taken by John Gladstone, father of the future Prime Minister. Another of the officers was Samuel Hope, a young Liverpool businessman and philanthropist. His sister, Maria Hope, was President of the new Ladies' Branch, which had collected in the previous three months over £7,000, most of it in subscriptions for books.

Maria Hope took the bold step of writing to Joseph Tarn at the Bible Society's London office, in February of 1819. The occasion was the rumour of Charles Stokes Dudley's resignation from voluntary service to the Society, at the time when his business troubles were beginning. She was 'well aware' that communication from a Ladies' Branch Society was not encouraged by the parent Committee, the rule having been 'painfully expressed' to her. But Dudley's departure would be an 'irreparable loss'. Maria Hope reported that she had recently answered seventy-four letters of inquiry about organizing Ladies' Societies, and frequently made journeys on behalf of the Society as far as Wales and Chester. These activities, she told Tarn, had 'arisen from a sincere desire on the part of my dear Father & myself to do the little we c[oul]d for the Society & we have no authority as yet but the example of our Lord to go about doing good'. They wanted to be granted some official status, not only to fund their travelling expenses, but so that they, like Dudley, could deter people whose evangelical energy was taking them in dangerous or inappropriate directions. Two months later, for example, Maria Hope and her father were at Bury, where the local Auxiliary had proposed to form a '*mixed* association ... not composed exclusively of Ladies, but the Collectors to be Ladies or Gent[leme]n indiscriminately'. Samuel Hope told Tarn, 'My father thought their presence might throw a little weight into the *right, i.e.* the *female* scale. The organization of the proposed measure would be so Hermaphroditisch, that I should expect it to be very unproductive, & I should fear its influence as an example.' Ten days later Hope was able to report that all had gone well, and a Ladies' Association was formed at Bury.

Maria Hope's father travelled with his daughter, who by the spring of 1819 was extending her visits as far as Newcastle, Stockport and even Edinburgh. She assured Tarn that Mr Hope was always 'able and willing to undertake the public part of the proceedings with which I have nothing to do at the formation of the Ladies Assoc[iatio]ns'. But privately she was very influential, knowing how much the women collectors wished for guidance at the first meetings to which they brought money – 'for it does not do to leave them like ostrich eggs in the sand'. Maria Hope and her group were very ambitious, building accommodation in Slater Street, Liverpool, which she hoped could eventually become a depot for the north of England, Scotland, Ireland and Wales. She told Tarn that her brother thought that printing could be done as cheaply in Liverpool as in London. But her hopes were quickly 'extinguished', by Tarn, who was undoubtedly becoming alarmed at the energy being generated in Liverpool.[54]

Despite the care taken by Maria Hope and her father and brother to cater to their neighbours' notions of decorum, there was strong opposition within the Liverpool Auxiliary Committee to the burgeoning Ladies' Associations. The entire collecting effort was in the hands of middle-class ladies, who managed their own collecting networks, bypassing the official Auxiliary (run by gentlemen) until it was time to send the funds to London. The Secretaries wrote in October 1819 to the parent Committee in London to request advice. Samuel Hope and R. T. Buddicom, who themselves supported the Ladies' Associations, set down both sides of the argument to be decided at Earl Street.[55] The two secretaries began diplomatically by quoting the expressed wish of one of the London Secretaries that women's co-operation should 'be active but unostentatious, like the blood which circulates unobserved through every part of the frame, and which is only to be seen in the hue of health which it imparts to the countenance, and the vitality and vigour which it communicates to the system'. But it was feared that organized Bible circulation by women might 'invade this sacred privacy and diminish that retired and unostentatious feeling which would "Do good by stealth & blush to find its fame"'. Assuming that no reasonable gentleman (or lady) in 1819 could disagree with such sentiments, Hope and Buddicom nevertheless proceeded to undermine them in the name of Christian piety. The difficulty was that Ladies' Societies had been formed only when efforts had failed to establish a Gentlemen's Association, which meant that 'the important task of distributing the Holy Scriptures among the Poor must either be accomplished in this most efficient way or left undone'. As the Secretaries put the problem in their practical way, 'defects in the plan of doing good can be of no moment compared with a plan which does no good at all'.

Some of the opponents within the Liverpool Committee thought it might be acceptable to send women in and out of the hovels of the poor as long as their purity was not defiled by contact with financial records. But their supporters pointed out that

Keeping Accounts in Books properly ruled and according to the simple and easy plan now adopted is found to be no difficulty to any Lady who has had a single Months trial, and not keeping Accounts would unavoidably occasion many misunderstandings and involve all their perspicuous Accounts in obscurity, and it is scarcely to be expected that Gentlemen involved in business, as is the case in large Manufacturing and Commercial Towns where Ladies' Branch Societies are formed either could or would attend monthly and punctually as the Ladies do, to this work of laborious Benevolence.

It was already apparent that men in these urban centres were not very punctual about Bible Society matters, so that Hope and Buddicom predicted 'the consequences of neglect would be, that every thing would run into confusion and the Ladies, chagrined by disappointments and restrictions &c, would give up *their* punctuality, and their zeal would languish. . .'. Nor would confusion of accounts and records be acceptable at Earl Street in London. The inescapable logic of Bible Society pragmatism argued that the distribution of the scriptures outweighed any other considerations.

The gentlemen of Liverpool, however, had additional concerns. Their unease with the public participation of women in the project of publishing cheap Bibles crossed the borders of gender into the question of social class and class conflict. In October 1819, memories of Peterloo were fresh. That summer the magistrates of Manchester had broken up a reform demonstration, and the day had ended with injury, death and political outrage. In these times, they felt, any public meeting was potentially insurrectionary.

Perhaps something might be said on the inexpediency of multiplying Public Meetings unnecessarily or giving the poor and uneducated a taste for attending them in times of such portentous aspect as the present; but independently of this consideration (and it is no mean one) it seems difficult to say what advantage is gained upon the whole. The Conductors of these Associations are Ladies, if they do not come forward to give the Books themselves they are at least the recognized Distributors, and must be present, probably actively assisting. Certain persons who receive these Bibles are either actually or virtually brought forward before their Neighbours, commended openly or by implication, and held up as objects of imitation (and the language held on these occasions must be general) when it may be that with the exception of the circumstance of having Subscribed for the Bible, they may not be such as it would be safe or right to follow.

Hope and Buddicom were conscious of the social force of evangelical enthusi-asm, telling the Secretaries that 'this is a professing Age in Religion and probably there may be some danger in increasing the form of Godliness without adding much to the power in these meetings for public Distribution of the Bible, public exhortation and public commendation'.

Nevertheless they refused to believe that public distributions might become occasions for radicalism. On the contrary: 'To us they appear to be the most effectual remedy against all the attempts of those who are endeavouring to upset the altar and overturn the throne.' And in any case 'none of these Meetings for Public Distribution have been held in this neighbourhood since these political disturbances commenced and therefore the objection here stated has no foundation in fact'. But their political anxiety was inextricably tied up with questions of gender. Only 'ladies' were willing to sell Bibles to the poor, and the danger that their efforts might foment political radicalism was offset by the potential of their programme to obliterate the secular attitudes underlying such beliefs. With such a prospect sanctioned by scrip-ture, and when women and their supporters were articulating the unarguable logic of evangelical pragmatism, the conventions about appropriate female behaviour began to break down.

And if their exertions tend to alienate the mind of our sex from an interest in the Bible Society and prove destructive to its prosperity, [Messrs Hope and Buddicom argued reasonably] that alienation of affection must be most unjustifiable so long as Gentlemen sleep on their post or only sit and cast the scowl of alienated affection on those who are up and doing. The remedy is always at hand. Break up the way before them and be as active in putting work into their hands as they are in performing it, and never necessitate them by years of delay to occupy the place where Husbands and Fathers and Brothers should have ostensibly sanctioned and aided their endeavours.

It is not difficult to imagine Maria Hope's intervention in the drafting of this document. It must have done a great deal to allay the fears of the Secretaries and Committee at Bible Society headquarters, who might otherwise have been alarmed by tales of public distribution and unladylike publicity. Instead they commended the women on their 'zeal and vigilance'.[56]

Bible Society women were careful of their reputation, but they were anxious that their contribution be recognized, if only so that others might follow in their footsteps. J. G. Gurney warned Tarn that the Ladies' Associ-ation in Norwich was quite independent of the Auxiliary: 'They must not be inserted [in the annual *Report*] as a Branch Society as their institution was previous to ours and they stand very much upon punctilio ... [T]heir connexion with us is that they pay in their funds thro' our Soc[iet]y but in all other respects they are completely independent and must continue to be so stated as they have been.' In Newcastle, the women were concerned about inadvertently making 'an ostentatious display of zeal', lest they stir up resentment among the 'Gentlemen'. But Anna Maria Lee, of Cork, was looking for a female mentor. She wanted to go to Liverpool to sit at the feet of Maria Hope, and 'learn ... the System and proper mode of conducting the Bible Society, as I fear we are far behind hand in regularity, system and punctuality, never having been instructed in the mode of conducting business, all engagements of the kind were new, and required patient attention ...'. Two months later she had founded her group, and warned, 'Should the gentlemen interfere with our rules and limit our grants, they will sow discontent and raise party spirit.'[57]

With the experience of the Liverpool and other Ladies' Branches in mind, we may ask what made middle-class women go out in all weathers, into some very unsavoury places, to collect for the Bible Society. What motivated them to organize meetings and allocate funds, to galvanize the energies of husbands and brothers, all the while leaving themselves open to criticism in terms such as those of H. H. Norris, who called them 'an *Amazonian* troop of female heroes'?[58] It is too simplistic and condescending to say that Bible work was an 'outlet' for women's frustrated natures.[59] It was, rather, a patch of territory in church and community where women could carve out for themselves a project in which they could work relatively unhindered. These findings make it necessary to take issue with Leonore Davidoff and Catherine Hall, and their study of gender and class formation, *Family Fortunes*. The authors reiterate the ideology of 'separate spheres' as an explanatory model for contemporary relations between men and women, with evangelical religion as a very powerful motive. They claim that women did not exert 'real social power' in the first half of the nineteenth century. This is to accept contemporary rhetoric at its face value. Within the Bible Society, at least, women were active organizers, persuasive collectors and powerful contributors. Though punctilious about their treatment, they did not see fit to engage in a public struggle with the men of the organization over the appropriate roles for people of their sex. But this fact should not be allowed to obscure the very real contribution of women to the Society's work and its finances, or the sparse evidence, much of it between the lines of letters and published reports, of friction between BFBS women and their fathers, brothers and husbands. A conclusion that women were subservient in societies like the BFBS makes it difficult to see the many creative ways in which women used the popular activity of Bible distribution to achieve desired ends.

Women were clearly the backbone of the Society, as they were in the contemporary abolition movement. Their dogged collecting and perennial enthusiasm no doubt kept the Auxiliary alive at Liverpool as in many other towns and cities. The name of the BFBS could perhaps be reformulated as the (Women's) British and (Men's) Foreign Bible Society. Men, exclusively, were members of the Committee, and male clergymen Secretaries staffed a publishing programme that was funded largely from the exertions of female collectors. Clearly, women's participation in the Society is one of the keys to understanding its place in nineteenth-century culture. Involving themselves in commercial transactions of a kind that 'ladies' were supposed to be too genteel to manage, the women of Liverpool and elsewhere took the unladylike aspects of the Bible transaction in their stride, and created a demand for cheap Bibles that the gentlemen at Earl Street were hard put to supply.

It is very difficult to develop a picture of the ordinary day-by-day operations of Bible Associations. The procedure, we are told, included collecting subscriptions and arranging an annual meeting where some of the copies that had been purchased were delivered. But Maria Hope did not recount to her correspondents at Bible House exactly what happened when she appeared at working-class homes in Liverpool, and most collectors did not write about their work at all. We know very little of the conversations on the doorsteps, and around the Committee tables, when the details of the Bible transaction were worked out in practice. The combined texts of Dudley's *Analysis*, of annual *Reports* and of official histories provide no reliable information on this process. Instead, these documents include numerous affecting sketches of Bible recipients preserved from drunkenness, prostitution or political radicalism. Such reports are unsatisfactory from the historian's point of view, since the observers are mostly biased, and the rhetoric designed for animating volunteers or for raising funds.

It may be impossible to obtain anything but a fragmentary sense of the Bible transaction at the level of working-class people. One case history of a sort, however, is available. The story of Richard Channor is an episode in the history-from-below of scripture distribution. Assize records, as well as an article in the Society's 1821 *Monthly Extracts*, record the exploits of a Regency confidence artist who collected pennies from the poor in the name of the Bible Society. Channor's collecting was offensive to the Committee and officers of the British and Foreign Bible Society, and as we shall see they moved strongly to stop him. But the publicity given to his activities helps to illuminate the normal process of scripture distribution, taken for granted by Earl Street and its respectable Auxiliaries, but not otherwise recorded for posterity.

The Bible transaction, as it unfolded on the doorsteps of Bermondsey, seems to have been a businesslike contact, devoid of preaching and prayer, one that merely offered a manifestly desirable commodity at a price that was not only a bargain but was broken up into affordable weekly instalments. On 11 September 1820, the following events occurred at the working-class home of James and Anna Barrett of the parish of St Mary Magdalen in Bermondsey.[60] Mrs Barrett was greeted by a caller, Richard Channor, dressed as a labourer. He told her he represented the Rev. John Townsend of Jamaica Row, Bermondsey, whom she knew to be president of the Bermondsey and Rotherhithe Bible Society, and asked her if she wished to belong to the Society.[61] Channor told Mrs Barrett that as a subscriber she might have a Bible for half price, which would be two shillings. She gave him a deposit of sixpence. The following week he returned for her next payment. He brought with him a Bible, not a new book but one he told her he had brought from Townsend's School to be repaired. Channor told Anna Barrett that the Bible which she was to have would be like the Bible he produced.

Unfortunately for Anna Barrett, Richard Channor was 'an evil disposed person', a confidence man, who had for some time been conducting a profitable fraud. Channor was convicted at the Surrey Lent Assizes in 1821 at Kingston upon Thames, on Saturday 7 April before Chief Baron Richards in the *Nisi Jurius* Court. Another victim was Ann Hodgkinson, wife of a buckram stiffner. Channor had claimed to belong to a variety of different local Associations, mostly in the East End of London. He was convicted of defrauding six persons in four parishes, and was accused of perpetrating the crime very widely indeed.[62]

It was not these humble working-class neighbours who brought Channor to court. On the contrary. The Auxiliary's own records show that the direct victims of Channor's fraud did not share the wrath of his prosecutors. The minutes of the Rotherhithe Upper Bible Association for 13 December 1820 remarked upon the 'forgiving disposition of the poor who had suffer'd most by that Imposter, instead of loading him with Invectives, they expressed themselves in terms of Pity, using an adage very common "never mind, – we shall be none the poorer, nor he the richer"'. In fact some families resumed the subscriptions the swindler had offered them in bad faith. Nor did the local Association's secretaries blame Channor. It was their own members who were at fault: 'No such fraud could be committed but from the laxity of the collectors.'[63] Instead, the court proceedings were initiated by members of the district Auxiliary for Southwark, L. B. Allen and J. Curling. They collected evidence, brought witnesses to Kingston on three different days, and incurred solicitor's charges of £215 1s 6d. The jury duly pronounced Channor guilty and he was sentenced to the usual punishment for such petty crimes, transportation 'beyond the seas', to Australia, for the term of seven years.

The parent Society and its Auxiliaries moved strongly to protect the reputation of the Bible Society, first by organizing the prosecution of Channor. It was equally important, however, for them to defend themselves against potential charges that it was inappropriate for a group of wealthy and powerful Christians to harass a poor and struggling worker, and cause him to be transported. After the case was reported in *The Times* (9 April 1821) in terms of a fraud on Hodgkinson only, for threepence, a letter from Henry Neave Rickman, a Secretary of the St George's Bible Association, assured the newspaper's readers that the judgment was not too severe. He asserted that the fraud had far exceeded 3d, and quoted the Common Sergeant's statement in court that Channor had been committing his crime for a long time and had gained several hundred pounds. It was necessary, claimed Rickman, to punish him 'in justice both to those societies whose names he used, and the poor who were exclusively the object of his depredations'. The April 1821 *Monthly Extracts* published by the BFBS carried a lead article by Rickman entitled 'Fraud on Bible Associations', which exaggerated Channor's crimes and solicited contributions towards the expenses of the trial.

The Channor affair is valuable evidence about the realities of the Bible transaction in the 1820s. Although Channor's unorthodox methods cannot be taken as typical, the response of the Barrett and other families to his approach corroborates BFBS claims that there was a willing market for Bibles among working-class people. The placable attitude of people in Bermondsey, after the fraud was discovered, may be interpreted as an attitude closer to the spirit of the Gospels than that of their 'betters' at Earl Street. When it turned out that Channor had taken advantage of the Society, they shrugged and reinstituted their subscriptions. But since a mechanism existed for the fraudulent subscriptions to be legitimized, the subscribers had nothing to lose by saying, 'never mind'. On the other hand, the Committee, backed by its senior metropolitan Auxiliaries, regarded the fraud as a very serious threat to their still-fragile reputation. They decided to prosecute to the full extent of the law, even at considerable expense, inconvenience and the risk of embarrassment. Then they used the *Monthly Extracts* to inform subscribers about the actions they had taken, and affirm the validity of their approach. Not only petty criminals like Channor, but also the business community and critics of local collection, would receive the message: the BFBS was not to be trifled with.

Beset by Channor's fraud in 1820, the crisis over circulation of the Apocrypha which climaxed in 1825, and the controversy about tests in 1832, the Committee were faced with the problem of maintaining the large complex organization the BFBS had become. The demand of Associations, through their Auxiliaries, for more and more books led to a stepping-up of production and a streamlining of packaging. But the management of printing and binding took place against a backdrop of managing the demand for cheap Bibles, which meant keeping track of the state of the local Societies. Bible distribution, organized on a model of gift and sale, voluntarism and commerce, had evolved in the hands of the ladies of Liverpool, the gentlemen of Southwark and others inspired by popular evangelicalism, all under Dudley's tutelage. Auxiliaries and Associations had undertaken local distribution, with spectacular results. But as the Society proceeded through the difficult years of controversy and schism, the London Committee became aware of a demand for cheap scriptures that was not being supplied with maximum efficiency.

They heard from other national organizations like the Sunday School Society and the Poor Law Guardians, whose leaders preferred to make centralized arrangements to supply their clients. The standard answer to these leaders was that, for the most part, Sunday Schools, workhouses, asylums and other institutions were to be supplied by local agency.[64] All too often, this answer was unsatisfactory.

Despite the great popularity of local BFBS activity, not every town and village maintained an active Auxiliary.[65] According to revised calculations in the 1835 *Report* there were approximately 269 Auxiliaries, 347 Branches and 1,541 Associations. These local societies were distributed over all the English counties and there was one in each major town and city. But like most voluntary societies, they were rather fluid organizations, declining and reviving again according to a number of variables, including local religious feeling but also the participation of strong individuals. Someone like Maria Hope in Liverpool would generate considerable enthusiasm, then depart to be married and leave disorder behind her. Perhaps even more important was the matter of contact with headquarters. Men like Richard Phillips and Robert Steven, both retired from all but philanthropic business, spent weeks at a time visiting and animating local societies. But until 1828 Charles Dudley was the only paid Domestic Agent, and the Secretaries could not always spare the time to travel. Consequently, a good deal of attention was paid to recruiting volunteer clergymen to attend and speak at Auxiliary annual meetings. Otherwise, contact with Earl Street was handled through the mails at a time before the efficiencies of the penny post were available.

By the 1820s, Dudley, Brandram and Hughes, and through them the Committee, were well aware of the problem of fluctuating commitment. Declining contributions could be attributed to all sorts of factors: economic (the price and wage problems of the period were notorious), philosophical (most of the wealthy Scottish Auxiliaries and some other branches and individual members cancelled their subscriptions over the Apocrypha affair), and organizational (the staff were constantly activating and reactivating flagging local groups). Even when Auxiliaries were active, however, there were problems with distribution. They were set up to supply individual copies to individuals on a residential basis. Efficacious as they were, they could not respond appropriately to institutional requirements. Women, as we have seen, had made it respectable to sell scriptures a copy at a time. But bulk transactions might well have raised criticism. A second problem was that each Auxiliary was jealous of its territory and its autonomy. Centralized arrangements, while they would have the effect of circulating more books, would interfere with local authority. The dual problems of fluctuating commitment on the one hand, and centralized demand for Bibles on the other, produced tensions that shaped relationships between the parent Society and its local Auxiliaries.

No. 91.

𝕾𝖚𝖓𝖉𝖆𝖞 𝕾𝖈𝖍𝖔𝖔𝖑 𝕿𝖗𝖆𝖈𝖙𝖘.

INTERESTING ACCOUNTS

OF THE

BIBLE SOCIETY,

With an Invitation to the Poor to promote its Object.

LONDON:

Published by W. KENT, 116, High Holborn,

Bookseller to the Sunday School Union Society;

And sold by W. Button, Paternoster Row, and A. Johnstone,
Grass Market, Edinburgh.

Price 1d. or 7s. a Hundred to give away.

Printed by W. Gilbert, Salter's Hall Court, Cannon Street.

Figure 5   Sunday School tract, *c.* 1813

One part of Dudley's programme for the late twenties was to establish Bible Associations in the villages. Besides dealing with the decline in Auxiliary support and responding to the political upheavals of the period, effort at the village level would help to serve Sunday Schools and other institutions without removing the transaction from the hands of local BFBS members. On 29 May 1829 it was decided to print an edition of 3,000 copies of suggested regulations for village organizations. They were to be found in the recommendations for 'Books and Papers' in Dudley's *Analysis*. After the pamphlet was set up in type, however, someone noticed that the 'Suggestions' were 'introducing a new principle in the Society, that of distributing Tracts, which, however excellent, may be liable to objection'.[66] This difficulty suggests another limitation created by the fragile politics of the Bible transaction: printed commentaries were dangerous, potentially divisive, and only direct personal agency was an acceptable organizational method. Unfortunately it was also expensive, exhausting and required a combination of dogmatism and diplomacy.[67]

The cholera epidemic of 1831 presented a new challenge to Bible distribution, and placed added strain on relations between central and local interests in the BFBS. The disease was highly infectious, and its effects were devastating, both for the individual victim and for the populace tormented by visions of a return of the plague.[68] Part of the movement to cope with the problem was a programme of circulating scriptures to victims of the disease. And in this crisis, the spiritual needs of dying people were deemed more important than the principle that scriptures must be paid for. And yet the BFBS still did not wish to give books away. The eventual compromise was the concept of 'loan stock'. The cheapest editions of the New Testament and Psalms were 'bound in unsprinkled basil letter & with the words "Loan Stock" impressed on the front cover in large letters; & copies to be numbered in succession on the Title page'. Supplies were provided at no charge to Auxiliaries and Associations, whose responsibility was to dole them out to local cholera victims.

An awareness that leather-bound books might be a vehicle for infection did not prevent this project. Robert Spence of North Shields wrote to Brandram and Hughes,

> The fearful pestilence having now reached our shores & spreading about in a manner that seems to baffle human intelligence to trace, occasioning amongst the most enlightened medical men a painful diversity of views and opinions, it appears undesirable for books that may have been in the hands of those afflicted with a disease which is enveloped in so much mystery to … run the risk of spreading the disease.

Spence suggested that the loans should never be reclaimed, since the distribution would primarily occur 'among that class of person who from their circumstances & habit of life will be generally found most exposed to the ravages of this and other diseases many of which are highly infectious & likely to prove communicable by books that have been for some time in their possession'.[69] The germ theory of disease was not yet well understood or generally accepted by the medical profession. Spence's sensible advice was ignored, in spite of the high percentage of medical professionals who were Committee members. Instead local Auxiliary secretaries were reminded that 'the importance of permanent LOAN STOCKS, as providing for the immediate supply of every destitute family without incurring the disadvantages of gifts, is daily becoming more evident'.[70]

If gifts were disadvantageous, even more worrisome was the possibility that generosity might be exploited by the unscrupulous. There was a constant risk that poor people might pawn their Bibles. Letters during 1834 raised the alarm. James Phillips reported that a Worcester pawnbroker, whose late father had operated the same trade at Reading, had on hand eight New Testaments stamped 'Reading Loan Stock'. George Hulme of the Reading Auxiliary was pessimistic about the chances of prosecution, since those who had pawned their books 'were in a state of great poverty and have since left the country'. Thus the case would be impossible to prove in court. He asked Brandram for advice, on the grounds that loan-stock Bibles were technically the property of the parent Society, not of the local.[71] There was no action taken, perhaps because Brandram was too shrewd to expose the Society to the publicity that would result from prosecuting paupers for pawning the scriptures. But the concern remained. Year after year annual *Reports* assured subscribers that pawned Bibles were a myth invented by the Society's enemies, that in fact only a negligible number had been found in the course of assiduous searches of pawnbrokers' stock. The principle of loan stock was a useful way to supply the demand of visiting societies in London. These organizations, instituted to assist the 'destitute poor in the Metropolis', included the Christian Instruction Society, District Visiting Society, City Missionary Society, Pastoral Aid Society and others. They would have been willing to accept stocks of books for retail to their clients, but such a policy would have alienated the powerful metropolitan Auxiliaries. Still, the locals were not meeting the need. The very demand of visiting societies was proof that, in spite of Auxiliary activity, London was far from being supplied with cheap scriptures.

In fact the energy and enthusiasm of Auxiliary participation had begun to decline, at least in the Greater London area, by the mid-twenties. Dudley wrote to Andrew Brandram in May of 1825, demanding that 'some measures be adopted for checking the progress of the *Dry-rot* throughout our Metropolitan Auxiliaries & their connected Associations'. He gave figures to show that the receipts of most London-area Auxiliaries had declined to less than half their previous decennial averages.[72] The fact that this decline was happening in London was especially significant to Earl Street. Many members of the parent Society Committee retained strong, perhaps primary loyalties to their local Auxiliary and were unwilling to see territorial prerogatives infringed upon. The figures in the appendix show that Auxiliary contributions declined from 47 per cent in 1815–19 to 28 per cent in 1820–4 and remained under 30 per cent for the rest of the period. In absolute terms the contributions were very large, but they had declined when compared with the burgeoning income of the initial decade.

Some business people might have attributed the drop in income to the fact that the market had been, to a large extent, supplied. Surely the demand for cheap scriptures was not infinite. But the 'demand' for cheap Bibles was often an emotional, not an economic fact. The proof of demand was not the lack of a text within a household or family, but rather infidelity and uncouth behaviour by members of that family. Further evidence for this sort of demand was apparent to evangelicals who were worried by the larger political affairs of the decade. A succession of events – including the Queen Caroline affair in 1820–1 and escalating to the reform agitation in 1832 – sparked again the dread of revolution. The financial panic of 1825 stimulated fears of financial ruin, of bankruptcy or commercial failure. For many people, such fears could still be laid to rest by a commitment to the idea of Bible distribution.

But if the demand remained, the expectations about how it was to be supplied were beginning to change. The new distributors, people associated with scripture-reading and district-visiting societies, were unwilling to abide by the BFBS rules of 'without note or comment'. Moreover, they wished to be supplied with books they could pass on directly to the needy poor, not to get involved with the complex bookkeeping of collectors, Associations, Auxiliaries and their parent Society. The problem of meeting the needs of London philanthropists without offending the sensibilities of Auxiliary leaders was dealt with by an attempted compromise. Visiting societies were authorized in 1838 to apply to local London Associations for loan stock, which was supplied to the latter from the Earl Street headquarters. The books were cheaply bound, on common paper and stamped with the information that they were loan stock, property of the BFBS. Each society was asked to put its own distinct mark inside the books, to number each volume to correspond with a registry, and to account for each book monthly to the BFBS.[73] Not surprisingly this complicated arrangement proved 'inconvenient', and the organizations were permitted to apply directly to the Earl Street depository. Although local Auxiliaries still maintained control over distribution outside London, Earl Street had outflanked its metropolitan Auxiliaries.

When it came to supplying Sunday Schools with scriptures, the BFBS found its Auxiliary-based distribution system inadequate to meet the demand, which was enormous. The growth of these institutions, and their importance to the education of working-class children, is well documented in Thomas Laqueur's *Religion and Respectability*. Sunday Schools were large (from about one hundred students to over a thousand) institutions where instruction was offered to children whose parents could not afford other schooling, on the one day when the children were not at work. They learned reading and writing, as well as religious subjects, so that 'within the context of a working-class childhood, three to five hours of instruction each week for an average of four years ... had a significant impact on the creation of mass literacy in nineteenth-century England'.[74] Since April 1818 the BFBS had provided books to charity schools, either to supply the classroom or to provide individual scholars with their own Bible or New Testament. But the schools had to find a local Auxiliary, and perhaps remind the executive that they were authorized to supply books below the cost price. By January 1825, as schools proliferated, this arrangement had become unworkable. When some new cheap editions were prepared, it was resolved to authorize local Auxiliaries 'to supply Sunday Schools with [the new editions] as School Stock exclusively: and that this Society will supply the required number at the prices which the Committees of such Auxiliary or Branch Societies may deem expedient; such prices being not below the Reduced prices of the Society'. The onus had moved from the schools to the Auxiliaries, but no financial considerations were made at headquarters. This arrangement, however, still presumed that Auxiliaries were permanent local institutions. In many communities the depot was someone's home or business, and if local enthusiasm had waned supplies were likely to be low, and contact with London minimal. Some communities had an active Sunday School but no Bible Society. In 1829, the arrangements were partially centralized. The Sunday School Union was permitted to order books for school stocks from the central depository, for schools located in areas with no Auxiliary.[75]

Throughout the thirties the tension between central and local interests simmered. A glance at the condition of England in the late 1830s was enough to demonstrate to evangelicals both within and outside the BFBS that Bible distribution had to be stepped up. Any visitor to any slum was guaranteed to discover at least one individual who lacked a copy of the scriptures and admitted that she or he would like the situation to be remedied. Sunday School teachers wanted books for their students and were frustrated by having to negotiate with local Auxiliaries.

The next event in the increasing conflict of interests between the Auxiliaries and the parent Society was a drastic price reduction. A Committee meeting late in 1839 decided to allow books to both day and Sunday schools at greatly reduced terms: Bibles at 1s 6d instead of 2s, and Testaments at 6d instead of 1s 2d. These prices failed to cover the cost of printing, binding and the depository. Nevertheless, it was resolved,

That the aspect of the times, taken in connexion with the well ascertained fact that all previous exertions, made in whatever quarter, have not succeeded in furnishing the people at large with adequate supplies of the Scriptures, makes it an imperative duty to see whether some further measures ought not to be adopted with a view to place the Bible, or at least the New Testament, within the reach of all who are capable of reading.

The new policy meant that the books were offered to schools at just over half their production cost. In addition, the restriction of keeping such copies for school stock was withdrawn; teachers and administrators could give children the books to take home. The generosity included a resolution that 'considering the very great boon that will thus be conferred upon all Schools, the Subcommittee express a strong hope that the managers of such Schools will, as much as possible, guard against any abuse of the Society's bounty'.[76]

The Rev. M. Castledon of Woburn heard the news and immediately wrote to the BFBS Secretaries. His letter is a witty reminder of the political context in which the event occurred:

I have just received your circular ... relative to the reduction of prices of books to Sunday Schools accompanied with an alarming communication, 'the *"portentous"* aspect of the times.' Why, What's the matter? Is the aspect the Whigs cannot be turned out? Is it, that Ireland like Scotland, is about to be released from a form of worship she won't have? The Queen's marriage? Some say to a Papist! Is it the Penny Post? Stoppage at the Bank? etc. etc. The Chartists? who are about to be hang'd and which they richly deserve. But perhaps 'the portentous aspect,' means, the *repeal* of the corn laws. God grant it may be this! and then there is a blessed foreboding of good to the hungry and distressed.[77]

The Committee was powerless to repeal the Corn Laws, but it was under heavy pressure to extend distribution. Short of undercutting the monopoly held by its own Auxiliaries, and thus destroying the popular commitment to the Bible transaction, the only way to do this was to reduce the price of its cheapest Bibles. The Society also required that the cheap editions be available through their local depots. They hoped that supporters would not only handle the distribution of books on the new plan, but would rise to the occasion with generous free contributions to help offset the expected losses.

The Sunday School Union was naturally very interested in the new arrangements. Not to be confused with the Sunday School Society, the Union was an organization of teachers which 'had banded together to secure books, discuss problems, and enjoy each other's company'. There were branches in London and in the provinces. Publishing, as in the Bible Society, accounted for most of the Union's budget.[78] William Watson, a leading member of the Union, wrote to express gratitude for the concession to Sunday Schools. He regretted, however, that no provision had been made to centralize further the system of distribution: 'There are a vast many schools in obscure situations which are doing much good and yet are very much shut out from any advantages of this sort. They are compelled to find their way to us to obtain elementary books for instruction and I trust thus the Committee will facilitate the means of sharing in the advantages now offered.'[79] Watson's attitude made sense for his own Society, but he failed to understand the importance of accountancy and indebtedness in the link between parent and local Bible Societies. The complex arrangements whereby a 'moiety account' for books and a 'free contribution' account for general support were maintained, permitted the Earl Street office to fund its foreign publication project out of the activities of local Societies.

As we have seen, it was because of Auxiliaries and the way cheap Bibles had always been funded that the Society had rich reserves. The only way for these to be maintained during a price reduction, however, was for Auxiliaries to make separate collections and contribute generous amounts of 'compensation' to the Earl Street coffers. Otherwise the foreign project would suffer. The Committee tried to challenge its local Auxiliaries with the needs of Sunday School students, hoping to solve the economic difficulty by reviving popular enthusiasm for the Bible transaction. But in 1840 very few Auxiliaries followed the example of Southwark and mounted fund-raising campaigns to help offset the price reductions. Most grabbed as many cheap copies as possible in what struck many observers as an unseemly way.

Writing in confidence to his fellow Secretary, George Browne told Andrew Brandram: 'I do mourn over these reductions.' Browne's letter shows the two sides of the issue: 'When faith is weak – unhappily more than seldom – I tremble for your funds: this self devoted nihili-nihification of the price at home must, I fear, – (it is so eagerly and universally laid hold of) shorten the hand, or diminish the handfuls of other countries. I have not heard any great alacrity towards compensation.' Browne was well aware that the nihilification (setting aside or slighting) of the price of domestic Bibles had very serious economic implications. On the other hand, he was out in the field, in Cambridgeshire and Lincolnshire, and like any other evangelical he felt himself to be living in portentous times:

But one is reconciled to the reduction of price, on behalf of Wisbech – a place where . . . Satan has 'had his seat' & 'dwelt,' through socialism . . . It is curdling to think of the fact, that an Infant school on infidel principles was established there, – & that mothers would be forced (is it the right word?) to send 150 children, to learn blasphemy with the alphabet, & to spit upon Christ from the very cradle! But your cheapening measure has enabled the Branch to 'fight against them with the sound of the Lord's wrath' – the school is now broken up & the premises secured by those who will turn it from its purpose of darkness to light – & from the power of Satan unto God.[80]

As a BFBS insider, Browne felt ambivalent about the value of the new plan.

Some subscribers, however, were clearly opposed to the price reduction. They believed it would be all the more difficult to fight against infidelity with reduced prices, and they began to wonder if there was such a thing as too low a price for a Bible. Not only would foreign countries suffer, but 'a more effectual course could not be adopted for alienating . . . the warm hearted sympathy of [loyal members]'. This was the view of a London supporter, J.

Brown, who told the Secretaries that if prices were reduced there would be no check on abuses: 'you at once loosen the hold which we now have on many members of our association Committees ... moreover, can you suppose that our members will be content to become merely the drudges to procure *free* contributions, in order that others who do not labour, may pluck & distribute the fruit?' The delicate balance of Bible Society economics was being upset. Another Southwark member warned that Auxiliaries would not only lose the prestige of being the distributors of Society Bibles, but they would lose the volunteer resources of Sunday School teachers on their committees: 'once render their managers and Teachers independent of us, and we may seek their help in vain'.[81]

The politics, as well as the economics, of the Bible transaction at the local level were fragile. Those who supported the price reduction were also concerned, but they hoped to circumvent the dangers by careful attention to the physical appearance of the books in question. It was felt that each volume of the new release had to project everything that was meant by the evocative word 'cheap': inexpensive, utilitarian, plain but strong, and with an austere flavour of the workhouse. An important aspect of the price reduction concerned the outward appearance of the books and the strength of their binding. Here is how the reduction was characterized for supporters in the *Monthly Extracts* and in the annual *Report* for 1840:

Your Committee are sure that you will join them in the delightful reflection, that in thus cheapening the sacred volume, we do not lessen its intrinsic worth – it is but the casket that is homely, the gem still retains its purity and richness: the peasant, or the peasant's child, when taking the *cheap* Bible in his hand, looks upon the same great truths ... as meet the eye of the prince when he bends over the vellumed page, or touches the gilded leaf.[82]

The BFBS Committee asked its supporters to embrace the idea of a drab new design and format for the text. At the same time it was necessary to build in guarantees that the Society's benevolence would not be exploited by booksellers or pawnbrokers.

The 'homely casket' was marked with a stamp that became a clear message of condescension. As part of the planning for the 1840 reduction, it was 'Resolved ... to have stamped on the outside of the Nonpareil Bible, the words "sold at 1*s* 6*d*," and on the Brevier Testament, "sold at 6*d*" – with the following addition to each, "to the Poor and the Children in Sunday & Day Schools".'[83] There was to be no question of booksellers turning a profit on the Society's generosity. William Watson wrote on behalf of the Sunday School Unions to 'plead most earnestly to solicit that no mark may be placed on the books which will make it a degradation to the children to receive them'. He continued by congratulating the Committee on a noble enterprise, and added, 'I should deeply deplore that any thing should be done to take away from the graciousness and utility of this act. While we endeavour to meet the circumstances of the Poor we must endeavour to prevent a feeling of pauperism amongst them which must tend to deteriorate their character.'[84] But Earl Street did not respond to Watson's sensitivity. The Secretaries were unwilling to trust people outside their circle of influence not to 'abuse the liberality of the Committee'. Whenever a fraud was discovered they tried to trace the source of the books, but it was easier to let each volume speak for itself.[85] The stamp was to become known as the 'charity brand' and clearly to label owners of books so marked as objects of philanthropy.

By August of 1840 the reduction was suspended, 'it being found utterly impossible, with a due regard to the other claims of the Society, to sacrifice so large a portion of the "Free Contributions"'. The loss for the six months February–July was £14,410 on 382,377 copies. Browne told Brandram, 'I was sure the sixpenny system would never do, from the moment I observed the general convulsive grasp that was made at the offer, whilst Southwark stood almost alone in the way of indemnity.' Dudley agreed: 'The *Experiment* has been tried, & it was high time it should have ceased. The power of removing the Suspension is in their own hands, & *now* we shall see whether Catholic Christianity or Denominational Selfishness is to Kick the Beam.'[86] The founder of BFBS Auxiliaries could be as caustic about their weaknesses as he sometimes was about the lack of support they got from London.

The price reduction of 1840 was the result of a fortuitous combination of circumstances: not just the demand from Sunday Schools, but also the use of cheaper machinery and materials at the Presses. Even more important was a campaign of political pressure against the 'Bible monopoly' of the Queen's Printer and the Universities. The following spring the BFBS was able to resume selling books at very cheap rates. As we shall see in chapter 3, this was made possible by circumstances outside the Society's control: the three Presses authorized to print scriptures in English and Welsh reduced their prices.

The perspective here is on the significance of cheap Bibles to evangelical activists in local Auxiliaries and Associations, and to their contemporaries who taught and organized Sunday Schools. During the years up to 1840, images of the Bible-starved poor had been juxtaposed in middle-class minds with concerns about the Poor Law, about paternalism and utilitarianism, about incipient radicalism, and about the potentialities of literacy. The Bible transaction was more than just a publishing venture, people believed: it was the best hope for national and international salvation.

With the tremendous optimism generated by the idea of Bible distribution in mind, some preliminary conclusions are possible. It is clear, first of all, that the price of books determined the economics of the Bible transaction at both local and international levels. The Society, as we shall see, took advantage of new technology at the printers and were untroubled by using sweated labour at the bookbinders. These policies meant that as time went on books could be produced more and more cheaply. But if they were distributed by agencies, like Sunday Schools, outside of the BFBS network, they did not generate any voluntary funds for the foreign project. And even inside the Society's system, lower prices meant a smaller budget for all categories of expenditure.

The political and social aspects of popular participation in the Society's project are also significant. The initial demand for cheap Bibles came not from the expected consumers, but indirectly from wealthier people. Local Ladies' Association members tried to convey their message about the value of a Bible transaction to working-class purchasers by the 'system' of penny-a-week subscription, with all the benefits it was supposed to include. Until the thirties, Bible Associations were eagerly organized and funds poured into Earl Street, where the Secretaries and staff had their hands full in meeting the demand. Later, by 1840, the nuances of the Bible transaction – political, economic and social – required a change in the book as physical object, not just in its distribution. The cheap BFBS Bible had to be designed, as well as priced, very carefully, to convey a critical cultural message. It had to be low enough in cost to be accessible to poor people, but not so low as to tempt them to devalue its contents. Or worse, to tempt booksellers and pawnbrokers to make a profit on it. To this end it was published in drab covers, and the reduced-price stamp marked it as a philanthropic gift.

The demand for cheap Bibles was a social phenomenon, a response to the economic and political tensions of the age in which it flourished. But as we shall see, cheapness was interpreted in a much more businesslike and matter-of-fact way by the printers and bookbinders who supplied the Society with the books in question.

3 · THE BFBS AND ENGLISH PRINTERS, 1804–1864

THE BIBLE TRADE in early nineteenth-century England was a 'little world of the book': a small circle of experienced printers, binders and booksellers, many of them personally acquainted, and all of them sharing an understanding of how their craft worked and what its products should look like.[1] This world had London as its centre, and extended to Cambridge and to Oxford, the two ancient seats of learning that were also entrusted with the privilege of printing the Bible in English. In 1804 when the Bible Society began, the Bible trade and the craft of printing had not changed much since William Caxton first printed a book in England in 1476, or since Thomas Berthelet first printed the Bible in 1535. Metal type, in limited supply, was set by hand a few pages at a time: paper was handmade and scarce: the presses, built of wood, were slow and required the attention of trained and experienced printers. Once books emerged from the printer's shop they had to be bound, and then to find their way to owners and readers through the labyrinthine network of eighteenth-century bookselling. In the next fifty years a great many changes precipitated the mechanization and the consequent massive expansion of the book and printing trades: population growth, increased literacy and education, political radicalism and agitation for social reform. One such transformation was the zeal of evangelical men and women for supplying the scriptures to others, and the complementary receptiveness of readers who decided to accept them. Thus it was that the impatient enthusiasm of the Bible Society, with its repeated demand for more and more books, cheap books, on strong paper, in vast quantities burst upon the traditional craft practices and cautious business methods of the English book trade.

The Bible, the first substantial book ever to be printed, is not like any other book. Massively long and perennially marketable, this unique text exacts scrupulous accuracy even while the tradition of producing a variety of formats sets accuracy at risk. For printers, these criteria mean that the lucrative contract to print Bibles can only be managed by someone with plenty of capital and a well-organized shop. P. M. Handover, in *Printing in London*, outlines the situation.

To many people in this country the Bible is a sacred book, perhaps even the inspired word of God, and that fact is relevant; but to its publishers the Bible is a book with certain physical features that make it different from all other books. First: the

Authorized Version contains 774,746 words. Compositors and pressmen will quickly work out what that means in terms of ens, in paper orders and machining time. Secondly: there exists a considerable and constant demand for the Bible. Thirdly: the Bible must be produced without a single misprint. And fourthly: the Bible is required in the whole range of sizes, from folio to the smallest.

Handover explains that this situation makes Bible printing 'highly specialized', so that it attracts 'the most shrewd businessmen in the trade'. A contract to print the scriptures requires 'a talent for organization and a keen analytical mind'.[2]

This organized and analytical printer, before the nineteenth century, would have had to set up the book a few pages at a time. Even though reprints might be required, no printer had enough type on hand to set up such a large book in one unit. They were always running out of sorts – of individual types – and needing either to cast more (which was expensive), or to print off earlier pages, distribute the type, and start again. This inevitably meant errors, and the 'He' and 'She' Bibles (for a transposition of pronouns in Ruth 3:15.), the 'Wicked Bible' ('Thou shalt commit adultery'), and the 'Vinegar (for vineyard) Bible', now collector's items, were in their day a disgrace to their printers and a potential threat to the immortal souls of their readers.[3]

The problem of resetting and consequent corruption of the text had been anticipated and dealt with in Germany, by one extraordinary publisher. In 1710, at Halle in Saxony, the *Cansteinsche Bibelanstalt* was established by Karl Hildebrand Baron von Canstein. He has been called 'a one-man Bible Society almost a hundred years before such institutions became common elsewhere'. Canstein's charitable contribution to cheapening Bibles while maintaining their accuracy was this. After the type pages had been composed he kept them standing, unavailable for any other printing, and invulnerable to the introduction of further errors. Because errors could be caught and corrected without new ones being introduced, Canstein's Bibles improved, rather than deteriorated.[4] In England, however, even the wealthiest and most generous philanthropist could not have emulated Canstein, because Bible-publishing was controlled by the state and limited to three 'privileged' Presses, all of which regarded the frequent resetting and reprinting of Bibles as normal, and all of which earned substantial profits from their monopoly.

The development of the Bible privilege demonstrates, in the context of British history, the economic and political realities of holding this coveted licence. The restriction of printing the Bible in English and Welsh to the two Universities and the Royal Printer dates from the sixteenth century. The King's or Queen's Printers (there were separate royal printers for England, Scotland and Ireland) held the privilege by patent, under the Royal prerogative. In addition, Cambridge University (in 1629) and later Oxford (1636) were granted Charters that confirmed or affirmed their right to print Bibles and Prayer Books. The rationale was that as learned bodies the Universities could control the accuracy of the text in a way that a merely technical printer licensed by the Crown could not.[5] The first Royal printer to receive a patent conferring the exclusive right to print Bibles and Prayer Books, as well as statutes, proclamations and other government documents was Christopher Barker, in 1577, under Elizabeth I.[6] His son and heir, Robert Barker, undertook the production of a new translation, authorized by James I and first published in 1611. The enormous expenses of the revision and collation meant that Barker, in financial difficulties, lost control of the patent just at the moment when the demand for the new version was making it so valuable. It was Bonham Norton and John Bill who took over, moving the Royal Press to Printing House Square in Blackfriars. In 1634 the patent came under the control of 'that ruthless triumvirate', Miles Flesher, John Haviland and Robert Young, who controlled more than a fifth of the printing presses in London at the time. They made a fortune out of publishing the Authorized Version in many sizes and formats, so that the Puritans in Parliament consequently developed a strong aversion to any monopoly in the printing of the Bible. The situation was confused during the Protectorate: although the patent had been abolished, the legal right to print Bibles without restrictions did not also include the capacity to operate the Blackfriars Printing House or to finance such large undertakings. Badly printed Bibles abounded: a bishop preparing for a sermon in St Paul's purchased a copy in one of the neighbouring bookshops and found that his chosen text was missing altogether.[7] In this situation, as earlier, the University Presses claimed to offer to the public versions that were more accurate than those produced in London.

The Royal Charters of the Universities included the right to print 'all kinds of books', an ambiguous provision that brought them into conflict with the apparently exclusive privilege of the London Royal printers. This began as early as 1591 when John Legate, printer to the University of Cambridge, printed a Bible and a New Testament, and continued into the eighteenth century. Sometimes the Royal printer paid the Universities to forbear from printing Bibles and Prayer Books; at other times the Universities engaged in litigation to protect their claims. And the University Printers sometimes leased their privilege to London printers who were members of the Stationers' Company.

At the Restoration, Christopher Barker III and John Bill II, descendants of earlier Royal printers, were granted, but did not personally exercise, the patent. Instead they sold shares in it, and the actual printers were Henry Hills and Thomas Newcombe. Friction with the Universities accelerated in 1673 when Dr John Fell, as Vice-Chancellor of Oxford, sponsored the publication of a quarto Bible. Hills and Newcombe took the University to court, and lost. They continued to engage in fierce competition until Hills made the mistake of allying himself with James II and the Roman Catholic cause. When William and Mary came to the throne in 1688, the rights of

Oxford (and subsequently Cambridge) were confirmed, and there was a new King's Printer in London, John Baskett. Baskett, who leased the Oxford privilege for a time, is remembered for his 'Vinegar Bible' printed at Oxford in 1717, and known as 'A Baskett-ful of Errors'. His heirs sold the patent in 1769, to Charles Eyre who entered into partnership with William Strahan, a Scottish printer. They moved the King's Printing House to New Square, between Fleet Street and Holborn, and began to make enormous profits out of the Government printing occasioned by the wars with America and with France. Their profits at the beginning of the nineteenth century were estimated at 216 per cent, about £13,000. When the Bible Society began, Eyre and Andrew Strahan (William's heir) were not printing the scriptures at all, being completely engaged with Government printing. They did, however, license some other printers to publish Bibles under their patent. Their wealth meant that when Eyre and Strahan were called upon to begin printing Bibles for the BFBS, they could invest heavily in equipment and materials and move quickly to become a major supplier.

The fortunes of the two University Presses, on the other hand, were at the turn of the nineteenth century largely dependent on the printing of Bibles and Books of Common Prayer. The Royal Charters, investing them with the right to print books, were good sources of income for both Universities. At Oxford the Press was divided into the 'Learned Side' and the 'Bible Side', both operated by a partnership agreement, between the University on the one hand, and Cook, Bensley and Dawson as 'managing partners' on the other. Joshua Cook and William Dawson were booksellers, of Oxford and London respectively, while Thomas Bensley was a well-known London printer with a shop in Bolt Court, off Fleet Street. They were replaced in 1810 by a new partnership of Samuel Collingwood and Joseph Parker, a printer and a bookseller of Oxford, and Edward Gardner, a bookbinder in London. Collingwood was to be the chief link between the Press and the BFBS, and he also became involved in the local Auxiliary. As Peter Sutcliffe observes, 'The relative importance of the two sides of the Press can be seen from the bills for paper in 1814: the Learned Press paid £1,003, the Bible Press £19,073.'[8]

The Press at Cambridge was smaller than at Oxford, but equally dependent on Bible publishing. At Cambridge a single 'University Printer' managed the Press and reported to a governing body, the Press Syndicate. As we have seen, the local BFBS Auxiliary in the town and University was sponsored in 1811 by prominent evangelicals including Isaac Milner and Charles Simeon. By that time the University's printers were already fully engaged in printing Bibles for the parent Society. Richard Watts, who had learned the trade publishing newspapers in Oxford and London, was University Printer from 1802 to 1809. Watts promoted an important technological change at the Press when he introduced stereotyping in 1804, arranging with Andrew Wilson to share the 'stereotype secret', in exchange for financial considerations.

Distribution was handled by agents, such as John Deighton who sold for the Press in both London and Cambridge, until 1811. John Smith was elected printer in 1809, and Watts moved to Broxbourne, near London, where he printed foreign-language editions for the Bible Society. John William Parker, originally from the London firm of William Clowes, served as Printer from 1836 until 1854, in partnership with Clowes, commuting between London and Cambridge.

Finally there were the ordinary printers, mostly in London, who printed versions of the Bible in English other than the Authorized Version, such as Bibles furnished with commentaries, or alternative translations from the original languages. Printers were free to produce, and readers to use, such versions, but they did not bear the *imprimatur* of Royal and ecclesiastical authority. These printers also produced editions in foreign languages for use at home or for distribution abroad. Little is known about most of these craftsmen and their shops, beyond the appearance of their imprints on title-pages. Samuel Bagster of London was an exception. His firm was founded in 1794, and printed polyglot editions and Bibles with notes and aids to prayer and study. But these were of no interest to a Society devoted to circulating the scriptures in versions they described as 'without note or comment' and 'sanctioned by public authority'.

The Bible Society's Secretaries and Committee were not members of the small fraternity of Bible printers, or even familiar with the customs of the contemporary book trade. Untroubled by their lack of experience, they approached their task with dedication, zeal and an overwhelming determination, and set about publishing Bibles in England. As they learned the trade, they adopted some of its conventions, disregarded others, and changed its pattern by the force of their demand for printed books. As we have seen, they had two groups of printers to work with. English Bibles – so much in demand to supply the local Auxiliaries and Ladies' Associations – could only be had from the privileged presses. But for books in foreign languages, there was open competition among those London and provincial printers who commanded the resources to handle a large and complex job. The Society lost no time in organizing a Subcommittee on printing. Formed within a month of the founding meeting, it was chaired by one prominent evangelical who did know his way around the book trade. This was Joseph Butterworth, the law bookseller. He had already subscribed with a generous 5 guineas, anxious not to appear ostentatious, but well aware that his 'own particular knowledge of the vast expence [*sic*] of Paper & Print might lead [him] to think differently of the *necessary* Subscriptions than some other Persons'.[9] Members of the Sub-committee from the clergy were the Secretaries, Joseph Hughes, Josiah Pratt (later John Owen) and C. F. A. Steinkopf. Lay members were William Alers (banker), Zachary Macaulay (merchant), Samuel Mills (leather dealer) and Joseph Reyner (cotton importer and shipper). The latter owned a warehouse which was to be convenient for storage and shipping until the Society obtained its own premises. Together they determined a policy of increasing the number of Bibles published and circulated in England, while maintaining high quality and low prices.

In 1804 the most likely way to do this was to make a commitment to the new technology of stereotype, which, according to its chief promoter, Andrew Wilson, inaugurated a 'new era in the history of Literary Science'.[10] The Bible was a prime candidate for stereotyping, a process by which pages of type were cast as permanent metal plates and stored for reprinting. A group of pages making up a forme were set up in type, and a plaster-of-paris mould taken of them. A thin layer of lead was poured into the mould to make a single solid plate of each page for the press, rather than each enclosing thousands of individual pieces of type. The innovation would ensure accuracy and – everyone hoped – drastically reduce prices by avoiding the necessity of resetting type every time the book was reprinted. This method had recently been re-discovered by Earl Stanhope, after an initial attempt by William Ged in the eighteenth century had failed to gain acceptance, and was being exploited economically by Stanhope's 'practical man' Andrew Wilson, a 'respectable printer' of London.[11] Wilson had recently (20 April 1804) made an agreement with the Syndics of the Cambridge University Press and the University Printer Richard Watts, to share with them the stereotype secret. They agreed to pay him one third of the money saved by the process.

The members of the BFBS Committee were delighted with the idea that textual accuracy could be ensured, avoiding the repetition of a costly process. They seem to have believed that God (it could not be mere coincidence) had provided the invention just in time for the first printings. These merchants, lawyers and businessmen did not hesitate to risk an untried technology. In fact the Society waited until the Press was equipped for stereotyping to place its first massive order, in November 1804, for 6,000 Bibles and 5,000 New Testaments in English, 20,000 of the long-awaited Welsh Bibles and 5,000 New Testaments in Welsh, all to be executed in stereotype.[12]

If the Society was to spend responsibly the funds entrusted to it, its executive would have to become familiar with the jargon of printers. Assistant Secretary Joseph Tarn was soon corresponding with Wilson, inquiring about the number of plates required for a pocket edition of the scriptures (280 for the New Testament and 560 for the Old), how many could be produced in a day (about three), and what they would cost (£600–700 for the initial set, and over £100 for subsequent sets, to be paid by the BFBS).[13] It was becoming clear that publishing Bibles was a bulky, slow and expensive process. Nor was the new technology implemented smoothly. On 28 October 1805 Watts wrote that he had sent out the second thousand of the Brevier duodecimo Testament, of which 5,000 had been ordered nearly a year before. He said: 'I need not conceal from you that Stereotype Printing at Cambridge

79

has still to struggle with many disadvantages: and that we cannot get on with our press work so fast as was expected.' Stereotype was not immune from typographical errors. For example, Watts had to explain to his exacting clients how 'The words "to remain" (a direction applicable in the margin of the 8vo proof to a comma) must have been ignorantly inserted by the compositor's supposing his instructions a part of the sentence; and the mistake as foolishly copied into our 12mo edition.'[14] At the same time Watts stressed that stereotyping would not reduce the price of producing the editions, but that the quality was improved.[15]

This was not good news to the Bible Society. Cambridge had estimated a price of 8d for the pocket-sized duodecimo Testament, but they charged a shilling. John Owen, the Church of England Secretary, wrote to describe the Committee's chagrin. They had been led to believe that stereotype would save one-third of the usual cost of printing. Moreover, 'This estimate ... has been pretty generally notified to the Members of the Society, and has also served as a rule for guiding the Committee in their different arrangements for purchase & distribution.' A 50 per cent increase 'must involve the Committee in much embarrassment, and subject them to considerable animadversion with their constituents & the Public'.[16]

At this stage the two Universities co-operated to determine the appropriate prices for Bibles. Both were accustomed to dealing with the Society for Promoting Christian Knowledge. The SPCK did not correspond directly with the printers, but worked through their London booksellers Francis and Charles Rivington. The latter was 'the leading theological publisher in London', at the sign of the Bible and Crown in Paternoster Row.[17] But the Press at Cambridge found that the upstarts in Earl Street demanded more books and further discounts than the SPCK. Cambridge publishers conferred with their opposite numbers at Oxford, and agreed to maintain prices and allowances. At the same time the two University Presses decided that 'the name of any particular Society be not inserted in the Title page', a policy that was not to last very long.[18]

The Society's appetite for printed scriptures continued to grow. Throughout 1805 and 1806 Tarn corresponded with Wilson and Watts about the plates for the Welsh Testament, which also came under the Bible privilege. There was pressure to complete this edition, since it had been called for by the charismatic Thomas Charles of Bala to meet the need of people like Mary Jones. Furthermore it was a way for the BFBS to establish its reputation for energy and commitment, as superior to the slackness of the SPCK. However there were format problems, typographical errors ('so glaring as to be evident even to the country people'), and disputes over the price.[19]

Wilson, by this time, was engaged in a conflict with the Syndics of the University Press at Cambridge that concerned his remuneration for sharing the secret of stereotyping. Among other tactics, he refused to allow the Press permission to use the plates he had made for the Welsh New Testament. In order to facilitate publication by getting Wilson to release the plates, the BFBS Committee advanced to him a sum of £300, on loan, to be repaid out of the moneys due to him from the University. Wilson gave them an order on the Vice-Chancellor for the amount. The Vice-Chancellor, Joseph Turner, replied rather frostily, 'I apprehend there is not the smallest probability of our coming to a settlement with him [Wilson] during the fortnight I have to remain in office.'[20]

Apart from the technical and financial frustrations of publishing by stereotype, the Wilson affair of 1806 exemplifies the Society's developing approach to business arrangements. The entrepreneurial Andrew Wilson recognized, no doubt much sooner than the Cambridge Syndics, that the new Society was going to control Bible publishing in England. He wrote to the Secretaries suggesting that he be appointed their official Bookseller and Printer. Wilson did not say what he proposed to do about his lack of a Royal Bible patent or University charter. Tarn hastened to assure Wilson that they valued his contribution to the interests of the Society, but noted that he had not explained 'whether in soliciting the appointment of Printer to the Society you propose to preclude them from availing themselves of any opportunity of Competition, which may present advantages that the Commercial part of the Committee know how to appreciate...'. He replied that his invention was a 'grand national object', and made it clear that he wanted some sort of official recognition, and that a public institution like the Bible Society could testify to 'the moral and intellectual, as well as financial value, of the Stereotype Invention'. They declined formally a week later, offering Wilson the cold comfort that 'when a proper opportunity occurs for the Society to render you any essential service in aid of your exertions, the Committee will gladly embrace it'.[21] This incident illustrates the way that Wilson was dealing with the Cambridge Press, as well as with the Bible Society. It demonstrates both his and the Committee's growing awareness of their unique position in the domestic Bible market-place. They had come early to an appreciation of the advantages of an arms-length relationship with the printers of English and Welsh scriptures. It also indicates an early commitment to the principle of non-interference on the part of the Committee with someone else's contract, which appears again in their response to the bookbinders' agitation. They were delighted with the abstract idea of stereotyping, and willing to be patient until it became a practical possibility. But they did not think of it as the private property of Andrew Wilson or of anyone else.

Joseph Hughes had asked 'If for Wales, why not for the world?' and the idea of supplying scriptures in languages where few copies existed, to readers whose whole nation was destitute, motivated the Society to publish in foreign languages as well as in the languages of the British Isles. As early as April of 1804, the BFBS had appointed a Subcommittee to open a foreign correspondence. Granville Sharpe, whose collection of printed Bibles was well known, was asked to prepare a list of existing versions (other than those in English, Latin and Ancient Greek).[22] The very first foreign edition published by the Bible Society was the Gospel of St John in the Mohawk language for native people of Upper Canada. No reference to its printing (by Phillips and Fardon), however, appears in the records of the Subcommittee.[23] The first two European languages considered were French and Spanish. England was at this date at war with Napoleonic France and its Spanish allies: the country was preparing for invasion, with beacon bonfires alight on the hilltops. But it was eminently characteristic of evangelical approaches to political and military problems that the Bible Society became concerned with French and Spanish prisoners of war, in English hands or about to be captured.

Although the first few French and Spanish editions were purchased ready-printed, the Society was preparing to publish its own. Before foreign versions could appear, however, the Subcommittee had to select good translations upon which to base their texts. Only Protestant translations were acceptable, and Sharpe and others were called upon to distinguish between competing texts and save the Society embarrassment. On 18 December 1805 the Sub-committee voted £100 to purchase (from Thomas Boosey of Bread Street) copies of David Martin's version of the New Testament in French, and have them bound in sheep to be sold for 2s 6d.[24] With a supply in hand, there was a recommendation to the General Committee to consider printing an edition of the entire scriptures in French. A few days later (26 December), Foreign Secretary Steinkopf was requested to canvas French Protestant ministers for their opinion of the best edition, while Josiah Pratt was to go to three printers for estimates. These were Richard Edwards, Richard Watts and (probably) Charles Whittingham.[25]

The same day it was decided to print the New Testament in Spanish, in the version of Cipriano de Valera published in Amsterdam in 1602. Joseph Reyner produced the name of J. Uzielli of Sun Street, Bishopsgate Street, 'a respectable Foreigner, well versed in the Spanish language', to supervise the press. Meanwhile estimates for 2,000 copies of the New Testament in Spanish had been received from Richard Edwards and from Samuel Rousseau, of Wood Street, Spa Fields. The latter's (lower) estimate was accepted, with an extra 1,000 copies of St Matthew's gospel to be struck off, 'done up in strong dark blue paper', and sent to Reyner for distribution among Spanish prisoners of war. The paper for this large edition was not handled by Rousseau, but ordered by the Bible Society from Key and Co.[26]

Four days later, the Subcommittee met again. Their decisions show how quickly they were learning to deal with the complexities of the publishing business. The order for paper to Key was countermanded, since Messrs Tucker quoted 2s less per ream. Boosey's French Testaments were sent to George Lister, for binding in sheep. Meanwhile Steinkopf raised the possibility of ordering Protestant Bibles in French from Basle, where the German Bible Society was established.[27] But this would only be practicable if the British government would permit the books to be imported free of duty. John Owen was detailed to find out. The preparation of the Spanish New Testament had advanced: the 1602 edition had been chosen, and Uzielli was to collate it with the 24mo edition of 1625, for a fee of one guinea per sheet. Another printer appeared with an offer for the French version: Andrew Wilson, who in addition to advising the University Presses on stereotype ran a shop in Duke Street, Lincoln's Inn Fields, was asked to estimate the cost of setting up the French Bible in Nonpareil type and preparing stereotype plates.

At the next meeting, 6 January 1806, Owen reported that the duty on books from Basle would be remitted by the government, but the problem of supply was not so easily solved. Carl Steinkopf, in correspondence with his evangelical brethren of Switzerland, had discovered that supplies were limited there. Only 800 to 1,000 copies could be spared, and even this number would tend to increase the price at Basle. The Subcommittee resolved not only to leave the books where they were, but to give £50 to the Basle Religious Society for the purpose of purchasing and distributing Bibles in French at a low price.[28] As for the French Testament to be printed in London, estimates had been received from Thomas Rutt for printing on common types, as well as from Wilson for stereotype. Not surprisingly, Wilson's was 'considerably higher'. The apparent long-term advantage of stereotype overcame the appeal of short-term savings, however, and Wilson was asked, on 13 January, to make proposals for three sets of plates. These appeared on the 27th, with a boldness that we now recognize as typical of Wilson's approach to customers. He could not undertake, he told them, 'in the present stage of the Stereotype business' to make a third set of plates for less than the full price of the types (6s 2d per pound). He offered instead to make a set for the Society at half that price, 'on condition that he should be allowed to make a set for himself for home Consumption'. The Subcommittee agreed, and Wilson undertook to finish the Bible in the present year.[29]

But Wilson was only the printer. The text was selected the same day, Martin's version, in Pierre Roques's edition of Basle 1772.[30] On 24 February there was a communication from Mr Des Carriers of Camberwell, who had been entrusted with correcting the proofs. He wanted to improve the orthography, according to standards set by the French Academy. Already reeling from SPCK criticisms of alterations in the orthography of Welsh Bibles, the Committee responded cautiously, asking for examples of the proposed changes. They had their own body of European experts to consult, whose standards were scriptural rather than linguistic. On 21 March, Steinkopf was asked to seek advice from Basle, and Des Carriers to discontinue his work temporarily. The situation was further confused in September, when a new edition of the French Bible appeared in Geneva. Steinkopf, comparing the translation with Martin's, found it 'rather paraphrastical than literal'. But although the text of this edition was rejected, its spelling was selected as the standard for Des Carriers's correction of the Martin/Roques edition of 1772. On 13 October, the intractable translator submitted a single corrected sheet: contrary to instructions 'he had altered many words for better French'. Andrew Wilson, moreover, announced that forty of the 324 plates had already been cast according to Des Carriers's corrections, but the Committee was adamant: the plates were to be corrected by a return to Martin's text. Two weeks later they heard of a further translation of the French Bible, made in Paris as recently as 1805 under the auspices of the London Missionary Society, and based on the eighteenth-century Protestant version produced by J. F. Ostervald. While it was being considered by trusted bilingual clergymen, Wilson was asked to suspend the printing of the edition prepared, corrected and re-corrected by Des Carriers. By November, positive reports had been received on the new translation and it was resolved to adopt this version for the stereotype edition, 'omitting the preliminary discourse, correcting the typographical errors, and such mistakes, as, according to Mr [Adam] Clarke's representation, have crept into it with respect to misprinting the Italic words'.[31]

At the same time, the Committee was grappling with remarkably similar problems of text, translation and typography with respect to the scriptures in Spanish. In January 1806 Rousseau had started to print from the 1602 edition when he was ordered to suspend his work, 'some doubts having arisen whether it would not be expedient to Stereotype it'. Meanwhile William Blair, another Bible collector, had written to recommend yet another text of the Spanish scriptures (1708) for publication, and to offer the use of his copy and his assistance in revising the proofs. On 13 January the later edition was adopted, with Rousseau basing his printing on a copy presented to the Society by Mr Johnson of Bristol, while Blair's copy of the same edition was given to Uzielli for the corrections. In October Uzielli, like Des Carriers the previous February, was discovered to have incorporated variations in the corrected proofs, variations which he 'vindicated' on the strength of his expertise as a linguist. The Committee decided to suspend printing until 'the nature & propriety of those variations were ascertained'. On 30 November, after a consultation between Reyner and a Mr Goslen, who knew Spanish, they resolved not, after all, to deviate from the New Testament published in Amsterdam in 1602. Rousseau was permitted to resume printing, but his days were numbered. William Blair, by now a member of the Committee, was unsatisfied with his work, telling Tarn that the printer had 'made very frivolous and unsatisfactory excuses for the tardiness and bad printing', and that he should not be employed again.[32] The order was reduced to 3,000 copies, Andrew Wilson having offered to stereotype the Spanish New Testament in a larger type (Brevier in a duodecimo format, for £160) for subsequent printings. This story ends with a letter in November 1807 announcing that the books were well received in Spain, and seen even by the normally hostile Roman Catholic priests 'as good and fair copies'. HMS *Serapis*, headed for Gibraltar and already taking English Bibles and Testaments to the Garrison, would also take 200 New Testaments in Spanish. It was feared that the copies sent to Portsea on the first of July were 'probably still waiting for a Conveyance'. Such were the hazards of international publishing in a time of war.

In the years after 1807, the Society published scriptures in Italian (printed from types by Heney and Haddon in 1808 and stereotyped by Rutt in 1811), in Portuguese (from types by Heney and Haddon in 1809, with a new edition by John Tilling in 1810),[33] and in Dutch (in stereotype by Brightley in 1809, and again in 1812 by Hamblin and Seyfang). There was a Danish Bible (printed by John Benjamin Gottlieb Vogel in 1809, with another edition in 1814 by Hamblin and Seyfang) and a version in both Ancient and Modern Greek (printed from types by Tilling in 1810, and in stereotype by Rutt in 1814). Thomas Rutt printed a stereotype New Testament in Manx, the language of the Isle of Man, in 1810. And Samuel McDowall printed the Gospels in the 'Esquimaux' language in 1813, with further books added in later years at the request of missionaries. There were difficulties over the German Bible similar to the editorial problems in French and Spanish; printing began with a New Testament in 1811 or 1812 by Vogel and Schulze. And heroic efforts of research, collation and editing were required to print the Psalms in Ethiopic, the liturgical language of the Abyssinian Church. The printing work went to Messrs J. and T. Clarke of St John's Square in 1813, and was completed in 1815. This is not the place for a detailed account of the printing of each of these books. Instead the narrative of the adventures of the BFBS with Andrew Wilson and other printers of the French scriptures, and with Charles Brightley and the Spanish scriptures, recounted below in detail, may serve as examples of the Society's dealings with non-privileged printers, and of the very volatile nature of the printing trades in the early years of the nineteenth century.

Considering their unwillingness to make special concessions to Andrew Wilson, the Subcommittee must have been delighted to hear from another stereotype printer, Charles Brightley of Bungay in Suffolk. Brightley came up to London at the Society's expense and attended a Subcommittee meeting on 21 July 1808, where he showed the members two plates, one entirely new and the other which had worked 50,000 impressions, demonstrating that there was 'scarcely any visible difference' in the proofs. He offered to charge the regular London prices for casework, nothing for casting in stereotype and keeping the plates in repair, and a healthy 12s to 20s per thousand sheets for presswork. He was given a Spanish New Testament to stereotype, in

Bourgeois instead of the smaller Brevier type offered by Wilson, keeping to the request that this edition should be 'an elegant one'.[34]

As we have seen, Thomas Rutt of Shacklewell lost the job of printing French scriptures to Wilson and his stereotype process. Rutt was heard of again in May 1809, offering to cast stereotype for the Society. Unlike the unfortunate Rousseau, he became a regular printer for the BFBS, later associating himself with Eyre and Strahan in the royal printing office. He must have impressed Joseph Tarn as trustworthy. At a meeting on 15 June 1809 it was decided to give him the job of a stereotype New Testament in Manx. The next month, his price was used as a standard to judge the quotations of others. And in August he was consulted about the quotation of Vogel, who had offered to print in German for the Society. Six years later he was building a new 'Bible office' and stereotype office, and his son, Thomas Rutt junior, was on his way to St Petersburg with a stereotype press to print for the Russian Bible Society.[35]

Meanwhile the French New Testament, suspended by a change in text at the end of 1806, was still out of print. Not surprisingly, Adam Clarke reported a multiplicity of errors in the page proofs, now in Andrew Wilson's hands, and the Subcommittee decided to have them corrected by an academic, Professor Bentley of King's College Aberdeen. Steinkopf would collate Bentley's corrected sheets with Des Carriers's proofs. Wilson made the necessary alterations in his plates and the book was finally offered for sale in May 1808 at 2s 9d.[36] The next challenge was the whole Bible, but for the Old Testament the Subcommittee turned to Charles Brightley, whose terms were liberal, and who as an unknown quantity promised to work more speedily and be more tractable than Wilson. In December 1808 he undertook to set up and stereotype the Old Testament on his Nonpareil types, which were judged to match closely enough to those of Wilson, promising also that his plates would be the same thickness as Wilson's. Meanwhile Reyner reported on the increasing market for the books in question. There were 32,857 French privates in the United Kingdom as prisoners of war, and a further 2,101 officers on parole. For the latter the BFBS required 3,000 copies of a superior edition of the New Testament.

Unfortunately Brightley had to admit defeat six months later, asking to transfer the job to yet another company hoping to make its fortune in stereotype, Heney and Haddon, of Finsbury.[37] The Subcommittee asked Rutt to quote again, but eventually awarded the printing of the Old Testament in French to Heney and Haddon in July 1809. The firm was unable to handle the technological and financial demands of the new printing process. Richard Watts, who had just left Cambridge to establish himself as a London printer, was called in to a meeting in January 1810 and asked to give an opinion of their work. He found the plates 'very defective'. Many letters and words were imperfect 'being uneven on the surface, some filled with metal, and others corroded and destroyed'; the plates were of irregular thickness, which would make it difficult and expensive for printers to make them ready for working; and the metal was softer than it ought to be, a circumstance that Watts traced to poor casting. John Haddon, who had by this time dissolved his partnership with Heney, willingly relinquished the job for a gratuity of £20. Both Watts and Rutt quoted for the Old Testament in French, but the former found that he was not ready and Rutt was offered the work.[38] In 1811 a French Bible appeared, with Rutt's imprint on the Old Testament and Wilson's on the New.

Brightley, however, continued to print the Spanish New Testament, writing to Joseph Tarn from time to time to explain the difficulties under which he laboured. In August 1808 he complained that the paper ordered by the Society was highly bleached, which he advised Tarn would lose its colour and cause the ink to yellow. 'I never saw paper so much bleached before. I believe it is made of a colored [sic] rag.' In another letter, Brightley offered to make paper, offering to instruct Tarn in the criteria for judging this commodity. He objected to a request that he send duplicate proofs to London, for Uzielli's editing, because the plan 'runs so on sorts that my present letter will not set up more than 12 pages'. He explained that this amount of text would take his compositors two days to set up and correct (their unfamiliarity with Spanish extended the time); the proof would take 'at least each 4 days backward & forward . . . consequently we must proceed very slow'. He offered instead to read the proofs in his Bungay shop, and pay for any necessary resetting that could not be traced to Uzielli's carelessness. He admitted later that proofreading was not the only difficulty of printing in the country: it was impossible to get staff to work for a short time, or to purchase a few sorts to fill a gap. He sent several completed sheets to London in December, complaining again of the poor quality of the paper, and admitting that 'casting of stereotype is undoubtedly an improvable art . . . the art has still many defects which neither the property or genius of Lord Stanhope has been able to conquer any more than myself'. Moreover his foundryman was dying ('still alive, but on the confines of Eternity') and this would lead to further delays in casting.[39]

The books were finally finished, and a reprint was ordered from the Society's plates, still in Brightley's care, in February 1811. This time he failed to produce and the Subcommittee, outraged at the expense they had incurred, closed their account with him in September 1811, charging the printer for part of the difference between what they would have paid him to print the Spanish Bible on movable types, and what he actually received for the now-useless plates. The new edition was printed by the Deaf and Dumb Institution, supervised by James Powell and edited once again by Uzielli. Their edition was used until 1816, when it was out of print and under criticism for inaccuracy. Presumably the Spanish-speaking consumers had become more critical. Another reprint was commissioned, this time from Peter White, of New Street, Bishopsgate.[40]

In the production of all these Bibles and parts of Bibles, we have seen the Subcommittee on Printing seeking the most efficient methods possible for composition, aiming for (though not always attaining) a high degree of textual accuracy and then casting the texts in metal to preserve their accuracy. But stereotype plates did not improve the speed of the printing process. The plates cast by Andrew Wilson, Thomas Rutt and others had to be printed on the iron press, invented by Lord Stanhope in 1800. While the Stanhope press was more precise and durable than the old wooden press, it was no faster. Thus the introduction of the steam press was of great interest to printers whose customers were interested in increasing the speed of production. The Bible Society was one of the first publishers to experiment with steam power. Another was John Walter, publisher of *The Times*, who commissioned a printing machine from Friedrich Koenig, which was patented between 1810 and 1816, and started working in 1814. Most book-printers, however, were content to print by hand until the 1830s. It was only the publishers of newspapers, and of books in very large editions, such as Bibles, who found it worthwhile to experiment with the first tentative efforts at machine printing.

Koenig's press is the best known to historians of printing and publishing. William Nicholson, an English inventor, patented a machine in 1790, but it was never built. Two other printing machines, however, were patented in November 1813, one by an Edinburgh printer called John Ruthven. The second patent was granted jointly, to Richard Mackenzie Bacon of Norwich and Bryan Donkin of Bermondsey. Bacon was a printer and Donkin an engineer. Their machine is remembered for its fine workmanship, its defective inking and its paralysing complexity. In Marjorie Plant's summing-up in *The English Book Trade*, 'within a few years it was described as obsolete'.[41] In that few years, however, Bacon and Donkin entered into a contract with the BFBS, which the Society hoped would expedite the production of Bibles and thus hasten the deliverance of world heathenism. In December 1813, the Subcommittee heard from the solicitor Thomas Pellat about Richard Mackenzie Bacon of Norwich (Donkin's name figures very little in their records) and his newly patented machine. Aware of Nicholson's and other precedents, Pellat cautioned the Subcommittee against using 'a Machine which encroached on any former Patent'. The Subcommittee, however, had already decided 'that Mr Bacon is a person of unquestionable responsibility'. He promised to print at 30 per cent below the price now paid for printing, and was willing to sign a contract specifying his services. He would also compose and print from movable types, and even make his own paper, 'he being the acting partner in a large Machine-paper Manufactory'. Several members had been up to Norwich and seen Bacon's machine and paper for themselves.

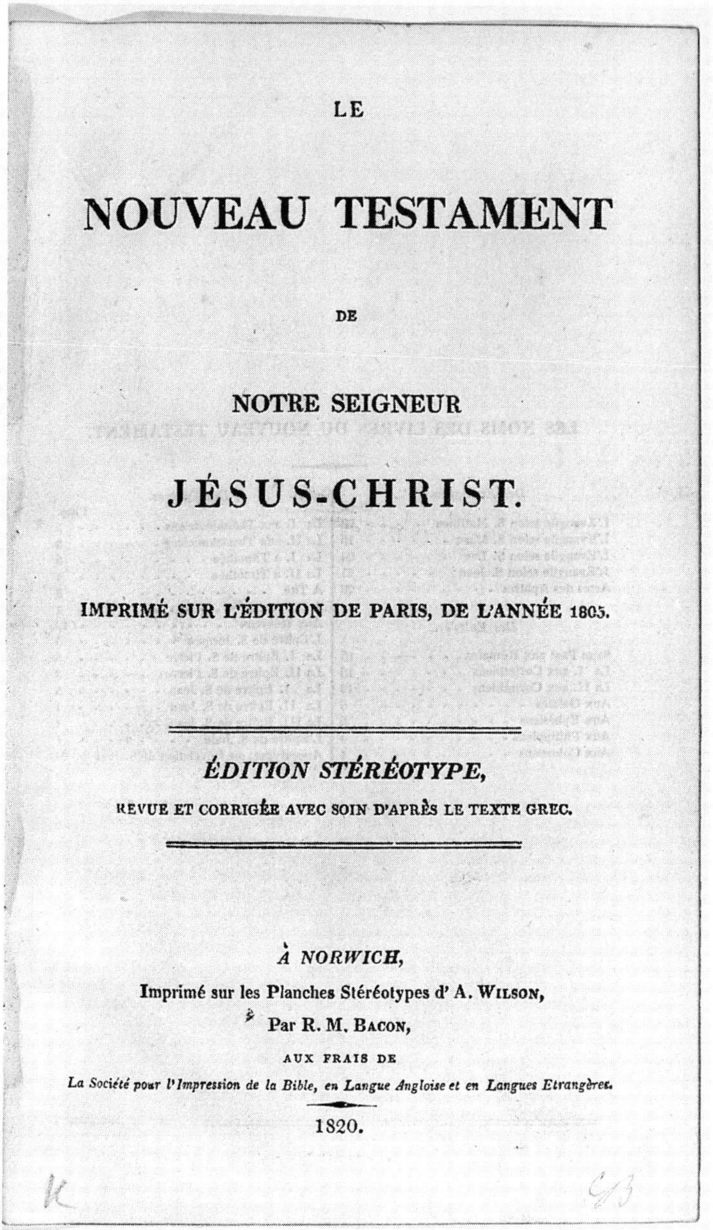

LE

NOUVEAU TESTAMENT

DE

NOTRE SEIGNEUR

JÉSUS-CHRIST.

IMPRIMÉ SUR L'ÉDITION DE PARIS, DE L'ANNÉE 1805.

ÉDITION STÉRÉOTYPE,

REVUE ET CORRIGÉE AVEC SOIN D'APRÈS LE TEXTE GREC.

À *NORWICH,*

Imprimé sur les Planches Stéréotypes d' A. WILSON,

Par R. M. BACON,

AUX FRAIS DE

La *Société pour l'Impression de la Bible, en Langue Angloise et en Langues Etrangères.*

1820.

Figure 6 Title-page of New Testament in French, printed from stereotype by Richard Mackenzie Bacon in Norwich, 1820.

They resolved to 'redeem' Andrew Wilson's plates for the French Brevier New Testament and have Bacon print 20,000 copies from them, at 30 per cent below the present price of 17s per thousand sheets.[42]

Two days after these decisions, Bacon attended a meeting where his salesmanship and charm apparently silenced any remaining doubts. He showed them samples of Demy paper from the mill he owned in partnership with Simon Wilkin, and quoted a good price. It was resolved to have a formal agreement with Bacon 'written upon a proper stamp, and signed', by the printer and by Joseph Tarn for the Society.[43] All went well at first, although Bacon, pleading other large orders, petitioned to purchase the paper for the French New Testament 'in the London market under the superintendence of Mr Tarn; he paying the difference if any in the price'. By July 1814, there was a letter from Bacon. The machine had finally 'got to steady work', but there were two difficulties. The type on one plate was battered, and he requested a replacement. 'The next evil is the title which bears Mr Wilson's imprint. I would wish my name and the machine to be introduced instead of his.' Andrew Wilson supplied the necessary plate and the revised imprint, but sounded the alarm about Bacon's process. He observed not only the battered type, but also '*bites* in abundance at the tops and bottoms of the pages. These batters, and bites, must infallibly destroy the plates; and I am vexed to see them, because I really wished success to his machine, and by Mr Bulmer's advice was about to open a negociation [*sic*] with Mr Bacon for one of them.'[44]

From then on, the printing of the French New Testament at Norwich, begun with such high optimism, was plagued by a succession of failures. Bacon sent a few sheets at the end of July, but he found the unequal thickness of the plates to be a major problem. When sheets were printed on one side only, they were kept wet too long, running the risk of spoilage. In December he groaned, 'I have had much to contend with in this new experiment and the plaster of Paris has played me such evil tricks that I decided to make the paper myself for the rest of the edition.'[45] The next October, Pratt visited Bacon at Norwich to inquire about the 20,000 books ordered nearly a year before. The problem of unequal plate thickness had been attacked by a new invention of Donkin's, a machine for planing their backs. Pratt reported to his principals that Bacon now foresaw no further obstacles. But when next we hear of him, a further year on in October 1816, Bacon was bankrupt, and his solicitor was asking what to do with BFBS plates and paper in his possession. The Society finally received £44 11s 5d as a first and final dividend on the sum of £202 16s od he owed the Society. As for the books, they had to be disposed of. Richard Cockle, the Depositary, submitted sheets 'of which no complete books have been furnished; the quantity of sheets are exceedingly various of the several signatures, and many are printed only on one side'. When paper manufacturers bid to purchase these sheets for recycling ('remanufacture'), a large percentage were found to be rotten.[46]

The story of Bacon and his 'patent machine' illuminates the frustrations, for publishers like the Society and inventor-practitioners like Richard Mackenzie Bacon, of implementing innovations in the printing business during the early nineteenth century. Technology that worked well on a trial run, with plates cast to order, inevitably broke down when the steam press was loaded with Wilson's old plates, which were themselves among the earliest products of 'the stereotype art'. Every aspect of the process was being transformed. And the Bible Society, still very young and not yet wealthy, was deeply engaged in these audacious experiments.

The composition and printing of scriptures in foreign languages was complex and difficult, but the quantities required, though large, were insignificant in comparison with the demand for cheap Bibles in English. In 1809, after four years of experience with the Cambridge Press, the Society entered into discussions with the University Press at Oxford, which would eventually become its largest supplier, and with the King's Printer in London. The printers at Cambridge were falling behind the demand of Bible Associations. And the Committee may have believed they were becoming too complacent. An order of 20,000 New Testaments in Brevier type left the Committee 'extremely dissatisfied with the paper', asking for a reduction in price, and resolving to make contact with the King's Printer.[47]

It was Oxford, however, that became the Society's second supplier. Bensley and Collingwood, too, had negotiated with Andrew Wilson and for a fee of £4,000 they acquired the ability to make and print from stereotype plates. In September 1809, word reached the Committee of 'a beautiful pocket edition of the Bible ... lately stereotyped at Oxford', a specimen was procured for consideration, and an order was placed. The books were expected from Oxford in February 1810, but the Press had difficulty in meeting the Society's demand. In his first letter to the BFBS William Dawson, the University's London partner, apologized for the delay in supplying the 24mo Nonpareil Bibles ordered, which 'altho' fully stereotyped, and compleated in that particular, are not worked off ... chiefly on account of not being able to finish the paper, already made, the weather being so much against the finishing it ...'.[48] Weather problems were to beset the Society and its printers for many years.

Cambridge having refused to reduce the price of unsatisfactory books, the Committee in turn (the decision is recorded in the next minute) decided to get in touch with the representatives of His Majesty's Printer in London, in April 1809. As we have seen, Eyre and Strahan, printing in New Square under the supervision of partners Andrew Strahan and William Preston, held the Royal patent, and had been too busy making vast profits out of Government printing to publish many Bibles. The initial negotiations were awkward. First Lord Teignmouth, the President, was requested by Joseph Tarn to get a third party, Robert Thornton, to enquire if the King's Printer would print stereotype editions. This may not have happened, and we find Tarn taking matters into his own hands nearly a year later. He wrote to the King's Printer in February 1810 'on the fly leaf of one of our Abstracts, conceiving the present to be a good opportunity of introducing the Society to his notice'. Harassed by disappointed customers, and thwarted by the delays at Oxford, he asked if Eyre and Strahan could supply a specific edition, Bibles with marginal references. They replied two days later, offering to render any assistance required. Joseph Butterworth asked if they would work the Society's own plates at trade prices. The King's Printer agreed to undertake orders from the BFBS '*provided it will not interfere with the Universities*'.[49] In the Society's view, there was business enough for all three of the privileged Presses.[50] It was not until 1811 that Strahan was asked to work a set of plates the Committee happened to have in London. (The Universities sometimes insisted that new plates, made specifically to meet the BFBS demand, be paid for by the Society, which insisted in turn on keeping its property at Earl Street where unauthorized impressions could not be made.) Even then the University printers tried to keep the King's Printer out of the business by promising to supply the required books, and the BFBS agreed to suspend the application to London. But in January 1812 they gave a firm order for 10,000 Nonpareil Bibles and 20,000 Brevier Testaments, and by April the Press was planning to double the size of its premises to meet the Society's demands.[51] Before long the King's Printer was competing equally for business and often surpassing the production of the University Presses.

The demand that Earl Street imposed on the three printers was a function of the demand made upon the BFBS Committee and Secretaries by the new Auxiliary Societies. Eyre and Strahan's building and staff were not large enough even for the first order. Cambridge too was increasing the press capacity 'in order that none of the Stereotype editions should remain out of print'. But to bespeak one of the new iron presses made to order, installed and put into operation took time that the Bible Society was increasingly impatient to allow. Committee members were impatient and frustrated at the lengthiness of the process of book-production. Drying was a particular bugbear: on the hand-press, paper was printed wet, so that books had to be properly dried before shipping, but the process caused delay. Zachary Macaulay suggested the Committee ask the Presses 'if their Bibles might not be expedited in their delivery by the adoption of the mode of drying by steam, successfully used by Messrs Williams & Co, of Smithfield'. Meanwhile Joseph Tarn kept track of part-books that would otherwise have lain unused at the binders. He required that Cambridge produce several individual sheets and also title-pages for Brevier Testaments, to complete otherwise useless books.[52]

All three Presses presented difficulties with quality control. We have seen how often editions in foreign languages turned out to be inaccurate in spelling, infelicitous in translation, or even downright heretical. Nor were

Table 4. *Proportion of Cambridge Press Bible business covered by BFBS*

Year	Total receipts £	Sales of Bibles and Prayer Books	Sales to BFBS	Sales to BFBS as % B and PB receipts	Sales to BFBS as % all
1806	450				
1807	3,687				
1808	5,534				
1809	5,639				
1810	6,068				
1811	15,847	12,893	5,407	41.9%	34.1%
1812	23,836	19,596	8,198	41.8%	34.4%
1813	24,064	19,961	14,744	73.9%	61.3%
1814	25,267	21,432	13,335	62.2%	52.8%
1815	27,918	23,384	12,815	54.8%	45.9%
1816	26,765	22,003	10,272	46.7%	38.4%
1817	19,090	15,602	4,251	27.2%	22.3%
1818	17,025	13,924	2,951	21.2%	17.3%
1819	19,415	15,318	3,804	24.8%	19.6%
1820	15,649	11,964	n/a		
1821	11,877	8,125	1,402	17.3%	11.8%

Sources of information in archives of the Cambridge University Press: Total receipts of Press. From Press Accounts 1811–24 (Pr.P.1.). Sales of Bibles and Prayer Books from 'Analysis of the Receipts of the Press from Michaelmas 1811' (Pr.P.1). Sales to BFBS. From University Audit Book 2(4) (1787–1822).

books in English exempt from criticism. Cambridge sent out sheets of Brevier Bibles with some of the plates wrongly imposed so that there was no proper margin at the head. The binders were directed to 'cut out the leaf of such sheets and to paste it in its proper place, the expense of the same to be charged to the University'. Similarly the King's Printer sent up Brevier Testaments in which it appeared 'that not only the Press Work is bad in the extreme, but that the pages are much out of Register; and that in gathering, even the very waste has been made up into books, inasmuch that sheets are put in which have been laid quite obliquely on the forms'.[53] The Committee tried to balance considerations of quality and of cost. But quality often had to give way to the demand for books in quantity, and in these early years it was all that the combined power of the three Presses could do to keep up with the Society's demand.

   All three were also, almost certainly, enjoying the greatly increased revenue that resulted from the popular Bible transaction. Detailed figures for this period are not available, but table 4, constructed from Cambridge Press records, shows how important was trade with the BFBS to the University

Press. Cambridge has the richest records, really the only records of the three privileged Presses dealing with the Society. Eventually, however, it claimed the smallest proportion of the orders, after Oxford (almost half) and London (more than a third).[54] John Smith, the Cambridge University Printer, wrote in 1817 to ask why the Society's orders had fallen off. Tarn answered first that the country was 'more fully supplied with Bibles' and hence the demand had diminished, by almost one quarter. (This occurred after the initial rush of Auxiliary expansion, and before the demand had settled down to a steady flow of books.) But in addition, Cambridge's edition of the popular Small Pica Bible was 'perhaps the most incorrect Bible in your Stock' and still had only single line heads to the chapters. London and Oxford could provide better ones. Another edition, the Minion Bible, had broken letters, so that 'although a bold and acceptable Type, we cannot receive it in that state'. Tarn could attest to this from his own experience, 'having one of these Bibles in daily use ... I find these defects occur so continually as appears irremediable without casting new plates'. A new edition of the Brevier Bible was, disappointingly, not so readable as the old – 'the letters appeared to be confused and rendered dazzling, by the ink having run round the edges of them'. Tarn assured Smith that the Society was not getting any better price or allowance from the other Presses.[55]

In its initial dealings with the privileged Presses, the BFBS was a demanding customer. These evangelicals, unlike the SPCK, were not prepared to wait for the means of salvation to be set up, run off, dried and shipped. They applied their pragmatic and entrepreneurial approach to business to the publishing enterprise they found themselves engaged in. Like modern printers' customers, they wanted the work done 'yesterday'. As well as hounding their suppliers about deadlines and quality control, they were fully prepared to exert the economic pressure of the large customer. As we have seen, they were intensely interested in the application of steam power to the printing process, signing an agreement – prematurely as it turned out – with Richard Mackenzie Bacon in 1814. And a London printer, Thomas Bensley proposed his 'Patent Machine' to print the Society's 13th *Report* in 1816, but the Committee were not satisfied with specimen pages and gave the work to Tilling and Hughes's Stanhope press. At the same time they resolved 'on a future occasion to consider the expediency of employing Machine Presses should they be brought to a proper state of perfection in the execution of the work'.[56] The King's Printer, Eyre and Strahan, were the first of the privileged presses to take up the challenge, acquiring their first steam engine and cylinder printing machine in 1819, which presumably they used to print Society Bibles and Testaments along with their Government work. But it was to be more than twenty years before the University Presses first experimented with machine printing.[57]

But while the Subcommittee on Printing made aggressive approaches to the inventors of steam-printing machinery, they did not publicize their attitude. In 1821 when Bensley added the words 'printed by machinery' to the title-page of a Gaelic Bible, he was directed by the Committee to omit the notice in future.[58] The reason, which was not given, may have been simply a reluctance to provide free advertising. We may also speculate, however, that the Committee did not wish to risk any possibility that subscribers would associate their policy of using machinery with the contemporary scandal of unemployment and destitution among hand-press printers. Committee members and the Secretaries were well aware that their attitude to business would be considered inappropriate by some of their subscribers in the mass evangelical market, for whom ends were not to be justified by means. We shall see in chapter 4 that when the Society's bookbinders asked for relief from modern methods and machinery, many subscribers thought their request was justified. They reasoned that a Bible publisher should not 'grind the faces of the poor', and hence might be expected to tolerate the slow and expensive methods of handwork craftsmen. Anticipating this sort of reaction, perhaps, the BFBS took care not to publicize its more controversial uses of technology.

Both Stanhope and machine presses required a dependable supply of paper, another commodity that was scarce in the early nineteenth century. The problem in this case was not machinery, but raw materials. Some printing paper had been made by machine (the Foudrinier and Dickinson paper machines) in London since the turn of the century. But the best materials for papermaking, white linen and cotton rags, had to be imported from places like Hamburg. Until the French wars were over, restrictions on continental trade prevented English papermakers from importing rags collected in European cities. Papermakers turned to coloured and second-quality rags, and adopted the new technology of chlorine bleaching to whiten their product. The first experiments sometimes produced a poor quality paper with a tendency to fox (develop brown stains).[59] More distressing, from the Society's viewpoint, was that the new paper was not strong enough to withstand the wear and tear that ardent evangelicals imposed on their Bibles and Testaments. Once again the BFBS found itself in the vanguard of technological experimentation.

We have seen how Brightley criticized the paper he was asked to work in 1808, and how Bacon promised in 1813 to supply improved paper from his own mill. The Society, as publisher, consumed large quantities of paper, dealing directly with both manufacturing mills and wholesale stationers. The paper for foreign-language Bibles and for annual *Reports* and other documents was purchased by Joseph Tarn and delivered to the printers. The BFBS was also shipping English paper to India for printing abroad. Among the suppliers of printing to the Society, only the privileged presses controlled the sources and quality of paper for the Bibles they produced.

By the end of 1815, with European trade reopened, the supply of rags had improved and the cost of paper had consequently dropped. The BFBS proposed a commensurate reduction to the privileged Presses, and both Cambridge and London declined. (Oxford was not approached until later, November 1816.) Smith at Cambridge merely denied that prices had dropped. Eyre and Strahan rather condescendingly informed the Committee that:

We are aware that lots in the hands of Stationers have been sold lately at reduced prices, from a Stagnation in the Demand; yet as no reduction has taken place in the kind of Rags from which our kind of Paper is made, the makers cannot afford to reduce their Price. We beg to observe also, that though our present Charge be the same as in 1812 the Colour and Fabrick of the Paper are superior, which is virtually so far a Reduction of the Price.

As for the notion that the introduction of stereotype could have meant savings of one third, 'we conceive must have proceeded from some erroneous Calculation, for in all cases the Paper and Presswork exceed two thirds of the Expence'.[60]

Tarn and his Committee were well aware that stereotype had not fulfilled its early economic promise. They were equally convinced that they did not want superior paper if colour quality was achieved by bleach, which drastically reduced tensile strength. Moreover they knew that the King's Printer was deceiving them. Tarn replied that the

expectation of a reduction ... was founded upon the terms of the purchases made by the Society during the last two years; within which period they have bought for exportation and other purposes several thousand reams. And that a Member of the Committee ... had received information of a very considerable reduction in the general price of paper from [two specifically named papermakers].[61]

The commercial gentlemen of the Bible Society Committee, printing their foreign versions and promotional literature, and shipping reams of paper to missionaries abroad, were not about to be placated or deceived by Messrs Eyre and Strahan. Furthermore the Committee found the paper supplied by Eyre and Strahan to be highly bleached – a treatment 'which they consider as injurious to the durability of the books'. This was an understatement. A history of papermaking notes that in 1816, 'of a quantity of Bibles printed by the British and Foreign Bible Society, one was found two years later crumbling to dust, although it had not been used, owing to the process used in bleaching the paper at the mill'.[62]

Early in 1817 the Committee took the paper question into their own hands. A Memorial from the Maidstone Bible Association complained that the texture of the paper caused English Bibles and Testaments to 'come to pieces' even though they were 'well sewed and bound'. The printing Subcommittee responded that the paper choice was decided by the privileged Presses.[63] In fact they had no intention of submitting to the authority of the patent-holders in this crucial matter of book quality. Bibles purchased by the Auxiliaries and Associations had to be durable. The Subcommittee circulated a notice to paper manufacturers, requesting samples. After a lengthy survey, the Society's requirements were established and circulated to papermakers. They required a weight of '21£ to 22 lbs for 20 inside quires, ... the Rags to be of a strong texture, free from sheaves, macerated with Dull Tackle ... free from any bleach, unless it be that of bleaching Salts used in washing the Rags, which must be afterwards well washed out with pure Water'.[64] Further consultation with papermakers confirmed the decision not to use bleach:

a more substantial Paper can be made from Hamburg rags than from any English ones; and ... the advantage usually obtained by bleaching may be acquired in a sufficient degree for the purposes of this Society by using one third Hamburg *best* superfine rags to two thirds of Hamburg superfine, without any bleach, in lieu of using the whole of the latter with bleaching Salts.[65]

These new standards were established empirically, based upon the Subcommittee's personal experience with printing paper and on their considered judgment of the advice they had solicited from the trade. Some printers, especially at the privileged Presses, found the paper made to Society principles to be unsatisfactory. They also learned that the Society was adamant in requiring adherence to its standards, and prepared to impose them on reluctant printers.

Strahan in London, Smith at Cambridge and Collingwood at Oxford all received letters announcing the Society's new standards and requesting that the Presses comply. Tarn suggested that the BFBS might provide its own paper.[66] He wrote again to explain the 'extremely simple proposition' to Smith, at Cambridge, assuring the printer that Oxford had 'most cheerfully acceded'. Smith agreed, but Eyre and Strahan did not. They insisted on 'an effectual control over the manufacture of the Paper'. This was permitted when they agreed to use a manufacturer who would produce 'upon the principles adopted by the Society' – one of Key and Brothers, Magnay and Co. or Francis Bryant.[67]

Rather than leave the choice of paper in the hands of the privileged Presses, the Committee decided to consult with an expert who happened to be one of their own members. Luke Howard (1771–1864), a Quaker, was a chemist and meteorologist, Fellow of the Royal Society, who served the Committee every year from 1813 to 1825, including participation in the printing, foreign and depository Subcommittees. Howard undertook a careful investigation of manufacturing processes. In a report submitted in September 1818, running to six pages transcribed in a BFBS minute book, Howard described the result of his visit to the plant of Messrs Longman and Dickinson, who manufactured paper for Eyre and Strahan.[68] He was inspecting 'the effects of bleaching on the tenacity of Printing Paper'. Defining tenacity as 'the property of resisting rubs and strains', Howard insisted that his observations were 'dictated more by principles which appear self evident, than by any practical knowledge of the art of Paper making'.

While whiteness and smoothness might be desirable to some publishers, 'the use of a book in unskilful hands is a continued trial of its perfection in this respect'. And the BFBS market constituted 'that description of persons, to whom *durability enhances twofold the value of every gift or purchase*'. Howard explained the process painstakingly, drawing analogies to the more accessible trade skill of basketmaking. The fibres of the paper needed to 'retain *their original length and soundness in the rag*', just as a basketmaker who would have no objection to peeling his rods (analogous to bleaching out the colour) could not make strong work by cutting them into short lengths. He went on to explain the botanical properties of cotton, so that each Committee member could see why this raw material was inferior to rags based on linen – that is flax and hemp. Howard informed his colleagues that 'in justice to the art of Chemistry' they could not fairly ask for bleach to be omitted from the process. His advice was to insist upon sound rags, and refuse cotton and coloured materials. Most important, Howard established a standard of tenacity, and described in detail the necessary equipment and method.[69] It is difficult to compare Howard's specifications with those of experienced papermakers. Histories of papermaking do not lay much stress on the problems of bleach, which were soon superseded by the need to find new materials to replace rags.[70] What is significant is the BFBS's recruiting and use of an expert who could help in their day-to-day business, and their inclination to trust a new-style, and self-confessed 'impractical' chemist over the traditional craftsmen of the paper industry and the experienced printers of the privileged Presses, especially when the latter had a vested interest. Howard's investigation also eased the awkward problem of the King's Printer's refusal to accept paper from the Society, since Longman and Dickinson's 'strongest paper' was pronounced acceptable. Criteria were established for other papermakers. But there was no magical cure to the problems of bleach. Printers and papermakers continued to complain about the Society's standards, and the Society kept trying to enforce Howard's criteria on the industry.

The Bible Society Committee approached the problem of paper supply and tenacity with earnest determination. Old books and unusable sheets in the warehouse were recycled for new paper. And when their evangelical colleagues in the Church Missionary Society received some flax from New Zealand, the CMS submitted it to the BFBS for an experiment in making paper. The test was solemnly carried out but the cost was too high.[71]

The question of paper was a source of tension between the Society and the University Presses, since the latter remained unsatisfied with the material supplied to them. The Society, moreover, refused to admit any defects in the paper, blaming the printers instead for bad presswork. The Committee could not very well refuse an 'extremely ill printed' job from Cambridge which had been executed on their own paper, but Tarn intimated that the problem was caused by a printing machine. This suggestion was met by a diatribe from John Smith: because of bleach, the paper was too harsh for the pressmen to work. 'On taking up the first bundles for printing after the paper had been prepared in the usual way, they steam'd like a lime kiln! – and would not keep for more than two days at the most.' The printed sheets mildewed so rapidly that they had to be perfected (printed on the reverse side) very quickly if the paper was to be preserved. And even after apparently spoiled sheets had been discarded, 'many spotted sheets still remain[ed] – as the quires were found to change on the drying-poles'.[72] Joseph Parker, the Oxford printer, wanted to insert on the title-pages of Bibles, 'printed on paper furnished by the Society'. The University Presses had Delegates (Oxford) and Syndics (Cambridge) to answer to, and all three Presses were subject to the preferences of customers. By 1821 the Universities were again supplying their own paper, having solemnly promised to have it made entirely of unbleached Hamburg rags.[73]

The BFBS had less influence over the design and format of printed Bibles than it did over matters of printing technology – of stereotype plates, of steam presses and of paper quality. In the early days, when all these processes were still at the stage of development or in short supply, little thought was given to the more subtle elements of book design. As we shall see, the Committee were on the whole conventional about format, not venturing into illustrated books, and even resisting for many years requests to publish a Family Bible. But they were nevertheless concerned, on behalf of their subscribers, that their Bibles be designed effectively.

What did Bible-Society Bibles look like? The questions we might ask, as we examine the books today, are similar to those that Joseph Tarn would have asked the printers, as he was commissioning new editions. They include the size of the typeface, its design, its physical properties. They also stretch to the layout of this type on the page – how wide are the margins and the gutter between the columns? What is the relationship between the type of the headings and that of the text? How are chapter headings and the text of summaries and arguments at the heads of pages to be handled? There are questions of quality: is the type page smooth and readable, or do broken letters and bad inking interfere with reading? Are the type pages in or out of register – that is are they printed straight on the leaf or not? What about the paper? Is it smooth, white and above all strong enough to stand up to intensive reading? These are the issues that Beatrice Warde, the great student of typography and bibliography, was thinking of when she created her celebrated metaphor of the crystal goblet. Just as a crystal goblet permits one to enjoy the colour and taste of wine (as compared to a gold one that obscures these things), good type unobtrusively contributes to the enjoyment of a book without distracting the reader from the text.[74] The Bibles and Testaments that the Bible Society required from their printers might be characterized as kitchen glasses, cut solid and stubby, and not perfectly translucent. The manner of their production was geared to the economic requirements of working-class readers, as mediated by the preconceptions of evangelical business people. They were printed in great quantities, and distributed by volunteers at affordable prices.

The layout and design of the English Bible page had become standardized by this time, with the space-saving two-column format dictated by the division of the text into numbered verses. M. H. Black has shown how there gradually developed a book with white-space at the book- and chapter-headings. Centred at the heads of pages were the book titles and running chapter-numbers; to facilitate quick reference there were also 'arguments' (cues to the subject-matter on each page) usually printed in italics. Also in italics were printed summaries at the beginning of each chapter. Page numbers were usually but by no means always provided, in Arabic.[75] These were the more subtle features, not consciously recognized by most users of the printed scriptures, but nevertheless taken for granted as defining how the Bible ought to look.

However, despite these common properties, a large lectern Bible does not look much like a small pocket edition. Printers and their customers differentiated among the various editions by their format, the means used to distinguish most books in the period of hand-printing. The format depended upon the arrangement of type pages on the large sheets used for printing. Thus a folio was folded once, and produced very large leaves, perhaps as much as 46 x 30 cm. Folio Bibles were used mostly in churches. The quarto, folded twice, into four, was up to about 30 x 23 cm. There were several sizes of octavos, eights, measuring up to 23 x 15 cm. Similarly duodecimos, twelves, up to 23 x 10 cm, followed by twenty-fourmos, thirty-twomos and so on. The dimensions of the sheet of printing paper, and the way in which it was folded, determined the measurements of the leaf. Because printing paper came in Demy, Medium and Royal, as well as other less common sizes, three octavo Bibles of slightly different sizes were also distinguished by these names.[76]

Not only the size of the paper sheet, but also the size of the type varied considerably. At the beginning of the nineteenth century, printers and the typefounders who supplied them used traditional names to differentiate between smaller and larger types: Pica, Pearl, Brevier (pronounced 'Brev*eer*') and Bourgeois (pronounced 'Bur*joyce*'), etc. The Society placed its orders for scriptures accordingly, and when they began to offer books for sale to their subscribers, adopted a similar pattern of description, suppressing the printer's name and mentioning only the format. Thus the earliest English books offered for sale in 1811 were listed as Nonpareil 12mo, while both French and Spanish Testaments first appeared in Brevier. The information provided, however, was not always clear to purchasers. A subscriber wrote from Exeter in 1810 to inquire

Whether ... it would not be an improvement & gratification to the Public, if the several descriptions of Bibles &c. were printed in the Reports, in the same type ... [T]he Subscribers by that means would know what Bibles &c. to send for, as most proper for the persons to whom they mean to give them; for I presume scarce one in an hundred of the people in the Country know what Brevier or Pica &c means.[77]

A variation of this proposal was adopted and 'Specimens of Type' (see figure 7) began to be included in annual *Reports* and the *Monthly Extracts of Correspondence*. In 1818 10,000 copies of this popular page had to be printed for Bible Associations. At the BFBS's request, the Presses began in 1820 to specify the typeface used on the title-page of each Bible.[78]

While other clients of the University Presses may have been expected to be familiar with typefaces, the new Bible market of the Society was typographically illiterate. In 1818, for example, it was discovered that 'the black letter [i.e. Gothic print] Titles at the Tops of the Pages in the Oxford Pica Testaments are unintelligible to the poor and ... a very considerable number had on that Account been refused by the Associations at Liverpool'.[79] The English printers were asked to supply books in Roman type henceforth. But other clients had different traditions. For the Danish Bible printed in 1810, John Benjamin Gottlieb Vogel had supplied types in the 'German or Gothic character'.

There were some proposed exceptions to the Society's tendency to adhere to a conventional book design. As early as 1804 Granville Sharp proposed the 'additional elegance' of printing books without chapter headings. Even more radically, Sharp suggested that octavo Bibles be divided into about seven parts: 'In a Family possessing such a Bible, several persons may read & be instructed in different parts of the House or Garden with one single Copy of the Bible at one and the same time.' This pious and practical notion was judged 'not expedient'. Sharp repeated it in 1812, also suggesting that printing might be cheapened by omitting breaks between the chapters and verses.[80] The notion of a 'paragraph Bible' was not raised again until the 1860s.

Sharp was inspired to innovative book design by his conviction that the Bible is not like any other book: it is very long and cannot summarily be abridged or compressed. Practical printers and type designers also know this. Beatrice Warde estimated that the Bible text would fill 'five stout volumes' if printed in paragraphs, in one column, and in standard-sized type. M. H. Black characterized the problem as 'putting a quart into a pint-pot', while Kurt Weidemann, a contemporary type-designer creating the new 'Biblica' face for a German Bible in 1981, was faced with 'managing the enormous amount of text in the Bible'. He observed that 'The designer must ... consider the handiness of the book and should attempt to eliminate any

SPECIMENS OF THE TYPES OF THE SOCIETY'S BIBLES AND TESTAMENTS.

DOUBLE PICA TYPE.

LONDON

O give thanks unto the LORD, for *he is* good: for his mercy *endureth* for ever. *Psalm* cvii. 1.

OXFORD.

O give thanks unto the God of gods : for his mercy endureth for ever. *Psalm* cxxxvi. 2.

ENGLISH TYPE.

For God so loved the world, that he gave his only begotten Son, that whosoever believeth in him should not perish, but have everlasting life. *John* iii. 16.

PICA TYPE.

And the sea gave up the dead which were in it; and death and hell delivered up the dead which were in them: and they were judged every man according to their works. *Rev.* xx. 13.

SMALL-PICA TYPE.

O Zion, that bringest good tidings, get thee up into the high mountain; O Jerusalem, that bringest good tidings, lift up thy voice with strength; lift *it* up, be not afraid ; say unto the cities of Judah, Behold your God! *Isai.* xl. 9.

BREVIER TYPE.

And they came to a place which was named Gethsemane : and he saith to his disciples, Sit ye here, while I shall pray. *Mark* xiv. 32.

MINION TYPE.

Let the wicked forsake his way, and the unrighteous man his thoughts: and let him return unto the LORD, and he will have mercy upon him; and to our God, for he will abundantly pardon. *Isai.* lv. 7.

NONPAREIL TYPE.

Trust in the LORD with all thine heart; and lean not unto thine own understanding. In all thy ways acknowledge him, and he shall direct thy paths. *Prov.* iii. 5, 6.

PEARL TYPE.

How beautiful upon the mountains are the feet of him that bringeth good tidings, that publisheth peace ; that bringeth good tidings of good, that publisheth salvation ; that saith unto Zion, Thy God reigneth ! *Isai.* lii. 7.

RUBY TYPE.

I was glad when they said unto me, Let us go into the house of the LORD. Our feet shall stand within thy gates, O Jerusalem. *Psalm* cxxii. 1, 2.

DIAMOND TYPE.

Let the word of Christ dwell in you richly in all wisdom ; teaching and admonishing one another in psalms and hymns and spiritual songs, singing with grace in your hearts to the Lord. *Colossians* iii. 16.

psychological fear of the reader toward the very length of the Bible text. Every book, indeed, should be designed for optimum lifting and holding by the human hand.'[81] The nineteenth-century designers and publishers were not worried about 'psychological fear', but they had still to confront the problems presented by a book of almost 800,000 words, where the issues of readability, portability and price had to be balanced. So did their patrons at the British and Foreign Bible Society.

The Society published the English-language scriptures in such a bewildering variety of formats in the nineteenth century that a comprehensive analysis of the books as physical objects would extend far beyond the limits of the present project.[82] A reasonably detailed investigation of the design and production of their volumes is possible, however, if we focus on the production of one popular book, in the first twenty or so years of its publication. The Small Pica edition (see figures 8–11) has been chosen because this typeface was just coming into its own as a standard. Stower's *Printer's Grammar*, a contemporary handbook, stated in 1808 that

now small pica and bourgeois are more generally used than any other letter, except pica, which is considered the standard size, as all leads are cast, and measures made, to its m's. Its face is neither too small for the eye, nor its size too large, so as to extend a work unnecessarily. Minion is a letter become almost useless, except on newspapers, it being so nearly allied to brevier, a much neater type. Nonpareil and pearl have lately been much employed in miniature editions of some of our standard works ... Diamond is only a pearl face upon a smaller body, and seldom used.[83]

The Society printed Bibles in all these sizes, often selecting Small Pica and Brevier, and demonstrating a great interest in the possibilities for compression offered by the new small types.

Small Pica type measures about eleven points, which is comparable to the conventional typesize of book publication today. Its merit in the nineteenth century context was that it was large enough to be read in an underilluminated cottage, by someone whose eyesight had deteriorated.[84] And Joseph Tarn discovered that it could convey the whole text of the Bible in one volume. Tarn explained the situation to Eyre and Strahan in 1814:

Since the University of Cambridge commenced the delivery of the Small Pica Bible, in April 1812, the Society has received from thence more than twenty thousand copies; and, I believe, Six Presses have been constantly employed thereon ... yet such is the demand that when the last 4000 were delivered the orders at our depository exceeded, I believe, 5000; and, although an edition of 5000 copies is about two thirds finished at Press, we have reason to expect that by the time they are completed the orders will exceed that number.

Tarn was well aware of the reason. The Bible Associations wanted a book in a relatively large format, certainly larger than had originally been marketed.

This vast demand arises from the formation of Bible Associations, the number of which is increasing throughout the Country: and the poor people very laudably adopt a Bible which will serve them as they advance in life: and having once seen the Small

Pica they contribute their pence to purchase that edition, at the Societies [*sic*] prices, in preference to any other.[85]

The evangelical zeal of Society members, and the response to that enthusiasm among the British working class, was modifying the policies of printers, and changing trends in typography and book design.

The earliest Society Bibles had been small Nonpareil duodecimos. The first discussion with Cambridge printers of a larger face was in June 1807, when Richard Watts showed the Society a 'full faced small Pica type, in 8vo, which he recommended in preference to Pica, as it would come within the limits of two volumes'. But the management of two-volume books would have created problems with warehousing, shipping and distribution. Tarn had sample copies of the new sheets in both sizes (Pica and Small Pica) bound in single volumes and found that the Pica was 'inconveniently bulky'. Small Pica was fixed upon as the Society's standard large type for the popular octavo format. The order of 15 June 1807 for 20,000 copies (designed to be bound in two volumes) was countermanded in favour of one for 5,000 with 'the scale of the pages enlarged so as to bring it into one volume'.[86] The 'scale' was presumably Medium, rather than Demy, octavo paper.

There was some resistance at Cambridge to Tarn's orders for redesigning the pages of the Holy Scriptures in this inelegant and pragmatic fashion. Watts would have been accustomed to make this sort of decision in consultation with his master craftsmen, and may have felt aggrieved at Tarn's intervention. The Society's order was duly received at Cambridge and Watts was required to 'prepare types for stereotyping an octavo Bible in small pica'.[87] The Society increased its order to 10,000 in March 1808 (requiring that 'more margin might be left at the back and less at the front'), but a month later they had to refuse Watts's suggestion that he print a Pica Bible instead. His other major customers, the University's agents and the London distributor Rivington's, preferred the larger type. Patiently the BFBS observed that such a book would be upwards of 1,000 pages, too large for one volume, 'and consequently unsuitable for the purposes of this Society'. In May John Owen had to write to the Syndics:

In deference to the opinions of your agent who recommended the large instead of the small *Pica* for the proposed 8vo Bible, the Committee caused, as the Minute states, a Copy of your 8vo Pica Bible to be bound in one volume; and the grotesque as well as inconvenient book which it formed, evinced, that no type larger than the small Pica, of which a page had been set up and approved by your Printer and yourselves, can be used in printing a Bible which will admit of being bound in one volume octavo.

Owen finished by stressing 'the impatience which the public discover for such a Bible as the *Small Pica*'.[88]

The Syndics of the Press at Cambridge issued most of their books in folded sheets in temporary bindings. The experimental and user-oriented approach to book format adopted by their clients in London may have seemed quite unconventional to them. But at length they resolved (again) that the Small Pica Bible be stereotyped and copies were produced.[89] The new book came to well over 1,000 pages (1,292), with fifty-three lines per page.[90] It was printed on Demy paper (leaves 21.6 x 13 cm) and on Medium (22 x 14 cm). The Demy edition is a sample of the sorts of problems in quality control that Tarn had to grapple with. The print is unclear, with letters either faint or over-endowed with ink. It is printed out of register so that the arguments (running cues to content) are at the very top of the trimmed page. Several weights of paper are used in the book, so that some signatures are printed on heavier, coarser sheets than the rest. These may have been the books that eight years later were criticized as 'perhaps the most incorrect Bible in your stock'.

Eyre and Strahan, at the Society's request, got into the lucrative Small Pica Bible market in 1814. By this time Thomas Rutt of Shacklewell was working with them. When the London printers designed their Small Pica books, they created a 54-line page and printed it on a larger sheet than Cambridge's 53-line. Their Royal octavo leaves ranged in size from 22.9 to 26 x 14 to 14.8 cm. This permitted them to reduce the book by ten leaves, to 1,272 pages. At the same time the text was made more accessible to readers, since this edition included 'the full heads to the chapters'.[91] Presumably the same plates were used for the 'Small Pica quarto Bible, with broad margins for writing upon'.[92] The type page, the line count, the number of leaves are all identical with the other London books of this vintage. But the leaf was a massive quarto, 29.6 x 23 cm. As advertised, there were indeed broad margins, since the type page took up only 19.6 x 11.3 cm. But there is more to book design than dropping a page of type down on a sheet of paper. The resulting page does not invite note-taking in the way that, for example, heavily leaded lines and generous well-proportioned margins would do. This edition remained on the Society's price list from 1817 until 1840. The price started at 2½ guineas, declined to 2 guineas in 1822 (bound in boards), and eventually to £1 10s, bound in coloured calf.

The discussion of Small Pica Bibles could be continued, by examining the marginal-reference editions produced at London and Oxford. And the design discussed above was refined by London in the 1860s, to produce a 57-line edition of the Small Pica octavo without referen·es, on 1,192 pages.[93] Although only a few pages less, this book is about half as bulky as the older editions, because the quality of the paper improved. Typography, printing and paper, the three aspects of book production, all worked together to create the volumes experienced by BFBS readers.

The Society during its first twenty years was turning the conventions of book production upside down to meet the exigencies of the evangelical project. Producing both foreign-language and English Bibles, the pragmatic Subcommittee urged its printers to experiment with design and materials to

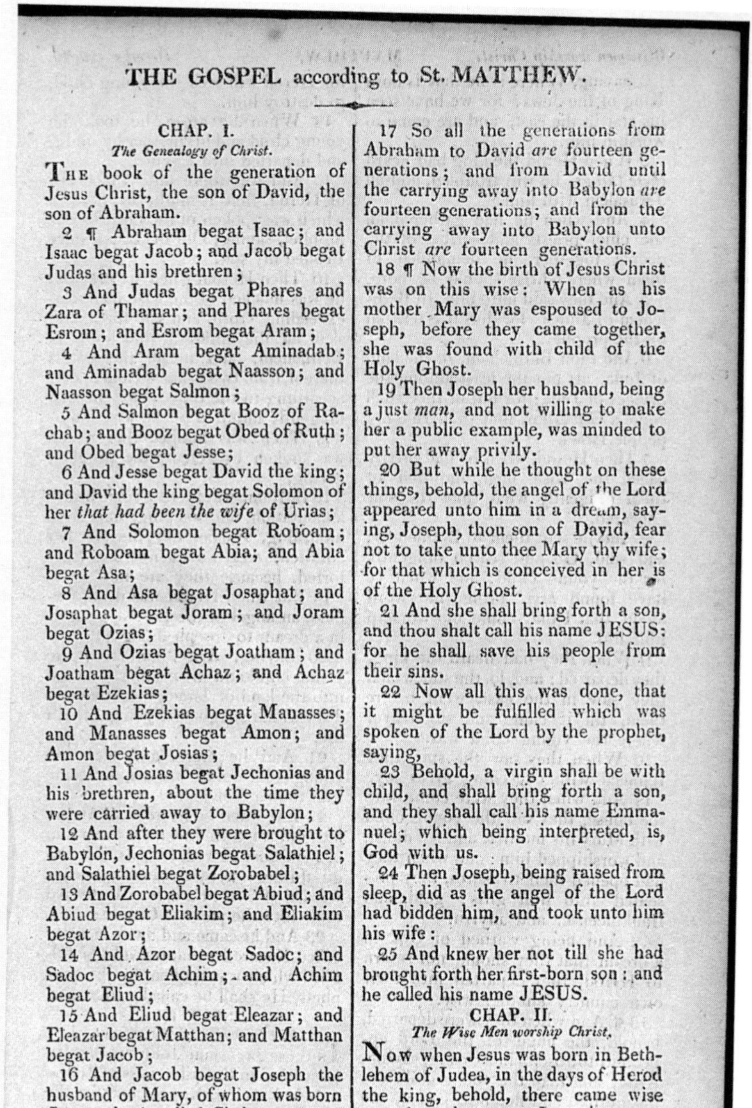

THE GOSPEL according to St. MATTHEW.

CHAP. I.
The Genealogy of Christ.

THE book of the generation of Jesus Christ, the son of David, the son of Abraham.

2 ¶ Abraham begat Isaac; and Isaac begat Jacob; and Jacob begat Judas and his brethren;

3 And Judas begat Phares and Zara of Thamar; and Phares begat Esrom; and Esrom begat Aram;

4 And Aram begat Aminadab; and Aminadab begat Naasson; and Naasson begat Salmon;

5 And Salmon begat Booz of Rachab; and Booz begat Obed of Ruth; and Obed begat Jesse;

6 And Jesse begat David the king; and David the king begat Solomon of her *that had been the wife* of Urias;

7 And Solomon begat Roboam; and Roboam begat Abia; and Abia begat Asa;

8 And Asa begat Josaphat; and Josaphat begat Joram; and Joram begat Ozias;

9 And Ozias begat Joatham; and Joatham begat Achaz; and Achaz begat Ezekias;

10 And Ezekias begat Manasses; and Manasses begat Amon; and Amon begat Josias;

11 And Josias begat Jechonias and his brethren, about the time they were carried away to Babylon;

12 And after they were brought to Babylon, Jechonias begat Salathiel; and Salathiel begat Zorobabel;

13 And Zorobabel begat Abiud; and Abiud begat Eliakim; and Eliakim begat Azor;

14 And Azor begat Sadoc; and Sadoc begat Achim; and Achim begat Eliud;

15 And Eliud begat Eleazar; and Eleazar begat Matthan; and Matthan begat Jacob;

16 And Jacob begat Joseph the husband of Mary, of whom was born Jesus, who is called Christ.

17 So all the generations from Abraham to David are fourteen generations; and from David until the carrying away into Babylon *are* fourteen generations; and from the carrying away into Babylon unto Christ *are* fourteen generations.

18 ¶ Now the birth of Jesus Christ was on this wise: When as his mother Mary was espoused to Joseph, before they came together, she was found with child of the Holy Ghost.

19 Then Joseph her husband, being a just *man,* and not willing to make her a public example, was minded to put her away privily.

20 But while he thought on these things, behold, the angel of the Lord appeared unto him in a dream, saying, Joseph, thou son of David, fear not to take unto thee Mary thy wife; for that which is conceived in her is of the Holy Ghost.

21 And she shall bring forth a son, and thou shalt call his name JESUS: for he shall save his people from their sins.

22 Now all this was done, that it might be fulfilled which was spoken of the Lord by the prophet, saying,

23 Behold, a virgin shall be with child, and shall bring forth a son, and they shall call his name Emmanuel; which being interpreted, is, God with us.

24 Then Joseph, being raised from sleep, did as the angel of the Lord had bidden him, and took unto him his wife:

25 And knew her not till she had brought forth her first-born son: and he called his name JESUS.

CHAP. II.
The Wise Men worship Christ.

NOW when Jesus was born in Bethlehem of Judea, in the days of Herod the king, behold, there came wise men from the east to Jerusalem,

989

Figure 8 Page from a stereotype Bible printed in medium octavo format on Small Pica type, by the University Press at Cambridge, 1810.

meet the needs of readers. Small Pica is just one example. In the very small typefaces, the issue of readability was sacrificed for portability. One cannot help but wonder how difficult it must have been to 'read, mark and inwardly digest' a Pearl Bible with its minute type. There is a copy of this book in the Bible Society's Library, however, with a well-worn binding and numerous marginal pencil markings. Despite its thin, yellowed paper and its very compact type page, the evidence is that someone read it carefully.[94] The Society was prepared to cater to a demand for Bibles and Testaments in a variety of formats, and to insist that the privileged Presses supply them with the best product possible.

In the mid-1830s, the number of formats in which the BFBS offered Bibles for sale increased drastically. As we shall see in the next chapter, questions about format extend to binding design in a dramatic way. But the page dimensions and typesize were also affected. The explosion of formats was the result partly of consumer demand and partly of improved supply. The Liverpool Auxiliary requested New Testaments in type larger than Pica in July 1826. The University Press at Oxford duly supplied books in their 'English' type, octavo, in March 1834, and the next year Cambridge was offering specimens of an improved 'English' edition, in quarto with marginal references. When Cambridge decided on a fresh edition in this large type, the Society was allowed to select the typefounder to be used.[95]

In 1831 the Cambridge Syndics decided to produce a new octavo Bible with references in the popular mid-sized Brevier type. The order was delayed because the Press wished to collate the text carefully with the 1611 folio edition, but the Bible Society had already ordered 10,000. When the delay occurred substitutes were ordered from the King's Printers.[96] Despite this evidence of commendable scholarly caution, however, the Cambridge Press records show a steady stream of orders for new editions, new type and reprints.

The tiny Pearl type was now coming into its own. 'Pocket editions' in small type had been sold by the BFBS since 1811. 'Pocket' size was actually 24mo, the format of the Oxford Press Bible discussed above. By 1837 C. S. Dudley was reporting a market for a larger-paged octavo edition, where the small type would leave room to print marginal references. Circumstantial as ever, he reported 'the numerous demands for it in certain parts of the West of England'. Once again, the Queen's (Tarn had to cross out King's in his minutes) Printers won the order.[97] The books began to be sold in 1839.[98]

Even smaller type became practicable, and Ruby and Diamond Testaments were prepared by the Presses. Two thousand Diamond 32mo Testaments ordered from Oxford in 1841 became 50,000 in March 1842 (18,000 from the Queen's Printer and 32,000 from Cambridge). Another 50,000 were ordered the next month, 'the last order having been so rapidly reduced' (25,000 from each), and by October 100,000 more were ordered. This time

THE GOSPEL according to St. MATTHEW.

CHAP. I.

1 *The genealogy of Christ from Abraham to Joseph.* 18 *He was conceived by the Holy Ghost, and born of the Virgin Mary when she was espoused to Joseph.* 19 *The angel satisfieth the misdeeming thoughts of Joseph, and interpreteth the names of Christ.*

THE book of the generation of Jesus Christ, the son of David, the son of Abraham.

2 Abraham begat Isaac; and Isaac begat Jacob; and Jacob begat Judas and his brethren;

3 And Judas begat Phares and Zara of Thamar; and Phares begat Esrom, and Esrom begat Aram;

4 And Aram begat Aminadab; and Aminadab begat Naasson; and Naasson begat Salmon;

5 And Salmon begat Booz of Rachab; and Booz begat Obed of Ruth; and Obed begat Jesse;

6 And Jesse begat David the king; and David the king begat Solomon of her *that had been the wife* of Urias;

7 And Solomon begat Roboam; and Roboam begat Abia; and Abia begat Asa;

8 And Asa begat Josaphat; and Josaphat begat Joram; and Joram begat Ozias;

9 And Ozias begat Joatham; and Joatham begat Achaz; and Achaz begat Ezekias;

10 And Ezekias begat Manasses; and Manasses begat Amon; and Amon begat Josias;

11 And Josias begat Jechonias and his brethren, about the time they were carried away to Babylon:

12 And after they were brought to Babylon, Jechonias begat Salathiel; and Salathiel begat Zorobabel;

13 And Zorobabel begat Abiud; and Abiud begat Eliakim; and Eliakim begat Azor;

14 And Azor begat Sadoc; and Sadoc begat Achim; and Achim begat Eliud;

15 And Eliud begat Eleazar; and Eleazar begat Matthan; and Matthan begat Jacob;

16 And Jacob begat Joseph the husband of Mary, of whom was born Jesus, who is called Christ.

17 So all the generations from Abraham to David *are* fourteen generations; and from David until the carrying away into Babylon *are* fourteen generations; and from the carrying away into Babylon unto Christ *are* fourteen generations.

18 ¶ Now the birth of Jesus Christ was on this wise: When as his mother Mary was espoused to Joseph, before they came together, she was found with child of the Holy Ghost.

19 Then Joseph her husband, being a just *man*, and not willing to make her a publick example, was minded to put her away privily.

20 But while he thought on these things, behold, the angel of the Lord appeared unto him in a dream, saying, Joseph, thou son of David, fear not to take unto thee Mary thy wife: for that which is conceived in her is of the Holy Ghost.

21 And she shall bring forth a son, and thou shalt call his name JESUS: for he shall save his people from their sins.

22 Now all this was done, that it might be fulfilled which was spoken of the Lord by the prophet, saying,

23 Behold, a virgin shall be with child, and shall bring forth a son, and they shall call his name Emmanuel, which being interpreted is, God with us.

24 Then Joseph being raised from sleep did as the angel of the Lord had bidden him, and took unto him his wife:

25 And knew her not till she had brought forth her firstborn son: and he called his name JESUS.

971

Figure 9   Page from a stereotype Bible printed in royal octavo format on Small Pica type, by Eyre and Strahan (the King's Printers), London, 1815.

THE GOSPEL according to St. MATTHEW.

CHAP. I.

1 The genealogy of Christ from Abraham to Joseph. 18 He was conceived by the Holy Ghost, and born of the Virgin Mary when she was espoused to Joseph. 19 The angel satisfieth the misdeeming thoughts of Joseph, and interpreteth the names of Christ.

THE book of the generation of Jesus Christ, the son of David, the son of Abraham.

2 Abraham begat Isaac; and Isaac begat Jacob; and Jacob begat Judas and his brethren;

3 And Judas begat Phares and Zara of Thamar; and Phares begat Esrom, and Esrom begat Aram;

4 And Aram begat Aminadab; and Aminadab begat Naasson; and Naasson begat Salmon;

5 And Salmon begat Booz of Rachab; and Booz begat Obed of Ruth; and Obed begat Jesse;

6 And Jesse begat David the king; and David the king begat Solomon of her *that had been the wife* of Urias;

7 And Solomon begat Roboam; and Roboam begat Abia; and Abia begat Asa;

8 And Asa begat Josaphat; and Josaphat begat Joram; and Joram begat Ozias;

9 And Ozias begat Joatham; and Joatham begat Achaz; and Achaz begat Ezekias;

10 And Ezekias begat Manasses; and Manasses begat Amon; and Amon begat Josias;

11 And Josias begat Jechonias and his brethren, about the time they were carried away to Babylon:

12 And after they were brought to Babylon, Jechonias begat Salathiel; and Salathiel begat Zorobabel;

13 And Zorobabel begat Abiud; and Abiud begat Eliakim; and Eliakim begat Azor;

14 And Azor begat Sadoc; and Sadoc begat Achim; and Achim begat Eliud;

971

15 And Eliud begat Eleazar; and Eleazar begat Matthan; and Matthan begat Jacob;

16 And Jacob begat Joseph the husband of Mary, of whom was born Jesus, who is called Christ.

17 So all the generations from Abraham to David *are* fourteen generations; and from David until the carrying away into Babylon *are* fourteen generations; and from the carrying away into Babylon unto Christ *are* fourteen generations.

18 ¶ Now the birth of Jesus Christ was on this wise: When as his mother Mary was espoused to Joseph, before they came together, she was found with child of the Holy Ghost.

19 Then Joseph her husband, being a just *man*, and not willing to make her a publick example, was minded to put her away privily.

20 But while he thought on these things, behold, the angel of the Lord appeared unto him in a dream, saying, Joseph, thou son of David, fear not to take unto thee Mary thy wife: for that which is conceived in her is of the Holy Ghost.

21 And she shall bring forth a son, and thou shalt call his name JESUS: for he shall save his people from their sins.

22 Now all this was done, that it might be fulfilled which was spoken of the Lord by the prophet, saying,

23 Behold, a virgin shall be with child, and shall bring forth a son, and they shall call his name Emmanuel, which being interpreted is, God with us.

24 Then Joseph being raised from sleep did as the angel of the Lord had bidden him, and took unto him his wife:

25 And knew her not till she had brought forth her firstborn son: and he called his name JESUS.

Figure 10   Page from a stereotype Bible printed in quarto format on Small Pica type, by Eyre and Strahan (the King's Printers), London, 1816. This is the octavo edition illustrated in figure 9, printed on large paper 'with broad margins for writing upon'.

THE GOSPEL ACCORDING TO
St. MATTHEW.

CHAPTER I.

1 *The genealogy of Christ from Abraham to Joseph.*
18 *He was conceived by the Holy Ghost, and born of the Virgin Mary when she was espoused to Joseph.*
19 *The angel satisfieth the misdeeming thoughts of Joseph, and interpreteth the names of Christ.*

THE book of the "generation of Jesus Christ, the son of David, the son of Abraham.

2 Abraham begat Isaac; and Isaac begat Jacob; and Jacob begat Judas and his brethren;

3 And Judas begat Phares and Zara of Thamar; and Phares begat Esrom; and Esrom begat Aram;

4 And Aram begat Aminadab; and Aminadab begat Naasson; and Naasson begat Salmon;

5 And Salmon begat Booz of Rachab; and Booz begat Obed of Ruth; and Obed begat Jesse;

6 And Jesse begat David the king; and David the king begat Solomon of her that had been the wife of Urias;

7 And Solomon begat Roboam; and Roboam begat Abia; and Abia begat Asa;

8 And Asa begat Josaphat; and Josaphat begat Joram; and Joram begat Ozias;

9 And Ozias begat Joatham; and Joatham begat Achaz; and Achaz begat Ezekias;

10 And Ezekias begat Manasses; and Manasses begat Amon; and Amon begat Josias;

11 And Josias begat Jechonias and his brethren, about the time they were carried away to Babylon:

12 And after they were brought to Babylon, Jechonias begat Salathiel; and Salathiel begat Zorobabel;

13 And Zorobabel begat Abiud; and Abiud begat Eliakim; and Eliakim begat Azor;

14 And Azor begat Sadoc; and Sadoc begat Achim; and Achim begat Eliud;

15 And Eliud begat Eleazar; and Eleazar begat Matthan; and Matthan begat Jacob;

16 And Jacob begat Joseph the husband of Mary, of whom was born Jesus, who is called Christ.

17 So all the generations from Abraham to David are fourteen generations; and from David until the carrying away into Babylon are fourteen generations; and from the carrying away into Babylon unto Christ are fourteen generations.

18 Now the birth of Jesus Christ was on this wise: When as his mother Mary was espoused to Joseph, before they came together, she was found with child of the Holy Ghost.

19 Then Joseph her husband, being a just man, and not willing to make her a publick example, was minded to put her away privily.

20 But while he thought on these things, behold, the angel of the Lord appeared unto him in a dream, saying, Joseph, thou son of David, fear not to take unto thee Mary thy wife: for that which is conceived in her is of the Holy Ghost.

21 And she shall bring forth a son, and thou shalt call his name JESUS: for he shall save his people from their sins.

22 Now all this was done, that it might be fulfilled which was spoken of the Lord by the prophet, saying,

23 Behold, a virgin shall be with child, and shall bring forth a son, and they shall call his name Emmanuel, which being interpreted is, God with us.

24 Then Joseph being raised from sleep did as the angel of the Lord had bidden him, and took unto him his wife:

25 And knew her not till she had brought forth her firstborn son: and he called his name JESUS.

CHAPTER II.

1 *The wise men out of the east are directed to Christ by a star.* 11 *They worship him, and offer their presents.* 14 *Joseph fleeth into Egypt, with Jesus and his mother.* 16 *Herod slayeth the children:* 20 *himself dieth.* 23 *Christ is brought back again into Galilee to Nazareth.*

NOW when Jesus was born in Bethlehem of Judæa in the

Figure 11 Page from a Bible with marginal references, printed from standing type in octavo format on small Pica type, by Eyre and Spottiswoode (the Queen's Printers), London, 1865.

Oxford was required to supply 30,000, Cambridge 14,000 and the Queen's Printer 56,000. The books, which cost the Society 3d per copy unbound, were sold at 6d bound prettily in roan with gilt edges. The next summer the Cambridge Syndics agreed that 'Mr Parker do procure the Type for and set up a 32mo Diamond Bible'.[99] The popularity of the small-type New Testament presumably made it worthwhile to set up the Old.

Not all of the new editions were stereotyped. By the thirties typefounders were able to produce in quantity, and Presses could find room to store the great blocks of movable (but stationary) type. The quality was higher than that of the awkward stereotype plates, which were fragile and tended to shrink. The Cambridge Press business records show agreements 'to set up in Type the Pica 8vo Testament, & to keep it in Type', and 'that such an addition be made to the font of Type (Nonpareil) as will be sufficient to set up the entire Bible in Standing Type'. By 1838 the Subcommittee had experience of 500,000 impressions being printed from standing types, and in 1847 it was noted that most of the English editions were thus printed.[100]

Improvements in the design and printing of the Bible, however, did not ensure typographic or textual accuracy. We have seen how in the early French and Spanish editions, linguists and clergymen were at odds with each other over the correct rendering of foreign words. Not even the English Bible was exempt from errors, but in a nation where the Bible privilege – which some critics were calling a monopoly – was based on the assurance of accuracy, the merest slip of the compositor's stick might became a subject of ideological and political debate.

The BFBS Committee responded courteously to local subscribers who discovered typographical errors. Miss E. Richardson of Walton near Hull, for example, noticed in 1840 the omission of the word *from* in Isaiah 60:4 in an 1836 Eyre and Strahan Pica quarto Bible. Spottiswoode assured the Society the error had been detected after the first impression and immediately corrected. He believed his vigilance and constant re-examination of the books were 'a sufficient guarantee against any typographical error remaining long in them'.[101] The Subcommittee tended to agree with members who wished to remove anything (except marginal notes) that could possibly be construed as a note or comment. Thus when the Cornwall Auxiliary wrote to disapprove of the tables appended to some editions, the Committee decided immediately to direct the authorized printers to omit these tables, which had been used to 'fill up a blank page'. But when a letter of severe textual criticism came from Thomas Curtis, Secretaries Brandram and Hughes merely passed the problem on to the privileged Presses.[102]

The Rev. Mr Curtis, a dissenting minister of Islington, told the Society in January 1832: 'you are circulating grossly inaccurate copies, if copies they may be called, of the Authorized Version. . .'. He claimed to have identified thousands of errors, not counting mere typographical ones. 'Then the Margin of all the Modern Reference Bibles has, wholly contrary to *your* excellent fundamental Laws, and King James's original Instructions, numerous *Notes* and *Comments* . . . sometimes flatly contradicting the Text.'[103] The debate over a test of Trinitarian belief as a criterion for membership was in full swing. The possibility of another upheaval, perhaps another schism along the lines of the Apocrypha controversy, must have been in the Secretaries' minds. The representatives of the three Presses, however, could not avoid responding to Curtis. They assured him that the problem had been dealt with in 1769, when the Oxford Delegates commissioned Dr Benjamin Blayney to prepare an edition which thereafter became their standard. Patiently they reminded him that the text of 1611 could not easily be recovered, since it existed in numerous competing editions.[104] Curtis fumed on, organizing a committee of clergymen and publishing a pamphlet, *The Existing Monopoly*, addressed to the Bishop of London in 1833. The Bible Society Committee declined his offer to show them nineteen interleaved volumes of 1611 with variant translations. They left it to the Presses to deal with Curtis, whose eclectic editorial standards were shared by few. As the King's Printer put it, 'There appears to be some delusion on the part of Mr Curtis . . . he seems to have found a standard from *nineteen* different Bibles, which may have led to some misunderstanding.' Eyre and Spottiswoode, like the Universities, used Blayney as a standard, and were convinced of the 'general faithfulness' of their editions.[105]

The Bible patent had its advantages at times like this, when it shielded the Committee from textual and doctrinal criticism. But later in the 1830s and again in the 1840s, the Royal patent itself, along with the privilege of the Universities, came under criticism. In an age when many people were becoming convinced of the benefits of free trade, in bread (the Anti-Corn Law League was established in 1838) as well as in Bibles, the 'privilege' of printing the scriptures was often considered to be a 'monopoly'. Curtis entitled his critique *The Existing Monopoly*, and sanguine freetraders were confident that textual accuracy would be maintained, even increased, in an open market. No other reason could be justified, in their view, for preserving a corrupt 'monopoly of the word of God'. Nonetheless it was maintained, in large part, arguably, because of the support of the British and Foreign Bible Society. They had become accustomed to dealing with three Presses, and the limited monopoly suited them well. Table 5 shows the relative quantities of books acquired from the three printers. The privileged Presses and their best customer had worked out a *modus vivendi* that involved limited competition. This left them all free to concentrate on matters of format, of text and of price, until the privilege itself came under attack from freetraders.

In 1832 was held the first of three Select Committees of Parliament on the King's Printers' patents. Evidence was taken from Sir David Hunter Blair, who held the Royal patent for Scotland, and his printer, William Waddell, who had been supplying all the books to their country since 1825. Like their

Table 5. *Privileged Presses' shares of BFBS orders, 1826–30*

	Number			Percentage		
	King's	Printer·Oxford·Cambridge		King's %	Printer·Oxford·Cambridge %	%
1826	64,314	87,755	20,265	37.3	50.9	11.8
1827	37,680	86,676	16,710	26.7	61.5	11.8
1828	123,455	169,032	52,010	35.8	49.1	15.1
1829	105,816	65,947	65,856	44.5	27.8	27.7
1830	87,759	94,667	60,987	36.1	38.8	25.1

Figures from Select Committee Report, 1832. Supplied to the Committee by Richard Cockle, BFBS Depositary, 21 November 1831.

opposite number in England, they claimed to be publishing the scriptures as cheaply as possible, and noted that they seldom used stereotype, finding that standing type afforded the same standard of accuracy.[106] Andrew Spottiswoode, the King's Printer for England (in the firm Eyre and Spottiswoode which had succeeded Eyre and Strahan) said much the same thing. But there was an opposing view. Ardent freetraders argued at these hearings that the reluctance of the privileged Presses to stereotype was the result of the 'apathy' of the monopolists. Robert Besley, a typefounder, stated that

the advantages of stereotyping with all other standard works have been derived by the Public. In the case of Bibles and Testaments, the monopolists have kept the advantage themselves ... The Universities have gone a very expensive way to work about their books generally, that is, they have kept the whole of them set up in moveable type, in many cases.

But Joseph Parker of the Oxford Press explained that while stereotype cost about one-quarter less than standing type, plates yielded 100,000 copies, while the equivalent blocks of standing type produced 1,200,000 copies each.

John William Parker of Cambridge testified that the prices were regulated not by the Presses but by the Societies, the SPCK and the much larger BFBS, which established 'a sort of conventional price at which [they] wish Bibles of a certain size and description to be produced and the changes that have taken place with regard to that, are rather in the improvement of the quality of the book, than an alteration of its price'.

Opponents of the privilege did not attack the Bible Society and the SPCK directly. Instead they gleefully sought out and counted errors in the available editions (London printer George Langford said of one, that 'such inaccuracies would disgrace an auctioneer's catalogue printed in the hurry of business'). The Rev. John Lee, a minister in the Church of Scotland and a member of the Edinburgh Bible Society, gave his opinion 'that a watchful

Public, under the circumstance of a free trade, would be much more influential in preserving the pure Text, than an unwatched monopoly'. They claimed the monopoly bred apathy, which prevented adequate 'variety . . . to meet the taste of the inquiring world'. The 1832 Select Committee resulted in no direct changes of policy. Nor does any reference to it appear in the BFBS minutes, although one of its members was Sir Robert Harry Inglis, a former member of the Bible Society's Committee. And no representative of the Society testified at the hearings.[107]

There were hearings again in 1837, this time concerned only with the Scottish King's Printer's Patent. The Rev. Adam Thomson, minister in the Kirk of Scotland, of Coldstream argued that the patent not be renewed, but for open competition to take its place. Any 'monopoly of the word of God' was, he said, 'especially outrageous'. The solicitor William Ellis, a member and former director of the Edinburgh Bible Society, believed that 'Parliament could not hurt the feelings of Scotchmen more than by renewing that monopoly'. A more commercial opponent of the patent was John Childs, stereotype printer of Bungay in Suffolk, who complained that 'the selling of Bibles has ceased to be a trade to the booksellers, since the establishment of the British and Foreign Bible Society, which in conjunction with the Society for the Promotion of Christian Knowledge, distributes, I should think, more than 95 per cent of all the Bibles that are printed'. (Joseph Parker, of Oxford University Press stated that two-thirds of their orders were from Societies, and one-third from the trade.) Childs voiced his suspicion that the University Presses avoided stereotype – the great invention of the age – because of their monopoly. Sir Robert Inglis asked Parker the pertinent question about whether Oxford used stereotype plates. He replied: 'We do not stereotype generally those Bibles which are of the greatest sale; we use standing type . . . it is as perfect as the stereotype, and perhaps less liable to incorrectness, because less liable to damage and more easily corrected . . . [T]he stereotype plate is very handsome at first, but is very liable to deterioration.'[108] No official of the Bible Society testified at these hearings, which did not directly concern them. Bibles for Scotland had been supplied from Edinburgh since 1825, and the Society in Scotland had been independent since the Apocrypha schism the same year. None of these books could legally be imported into England.

As a result of this inquiry, the Queen's Printer for Scotland lost his patent when it lapsed in 1839. It was replaced by a Board for Bible Circulation, whose Secretary was the Rev. Adam Thomson. Thomson now embarked upon a campaign to abolish the English monopoly of the Queen's Printer. His ally in this effort was Dr John Campbell, a leading Congregationalist. Campbell wrote his attack on the monopoly under the pseudonym 'Jethro', calling for 'A System of Lay Agency . . . for the Diffusion of the Gospel Among Our Home Population'. Together they widened the attack on Spottiswoode to include the Bible Society. Thomson published his charges in open letters to Lord Bexley, the BFBS President, to whom he denounced the Society's management. He accused the 'richly-salaried agents' and Secretaries of 'pre-eminently extravagant expenditure' and of short-changing the needs of foreign readers by charging too much for English scriptures printed by the 'bibliopolist'. Moreover he charged 'the leading members of the Committee' with an 'ignorant hatred of dissent, and [an] illiberal treatment of dissenters'. Again, the evidence was their support of the monopoly, whose abolition, he claimed, was sought mostly by Dissenters.[109]

We saw in the previous chapter how the Committee attributed its price reduction of 1840 to 'the portentous aspect of the time' and the needs of Sunday Schools. Although officially, and even in the minutes of its meetings, the Committee was not involved with the Government's arrangements for printing the Bible, by 1840 it was impossible for the BFBS to ignore the campaign against the monopoly. The Society's answers to correspondents show considerable concern about the issue. There is no documented connection between the price reduction of 1840 and the anti-monopoly agitation, but many subscribers believed there must be such a connection. John Gray wrote on behalf of the Hexham Auxiliary, regretting that the price reduction had been suspended. As Gray read the evidence, the record of earlier Select Committees 'proves to a demonstration, that the whole *Twelve Thousand pounds* of loss ... has gone into the pockets of the Monopolists'. He demanded that the Committee petition Parliament 'to emancipate God's Word from the tricks and trammels of Monopoly'. Brandram replied, 'From what has appeared in the public press it seems almost impossible to avoid giving a party complexion to this Affair. In Dr Thomson's circular the Appeal to *Dissenters* is reiterated – and there is too much reason to fear that it will become an array of strength on each side!' Brandram begged Gray to be patient.[110] He wrote 'gloomy' letters to his colleagues, the BFBS agents W. Brackenbury and T. J. Bourne: 'this monopoly Question ... may involve modifications in some of our arrangements. It may affect public meetings very seriously.' He asked Bourne to 'slip up' to London on the mail train, 'breakfast here and cram yourself with Monopoly bread'. He instructed the agents to be discreet. Thomas Phillips, the agent for Wales, warned: 'Depend upon it this agitation will shake the country from its centre to its circumference.'[111] He was right. Opponents of the monopoly used the price reduction, and its subsequent suspension, as fuel for their assertions that the privileged Presses were fleecing the public.

The reduction of 1840 involved a loss for the Society, a loss that the Secretaries were determined to keep to a minimum. They requested from the printers several specimens of cheap editions of the scriptures (a Nonpareil Bible, a Brevier and a Nonpareil Testament) and resolved to order these in bulk: 5,000 copies of each edition from each Press, 45,000 books in all. Table 6

Table 6. *Loss to BFBS on cheap Bibles, 1840*

	Sheets	Binding	Total	Reduced price
Nonpareil Bible	1s 2d	8¾d	1s 10¾d	1s 9d
Brevier Testament	5¾d	5d	10¾d	9d
Nonpareil Testament	3½d	4½d	8d	6d

shows how they calculated the expected loss. The arrangement began on 1 January, with the provision of 'the prices being first duly stamped on the outside Covers'.[112] In February the prices were reduced further, to 1s 6d, 8d and 6d respectively. To the stock were added Pearl and Ruby Bibles from Oxford to be sold at 1s 6d.[113] By August, however, the reduction was suspended, because over £14,000 had been lost, and Auxiliaries were not forthcoming with 'compensation' to make it up.

The privileged Presses, particularly the 'monopolist', Andrew Spottiswoode, were hurt by criticism following the suspension. They were aware of public opinion, and probably chose to reduce their profit margins as an alternative to losing the privilege altogether. As one Society employee wrote in confidence to another, 'on the Cheap Bible Question or perhaps the Monopoly subject – the printers are awake, and I have no doubt we shall have a cheap Bible & Testament from them without robbing the Society'.[114] The 'nihilification', as Secretary George Browne put it, of 'the price at home', was handled smoothly by the privileged Presses, because their standards, as well as the techniques and technologies they used, had changed radically. Furthermore, they needed to show that they could be entrusted with the responsibility for producing the nation's supply of cheap Bibles. John W. Parker of the Cambridge Press wrote in December 1840 a letter that spelled out just how the prices of books could best be reduced. The design could be changed to facilitate cheaper binding:

I beg further to apprise you that these editions will be printed in such a form as to reduce the labour of folding and sewing the sheets to the lowest possible amount, while the strength of the work will be perfect, and the opening of the book rather improved than otherwise. Those editions therefore, may of course be bound at a proportionately low price.[115]

The BFBS was surprised, however, to find that the printers cut their losses as much as possible by reducing the quality of books. A few days after the first delivery there was a meeting in London, between Parker and some members of the Committee and staff concerned with printing. It appears from Parker's letter after this meeting that the Society had complained of reductions in quality in the much cheaper Bibles. The new cheap editions, he told them, differ very materially from those hitherto supplied at higher prices. As copies of the text of the authorized version, they are indeed identically the same, but in material and manufacture they are of a less costly kind, and are consequently inferior in quality to the second class books ... In order to produce those very low-priced editions we have employed ... the large steam machines, whereby we are enabled to print upon double-sheets, and this, I believe, has never before been done, in the production of Bibles. Further, the paper is reduced both in size and substance, the weight being now 15 instead of 21; and ink, & labour in getting up, being economised in a corresponding degree, the cost of manufacture may be considered as reduced as low as it ought to be, or indeed can be, consistently with security and permanency.[116]

The Society had to be content with this reality. Its cheapest Bibles were presented to the public in very 'homely caskets' indeed.

The 'monopoly agitation' affected the Bible Society only indirectly. But the campaign for free trade in Bibles cannot be understood without a realization that the 'monopolist' and his University colleagues were serving one major customer. Table 7, taken from a routine government report for the decade 1837–47, shows that the relative shares of the three Presses had not changed much since 1830, and that the Bible Society was responsible for circulating 60 per cent of their output. The Society had set up a situation where the three Presses competed against each other, in terms of price and quality, while at the same time they increased the volume of production so much that the Bible and New Testament were by mid-century no longer the profitable titles in the Press lists that they had been earlier. The 'monopoly agitation' was to reopen in 1860, when another Select Committee debated the justification for the Queen's Printer's monopoly. This time the BFBS reluctantly but inevitably became involved in the debates concerning the political economy of Bible publishing. The occasion, discussed in chapter 6, was an exception to their tradition of silent non-involvement, intended to keep them clear of controversy and criticism. It was because of this caution that the innovative influence of the Society upon the design, production, paper and textual accuracy of the scriptural text passed unnoticed during earlier debates on the subject.

The Bible transaction, inspired as it was by a popular movement to change the world by distributing books, had a profound effect upon the printing trades. The Committee at Earl Street and their executive staff were only the channel of the BFBS demand, which had its source in the enthusiasm of Auxiliary and Association members. Evangelical zeal, translated into orders for large numbers of books, stimulated the printers to introduce technical changes. Not only the three privileged Presses, but also London printers like Thomas Rutt and John Benjamin Gottlieb Vogel, and provincial printers like Richard Mackenzie Bacon and Charles Brightley, found a market for new methods. In the long term, both quantity and quality improved, even though the Society's eagerness to adopt the newest and most promising technologies sometimes left the Printing Subcommittee mired in difficulties. The new

Table 7. *Numbers of Bibles and Testaments printed, including numbers purchased by BFBS, 1837–47*

	Bible	Testament	Total	Percentages
Queen's Printer				
Books produced				of all books
	2,284,540	1,971,877	4,256,417	38.9%
Purchased by BFBS				of Press books
	1,314,031	1,352,604	2,666,635	62.6%
				of BFBS books
				41.4%
Oxford University Press				
Books produced				of all books
	2,612,730	2,062,250	4,674,980	42.7%
Purchased by BFBS				of Press books
	1,151,276	1,355,926	2,507,202	53.6%
				of BFBS books
				38.9%
Cambridge University Press				
Books produced				of all books
	895,500	1,111,600	2,007,100	18.3%
Purchased by BFBS				of Press books
	527,846	737,496	1,265,342	63.0%
				of BFBS books
				19.7%

Totals
Books produced by all three Presses 10,938,497
Purchased by BFBS 6,439,179 (58.9% of all books produced)

Notes: Figures taken from Parliamentary Papers. Number of Bibles and Prayer Books Printed published and sold ... in the years 1833–47 ... including number sold to BFBS (1847–8, vol. 82, xlix.1).

technologies of stereotype, machine printing and paper tenacity did not depend on the Bible Society, but the Society's demand accelerated their implementation.

The attitude of the BFBS to technology was complex. Stereotype, because it promised to maintain the accuracy of the text, was admired without reservation. The Society was talking about the excellence of stereotype long after the technology had been abandoned for standing types. They were just as enthusiastic about machine printing and unbleached paper, but not so publicly. The image of conservatism covered printing practices at least as radical as that of the new typographical method. The members of the printing Subcommittee were anxious to learn enough to be shrewd customers of the printing trades. In 1813 when a printer asked to be recompensed for the cost

Table 8. *Editions of the scriptures in the continental languages printed in England for the BFBS, August 1849–August 1851*

Number of copies	Edition and format	Print mode	Editorial expenses
3,000	French Bible 12mo	Plates	nil
5,000	French Testament 12mo Ostervald	Plates	£15
15,000	French Testament 48mo Ostervald	Type	£20
15,000	French Testament 48mo Martin	Type	£20
15,000	French Testament and Psalms 32mo Martin	Type	£25
15,000	French Testament and Psalms 32mo Ostervald	Type	£25
3,000	German Bible 12mo	Plates	nil
5,000	German Bible 16mo	Plates	nil
20,000	German Testament and Psalms	Plates	nil
2,000	German and Hebrew Old Testament	Plates	nil
6,000	German and Hebrew Pentateuch (2 eds.)	Plates	nil
2,000	German and Hebrew Prophets etc.	Plates	nil
2,000	German and Hebrew Psalms	Plates	nil
5,000	Greek Testament Ancient	Type	nil
25,000	Italian Bible 24mo (2 editions)	Plates	nil
5,000	Italian Bible 8vo Diodati	Type	£100
10,000	Italian Bible 8vo Diodati	Type	£100
10,000	Italian Testament 32mo Diodati	Type	£20
15,000	Italian Testament 32mo Martini	Type	£20
15,000	Italian Testament 48mo Diodati	Type	£20
15,000	Italian Testament 48mo Martini	Type	£20
15,000	Norwegian Testament 48mo	Type	nil
1,000	Spanish Testament 8vo	Plates	nil

of extra labour, Adam Clarke recognized that 'the Committee, among whom there is not one Printer, can not properly judge of the business'. He recommended that the question be referred to two or three friendly conscientious printers, adding 'Every labourer should have his proper hire: & we certainly would feel as much grieved to give a shilling too *little* as to give one *too much*.'[117] The Committee were hard-headed businessmen of the industrial revolution, questioning the competence of traditional practitioners and seeking ways to cut costs and increase efficiency. Collective biographical research confirms the fact that most members knew about printing primarily from their experience with Bibles. This *naïveté* was an advantage, juxtaposed as it was with commercial acumen and with commitment to the project. The members were always prepared to question the established practices of the trade. When Cambridge stalled on drying, for example, Zachary Macaulay suggested the use of machinery.[118] The controversy over the use of bleach in printing paper is also evidence of Committee business methods. They recruited Luke Howard, a scientist whose professional expertise was outside that of the printing crafts. The three suppliers of English scriptures found it impossible to take advantage of the Society's inexperience because it was so quickly transformed into expertise. Tarn and his colleagues became seasoned publishers in their first few years of doing business.

By 1845 Charles Stokes Dudley was exulting in what he called 'Railway Speed in printing!'[119] The Society's foreign publishing increased along with missionary activity, and Thomas Rutt, among other craftsmen, was making a fortune out of his skill and reliability as a Bible printer. Scriptures in the so-called 'Continental languages' remained in print in a wide range of versions and formats. Table 8 displays the volume of production of such books in 1849–51.

The Bible is not like other books, and the Bible Society is not like other publishers. The Committee and staff were part of the evangelical revival, and they were managers of a voluntary organization. But they were primarily publishers in their own right, confidently arranging for plates and paper and insisting upon very high standards of both quantity and quality. They influenced the course of development in the English book trades, not only in the printing shops, the typefoundries and the paper mills, but also in the workrooms of the bookbinders.

4 · THE BFBS AND LONDON BOOKBINDERS, 1811–1864

Like printers and papermakers, the bookbinders employed by the British and Foreign Bible Society were required to render books durable enough to withstand energetic perusal. The Society encouraged bookbinders to use machinery, exerted its economic influence to keep prices as low as possible, and incidentally precipitated a revolution in the practices of a traditional craft. In printing, however, the many changes that occurred because of BFBS demand received minimal publicity; they were known only to people working in the book trades. The bookbinders, in 1850, took their case to the world. Charges that the Society's workers were being exploited were met with cries of 'Scripture Slaves' and 'Bibles and Brothels', with scandalized subscribers and with cancelled subscriptions. When members of local Auxiliaries and Associations were told the Society was 'grinding the faces of the poor', they began to ask themselves – and demand of the Committee at Earl Street – if there was such a thing as a cheap Bible that was too cheap.

The subject of binding BFBS Bibles opens an opportunity that is unusual in the history of books. It is possible, in this case, to consider the format of books as historical artifacts in juxtaposition with documents concerning the labour relations involved in their production. Usually these questions are the province of bibliographers on the one hand and labour historians on the other, one group preoccupied with chainlines and watermarks, the other with picket lines and solidarity. But as Robert Darnton has argued, 'bibliography leads directly into the hurly-burly of working-class history; it provides one of the few means of analyzing the work habits of skilled artisans before the Industrial Revolution'.[1] And after. Trade bookbinders at the beginning of the nineteenth century were faced with machinery that lowered the value of their trade skills, and with employers who paid piece-work rates. Their employers, the 'Bible masters', were faced with patrons at Earl Street who were determined to reduce prices without trenching too much on the funds allocated to their foreign project. Finally, the BFBS Secretaries also came under attack from local Auxiliary and Association members, who had been encouraged to believe themselves personally involved in the Bible transaction, but who could not accept that cheap Bibles were manufactured by sweated labour. The whole situation was given a final twist by the rhetoric of gender, so that the feminine purity of bookbinders, not the dilution of their trade skills, became the issue of the day.

The BFBS offered Bibles to the nineteenth-century public in a multitude of bindings. Leather was traditional for Bibles, and the first books appeared in calf covers for well-to-do subscribers, while sheepskin served for the charity editions. These choices were later expanded. Sheepskin was available both as skiver, the very inexpensive and flimsy half-thickness material, and in the full-thickness roan. The latter was easily polished, so that it could compete with morocco and calf in appearance, while the price was much lower. Coloured calf was an attractive alternative, and the higher-quality leathers, Persian basil and morocco could be had for a price. At the bottom of the range, canvas and later bookcloth were also available. The name of the Society was impressed on the front covers with a stamp.

The packaging of the scriptural text was intrinsic to a social and economic transaction between a London Committee of keen businessmen on the one hand, and enthusiastic women and men organizing local Auxiliaries and Associations on the other. When subscribers selected books for their own use, or Auxiliary visitors for philanthropic circulation, their initial impression was formed by the binding. The materials and design of the packaging around the text clearly signalled the social assumptions of the BFBS members and leadership. The cheapest Bibles were designated by a 'charity brand', a stamp indicating that distribution at this low price was limited 'to schools and the poor'. At the other end of the Bible market, gilt edges and elaborately lettered covers appealed to a wealthier public. The bookbinding part of the publishing operation tells us a great deal about what Committee members and staff thought they were doing when they distributed scriptures 'without note or comment'.

What they were doing, as we have seen, was operating a large and successful business, making the shrewd and innovative decisions that allowed them to reduce the price of books to the very low levels of the 1840s. And there were no restrictions, no privileges, patents or charters hampering the BFBS Committee in its dealings with the bookbinders. The Society generated competition within the London bookbinding trades, making and breaking businesses as they bestowed and withdrew the Society's custom. Nor did the lack of a monopoly in binding the Holy Scriptures preclude controversy and criticism. The bookbinders' strikes of the 1840s placed the Bible Society squarely and unfavourably in the public eye. By that time the business practices of the BFBS had radically altered the London binding trades.

It was the binder who made the 'books' coming from the press in sheets look like books to people uninitiated in the mysteries of their production. The manufacture of Bibles and Testaments by the Society's printers finished with the production of large sheets, each side comprising eight, twelve, sixteen or more pages. The letterpress pages were distributed over these sheets in such a way that they might be folded into quires, then stitched up one side, while the edges were trimmed off the other three; the stitched and gathered quires were encased in covers. These procedures were the purview of the bookbinders. A history of one of the Bible Society's principal shops, Burn's, gives a thumbnail sketch of the binding business at the end of the eighteenth century:

The bookbinder of the seventeen-eighties [when Thomas Burn began] was a retail tradesman working at home with his own hands and employing such assistants as his business required. His best work would be single volumes, usually hand-tooled calf, gilt edges, done to suit the taste and pocket of private customers: his longest orders, thirteens and twenty-fives, (the odd copy, the quartern book, bound without charge), done in unlettered sheep, uncut edges, for booksellers and library suppliers.[2]

The Bible Society, printing books by the hundreds and thousands, needed bookbinders who could handle more than a dozen or two at a time.

The concept of 'publisher's binding' or 'edition binding' – where the publisher was responsible for covering all books as they came off the press – was quite new in 1804. Few publishers before the 1820s arranged for a whole edition of books to be bound. These arrangements were left to the retailer or to the customer.[3] The wealthier Committee members would have been accustomed to buy books unbound, in sheets or in temporary 'boards', and then to bespeak for each the binding used in their personal libraries. But the Bible Society's chosen market, people of the British working class and of the emerging middle class, were not accustomed (or able) to arrange for bookbinding. Foreign readers, too, had to be offered complete books, ready to use.

The bookbinding craft, like the printing trades, went through major changes during the first half century of the BFBS. At the beginning of the period there were few binders, and labour relations between masters and journeymen were amicable. According to a history of Kitcat's, another contemporary bookbinding business, 'As late as 1806 there were not more than 200 journeymen bookbinders in London, whilst the master bookbinders who belonged to the Stationers' Company numbered 124 – a grand total of about 320 working craftsmen.'[4] Within this small industry there were two separate craft cultures, the distinguished and the plebeian binders. The bespoke binders had premises in the West End, while the cheaper East End binders 'flourished in the City, convenient to the booksellers' district in and around Paternoster Row', binding educational books, Bibles, and books for distributors of novels and for the lending libraries. 'Here, speed and economy were the prime considerations and enterprise leaned towards a rudimentary mass production.'[5]

The London bookbinder Thomas Burn of Kirby Street was one of these. He worked mostly in the casual trade, binding small quantities of books at prices established by custom, and often having difficulty in collecting his accounts. All this changed in the summer of 1805, when a delegation of gentlemen from the Bible Society called upon him. They proposed that he tender for the binding of their books. Initially, Burn was suspicious. His 'first impulse was to refuse; he thought it was an attempt to get work done at less than a fair price, or an inducement to try and undersell his neighbours; but his wife pointed out that all he was asked to do was to state the terms on which he could do the work'. The diary of Sarah Bain, their granddaughter, provides this useful sidelight on the impact of the BFBS and their novel ways of doing business upon a settled and custom-bound trade. The Burns discovered 'how great was the advantage and the relief from the custom of settling all accounts monthly'.[6] But like their bookbinding neighbours they were to find that the BFBS drove a hard bargain.

Clearly the BFBS had an immediate, revolutionary, and even shattering effect on the traditional practices and customs of London bookbinding. The gentlemen of the Subcommittee for Printing and General Purposes were prepared to call for tenders, to request large quantities of work, and to pay their accounts every month. The single customers and small-time publishers who constituted the clientele of Burn and his neighbours did not have the financial resources or the commercial habits to do business this way. But for the large merchants and successful professionals of the BFBS, these were natural and desirable ways to proceed. A circular letter dated 18 August 1805 asked Burn and five others for 'the terms on which you are willing to do business for the Society (whose binding will be considerable) viz. The prices in Calf, and in Sheep, *done very strong* . . . specifying the times at which you would expect to settle, and the Discount you allow for immediate payment'. The others were John Bird, David Nelson, Thomas Payne, George Lister and the Philanthropic Society.[7] Eventually the BFBS had a group of regular binders among whom their work was shared: there were about eighteen by 1812, including most of the original six.

The requirement for extra strength, and the peculiarities of the new stereotype editions, made it difficult to settle on a price. The earliest communications with binders had to do with allowances for these considerations. For example David Nelson attended a printing Subcommittee meeting in November 1805 at the New London Tavern. He gave a practical demonstration of 'the difference in the trouble of folding a Sheet of Duodecimo printed in the manner that Testaments usually are, containing 24 pages in a Sheet; and one printed as the Stereotype editions now are, on a larger sheet containing 36 pages'. It was resolved to allow a halfpenny extra when the books were printed in eighteens, with thirty-six pages to fold as three half sheets.[8] The BFBS was introducing to these bookbinders the practical effects of new technology in the printing trades.

The consultations gradually produced a set of expectations, conditions the Society insisted on for their work, with respect to the costs and practices of the binders. Unlike the casual trade, a large contractor like the BFBS could and did set standards. In August of 1808, the Society's binders got together to present a Memorial requesting an advance in the price of books bound in calf leather, as the cost of materials had advanced. The Subcommittee's decision was deferred until standards could be set for the quality of binding required by the Society. Finally it was resolved to allow the advance to the regular binders, as the Committee had found by comparison that their quality was above the norm of the trade.[9]

However the BFBS required books in such great quantities that even their carefully chosen binders often delivered faulty work. A system was devised by which each binder was assigned a number of 'stars'. These were asterisks to be impressed on the front cover of each Bible, a specified number for each binder. When complaints were received, the damage could be traced to its source. When a book traced to John Bird of Hatton Garden was returned by a subscriber in 1810, for example, the binder was removed from the Society's roster. Bird wrote to beg for reinstatement. The Committee, he argued, had required that he use 'expedition . . . which I accordingly did, notwithstanding the very *wet* & improper state for binding I rec[eive]d them from the printing office, which not only much retarded, but likewise rendered it almost impossible for any person to work upon without the paper giving way both in the folding & sewing & consequently the leaves becoming loose'. Bird wanted a chance to explain to the Subcommittee, and to see the book that had led to the original complaint. He did not get one.[10] Leonard Benton Seeley, the Depositary, was asked in 1811 to keep a book in which to enter supplies received from the binders, '& to write against each parcel "well," or "ill, bound;" & that such book be laid before this Sub Committee whenever they meet at the Library'.[11]

By 1812 the Subcommittee for Printing and General Purposes established some 'general principles' to guide and control the quality of binding. The search for an ideal binding for their purpose is similar to Luke Howard's report on paper quality. Committee members established requirements and bullied craftsmen into changing their ancient practices. The Printing Subcommittee at this time included Edward N. Thornton, Josiah Pratt, William Blair, Granville Sharp and Richard Stainforth. Any of these clergymen or laymen might have taken this role; many of them were in close touch with Bible Associations, whose members were doing market research on every doorstep. So were Joseph Tarn, the Assistant Secretary, and Leonard Benton Seeley, the Depositary, who received books from the binders at his Fleet Street warehouse until the Earl Street Bible House was built in 1816.

The books had to be strong enough to withstand the intensive use that evangelicals made of their Bibles. The signatures of folded leaves must be attached firmly to each other by sewing, and to the leather cover by bands or by the new process of hollow backing. At a Subcommittee meeting in June of 1812, the requirements were established.[12] The specifications concerned the method of sewing and the strength of the bands onto which the printed and folded sheets were sewn:

1. That all books shall be Sewed up and down.
2. That all Bibles be bound either on Bands or with Hollow Backs, and that all above 24mo have Five Bands.
3. That no Bands be laid on, but that they be Sewed to the Bands.
4. That those with hollow backs be Rebacked and lined with strong Canvass, and the leather back stiffened with Millboard.
5. That all books have the Backs Hard.
6. That the Headbands be of striped Gingham or Cotton, over a Cord, and well Glued to the Back.
7. That all calf books be finished with a Double Pane.
8. That all calf books have the Boards bent with the hand, to keep close at the fore-edge.
9. That all Testaments in calf be on Bands.
10. That the Books in general be kept from blistering in the back.

The technology is explained and described by H. G. Pollard:

The disadvantage in a hard, smooth, tight back is that ... you cannot open it, without damage ... The remedy for this is the hollow back, a form of binding in which the cords are recessed but the leather back is not glued or pasted on to them, so that when the book lies open, the sides and the back all rest flat on the table, but the recessed cords bend upwards leaving a semicircular space between them and the leather back ... It is unusual to find an English book so bound before 1800.[13]

A few of these books may still be seen in the Bible Society's Library, often fraying enough at the spine to allow a glimpse of the cords and headbands.

At the meeting when the binding principles quoted above were established, the Subcommittee also made decisions about prices and costing for each edition of the scriptures. They insisted 'that Trade List Prices be paid for all Bibles and Testaments in the List, and others in proportion', and 'that it is understood that the Workmen employed on the Society's books be not engaged by Piece-work, unless in cases where they are under the vigilant inspection of their Employer'. Piece-work was becoming a point of contention within the binding trade. From the publisher's point of view, it was a question of quality control, but for journeymen bookbinders facing a devaluation of their trade skills, piece-work was a threat to livelihoods. We shall see, however, that the Society's opposition to piece-work was not maintained when the volume of work increased and when alternative methods of 'vigilant inspection' came into use.

The Committee had to employ binders, like papermakers, in large numbers. No single master binder could employ enough artisans to keep up with the books produced by the Society's printers, not to mention the demand of Bible Associations:

Every Binder employed, or to be hereafter employed, by the Committee, to deliver in a Sample of each English Bible, and Two Sets of each English Testament, bound according to the Society's Patterns, and at the List Prices, which Sample-copies, having been approved by the Comm[itte]e, shall be kept, and the Work of each Binder kept up to that standard.

The meeting concluded with specific arrangements:

That Copies of the several Books above mentioned be delivered to the following Binders, to execute as specimens agreeably to the foregoing regulations: – Mr Burn, Bielefeld, Seear, Collier, Buss, Birch, Ford, Claxton, Polworth, Hayes, Watkins, Kitcat. That Mrs Pettitt, of Angel-street, be continued as a Binder of Testaments in Cloth and Sheep. That Mr Bewsey be also continued as a Cloth-binder. That in consequence of the ill execution of the Books by the Philanthropic Society, after repeated remonstrances, no further supplies be sent to them, until directed by this Sub Committee. That, as it appears that a considerable advance will take place upon Leather, in consequence of the additional Duty on that article, One Penny be added to the Cost Price of each Bible and Testament in the Society's Catalogue.[14]

These minutes of June 1812 reveal the detailed attention given by the Subcommittee to the quality of binding. They now had fourteen master binders to keep track of. The fifteenth, the Philanthropic Society, must have been exasperating. The Subcommittee wished to support this charitable project, which was meant to provide work and wages to poor men, but not at the expense of shoddy work. They were well aware of their own position, having to defend their decisions about binding to the readers who would eventually use the books.

Bible-readers were demanding customers. We have seen how the English poor preferred Small Pica type to smaller faces, and how local Societies tried to accommodate them. These readers and their patrons in Auxiliaries also required correct and very strong binding. Hezekiah Jones wrote from Cadoxton in 1808 about New Testaments bound incomplete: 'it must be either the neglect or the wickedness of the binders: there is great complaint throughout this county & Monmouthshire ... & I am sure not the half is discovered yet'.[15]

The Secretaries tried to be sensitive to complaints from subscribers about poor binding. They were vigilant for neglectful or 'wicked' work, balancing quality control with a need to keep supplies flowing out to the provinces. They also realized, though, that such complaints could be based upon self-interest. A letter from Joseph Tarn to a correspondent at Manchester is illuminating. The anonymous correspondent had complained about both price and quality, comparing BFBS books unfavourably to those of the SPCK. Tarn assured the subscriber that the Committee

employ none but men upon whom they can rely as good workmen; they have, for several years past established a rigid inspection, – the binders are required to use the very best leather, they are allowed to use only a very small number of patches, and are required to line and sew the books in a manner superior to other binders: and the Society pays them accordingly; requiring each binder to have a private mark in the Stamp, by which we may instantly ascertain by whom a book has been bound.

Although of course the occasional blemish might be missed by inspectors, some of the criticism revealed self-interested motives:

we have repeatedly found that persons in different parts of the Country to whom the binding of Bibles for the district in which they live could prove a material advantage (even if taken at a very low price,) have cried down the binding of the Society's books and have also found fault with the price of them.[16]

This was a case where the financial aspect of the Bible transaction might have made a difference to a local Auxiliary. The Committee, however, preferred to entrust their bookbinding budget to Londoners under the eye of Joseph Tarn.[17]

The discussion of binding 'principles' raises the question of cloth binding, an important one for the history of the expanding nineteenth-century book trade. The cost of book production would have been considerably higher had leather not been replaced by cloth, beginning about 1825. Although leather was the traditional material for Bibles, we should not be surprised to find the Committee testing cheaper alternatives. Before bookcloth was invented, canvas was used for many school books and practical manuals. From the Society's pragmatic point of view, canvas was cheap and strong: perfect for the books being demanded by Auxiliaries and Associations. But many bookbinders found canvas unacceptable.[18] The difficulty with canvas, and with all fabric binding materials until bookcloth was developed, was that glue penetrating between the fibres made a stain. Canvas binders were also faced with the conservatism of booksellers, few of whom could be persuaded to try it. The Society had no such difficulty, since it enjoyed a near-captive market for its cheapest editions, and a progressive attitude towards new techniques. The Brevier 12mo New Testament was available in 1811 in cloth at 10d, sheep at a shilling, and calf at 1s 6d.

An article on early cloth bindings by Douglas Leighton assessed canvas as a failure, and bookcloth as an outstanding success. Leighton referred to a second attempt to find an alternative to leather on the one hand or insubstantial boards on the other. This was 'binding in the Vellum Manner', an adaptation of the technique of the vellum or account bookbinder to suit ordinary books. The Society tried this too, corresponding in July and August 1824 with Edward Hickson of King Street, who reported that 'he experienced much difficulty from the opposition of the Society [i.e. trades organization] Workmen who resisted the proposed union of Vellum with Leather Binding'.[19] This is the last we hear of the vellum technique, whose advantages presumably did not outweigh the resistance of workers in the trade.

There was little change in the conventional methods used on leather bindings. Calf and sheep were the primary materials of the first twenty years, and they required few trimmings. Lionel Darley, historian of Burn's shop, says that 'a favourite Bible Society style of binding then [c. 1810–15] was buff-coloured sheep on which a panel was stencilled in grey stain, on both boards, outlined with a chain-patterned blind roll. No lettering appeared on the cover; but even when lettering was required it would be hard to find a title making smaller demands on the finisher's craft.' Finishing was the branch of the binding trade involved with improving the appearance of the finished volume. The Society differed from other clients of the binders in demanding very high standards of strength, but not bothering about aesthetic standards.[20] Figure 12 illustrates a sample of a typical BFBS binding of the early nineteenth century.

The Society's close supervision of binding did a great deal to offset their lack of control over the printing carried out by the privileged Presses. Apart from anything else, it was a check on the printers' accuracy. In 1823 all three privileged Presses were informed 'of the great inconvenience that has arisen among the Binders in consequence of the very defective state of the Register of the several Editions lately received'. The next year the 'Directions for Binding' were further refined, and instead of 'stars' or other anonymous marks, each binder was required 'to affix his name, and place of abode, in the front cover of every book'.[21]

But the bookbinding operation was also the Committee's way of claiming the books as their own, assuring that BFBS-stamped covers would contain only BFBS-approved text. For printers a book was a gathering of sheets, collated and ready for the binder. But for the Committee members, as for their clients, a book was a volume inside hard covers, and they learned how to market it as such. Bound books were discrete packages, with the Society imprimatur. One important reason why the BFBS was committed to selling its books in packages was to ensure the circulation of 'the Bible without note or comment'. To send out books in sheets was to permit clients to bind up with the Old and New Testaments pages of the Apocrypha, or the metrical Psalms, or the Book of Common Prayer. Each of these was the beloved tradition of some members of the Society, and anathema to others. Long before the Apocrypha controversy reached its climax in the mid-twenties, it was clear to the Committee and Secretaries that bound books could not easily be infiltrated with controversial text.

In the earliest and most spiritually rigorous period of the Bible Society's existence, all that was required of bookbinders was durability and speed of execution. The design and format of bindings was of little concern in the days when John Bird was trying to bind wet sheets securely, and others were receiving books from the printers out of register, while the Society's Depositary called repeatedly for large quantities of books for distribution, and supporters like Joseph John Gurney in Norwich warned that 'poor people who have paid their money are very anxious – I might say very importunate for bibles'. The Society was as conservative about design as it was innovative about technology. An 1811 proposal to 'accommodate' members by binding pocket Bibles in various styles was accepted by the Subcommittee and rescinded the same day by the General Committee. A clergyman of Lynn who wrote in 1824 to suggest using clasps and ornamental bindings, was told that his idea 'appeared inexpedient'.[22]

Figure 12   Typical BFBS binding, *c.* 1816

But this approach changed in the 1830s, as the supply of strong binding was taken for granted, and as aesthetic considerations began to enter the consciousness of some members and subscribers. There was a demand not only for cheap books for distribution to the poor, but also for attractively packaged volumes for the personal use of people who supported the publisher's philanthropic project. During these years, the Bible Society's Committee took the twenty-one Bibles and twelve Testaments offered in the English language by the privileged Presses and caused them to be bound in a bewildering variety of covers: cloth, canvas, and leather of various qualities. The bindings were intended to alert contemporaries to their designated market: they delineated very clear distinctions of social class. Sheep, calf and canvas were for the poor; roan, morocco and coloured calf (with or without gilt edges) indicated that one supported the Bible Society and was not the object of its charity. Table 9 shows the variety of bindings in which a single edition of the Small Pica Bible (octavo without references) appeared, and how the prices varied accordingly.

The new materials made an impression. Books bound with gilt edges in the inexpensive but attractive new leathers looked shiny, textured and fresh after the dull tan (plain sheep or calf) of earlier editions. The plain bindings continued, however, in the charity books. The Society saved over £9,000 in less than three years by using canvas instead of leather for 60,000 Bibles and over 100,000 New Testaments destined for free grants during the mid-1830s.[23] After the 1840 price reduction such books bore stamps proclaiming the price as well as the user's social status: 'British and Foreign Bible Society, Sold under Cost, Fourpence.' But the BFBS was not only subsidizing the cost prices of cheap Bibles: it was also establishing that price. We have seen how it influenced the prices set by the privileged Presses at this time. The Society also used its economic power in the market-place to reduce the wages paid to bookbinders.

Because the BFBS dominated the market for cheap Bibles, it is important to look at the Society's influence on labour relations in the binding trades. In this field there was extensive use of semi-skilled labour and, as in printing, a growing concern about the incursion of machinery. As in printing, the Society could make or break a business by extending or withholding its trade. We have seen how the Bible Society's custom was the foundation of Thomas (and later William) Burn's prosperity. Two other binders, William Ford and Samuel A. Bielefeld, were less fortunate. These men had a conflict with the Depositary Richard Cockle in 1827. They printed a circular letter to the 'Governors & Friends' of the BFBS alleging Cockle's misconduct. The minutes merely record that their work was terminated. Several months later they were reduced to petitioning for reinstatement. William Ford said that his attention to BFBS work had prevented his developing any other clientele. Bielefeld, after binding for the Society for twenty-one years, had found no

Table 9. *Binding materials and prices, Small Pica 8vo Bibles without references, 1811–64*

Format	Material	Dates	Paper quality, lettering, edges	Price
Demy	Calf	1811		8/6
		1841–2	inferior, lettered	6/2
	Sheep	1841–2	inferior	5/2
Medium	Calf	1812–17		12/0
		1818–19		11/6
		1820		11/0
		1821		10/6
		1822–3		10/0
		1834–8		8/3
		1839–40		7/3
		1841–2	inferior	6/2
		1841–2	second quality, lettered	7/3
		1841–2	fine quality, lettered	8/3
	Sheep	1841–2		6/3
		1843–5		5/0
		1846–54	charity edition	4/9
		1856–64	lettered	2/6
	Coloured calf	1834–8	lettered	10/0
		1839–40	lettered	8/6
		1843–5		6/2
		1844	fine	8/3
		1846–55		5/0
		1856–9	marbled edges	5/0
		1860–4	fine, marbled	5/0
	Morocco	1842	fine, gilt	12/6
	Persian basil	1855		4/6
		1856–64		3/0
		1856–64	fine, marbled	4/6
	Embossed cloth	1860–4	(charity edition)	2/6
Royal	Calf	1813–18		21/0
		1819		20/0
		1820–1	fine	19/6
		1822–30		18/0

work for himself or his sons for seventeen months. Both petitions were refused. The books published from 1830 were packaged in the binding shops of Thomas Burn, George Collier, Cross, Hickson and Watkins.[24]

Individual efforts on the part of master bookbinders gave way to collective action by their journeymen, to what Ellic Howe and John Child, in *The Society of London Bookbinders*, call 'The Bible Disputes'. The Trade Society of Journeymen Bookbinders was by this time a well-organized union, but they were facing problems with mechanization and the accompanying trend to piece-work, which was dividing the membership. Many time-workers believed that all their dues were going to support out-of-work piece-workers, whose proper course would have been to insist upon being paid at time rates. Their Secretary, T. J. Dunning, was a brilliant organizer and rhetorician. Dunning was a prototype of a 'new model' unionist. An important part of his strategy was to get meetings of the Trades' Society out of public houses, and into places where decisions could be made without the influences of tobacco and beer. According to his biographers, Dunning's gifts included 'the power of reasoning, the capacity for lucid expression, and a personal magnetism that caused him to be almost worshipped by his followers'.[25]

Dunning and his union members, as well as their employers, were fully aware of the effect the BFBS project had on their prospects. More books were being bound, but at the lowest prices, piece-work, using machinery whenever possible, while competition among the workshops was manipulated. Master binder William Burn, for example, extended his workshop from Kirby Street to Hatton Gardens in the mid thirties: 'While workshop space thus increased, work itself showed a contrary inclination: the Bible Society, demanding ever cheaper prices, now shared its work among four binders. This led to the introduction of piece-work systems in the workshops and thereafter to bickering over rates for jobs that ended in the strike of 1837.'[26]

Although Lionel Darley rightly sees the BFBS influence as crucial to the labour history of binding, the SPCK was in fact the first Society to persuade master binders to reduce their prices, in 1826, an action that resulted in a strike. The union of Journeymen Bookbinders published an address, not only stating the distress of the working class in general and of bookbinders in particular, but calling into question the honour of the SPCK:

We cannot suppose for a moment that a Society composed of the most illustrious Characters in Church and State, and formed for the express purpose of disseminating the Holy Scriptures ... would sanction any measure which had the effect of reducing an industrious class of men to a state of pauperism. They therefore respectfully solicit an investigation, on the part of the Society, into the conduct of the ... Employers.[27]

The workers failed to shame the SPCK into taking action, and had to return to work at the same wages. The tactic was to be tried repeatedly against the BFBS, never successfully. But it had a profound indirect impact on the Society's reputation.

In 1832 the Journeymen Bookbinders of London and Westminster petitioned the BFBS Committee 'to discountenance the use of the Rolling Machine, as a substitute for Manual labour, in compressing the books bound for this Society'. This machine, which had been invented by William Burn in 1827 was 'an apparatus consisting of a heavy iron mangle designed to press flat sheets of printed matter before they were folded and sewn. [It] threatened the livelihood of the Beaters, a semi-skilled class of worker who used heavy beating hammers to flatten the surface of the paper.' The machine could compress an average-sized Bible to five-sixths its former size in one minute, as compared to twenty minutes beaten by hand.[28] In their petition the journeymen told the BFBS Committee that nearly fifty men, half of whom worked on Bibles, had been driven out of work by the rolling machine. They offered to set up a trial, comparing machine and hand work. In a later letter they pointed out that religious societies in the Baptist and Methodist connections had prohibited the use of machinery in their printing.[29] But the Committee members were more impressed with technological improvement than with the sufferings of the beaters. It was 'resolved that the point, which these documents embrace, appears to be one in which the Committee cannot interfere, it being a matter entirely between the Masters and their workmen'.[30] This policy of non-interference did not change the fact that the Society's ambitious project and the way they chose to implement it had already greatly influenced the customary structures and practices of the cheaper end of the bookbinding trade.

In 1833 there arose another Bible dispute, and another appeal from artisans to what they apparently took to be the charitable impulses of a religious society. According to the trade union records consulted by Howe and Child, the master binders had reduced quality as well as piece-work rates and also imported blackleg labour. When the British and Foreign Bible Society was memorialized, 'the appeal was callously neglected by the committee of the B.F.B.S., whose insistence upon cheap production had started the trouble, and whose continued pressure on the employers had vitiated any chance of a settlement'. According to Ramsay MacDonald's study of women in the printing trades, a compromise between the two sides was prevented when 'a representative of the Bible Society instructed the masters to hold out'. No record of this instruction has been found in the Society's minute books or correspondence.[31]

The 1833 dispute included concern about the position of women working in the binding shops. The memorial 'respectfully submit[ted] that the making it more difficult, and in some cases impossible, for females to earn an honest subsistence, by their labour, is in the same proportion to give potency to the seducers of female virtue'. The notion that women who failed to earn enough at honest labour might turn to prostitution was a powerful one. The BFBS Committee, however, ignored Dunning's appeal to their chivalry and respectability, and issued a document informing the public that its binders had assured them that 'competent and industrious men in our employ earn on an average 6*d* an hour or 30*s* weekly when in constant work; and women in the same description from 8*s* to 10*s* and upwards'.[32] The differential between men's and women's wages was not at issue. Ten shillings was widely regarded as a fair wage for a woman, but the memorial claimed that some were working for much less. It is important to note, too, that the women were not members of the Journeymen Bookbinders Trade Society. Dunning's appeal on their behalf was designed to help his fellow workers by indirection, by an appeal to middle-class sensibilities. Not all of Dunning's members understood and accepted the subtlety of this strategy, complaining that the women's interests were placed above their own. This strike was a long one, in which the bookbinders managed to stay off work from January to August. Howe and Child attribute this circumstance to the contemporary strength of trades unionism: 'the working class of Britain was united as it had seldom been in its history'.[33]

Yet another dispute developed in 1842–3, and again the Bible Society was appealed to. This time Dunning carried his campaign to the general 'religious public', by publishing pamphlets and writing to the newspapers. Presumably he calculated that others would be more susceptible than the Earl Street Committee to his rhetoric of female depravity in the Bible shops. He wrote to the Society in January 1842, enclosing a memorial complaining of price reductions on the Pearl Bibles, bound in roan leather with gilt edges. Dunning's 'Memorial' was published in some newspapers, including the evangelically oriented *Patriot*. This document too alluded to the sexual purity of women binders. It also stressed the luxurious nature of the books in question. By March at least three members had withdrawn their subscriptions in protest, and dozens of others were asking the Committee to justify its line of conduct.[34]

A letter from Mr S. Ranyard, a subscriber at Kingston, serves as an example of the criticism being stirred up by the Society's business methods. Ranyard had read the *Patriot*, and found the Society's reply 'very short and destitute of expressions of regard to and sympathy for the case of those who complained of suffering and oppression which might naturally have been expected from a religious body under such circumstances'. Ranyard begged his District Secretary to tell him the truth about the allegations. He concluded by noting that:

the binding chiefly pointed at was of those books which are most distinguished by external appearances, in fact, books suited to the affluent and not to the poor, the question rises in my mind, whether it is strictly within the provision of the bible Society to produce such books and by the aid of a powerful combination for a religious purpose, so to produce them that the rich shall obtain the utmost for their gold and the poor be driven by necessity to accept the smallest possible remuneration for their labour.[35]

The remark shows how the proliferation of new and luxurious formats was closely connected with the tension over labour relations.

The Committee asked the five master bookbinders to attend its 17 February meeting, impressed upon them the seriousness of the matter, and asked them to draft written replies to the Journeymen's circular. The master binders' letters merely stated the usual rates paid, time and piece-work, to men and women. The BFBS printed these replies without comment or self-defence, expressing a regret 'that the reply of their Secretary to a Memorial . . . should have been considered harsh and abrupt'.[36] This had to satisfy Ranyard and others. It was the maximum intervention the Committee was prepared to make between their contract binders and the journeymen and 'females' who did the actual work.

This 'Bible dispute' was not a strike. In an article written twenty years later, T. J. Dunning reminded the members of the Trade Society that this and the subsequent dispute of 1849 – 50 'took the form of controversies in print instead of "strikes"'. Similarly his biographers state that 'he saw that the result of disputes was neither influenced nor decided by the rights of the parties, but by their tactics and resources, as in a military operation'.[37] For Dunning, who was attempting to shape the Bookbinders into a modern trade society, the controversy in print was an excellent tactic. Printing and postage were resources much less expensive than strike pay. More important in the long run, someone with his rhetorical skills could appeal to middle-class public opinion. He was aware that the blind anger of journeymen exploited by the master binders over some aspect of their traditional methods, however justifiable, was incomprehensible to the general public, especially when that public was prejudiced against combinations of workers. With great subtlety, Dunning chose to play upon other values embraced by the middle class, the growing belief that women needed to be sheltered from a harsh world, and the equally powerful notions that had been shaped by their forty-years' participation in the Bible transaction.

The Committee believed their claim to impartiality was justified, because the disputes over binding were not between themselves and the master binders, but between journeymen members of a trades union and the five owners who did the Society's binding. None of the masters could afford to appeal to the BFBS for an increase in rates. On the contrary. They were competing fiercely for contracts to bind the new cheaply printed editions. The Society for its part wished to extend to packaging the savings they had already negotiated for the production of the new product. As contractors of labour the Committee members showed themselves to be as parsimonious as any other Victorian business operators, and just as likely to use the rhetoric of political economy and free trade to justify their actions. Their critics seized the opportunity to accuse them of grinding the faces of the poor and of driving women into prostitution.

As we have seen, BFBS prices for Bibles and Testaments were drastically reduced for nine months in 1840, to meet the needs of Sunday Schools, then raised again when Auxiliary members failed to donate enough charitable funds to cover the loss. Prices dropped again five years later, when the privileged Presses, in the circumstances of the 'monopoly' agitation, offered new editions of somewhat poorer quality at appropriately low prices. In the background to this unstable situation were cheap books printed in Scotland and beginning to flood the English market.

In January of 1845, some Committee members proposed a further reduction in the price of Bibles for the domestic market, a reduction to be effected by lowering the prices paid for bookbinding. They wanted to call for tenders, from the group of binders already doing the work, as well as from outside. Andrew Brandram, the Anglican Secretary, had to threaten to resign before this plan was set aside. In a twelve-page, closely printed pamphlet labelled 'entirely private and confidential' Brandram argued that this plan was not only unfair to the master binders with whom he and his colleagues had been working. It was also unnecessary for the Society's luxury Bibles to compete with the extremely cheap ones now available from Scotland. It looked, he said, 'just as if the Society were nothing more than a trading establishment struggling for existence, and obliged, like such establishments, not to be nice in the means pursued to maintain that existence'.[38] Brandram knew that the Society was already virtually setting the bookbinding prices, and that competition would cause the established shops to reduce prices to the point of deteriorating quality, or to 'an oppression of the workman – I mean the master binder'. Even in a confidential memo to the Committee, Brandram did not wish to get into a discussion of the wages paid to the men and women who actually bound the books. He concluded, 'I throw myself between the Committee and [the master binders].' His resignation was not accepted, but nor did the Committee stop behaving like a trading establishment.

In May of 1845, notwithstanding Brandram's opposition, the Committee decided that the 'mode for conducting the binding of the Society . . . should be by Contract'. Contract was a significant word in nineteenth-century business terminology, an important way of managing the volume of work and the supervision of staff on large projects.[39] In the case of the Bible Society, it meant an agreement to bind all books for a fixed price over a period of years, as against tendering for each separate job. The successful bidder could offer to bind individual copies for less than a smaller craftsman could, because he or she could institute economies of scale. But such economies were possible only if the large volume of BFBS work was guaranteed to pass through one shop. In several subsequent letters and in a newspaper announcement, Brandram explained the process of tendering the contract: 'We addressed ourselves to 16 parties of known respectability. It was not an absolutely open competition which might have induced some persons to offer proposals which they would only realize by oppressing their workpeople; we looked for respectability of character.'[40] Brandram in another letter confided to a correspondent 'I hate contract work. But I am sure if work is to be done (and it is the system of the day) by contract, the contractor must not be interfered with by those whom he contracts with.' He added that 'gentlemen of business [on the Committee] who have large experience of contract work are of our mind'.[41] Presumably Brandram would have preferred the control that was possible when the Society divided its work among a select group of master binders.

By July tenders had been called from shops interested in handling half the Society's binding. Lorina M. Watkins of 8 Paradise Row, Southwark, offered a further discount for the entire BFBS contract as well as competitive terms for half. Miss Watkins was the daughter of Thomas Watkins, who with his wife had bound for the Society on and off since 1812. Thomas left home some time in the 1820s and Mrs Watkins petitioned to be allowed to carry on the work, which was issued under the initials of her daughter, L. M. Watkins.[42] In the 1845 competition, Lorina Watkins's was the lowest tender of the sixteen 'respectable' bookbinders canvassed, and it was accepted. She 'expressed herself grateful ... and gave her assurance that justice should be done to the Society in the work committed to her'.[43]

Business boomed. At the time of the contract the expectation was about 2,000 books per diem, but by November the daily rate was 3,000 and increasing. When she was able to supply extra Bibles and Testaments for an exceptional demand in Manchester that month, C. S. Dudley called Lorina Watkins 'an honour to her Sex & Country', and added an outrageous pun: 'If she is not the Maid of *Orleans*, she certainly is the *Maid of Roan*, alias Rouen.'[44] Watkins applied for and received an allowance to acquire additional machinery and overlookers. In March 1848 the contract was renewed for a further three years.[45] Just as large volumes meant low prices for the BFBS and the Presses, the massive amount of work guaranteed to pass through her shop allowed Watkins to bind for less. She was no longer competing for work with William Burn and the other three master binders who had shared the Society's work. Burn was the only one of the four who did not go out of business.[46]

The BFBS had granted a monopoly to a single bookbinding firm, which allowed them to reduce the price of books. They did not think of it as a monopoly like that of the privileged presses, but as a triumph of *laissez-faire*, since Watkins had competed with other binders in a free market for the Society's exclusive contract. Despite the urging of Brandram and others, there was apparently a majority of Committee members who wanted the Society to compete in the whole spectrum of the Bible market, not just to supply cheap charity editions to the British poor, and foreign-language texts abroad. If prices were going down, the BFBS had to find a way to lower its own. It is clear, however, that the increased efficiency acted to limit flexibility and choice. When Miss Watkins reduced wages to her workpeople in the middle of the second contract period, the Committee was helpless in the face of a public outcry. And Andrew Brandram found himself defending a policy that he himself opposed on moral grounds, and had argued against as a practical proposition.

There erupted in 1849–50 a scandal over the wages and working conditions experienced by women working at Watkins's shop. These events present an excellent opportunity to investigate popular attitudes, towards both the

BFBS and the cheap Bible, at mid-century. It became clear that the Bible transaction was more than a matter of buying and selling books at moderate prices: indeed the level of cheapness appropriate to a religious society was for the first time called dramatically into question. Bible Auxiliary and Association members insisted that they too had a right to view themselves as parties in a labour struggle over the cost of bookbinding. They were concerned about the morality of the Committee's business methods, because they considered the ethics of labour struggles from a religious point of view, not simply as a commercial and business proposition.

The story of the dispute between Lorina M. Watkins and her staff of male and female bookbinders also constitutes an important and as yet unwritten chapter in women's history and labour history. Here was an unmarried woman, the proprietor and spokesperson for her business. In letters cited below, the fact that a 'contractress' was exploiting poor female workers seems to have provoked a special outrage. The control of a business by a female proprietor raises interesting questions that go beyond the limits of the history of books.[47]

The roan gilt-edged books that were to become famous in the Watkins dispute were undeniably popular, and competitively priced at 10d. Such books as the Pearl 24mo Bible became more ornate, and more competitively priced during the forties and fifties. New leather products were available. 'Persian basil', reputed to be stronger than sheep, could be finished either smooth or 'hard grained, similar to Morocco', and dyed.[48] Additional trimmings took the form of circuit bindings (metal edges around the covers), and later rims and clasps to protect and embellish the books.[49] Bookcloth had long since replaced canvas and become a respectable binding material. And bookbinding had become an industry employing large numbers of workers.

The affair began with the publication on 17 August 1849 of an *Appeal of the Journeymen Bookbinders of London and Westminster to the Committee, Members, Donors, and Subscribers, of the British and Foreign Bible Society, and the Religious Public in General, on the subject of Cheap Bibles*. It was an eloquently phrased public statement from the trade society on behalf of the women who worked in Watkins's shop. T. J. Dunning had received detailed information from one of them, Mary E. Zugg.[50] The *Appeal* began, 'That the Word of God should be distributed at the lowest possible price, is a proposition which no one will dispute; but ... it is contrary to every precept which it [the Bible] contains to do this by unlawful means – to produce this desired cheapness at the cost of those whose labour prepares this holy volume for its readers.'

Dunning stated clearly that he was not concerned with the price of 'School' Bibles and Testaments bound below cost for the use of the poor, noting that the difference between cost and selling price was made up by donations. But in the case of the desirable and fashionable Pearl Bible – bound in embossed roan with gilt edges – the contract price did not allow for any profit to Miss

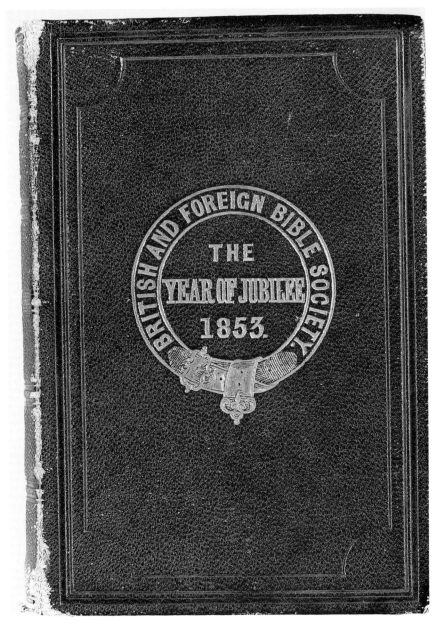

Figure 13 Binding to celebrate the BFBS Golden Jubilee, 1853.

Watkins. It could be sold by the BFBS at 10d only by sweating the women workers. Dunning stated that women could usually earn no more than 6s per week, working ten hours daily, Monday to Saturday, which was significantly less than that paid by the binders for the Society for Promoting Christian Knowledge. Moreover the women were fined so heavily for faulty work that their wages were further reduced. 'It is a melancholy circumstance', he claimed,

that the female labour should contribute to make the Bible cheap. Females often have not the power to plead their cause in such matters, and being helpless in many respects where their wages are concerned, they are trodden down until a state of things, such as described in the Song of the Shirt, appals the mind with the enormity of their injuries, their suffering, and their moral condition.

Dunning went further in his comparison of bookbinders and the needlewomen whom Thomas Hood's poem 'The Song of the Shirt' and Mayhew's revelations in the *Morning Chronicle* had brought to popular attention:

We are quite aware that there is no necessary connection between unchastity and poverty ... however ... instances incontestable, and, alas, almost innumerable, have been adduced of the wiles of the seducer having had greater potency from insufficient wages; ... we fear that some [cases of this description] can be adduced from the shop of the contractress of the British and Foreign Bible Society, of females who attribute their first departure from the paths of virtue to the insufficient wages paid in that establishment.

Dunning claimed that the Journeymen Bookbinders' quarrel was not with Watkins, but with the Committee of the Bible Society. He noted that their response to the 1843 dispute had been unsatisfactory ('what we then stated was met by counter statements, which we were not allowed either to examine or to know even their exact purport'). His appeal therefore was over their heads, to the religious public, in whose good faith he professed himself confident. Certainly the *Appeal* raised considerable alarm among members, alarm which was to reverberate for years.[51]

The women binders 'struck' work on 18 August, the day after the *Appeal* was printed, but before many of them had read it. They were duped into signing a document which they were told was a statement that they had nothing to do with the *Appeal*. In a subsequent pamphlet Dunning described how they were tricked: 'After they had all signed it, to the number of 64, the forewoman said, "Of course you know what you have signed? ... Of course you are aware that you have signed this paper to state to the Committee (of the British and Foreign Bible Society) that you are perfectly satisfied with the prices paid for the Society's work?"'[52] The forewoman then showed her employees the heading of the paper they had signed, and their strike the following day resulted from their failure to have the false statement returned or destroyed. That evening they went to Dunning for help, at the Monarch

Coffee House in Bloomsbury. He advised them to return to work, and also drew up a counterstatement for them to sign, and forwarded it to the Committee of the British and Foreign Bible Society. The BFBS archives contain the counterstatement, with its sixty straggling signatures, and a file copy of Andrew Brandram's frosty reply, 'as [our Committee] have not received the memorial, or whatever else it may be called ... I have no observation to make upon the matter'.[53] This remained the stated position of the parent Society, that 'they have no duty to perform [in the matter] excepting that of abstaining from meddling in it'. It was, in their view, an affair between the women workers and their protectors in the trades union on the one hand, and the 'contractress' on the other.

Officially at least: but behind the scenes the Committee and their Secretaries worked hard to mitigate the damage done by Dunning's publicity about working conditions at the Watkins shop. The *Appeal* was widely circulated. Not only was it reprinted in several newspapers, but the Trade Society sent copies to many BFBS subscribers. The archives of the Society contain a spate of correspondence from members and supporters whose consciences were aroused on the subject, while the file of outward-bound letters indicates that at least some of these were answered. On the first of September, George Cartwright of Lyme Regis, Dorset, wrote to Andrew Brandram:

Should [the *Appeal*] prove true it will deeply injure the Society as no one of Christian principles would like to sanction circulating the word of God at the expense of poor helpless women whose earnings are so cruelly cut down in the binding of Bibles (3 Shillings a hundred below the Christian Knowledge Society!!) Such low wages given by the Contractor (or Contractress!!!) appear very much like pandering to the vicious and selfish public, who in their morbid desire for cheapness, are reckless & indifferent to the misery & want of the Producers, who are thus forced (by a professing Religious Society) to work for the most inadequate wages, a sin condemn'd continually throughout the very Book we publish & take such pains to propagate.

If the British & Foreign Bible Society is to teach uprightness to the Chinese, just dealings to the New Zealander & the laws of Christ from Greenland's Icy Mountains to India's Coral Strand, you will I am sure agree with me, that, our work must not be open to the charge of hypocrisy in giving or rather withholding fair wages to the Poor workwomen whom the Bible Society employs.

The Rev. David Wheeler of Worcester spoke for many: 'I have often thought in our circumstances at least in Worcester, the gilt Edge Bibles were unnecessarily cheap – & that 1/- would have been given as readily as 10*d*.' The Rev. H. G. Bunsen, vicar of Lilleshall, Newport, Shropshire said the same thing, adding 'it seems ... inconsistent with our Christian profession'. Frederick Coombs, of Bush Lane, Trent, Cornwall, was not waiting for further reassurances. He wanted his name withdrawn from the list of subscribers: 'The contract system, I am convinced, is unjust toward the poor.' And Samuel Minton of Liverpool 'would as soon give a guinea to the

Propaganda as to the B & F Bible Soc – if there is any foundation whatever for such a complaint against it'.[54]

Other correspondents urged the Secretaries and the Committee to investigate the complaints: The Rev. Dr William Marsh of Leamington agreed that the Society had nothing to do with how the contractor executes the contract, but 'It appears that it would silence the mouths of Gainsayers if two or three of the London Com[itt]ee would ascertain the fact ... It is very desirable for Auxiliaries to have the power to answer explicitly such Charges, because the Jesuit is abroad.' And C. S. Dudley, on his peregrinations about the country, wrote from Manchester to warn his colleagues that 'The Book-binding question is producing *much* dissatisfaction ...'. After more details he continued: 'I wrote to Mr Cockle for some Copies of Miss Watkins's publications, in order that *some* answer might be given to the numerous inquiries ... but he can send me only 6 of each, adding that "you have no idea of the actual Cost of this Conflict to the Society's Binding Contractor, who must of course print & circulate it at her own cost".' Dudley was convinced 'of the impropriety & inexpediency of our becoming a Board for the regulation of wages, which should be left to find their own level; but on the other hand something should surely be done to attenuate, if we cannot *satisfy* the uneasiness of many valued friends. If the Committee decide on doing nothing, should not Miss Watkins be enabled to defend herself?'[55]

Apparently not. Despite Dunning's dire allegations that Cockle 'exercises as much control over the binding establishment as he would if it were in his own department in the Society's House in Earl-street', the published answers, with one exception, were in the name of L. M. Watkins. She addressed herself in the *Morning Herald* and other newspapers, 'To the Subscribers and Friends of the British and Foreign Bible Society', giving details of wages and practices. Dunning replied in another pamphlet, the *Address* of 10 October, which refuted Watkins's statement and announced that Dunning had made a proposal to the Bible Society. Since the wages book of Watkins's shop would be 'irrefragable' evidence of the true situation, he suggested that representatives of both sides examine it together.[56] Brandram declined this proposal, to the published 'astonishment' but probably not to the surprise of T. J. Dunning. Instead Watkins published a 'Tabular Statement', which purported to show the wages paid. Dunning analysed the document in order to prove to the Society that it was a fabrication, not accounting for the lowest-paid workers: 'regarded logically it is absurd; regarded morally it calls for terms we do not chuse to write'.[57]

The binders received valuable support from a stinging satire in *Punch*, which purported to report on 'a recent meeting of African savages ... a meeting conducted with the greatest decorum and resulting in most pious resolutions'.

The purpose of the meeting to take into consideration the benighted condition of certain individuals, known as the Committee of the British and Foreign Society. ... it was written in the paper, the Morning Tongue, that though silent, talked to the English nation . . . [that] the young women who folded and stitched the Bibles and Testaments for the Society – the Scripture Slaves as the old man called them – could not, one with the other, earn more than 5*s* 6*d* a week . . . 'The Committee of the British and Foreign Bible Society . . . offer manna to black man, and ashes to white girl.'

After more heavy ironies, *Punch*'s 'Little Bird' concluded: 'It is to be hoped that the benighted Committee of the British and Foreign Society, who sell cheap Bibles at the likely cost of female purity, will give patient ear to the teachings of the philanthropic savages.' Around the same time the London *Weekly Times* published an article under the heading 'Bibles and Brothels'.[58]

The Committee, however, still had loyal allies and formidable resources. Two local Auxiliaries announced their intention of inquiring into the affair. Brandram appears to have instigated these investigations. A letter to him from Edward Corderoy of the Southwark Auxiliary notes that 'we found that the Binding question was interfering with our Subscriptions – so that independent of your suggestion we must have taken notice of it'. Brandram told them that 'your [investigating] from an Auxiliary is a very different thing to the Parent Society taking such a step'.[59] The results of the investigations were published in the Bible Society's *Monthly Extracts from the Correspondence* on 28 February 1850. The Southwark Auxiliary Subcommittee reported that it had visited the workshop and inquired into the wages and other circumstances. The wages of a hard-working folder who was willing to put in a full week were found to range from 11s to 14s per week. To the sceptical astonishment of Dunning (see below) a wages book produced for their examination bore out these findings.

The Southwark delegation also looked into 'The Comforts and Conveniences', a subject that had been mentioned in the *Appeal*. Although they made no reference to the water on floors noted in the pamphlet, and although the drinking-water filter they were shown was a recent innovation, their praises were reserved for the moral aspects of the 'lofty, well lighted and well ventilated' workshops: 'the whole are well arranged, by their construction, for separating the men's from the women's department'. None of the tradesmen's or the workwomen's appeals had mentioned the problem. The Southwark Subcommittee were presumably, like Dunning with his claims of prostitution, seeking to appeal to outraged middle-class morality. The same *Monthly Extracts* published a second report, from Lieut. H. Coode (RN) and Robert Dixon Box, the Secretaries of the Westminster Auxiliary Society. They took up Dunning's challenge that 'there was no Workshop in the Trade wherein the comfort of the Work-people is so entirely disregarded'. On the contrary, 'the Deputation . . . have never seen workshops in any trade more replete with comfort than those built by Miss Watkins'.

However, one of the district Associations within the Westminster Auxiliary, the Seven Dials Association, dissented from this report. Dunning's final publication on the subject, the 'Reply', notes this fact, which fortunately may be confirmed, since the minute books of the Westminster Auxiliary are among those that have survived in the BFBS archives. A delegation from the Seven Dials Association had asked their Auxiliary Committee in November, at the height of the publicity, to investigate the situation. They told Coode and Box they would withdraw if the answer was unsatisfactory, and purchase Bibles elsewhere. It is clear from the minutes that this cool threat was a significant motive behind the Westminster investigation. After the visit to Watkins's shop on 10 December, the Seven Dials people decided that some of Dunning's charges had been answered, but those that had not must be referred back to the delegation for a second visit. This time members from Seven Dials were to be present.

Arthur Cribb, Secretary of the Seven Dials Bible Association, had apparently expected to attend, but was unable to go to the morning visit (which had originally been planned for 4 or 5 p.m.). He was replaced by two Association members who were, it turned out, less sympathetic than Cribb to the Bookbinders' appeal, and more amenable to whitewashing the Bible Society. The result was that the Seven Dials Association withdrew from the Westminster Auxiliary.[60] There is no record of whether or not its members continued with Bible distribution unaided by the parent Society. There is scarcely any record of the break at all – certainly not in the minutes and correspondence produced at Earl Street, or in the printed report of the Westminster Auxiliary. But subsequent reports show no activity for several years under the heading 'Seven Dials Association'.

Dunning, characteristically, knew all about it. He entered the argument one last time, with a pamphlet published in March 1850.[61] In twelve very detailed pages, Dunning accused Watkins of showing the Southwark Committee a false wages book. He adduced independent evidence in support of the claim, and reiterated the five attempts to get the Bible Society to agree to a joint opening of the disputed records, six months earlier. He had even applied to the Archbishop of Canterbury, one of the Vice-Presidents of the Society, who informed Dunning 'that he has never taken any part in the details of management [of the BFBS] or attended any Committee Meetings. He cannot, therefore, with propriety, interfere now in the question ... on which the Committee ... are alone able to judge correctly.' Gleefully quoting scripture passages about the inadvisability of grinding the faces of the poor, Dunning retired from the controversy. He had battles to fight within his own trade society, including a serious one with members who had opposed providing any support to the women bookbinders, since they were not members of the Journeymen's Society.

The evidence on both sides was complex and contradictory, involving issues of time- vs. piece-work, and prices paid to learners vs. experienced hands. Dunning's arguments, however, seem to have stood up, for the most part. He may have been wrong that the Bible Society Depositary was the puppet-master behind Miss Watkins's intransigence. But Dunning was right that the monopoly contract forced the price of binding down to a point that sweated the workers involved. And he was right about the kind of rhetoric that would appeal to 'the religious public'. He knew that his audience was not sympathetic to workers.

> Most of those to whom this is addressed will have heard of such a thing [a strike], and have, doubtless, associated it with everything that is atrocious. We entreat attention to this part, of our reply. Fishes in their agony cannot scream, and it often happens that workpeople are as unable to set forth the causes which have led to these occurrences. Hence the obloquy with which they are regarded . . . [I]t seldom happens that a strike occurs without some bitter wrong having been felt as its cause.[62]

It was Dunning's genius to use the fact that workwomen, cast as potential prostitutes, were a more sympathetic subject than their male colleagues.

The 'Bible Dispute' indicates that the Committee, acting as publisher, conformed to the stereotype of a hard-hearted Victorian employer. Dunning cited their policy of letting wages find their own level: 'Who does not know that this means that they have a right to all the advantages that the want and misery of a depreciated labour market brings to those who employ labour? No matter the vice that follows: it is our harvest, we have a right to it, and therefore "we ought not to interfere".' None of this should surprise us: we know the Committee was a collection of merchants and professionals who shared the business ethics of their contemporaries, and who demonstrably were very keen managers. But it was a shock to members who had created in their minds an image of an ideal 'religious society', whose leaders would always 'do what is right'. The press and letter campaign from the membership indicates that much of popular evangelicalism did not share their leaders' tough-mindedness. Many individuals were appalled that scripture circulation and female destitution could exist in juxtaposition. The Agent in Wales, T. Phillips, reported 'I am already sadly teased by the Bookbinders *Circular*. The *Ladies* begin to plead for them.'

Although the *Appeal*, *Address* and *Reply to a Letter* were all widely circulated (the *Appeal* was reprinted in November 1849), the bookbinders were at a disadvantage with respect to propaganda. The Bible Society Committee had in its power the *Monthly Extracts* and could easily suppress such information as the defection of the Seven Dials Association or the possible forgery of a wages book. More importantly, it had great reserves of public trust, so that for most members a mere reassurance was enough to quell their doubts. As Dunning said of his fellow workpeople, 'we do not possess that oft-times dangerous advantage of commanding belief, from our position in society. We have, therefore, been obliged to prove, or to give reasons for, everything.'[63] The BFBS did not address the situation directly, by increasing the payments for binding or even investigating Dunning's charges. Instead they operated an energetic publicity campaign to discredit the binders and assert the business morality of themselves and their 'contractress'. Being in the book trade, the journeymen binders were perhaps better able to take their campaign to the public than were other unions. But their opponents, too, were major publishers. The BFBS had ample resources to mount a publicity campaign.[64]

In the Watkins affair it is clear that the London Committee was sensitive to criticism from the provinces, but not to the point of engaging in unprofitable business practices. The same shrewd commercial instincts that they brought to relationships with the privileged Presses, the Committee also applied to the bookbinding business. But London master bookbinders, like London master printers, were not protected by any government monopoly – theirs was a fully competitive enterprise, subject to economic and technological fluctuations and unprotected by such formidable institutional structures as the Crown and the two ancient Universities. Although Brandram demurred, he was overruled by a Committee whose members saw no reason not to have work done by contract, when 'it is the system of the day'.

The Bible Society management reckoned themselves and the master book-binders to be the only legitimate participants in the Bible transaction. Neither the artisans nor their own membership came into their calculations. Popular evangelical enthusiasm was stirred when a trade union of Journey-men Bookbinders accused the BFBS of 'grinding the faces of the poor'. Having encouraged, and benefited economically from, the popularization of the Bible transaction, the Committee suffered from the backlash of outraged public opinion. When the Journeymen Bookbinders 'appealed to the religious public', there was a controversy, but no permanent change. The Committee's policy of selling books to middle-class people as cheaply as possible was checked by Dunning's revelations about the Watkins shop, but there was no lasting damage. Most members were content to believe the Secretaries' reassurances, and continued to acquire the books they wanted – along with a pleasant feeling that by doing so they were supporting the Society's foreign and charitable projects.

We may conclude that the Committee's management of bookbinding confirms the judgment of chapter 3: whether members and subscribers knew it or not, this 'religious society' was a major publisher. Even more than in book printing, the commercial magnitude of BFBS demand changed the shape of the London bookbinding craft. But if the Society was a mere publisher in the eyes of people occupied in the book trades, it was something much more significant in the eyes of its own members and subscribers. Articulating as it did the rhetoric of global salvation, the Society was, by mid-century, well on the way to becoming a Victorian institution. In the early days, it was cheap Bibles for the poor, and translations for readers abroad, that were the focus of activity. Bibles and Testaments in dull bindings of sheepskin or canvas emerged from the depository and into the streets. But later, a new definition of 'cheap' began to emerge. The tenpence book neatly

Figure 14 Binding to mark presentation by the BFBS to Sergeant's Temperance Hotel, Southport.

bound in roan with gilt edges had become a popular consumer commodity. The Society seems to have used these cheap Bibles for the wealthy to tighten the connections between donors and clients in its social transaction. People must have begun to feel that it would be disloyal to the parent Society to buy one's personal copies in a bookshop like any novel. This custom was nourished, starting in the early 1830s, by the headquarters Committee, whose members authorized a large number and variety of editions. A steady supply of books, neatly and attractively bound, streamed out of Earl Street, not only into the Sunday School classrooms, but also into the boudoirs, the reticules, the pockets and the parlours of Britain.

But subscribers at mid-century, especially those who responded sympathetically to Dunning's *Appeal*, began to wonder about the Society's policy of publishing such inexpensive Bibles for the middle-class market. The publicity about labour relations and the Society's response to it may be observed at the levels of Associations like Seven Dials, of Auxiliaries like Southwark and Westminster, and finally at the level of the Committee Room in Earl Street. From individual clergymen begging for reassurance, to loyal Andrew Brandram defending a policy he had opposed, Bible Society members were disturbed by the events of 1849–50.

Nevertheless the Society provided its own members and subscribers with books, and continued to do so in the face of criticism. The policy may be explained by considering the economics of publishing in conjunction with the financial structure of the Auxiliary-Association system. It cost very little to produce books in these more luxurious states, since the type and printing presses that supplied the charity market, already set up, could be used to produce books on higher quality paper at minimal additional expense. And Auxiliaries and their subsidiary Associations and Ladies' Associations controlled the domestic distribution of scriptures, with their contributions divided between the purchase of books in English and the foreign project. Perhaps it is enough to say that there was a demand: in the beginning, all classes of readers expressed a desire for more copies of the scriptures. The subscription system was designed to supply members with at least enough books to meet the needs of their immediate dependants. Even when Bible-distribution-as-philanthropy became enormously popular, the habit of acquiring personal copies from the BFBS remained. The patterns of demand and distribution in the fifties and sixties demonstrate that unlike the conflict and schism that scarred the earliest years, by the mid-Victorian period the BFBS had become an institution.

5 · THE BFBS AND BOOKSELLING, 1804–1864

THE TENTH ANNUAL report of the BFBS, in 1814, announced that a missionary to Africa had been shipwrecked. Among the goods taken by the 'natives' was a cargo of Bibles in Arabic. But Leopold Butscher of the Church Missionary Society was philosophic: 'my having been cast away, may perhaps be the saving of many of those into whose hands these Bibles have fallen, or shall fall in the future'. The distribution of the Society's books was not always so haphazard, but Butscher's experience was a powerful reminder of the parable that was to become the Society's emblem, the parable of the sower. Some copies of the Bible and New Testament were bound to fall by the wayside, on stony ground, or among thorns, but others were certain to fall upon good ground, to yield fruit and increase. All the Society could do was to put grain in the sower's pouch. The means of doing so varied from country to country, and changed over time.

As we have seen, the Bible Society's approach to both printing and bookbinding was generic: within the constraints of the Bible privilege, they used the same shops, machinery and methods as other publishers. When it came to distribution at home, however, the Society avoided the booksellers and hawkers who handled the retail sale of other books, the former to upper- and middle-class readers, the latter to poorer people who purchased litera- ture in the street. Instead, the Society found a way to reach both audiences, using each to create and enlarge the other. At the same time they created and preserved the special significance of a cheap Bible: to purchase one was to participate in the provision of scriptures to a global readership. Domestic distribution began with a subscription plan, whereby Society members whose interest in the project was immediate and practical could buy books at a substantial discount, for personal distribution in their local neighbourhoods. When it became clear that domestic circulation appealed to large numbers of people, individual subscriptions were largely supplanted by Bible Society Auxiliaries and their subordinate Associations, which collected funds locally, mostly in the form of penny-a-week subscriptions from working-class pur- chasers. These funds were transmitted to London and divided: half was returned in the form of Bibles and New Testaments at cost price, the balance applied to the foreign project. Foreign distribution was handled at first through the Bible Societies in European countries, assisted by travelling agents sent out from London. When the BFBS severed its ties with most of the continental societies after the Apocrypha crisis in the late 1820s, this pattern had to be replaced by alternative distribution systems. One successful method was colportage, whereby the Society's foreign agents (trusted, full-time staff) supervised a corps of travelling hawkers, called colporteurs, who sold Bibles and Testaments only. In Africa and Asia, the Society arranged with missionaries to distribute the books. Colportage was eventually used in Britain, but not until the fifties and sixties, after the enthusiasm of local Auxiliary members for direct distribution had begun to flag.

In London, the Society's popular Bibles in English were offered only through the Metropolitan Auxiliaries, while foreign-language versions were sold to the public from the Earl Street headquarters and from exclusive 'open depots'. This policy of specialized circulation permitted the Society to shape the distribution process as not merely a commercial transaction, but a cultural one, laden with significance. To purchase or donate, own or distribute, Society Bibles, was to participate in promoting 'the secret of England's greatness', in a satisfactorily tangible and practical way. But commercial booksellers suffered from the Society's policy, which by reducing prices to unprofitable levels, effectively cut them off from the trade in one of Victorian Britain's most popular books, the cheap Bible.

The bookselling trade in 1804, when the Society began, was not confined to retail sales. Bookselling included what we would now call publishing. Booksellers purchased copyrights from authors, or from authors' heirs or former publishers, and arranged for printing and bookbinding. These tradesmen also undertook retail sales of books published by authors themselves. They sold such books directly to the public in their own shops, and (at a discount) to fellow booksellers for a wider distribution. Many of these publishing booksellers specialized in one branch of literature: the best-known religious publisher was Rivington's.[1] In both London and the provinces, most general booksellers kept a stock of Bibles, and many supplemented them with a wide range of works on religious questions. A study of eighteenth-century provincial bookselling observes that 'the overwhelming impression is that stocks were dominated by theology, and that Bibles and Prayer Books were the one class of literature which could be guaranteed a place on the shelves of any country bookshop'.[2] Only some of these books were copies of the Authorized Version 'without note or comment', obtained from the privileged Presses. Versions furnished with notes and annotations were not covered by the Royal patent or the University charters. Thus, for example, Bowyer and Fittler of London published in 1796 a duodecimo Bible in two volumes, ornamented with engravings, while Fairbairn and Constable of Edinburgh produced in the same year a 'Pronouncing Testament . . . intended to facilitate the reading of the New Testament with Propriety'. It included explanatory notes by William Brown, a minister of Bedrule. Apart from these admissible infringements of the Royal patent and University charters, there were enterprising booksellers who circumvented the privilege by publishing Bibles in the Authorized Version with a few token notes, printed very low on the page and intended to be cut off by the binder.[3] These books were, however, relatively high in price. And potential readers still had to go into the shop to acquire them.

The most popular Bible-shop in London at the turn of the nineteenth century was Rivington's, in St Paul's Churchyard, with warehouses in Paternoster Row under the sign of the 'Bible and Crown'. The family had been in business since 1711. John Rivington (1720–92) allied himself firmly with the Establishment in the eighteenth-century religious upheavals, being on friendly terms with bishops and refusing to publish works by Wesley and Whitfield. He was appointed in 1765 as publisher to the Society for Promoting Christian Knowledge, and the office remained with the family for seventy years. John and his partner-brother James Rivington were succeeded by Francis and Charles, the two sons of John. Henry Curwen in his 1873 *History of Booksellers* observes that 'Dissent in itself was injurious enough to [John Rivington's] interests, but when Wilberforce and Hannah More succeeded in making a portion of the Church "Evangelical," upwards of half his customers deserted to a rival shop in Piccadilly.'[4] This was John Hatchard's, a meeting-place for literary and political conversation. Hatchard's Low-Church views brought him such authors as William Wilberforce, Zacharay Macaulay and Henry Thornton, as well as Hannah More. He was one of the people designated to receive subscriptions for the Bible Society in the pre-Earl Street days.[5] But despite the close association of Hatchard's evangelical authors with the BFBS, he was not offered the exclusive agency for the Society's books.

Booksellers normally acquired books published by the University printers from the London agents of each Press. These agents purchased books from the Presses at a discount and then retailed them to individual customers or in quantity. Cambridge had several London agents for the sale of the books they printed and published, including Bibles, New Testaments and Books of Common Prayer. These were prominent booksellers, including John Rivington, who acted until about 1832. In addition, some of the partners in the Press took responsibility for London sales. From 1802 until 1811 John Deighton, of the Cambridge family of booksellers and publishers, was appointed a University Printer, but apparently acted primarily as a publishing agent in Cambridge as well as in London. In 1829 when John William Parker took over at Cambridge as printer, his senior partner, William Clowes, looked after the London side of the business. Clowes had a printing and publishing business in the West Strand, which 'became in effect the Cambridge depository and agency – mainly for the sale of Bibles and prayer books'. In 1861 Rivington was again appointed London agent; he served until 1872. In that year,

Cambridge University Press ceased to handle its national sales through London agents, and the Cambridge Warehouse was opened in Paternoster Row.[6] Oxford, too, maintained a Bible warehouse in London, under the supervision of Edward Gardner, one of the partners of the Press since 1810 (along with Samuel Collingwood and Joseph Parker).[7]

The Society for Promoting Christian Knowledge was the Bible Society's chief rival. It was their failure to provide a cheap Bible for Wales that had generated the initial enthusiasm for an evangelical and nonsectarian Society. The SPCK had been distributing Bibles published by the privileged Presses since 1705. Most copies went to charity schools of various kinds, to the Army and Navy, and to workhouses. After 1765 and the agreement with John Rivington, the SPCK's books were distributed from his shop. Rivington attended their Bartlett's Buildings headquarters once a week, receiving orders and securing the Society's approval of his arrangements for bookbinding. This arrangement lasted until 1835 when complaints of unsatisfactory service, combined with theological disputes, ended the connection. The SPCK became its own distributor, from a shop in Great Queen Street. By this time the Society had developed a small network of district committees, similar to those of the BFBS but not nearly so successful. The pricing structure tended to impoverish rather than to enrich the parent Society.[8] And these district committees were limited to Anglicans, whereas everyone could participate in their local Bible Society.

The British and Foreign Bible Society went about its business in a different way, resolving very early that any connection with the bookselling trade would 'prove injurious to the interests of the Society'. Nor did they deal with the agents of the University Presses. From the beginning the volume of their orders was so large that they dealt with the Syndics of the Press at Cambridge, and the Delegates at Oxford. These arrangements were direct in the case of major decisions on costs and prices, new editions and reprints, while day-to-day arrangements were handled between the University Printers and the Society's Depositary. Because the largest payments made by the BFBS went to the privileged Presses, for Bibles and Testaments in English for domestic circulation, the Secretaries and Committee were interested in improving the terms on which they purchased books. Initially, Cambridge allowed the Society the same terms as the University's agents, 6 per cent as a regular discount, with a further 5 per cent for prompt payment. In addition, both agents and the BFBS were allowed 'the seventh copy', one free book in every seven. Oxford and the King's Printer matched Cambridge University's terms when they began to supply the Society.[9] In 1817, when the BFBS was established in Earl Street and beginning to demand that the Presses reduce their prices because paper had become cheaper, the terms were modified. Eyre and Strahan proposed to raise their allowance to 10 per cent, while both Universities proposed to give one book in five instead of one in seven, while continuing the original terms for volume discounts and prompt payment.[10]

Instead of using the book trade's network of shops and co-operative agency, the Bible Society established a 'depository' in London to manage its stock of books. In the earliest days this was the Little Moorfields counting-house of Thomas Smith, the collector. But as we saw in chapter 1, Smith was soon overwhelmed by the volume of subscription business and the first orders from local Auxiliaries and Associations. Joseph Tarn had his hands full with administration and accounts. In June 1808, Leonard Benton Seeley was appointed the Society's Depositary. He issued Bibles and New Testaments from his shop at number 169 Fleet Street, Blackfriars, until 1816. When the Society moved to Bible House in Earl Street, Seeley was replaced by Richard Cockle, his former assistant, who worked for the BFBS until his death in 1850. Cockle in turn was succeeded by an experienced assistant, James Franklin.

The fact that Leonard Benton Seeley was a bookseller did not contradict the Society's policy of exclusive distribution. It was clear that the BFBS depository was 'to form a distinct Department of his business'. Moreover, the person employed by him in that department was expected to 'post up the books and keep the accounts, and give attention to the general concerns of the Society'. This person, perhaps right from the beginning, was Richard Cockle. Seeley, like Smith before him, received a commission of 5 per cent on sales. This amount was built into the 'cost price' of Bibles and Testaments, along with the printers' and binders' charges. There was some dispute over how the Depositary was to be reimbursed for handling the books provided by the Society to schools and other charities as free grants. Seeley made it clear in December 1810 that he expected to receive the same commission on all work, with no further gradations and exceptions for special circumstances, and this was approved.[11] By paying a commission to Seeley, exclusively, the Society could control the retail distribution of its cheap Bibles.

Seeley was an able and experienced bookseller, unlike the incompetent and belligerent Thomas Smith. But even he found the volume of the Society's business difficult to manage. 'If the sale goes on as it has begun', he warned Tarn in 1808, '& the Binders send in no faster, I perceive that every third order will wait.' He asked if Tarn could 'teach the Binders the true meaning of that little world *Dispatch* – for my part I have been so used to it that I have now strong symptoms of a fit of illness coming on, merely from anxiety to be going on the way I know we ought & must'. He complained that Smith did not keep track of which members had paid for their subscriptions and for extra Bibles: 'if that is the mode he means to adopt . . . he may soon dispense my Stock to the 4 Winds & leave me to Whistle for the amount'. Tarn had little patience with Smith, but he begged Seeley not to be too hard on the binders, at least when making excuses to subscribers: after working hard to get supplies flowing from Cambridge into the binders' shops, Tarn found that Seeley had caused the discharge of eight or nine men from the several shops and this, Tarn felt, 'must give the Subscribers an idea that there is mismanagement on the part of [the BFBS's] Committee and Officers'.[12]

The new Society had to struggle with the problems of shipping and handling large quantities of heavy and yet fragile products, in a time when communications were upset by the military situation, and in any case not very sophisticated. In 1806 an order of 500 New Testaments from Cambridge went astray. Richard Watts had been asked to send them directly to Thomas Burn, the Kirby Street bookbinder. But the waggon, accidentally, delivered the order to Rivington's in St Paul's Churchyard. Watts had to admit that the rival bookseller had 'made use of them'. Perhaps, Watts suggested diplomatically, he was not aware that the books had the BFBS title-page. The Cambridge printer could not immediately redress the mistake, not having a further 500 copies. And the problems caused by dampness and cold affected distribution just as they did papermaking and the printing process: in 1814, for example, the conveyance of an order from Oxford was interrupted by the frost.[13]

The Bible Society hired the services of carters and waggoners when necessary, and paid for insurance and shipping charges on their books. But their status as a charitable organization often meant relief from the expenses of distribution. Joseph Hughes was able to announce in June 1809 that someone in the Transport Office had 'offered his services in sending the Scriptures to Foreign parts by trusty Agents to whom he has frequent access'. Five hundred Portuguese New Testaments were put at Mr Campbell's disposal, and he was asked to account for them. The same year, a 'respectable officer in the Royal Navy' reported: 'This unsettled way of life has given me many, very many, opportunities of scattering the Scriptures far and wide.' Two years later the Committee accepted with thanks the offer of William Napier, of the Grand Junction Wharf, White Friars, to become the Society's Wharfingers. There was to be no charge for this vital service. Napier further offered that 'as their Waggons are passing the Depository almost hourly', goods destined for their wharf could be collected.[14]

The Depository received books from the binders, packed up single copies for individual subscribers and large orders for local Auxiliaries, and sent them off by waggon, canal, coach and all the other diverse means at his disposal. He kept excess copies – mostly of foreign editions, the English ones moved too quickly – in the warehouse space donated by Committee members Thomas Hodson and Joseph Reyner. Reyner hosted the earliest Committee meetings at his premises in Lower Thames Street, near Old Swan Stairs. Joseph Tarn worked out of his home in Spa Fields, and the annual meetings were held at the New London Tavern. As the passion for Bible-circulating increased, the problems of managing the practical side of a publishing business grew large.

In December 1815, the Subcommittee on the depository recorded that a delegation had viewed 'commodious premises in Earl Street, Blackfriars'. By the middle of 1816 they moved in. The Presses were asked to change the imprint on the title-pages of Bibles and New Testaments: 'Sold to Subscribers only at the Society's House, Earl Street, Blackfriars, London.' At this time Seeley ended his appointment as the Society's bookseller. He turned the stock over to the new Depositary, his former assistant Richard Cockle, expressing regret and satisfaction, along with hopes for the Society's future prosperity.[15] Now all the Society's officers could be accommodated under one roof, and the Committee and Subcommittees could meet there too, to decide the policy of a growing organization. The break with Seeley and the other 'receivers' of subscriptions was not perfectly smooth. Three months after the new arrangements had been initiated, in September 1816, Seeley reported that he found it inconvenient and injurious to have to refuse to accept subscriptions from his clients who were used to doing their business with the Bible Society through him. He offered to receive them at no charge, as did John Hatchard. It was arranged that Anthony Wagner, the collector, would call at each shop once a month for subscriptions. But Seeley later demanded compensation of £1,400, of which the Society granted £350 and the arbitrator to whom the case was referred granted a further £404.[16] The booksellers Seeley and Hatchard, like binders who lost the Society's custom, found that their profits were reduced. Nor did booksellers resign themselves to the Society's control of such a significant part of their business as the Bible trade. Samuel Bagster, the publisher of polyglot Bibles, offered in 1824 to supply the BFBS, claiming that by doing so he would lose 'the present prospect by Merchants of an opening and extended market'.[17] In fact the Society had not left much of a market in Bibles for the rest of the trade.

Members of the Committee, on the other hand, were delighted with their Depositary, Mr Cockle, and his depository. In February 1818 it was calculated that the new system had saved £280 in the first year. And

The Committee and Officers of the Society in the meantime enjoy the advantage ... of being enabled to conduct the business in its several departments with a connection, a security, promptness, and correctness, which their most sedulous attention and vigilance could not have obtained for it under the former system of management, and (it may be added) the Institution itself is presented to the view of Foreigners and other persons of distinction in that respectable light in which the magnitude of the object which it pursues and of the operations which it carries on entitle it to be placed.[18]

As always, the Committee had to balance their desire for economical and efficient operation with the equally important matter of a 'respectable' image in the eyes of the world.

When books destined for the hungry market of local Bible Auxiliaries and Associations left Earl Street, they were sent to the designated depot in each community. This was often a church or chapel, sometimes a private home, and occasionally (as at Oxford after 1825) a bookseller. Books were distributed in single copies by the collectors when subscribers had completed, or almost completed, their payments. Some local Auxiliaries held public meetings, to the consternation of their critics, and books were presented there to loyal subscribers. Local Societies also received the books destined from Earl Street to Sunday Schools and other charitable institutions in their neighbourhoods.[19]

The system, though amazingly successful, was a fragile one, requiring constant vigilance and labour on the part of volunteers. Robert Steven made a tour of the North in 1820 and reported to Joseph Tarn from Stirling. In a confidential paragraph he admitted that he was 'not getting younger' and described how he often had to write twelve or fifteen letters before noon, including 'some long ones to meet objections'. Then he had to run 'from one meeting to another in the large towns'. Local members could be helped to deal with criticism, but such assistance cost precious time and energy. 'A single letter from a large town ... broke up a course of nearly 200 miles, & obliged me to a fresh correspondence, & from some of the parties it required perhaps 2 or 3 letters before I could get the links of the chain all joined again.' Steven concluded that his journey was 'not a jaunt of pleasure'. Fifteen years later another volunteer organizer despaired of Sheffield, where the population was contributing less than an average 2d per family per year, 'a sum really not equalling what each family will bestow on Trampers that call at their doors for charity'. The local leadership would 'investigate, appoint collectors, & carry on the collecting until the number of subscribers is exhausted & then investigate again. In other words', he said, 'they suffer the associations to die & then raise them from the dead.'[20]

In 1821 Charles Stokes Dudley was engaged to travel up and down the country, encouraging the formation of new local Societies and renewing the commitment of old ones. After 1827 he was assisted by a second Domestic Agent, W. Brackenbury, and soon by the Rev. W. Acworth (1828) and the Rev. Thomas Brook (1832). Thomas Sangster, who started work in 1834, was in charge of local societies in the Metropolis of London and vicinity. And the Rev. Thomas Phillips (1835) took Wales, Hereford and Monmouthshire for his territory. In 1848 there was a separate agent for the Manchester District, Jonathan Taylor. In addition to their more abstract task of rousing local enthusiasm, these agents saw to it that parcels of Bibles and Testaments reached their destinations safely and made sure they were stored and properly distributed to their purchasers. The system of local societies was efficient and profitable, but it entailed the expense of constant supervision from Earl Street. The clergymen and others who attended annual meetings required only their travelling expenses, but Dudley and his colleagues received a salary in addition to the heavy cost of their constant travels.

Although most of the foreign-language Bibles printed by the Society in

London were designated for distribution abroad, there was a steady market for them in the international port of London, and a group of merchants, naval officers and others who were anxious to press copies of the scriptures on seamen before they departed. But there were difficulties. At a meeting in July 1810, the Subcommittee on Printing and General Purposes discovered that people on foreign ships had refused to accept foreign versions when the books bore any marks that would show the recipient had been in an English port; such evidence 'would endanger the confiscation of the vessel', under Napoleon's stringent Milan decrees forbidding contact with England. Some lawyers on the Committee were detailed to consider whether 'the Society can, with propriety adopt cancel titles, and final pages to their Foreign versions after they have been printed with the regular Imprint, required by the statute', that is, cut out the BFBS title page and the printer's address, both required by the 1710 Copyright Act, and insert forged replacements.[21] In the end this policy was declared inexpedient, but the fact that it was considered at all, by so politically astute a Committee, in a time of war, shows how serious they were about scripture circulation.

If distribution within the British Isles was difficult, the circulation of Bibles abroad called for heroic efforts and costly agency. The Society made its initial contacts with European evangelicals through the Foreign Secretary, Carl Friedrich Adolph Steinkopf. He wrote to an associate, a Nuremberg merchant called Kiesling. Kiesling answered in feeling terms about the dearth of Bibles in Austria and Switzerland, and promised that a meeting would be held on Ascension Day (10 May, only a month after the London meeting) to found a German Bible Society. The London Committee granted £100 to the new organization, and 5,000 copies of a German New Testament were printed in Nuremberg. A group of Swiss supporters in Basle, instead of forming their own Society, 'joined their efforts' with the Nuremberg group. The Society in Switzerland informed Steinkopf and his English colleagues of their intention to print a cheap edition of the French Protestant Bible. The 'chief difficulty', however, would be 'to meet with suitable persons who would undertake the sale and distribution of such a Bible'. Comparing their country with Britain, they found 'an infinite difference': 'your's is rich, our's is impoverished; your commerce is still flourishing, our's is sinking; among you subscriptions and contributions are a very common thing, which is not equally the case with us'. They placed their hope in 'a pious member of the Moravian congregation, who traverses France at present, and who would be the very man that might render the most essential service in this respect'.[22] Thus was established the basis for the European system of distribution: individual travelling agents, supplied with books to be offered at random. It was quite alien to the British system of subscriptions and local societies.

Two years later the Nuremberg Society was transferred to its Swiss headquarters, in Basle. This became the centre of distribution, not only for

Switzerland and Germany, but for Napoleonic France. The Committee granted stereotype plates of the French scriptures, as well as generous donations of funds, to central Europe. A Prussian Bible Society, started in Berlin in 1805, obtained many of its books from the Canstein Bible Institution where cheap books were produced from standing type. In 1809 a Könings-berg Bible Committee formed, and began to distribute Bibles in Polish and Lithuanian. The Committee in London made massive donations to these efforts.[23] The tables in the appendix show that about 20 per cent of BFBS expenditure was allocated to scriptures in foreign languages in the early years.

In addition to the semi-independent Societies in Europe, the BFBS developed a network of unofficial agents who arranged either for donations or for the sale of Bibles at massive discounts. With the help of sympathetic chaplains, French and Spanish prisoners of war received copies in their own language, and convicts exiled to Botany Bay were provided with books. 'Not the cartels and the convict-ships alone, but missionaries, Government officials, travellers, settlers, schoolmasters were taken advantage of, to convey the sacred volume [abroad].' Distribution in the western Mediterranean centred on Gibraltar, where volunteers could be found at the British garrison; for the eastern Mediterranean the headquarters were in Malta.[24] This network circulated editions both in English and in other languages: Bibles in Gaelic to Nova Scotia as well as to Scotland, in Dutch to South Africa as well as to Holland, in Arabic to the west coast of Africa, in Spanish to the Canaries and in Portuguese to Madeira.[25]

Some of the Society's foreign agents, however, were salaried and full-time workers. John Paterson and Ebenezer Henderson were two Scottish ministers, Congregationalists associated with Robert Haldane. They travelled from Leith to Elsinore in August 1805, as missionaries from Edinburgh destined for India. Held up in Copenhagen through the winter, they began to preach there, abandoning their plans to travel further. The two missionaries supported themselves by teaching English until they were engaged by the Bible Society. Joseph Reyner, the cotton merchant whose warehouse also stored Bibles, arranged introductions for them to prominent Danes, and they undertook to manage the production and distribution of scriptures for Iceland. Paterson and Henderson travelled widely throughout Scandinavia, organizing Bible Societies and spending the London Committee's funds on type, paper and printing.[26]

In June 1812, Steinkopf left London for his first tour of the European Societies. His co-Secretaries were not by any means certain that he would return. He was away for six months, during which time he spent over £2,700 and laid the groundwork for the European part of the Society's project. He visited Halle in Saxony and contributed £50 towards the formation of a Bible Committee in connection with the Cansteinsche Bibelanstalt. He visited

Basle, then went on to Zurich, Stuttgart, Frankfurt, and other cities. He left sums of money in charge of selected agents, and ordered books printed at Halle and Basle that could be distributed by sympathetic clergymen. Then he proceeded, undaunted by military chaos, to St Petersburg and to Moscow. He sat out the siege of Moscow in St Petersburg, spending the time drafting a proposal for the Russian Bible Society and preparing the type for the Bible in Finnish. In the summer of 1815, Steinkopf made a second tour of the Continent, spent a further £4,000 and travelled a further 5,000 miles.[27]

The earliest efforts in France, while the two countries were at war, were made from beyond its boundaries. But in 1818 a Protestant Bible Society of Paris was formed, and in 1820 the British and Foreign Bible Society opened a Paris depot under the supervision of Jean Daniel Kieffer. Kieffer was Professor of Oriental Languages in the Royal College of Paris and held the post of Interpreting Secretary to the King of France.[28] His project was to supply the scriptures to the Roman Catholic majority of the French population. Kieffer supervised the work of several Paris printers, organizing the production of versions in French and several other languages. By 1825 he had opened depots in a number of towns, but it was not until after the 1830 revolution that the French agency became really active.

Kieffer's contribution to Bible distribution was the concept of colportage. Colporteurs were pedlars who specialized in scriptures. They carried books in a leather sack and effected conversions, or at least sales, by example and exhortation. Door-to-door distribution by colporteurs was successful in circumventing the opposition of the Roman Catholic Church to reach potential readers.[29] Kieffer told a correspondent in 1831:

It is quite an occupation, independently of our usual engagements, to supply these colporteurs. Every day we have reports of a curious and interesting nature; as our men go up the streets the people call from their shops, and are quite glad to be able to purchase their volumes. They assure me that they scarcely ever pass a corner of a street without placing one or more with the porters who are stationed there.[30]

When Kieffer died in 1833 he was replaced by Victor de Pressensé, who continued to refine the system. Colportage was even more successful in the rural south of France. A family of Toulouse bankers, for example, engaged colporteurs to travel from door to door and to visit fairs and markets, distributing Bibles and Testaments at a low price, to people who had always been discouraged by the Church from reading the scriptures personally. Colporteurs were never volunteers: means had to be found to support their work. But nor were they mere employees: their reputation for piety was part of their success story.

The connection between London and the European Societies was severed after 1825, when the conflict over the propriety of circulating the Apocrypha cut off the flow of funds from London. In most places, the national Societies insisted on being free to include the Apocryphal books with the canonical ones, while in Britain – however individual officers of the Society might feel about the question – it was impossible to countenance such policies and remain in existence. After the break, the British and Foreign Bible Society gradually built up a staff of continental agents who managed the printing and distribution of scriptures in major cities. Kieffer was in Paris, Robert Pinkerton in Frankfurt, Henry Leeves in Constantinople and Isaac Lowndes in Malta. William Pascoe Tiddy worked out of Brussels and Edward Millard from Vienna. Each of them sent home narratives of their adventures in the Bible cause, to be published in annual *Reports* and in the *Monthly Extracts of Correspondence*. Thus was kept alive the interest of British members of the Society in the distribution of scriptures abroad.

Tales of colportage were most popular. After 1837, de Pressensé and the Paris agency stopped using colporteurs who also distributed for other societies and hired a corps of forty-four exclusive agents. Many of them were former Roman Catholics, whose dedication to Protestantism included a commitment to putting the Bible 'without note or comment' into the hands of those to whom the papacy would deny it. They earned about £3 per month, travelling long distances, seeking lodging from their customers and often braving the hostility of priests. De Pressensé wrote that 'It has now become a fact well known to the authorities that the Bible colporteurs are men who on no account meddle with politics, and who commend themselves by an upright, peaceable, and exemplary course of conduct.' This was a narrow conception of the political, when colporteurs frequently resorted to smuggling their wares, and in Catholic countries were commissioned to function contrary to the state religion.[31]

The only limitation to tales of brave colporteurs was literary: most of the men themselves were unable to write about their work in English, and the agents who employed them were not endowed with any particular narrative skill. This changed when the Society sent George Borrow to Spain, not as a colporteur but as their agent. Borrow was a writer, hitherto unsuccessful and almost unpublished, interested in languages, in gypsies and in adventure. Between 1835 and 1840 Borrow travelled widely in Spain for the Bible Society, writing letters to Brandram describing his experiences. On his return to England he used these letters as the basis for *The Bible in Spain* (1843). The publication was very successful, 'one of the great books of mid-century Britain', and an important element in the creation of the public notion of how Bibles were distributed abroad. 'The soul of the Evangelical middle class had been stirred by this frank story of an intrepid missionary who had survived such dreadful hazards in order to distribute the New Testament to a benighted people whose need for it was obviously great. The book ... had penetrated the reader's moral defenses.'[32] Borrow was by no means a typical agent of the Bible Society, but his book nevertheless contributed a great deal to its reputation. A new generation of urban readers in the 1840s, inclined perhaps to take the Bible Society for granted, were stirred by Borrow's narrative of heroism and conflict.

Distribution 'at home' in civilized Britain, where Protestantism and the Bible were believed to be the secret of greatness, was not supposed to require intrepid missionaries or costly agency. Books sent by Richard Cockle in London to the depositories managed by local Auxiliaries, were circulated according to C. S. Dudley's 'system', to their purchasers. As we have seen, the system was fragile, and individual parts of it – the leadership of some Auxiliaries – often broke down and had to be renewed. But at the same time it was very effective overall, generating a massive income. After the printers' and bookbinders' bills had been paid, these revenues were sufficient to sustain the expensive structure of foreign agents and support for translation. Early suggestions that colportage be used in the British Isles were discouraged: it would be much more expensive to employ and license such agents than to prop up the old system of voluntary distribution.

The system worked best when there was a steady and balanced flow of books and of funds. In the early years when the printers and bookbinders had difficulty keeping up with the demand, there had been constant criticism, and concern that the Society would lose subscribers impatient to receive their Bibles. By the 1840s the balance had been established. Even the cheap books for Sunday Schools could be supplied without difficulty, sheep- or cloth-bound and stamped with the 'charity brand'. Then in November of 1845, Dudley announced to his principals in Earl Street that 'a great work' was going on in Manchester, 'though not precisely in the most judicious manner'. Andrew Brandram already knew about it, and he confessed that he 'trembled' at the thought.

After averaging a circulation of 5,000 copies per year, the demand of Manchester and its surrounding district rose to 10,000 annually in the early forties, then suddenly to 20,000 copies in one month, November 1845. The local Auxiliary was not aware of the situation until it was well advanced. Once informed, they tried to encourage it, although in the case of Ladies' Associations 'it might seem to trench a little on their proper sphere of labour'. They sat on the sidelines and watched the superintendents, teachers and senior students of the Sunday Schools, under the supervision of a 'zealous ... gentleman', sell Bibles and Testaments to the workpeople at the local mills and factories.[33] The editions preferred by Manchester readers were the 'roan gilt-edged' Bibles, a shilling a copy, being turned out in the Watkins factory.

Manchester was the cotton town where the Anti-Corn Law movement began, where Engels described *The Condition of the Working Class in England* in terms of exploitation and potential revolution, and where Elizabeth Gaskell set her novel *Mary Barton: A Tale of Manchester Life*. In the words of Asa Briggs, author of *Victorian Cities*, 'all roads led to Manchester in the 1840s'. Novelists, social commentators, reformers, industrialists and politicians all found the city a symbol of changing patterns of human relationships. The British and Foreign Bible Society, too, discovered in Manchester that their 'system', which had been revolutionary in 1820, was outmoded by 1845.[34]

The 'zealous gentleman' was James Dilworth, a merchant. He wrote to Brandram in October 1845, describing his plan for a large circulation of the scriptures in Blackpool. He had been selling books at the reduced prices and asking the wealthier classes for contributions to make up the difference. Dilworth feared that the local Auxiliary and its Associations 'may be found rather in the rear than in the lead of this work'. He also alluded to his conviction that the Bible Society had been foretold in the scriptures (Esther 4:14).[35] Sincere a Christian as Brandram was, this kind of extravagant piety would have sounded an alarm in his administrator's mind. He told Dilworth that he 'trembled' at the thought of such an unorthodox scheme of distribution. The 'Manchester man', as Dilworth came to be known at Earl Street, gave more details of his scheme. His son John had begun to operate in Salford, commencing by calling together a group of tract distributors, reporting to them the experience of Blackpool, and asking them to pray for guidance. 'The result', he announced, 'has been beyond all parallel.'

All labouring people – youths, for the most part in our Bible classes, & Teachers, pious holy people of both sexes. Their plan is before they go out with the Scriptures to place them on a Chair before them & to kneel down and pray for divine wisdom help & success. Upwards of 20 are engaged & they have sold 1500 copies within the last 12 days & the demand is increasing daily ... Another mode is to interest the millowners in whose service the mass of the people are employed. They, through the medium of the manager, or some pious workman, succeed and are likely to succeed to an extent quite unknown.

Dilworth went on to ask what terms Brandram was prepared to offer to colporteurs who had to make their living by the circulation of scriptures, although he preferred to use volunteers who worked '*without money or price* ... by the poor amongst the poor'. He exulted at the recent reduction in the price of books, and even at this early date warned that the local depository was 'sadly short of supply'.[36] Brandram and Browne must have been dismayed: prayer associated with Bible work, circulation at the reduced prices, and alienation from the local Auxiliary. All these elements had in the past put the Bible Society at risk of censure, of impoverishment, even of dissolution.

Early in November Charles Stokes Dudley was dispatched to Manchester. Although his first impression was that the manner of the work was not very judicious, the old organizer soon found himself caught up in the movement. Sixty-five years of age that year, he told a colleague that it 'surpasses anything I have ever witnessed. Woe to him who would check it!' Replying to Brandram's request that he consider the circumstances of the Manchester Associations he replied 'Verily *they* have not once been thought of by me. The danger is that your poor old friend should be carried away by the most extraordinary & *blessed* Biblical excitement ever witnessed in this Country; & they be deprived of the power of exercising the little judgment he possesses, in directing that excitement into right Channels.'[37]

Dilworth, meanwhile, was writing to Earl Street. His demands for more books were interspersed with marvels on the efficacy of prayer. Brandram sent him a copy of the American Bible Society *Report* for 1845, a document that cautioned against the dangers of undue religious enthusiasm on the part of Bible Associations. But Dilworth scorned anything that would diminish his work. 'If the Church of Christ had been awake to her responsibilities & to her power in Christ, the world would long since have been deluged with Bibles & with missionaries too ...' Although the work in Manchester had been 'done *chiefly* by the poor operatives themselves', Dilworth thought there was 'ample work for a well organized Bible Association'. But he found that very few people wanted to pay by instalments.[38] In an age when wages had increased and book-prices decreased, Bibles no longer had to be paid for a penny at a time, and there was no incentive to develop the pattern of trust and communication that the early Associations had endeavoured to build up.

In a formal report to Brandram and the Committee, Dudley confessed that he found it difficult to keep from being carried away by the 'atmosphere of mental & moral excitation' around him. He called the movement 'the most interesting case which has hitherto occurred in the history of our beloved Society – or at least in its *Domestic* annals', and attributed it to a combination of circumstances. This was a time of prosperity and general employment in Manchester, and the children working in factories had been receiving scriptural instruction in the Sunday Schools. Another factor was the 'unprecedentedly low prices & attractive appearance of the Books'. Dudley also believed that the movement was influenced by 'the re-action, or rather the revulsion of the Public mind from the absurdities & degrading influence of miscalled "Socialism"'. Above all, of course, divine intervention, brought forth by prayer, had caused the crusade. In a more private letter he responded to Brandram's misgivings:

We live in Railway times, & 'Onwards' must be our motto. But I am perfectly sure that such movements as that in Manchester may be made to *chime in* with our Association system, & I *much* prefer it to *Colportage*. Voluntary Colporteurs, acting under the advice of a Committee or of an individual & judicious collector, will do ten times more good than a stipendiary Colporteur – as I daily see.

A month later he was urging Brandram to 'quicken the supply', and warning him not to listen to those who say 'The case has not been made out.'[39]

Dudley's and Dilworth's demands were putting extraordinary pressure on Richard Cockle in the depository, and behind him on Lorina Watkins and her staff in the bindery, where a contract had just been signed. At first she stepped up production to 300 books per day, and Dudley called her 'the maid of Roan ... she deserves a Statue of Leather, Gilt'. But in December, when the demand of Manchester rose to over 1,000 a day, he calmly proposed breaking the contract and engaging 'additional Master, or Mistress Binders to meet the demand'. Instead the Depository and Printing Subcommittee required Watkins to procure (presumably by subcontract) an additional 100,000 copies of the roan gilt-edged Pearl Bible and Diamond Testament, all to be delivered within two months.[40] But two months later the shelves at the Manchester depository were still empty, Dudley told Brandram, although 10,000 copies could have been sold in the previous week. Worse than this, the 'Channel of the BFBS [had] proved too limited to convey the waters, [and] the Flood [was finding] its way through other canals'. Two rival depositories had been established, one a bookseller and one associated with the Scottish Board for Bible Circulation. 'Just in proportion to our inability to supply our Aux. Soc's', Dudley warned, 'will be the *decrease* of means to meet the increasing Foreign demands.'[41] This possibility had been in Brandram's mind all along, as he urged caution and spoke to Dilworth and Dudley of how he 'trembled' at the news from Manchester.

By the spring of 1846 the demand in Manchester had begun to diminish, but Dudley had yet to become completely disillusioned with James Dilworth. The Secretary prepared for publication a report of the extraordinary events in Manchester, and the General Committee routinely decided to print 5,000 copies for distribution, beginning with the annual meeting at Exeter Hall. But Dilworth objected to Dudley's interpretation of events. Dudley told Brandram, 'I believe Mr D. to be a good man, but wish he thought less of No 1.' And a few days later he remarked 'Either [Dilworth] is inaccessible by Common-sense, & demonstrative evidence, – or he is more the slave of Personal Vanity than any *Christian* with whom I ever before came in contact. I am just as thoroughly satisfied of the strict accuracy of the statement ... as I am that it is daylight at 12 o'clock at noon.'[42]

Dilworth's personal vanity might have been measured in proportion to his undoubted charisma, never a quality in high favour in Earl Street. In the overheated atmosphere of Manchester politics and social change, he created a movement that flourished for about four months and then died. It is not surprising that Sunday School teachers and students persuaded millworkers by the thousand to purchase a copy of the Bible or New Testament. There were more thousands of millworkers than most people knew about, and they had scant exposure to religious education or indeed to any contact with cultural life. It is only a little surprising that Charles Stokes Dudley allowed himself to be caught up in the movement. But he was always a field agent, constantly complaining that he was 'as ignorant of proceedings at Earl St as of those in Hong Kong'. As such, he regarded it as part of his job to be open to new procedures and practices in provincial towns and cities. It was up to Brandram and Browne to evaluate and control the innovations. In their correspondence over the 'Manchester movement', we see Dudley and the

Figure 15   'Welcome to Bible Distributors.'

Secretaries struggling with the awareness that while there was still a demand for Bibles and Testaments, it could not be supplied in the old way. More distressing than loss of funds, or criticisms from religious fanatics like Dilworth, was the awareness that local Auxiliaries could no longer be called upon to exercise restraint in the interests of Earl Street and the foreign project. They were independent now.

In 1848, three years after the Dilworth experience, the Manchester Auxiliary decided to engage its own agent and a staff of five colporteurs.[43] Thus it was that about twenty years after its institution in France, the system of colportage began to be used to sell scriptures in the British Isles. Not that the system was altogether foreign. Chapbooks and other inexpensive publications for the penny-and-under market were distributed by streethawkers. Hannah More had engaged these same hawkers to include her Cheap Repository Tracts in their packs.[44] In the 1840s, as it became more and more difficult to maintain the energy and commitment of local Societies, especially in the largest cities, the Society began to look for alternative means of distribution. But they were never to find any method as economical as the voluntary efforts of Ladies' Bible Associations.

When the Society celebrated its Jubilee in 1853–4, and began collecting a large special fund for the occasion, the first objective was the adoption of colportage throughout Great Britain during the Jubilee year. The fund generated £70,000 in donations, much of which was put aside to fund paid distribution in the towns and cities of Britain. Some colportage was rural but most was in cities, in the street, at corner stands, or from waggons. Manchester colporteurs visited wakes and fairs, sometimes selling 100 copies at a single fair. One London agent took his Bibles into public houses. When a colporteur was employed on the Great Northern Railway, the BFBS arranged for a free pass to facilitate his work. The annual *Reports* were now laced with anecdotes of hardy colporteurs at home as well as abroad. Margaret Fison, who chronicled many of these stories said, 'A Christian with Howard's philanthropy, Brainerd's devotion, Page's fidelity, and Milner's business accuracy, would make a model colporteur.'[45] It soon became clear that colportage was not supplementing but replacing the activity of volunteer Collectors. The only limit was the Society's ability to pay the colporteurs' wages. Back in 1840, Auxiliaries had complained that Sunday School distribution encroached on their preserves. Now they willingly handed over their districts to colporteurs, and even competed among themselves for grants to pay the new agents. In 1845, Brandram had been anxious about the precedent of a specialized programme of distribution in Manchester. Now Robert Frost, his successor, and George Browne were being asked to sponsor one, this time for the whole country. The original plan to restrict the extraordinary grants for colportage in Great Britain to the Jubilee year had to be revised. Local Auxiliaries continued to receive assistance, at reduced rates, to permit 'the seasonable and kindly visit of the Bible Hawker'.[46]

As paid agency, colportage made Bible distribution more like other forms of bookselling. In the absence of volunteer labour, the cost of selling the book had to be incorporated in the budget of its publisher. Partly because the Society was still unwilling to mingle its books with other publications, this item was very expensive. It averaged 3¾d per copy throughout the country (as high as 8½d in Norfolk), and as sales were very large, the grants were significant: between 1854 and 1869 they totalled £9,212, over 13 per cent of the total Jubilee fund. The Society still resisted a formal connection with the upper end of the bookselling trade; they declined an offer from the Leicester Square entrepreneur Bernard Quaritch in 1851.[47] But they found themselves in charge of a corps of travelling agents.

A further expense of colportage in England was the licence that had to be purchased for each individual agent, at a cost of £4 per annum. The BFBS tried in vain to use its influence to have the fees waived, calling them a 'heavy tax on this system of Christian benevolence'.[48] Many people, including Charles Stokes Dudley, found it difficult to believe that the legislation was intended to forbid distribution by publishers not seeking to make a profit.[49] In July 1850 the Society sought learned opinion on the subject, and were told that Bibles were not exempted under the Hawkers and Pedlars Acts.[50] Three days later, nevertheless, Henry Roberts, an architect and traveller who belonged to the Committee, presented a memorial to the Treasury praying for exemption. It was not granted. A letter from Sir Charles E. Trevelyan explained that the Lords of the Treasury could not comply with the memorial 'under the existing state of the law'.[51]

The question was raised again in 1853, and Lord Shaftesbury addressed himself to W. E. Gladstone, then Chancellor of the Exchequer. The President enclosed Gladstone's reply in a note to Browne, saying 'It would hardly be worthwhile, seeing his determination, to ask for an interview.' Gladstone had written:

Out of respect to the Deputation and its object I will certainly make an appointment should you continue to desire it. But the question is not new to me: the various considerations connected with it have been suggested to me from more than one quarter. It has therefore been my duty to examine them: and I have arrived at the conclusion that the question ought to stand over. I am friendly to the principle of the proposal: but I can not think that the limitation of it would be quite easy, and further if, as is probable, it should open up the whole question of Hawkers' Licences it would involve us in a probable loss of revenue which at present we could not venture to risk. You will say why should it open up that question: the answer is because it is not in a sound state and thus the raising any point connected with it would be hazardous. I hope therefore that, the matter not being of great importance, you will be of opinion that it had better stand over until we are in a condition, which I certainly hope to very soon be, to attempt something more like a general revision of our Stamp Duties.[52]

Gladstone, despite his sympathies with its philanthropic objectives, was well aware that the Bible Society was a business and a fact in British economic life. He also knew the matter was not 'of great importance', because the BFBS could afford to license its colporteurs.

The cost of licensing had to be met, because it was clear that Auxiliaries and their dependent Associations were no longer suited to the requirements of Bible marketing at mid-century. Canton refers to an 'inevitable process of disintegration', whereby local Societies became extinct at an alarming rate. Often new institutions were re-founded in the same community, but the momentum was lost. Times had changed. Even the most officious lady visitor could not with propriety penetrate her neighbour's kitchen and collect subscriptions from the servants, 'but the colporteur can offer his Bible for sale just as any other licensed person may offer his goods for sale'. Domestic Agent J. A. Page, of Manchester, said publicly in the 1854 Annual Report that 'where there is a declining Ladies' Association, and it is found that a revival cannot otherwise be effected, a colporteur should be employed as a canvasser for new subscribers'.[53]

The Auxiliaries were anxious to engage in colportage, especially if they could get grants from the parent Society to pay wages and expenses. Not surprisingly the new policy produced tension between parent Society and locals. Sidelights on this tension may be found in the correspondence between Earl Street and the Auxiliary in Birmingham during the late fifties. The Rev. John Angell James, venerable evangelical and secretary of the Birmingham Auxiliary, had written on behalf of his colleagues requesting advice. A bookhawker named Ardrey had offered to sell BFBS Bibles with other books. Secretary Samuel Bergne replied from Earl Street:

To sanction the disposal of our books with a miscellaneous collection such as the hawker in question proposes to carry, would give a latitude that would become very embarrassing, especially in cases where a person paid cash for all his purchases at a reduction from the cost price. What kind of control would it be possible to exercise over the publications he disposed of? And by the large discount we allowed, we might furnish the means of disseminating works which we should be far from approving. If such a plan as that on which you ask an advice should be sanctioned it would become a precedent pleaded in many localities and a serious inroad would be made upon our free contributors.

The old concern about juxtaposing the Society's Bibles with potentially controversial literature of any kind was still very strong. But increasingly it seemed that circulation could only be promoted by taking risks. Nevertheless,

The plan would we think clash, to some extent with our ordinary work. The hawker would of course push his sales wherever he could and not confine them to the poor, and by this means many who are now willing and able to pay full price for copies purchased would be able to buy at a reduction, while the Society would lose 12£ per cent on all such sales. The Committee cannot help thinking that the simplest and *safest* mode of carrying on the operation of colportage is to make that of this society distinct and complete in itself and quite free from any kind of admixture.

A member of the Birmingham Committee, Mr Duffield, replying to Bergne, pointed out some of the problems being experienced in the manufacturing city. He calculated that free contributions had not kept pace with sales in the previous ten years, nor had the increasing wealth of Birmingham been matched by the income of the Auxiliary. He saw 'two plain reasons' for the situation, the first being that individual denominations were operating parallel or similar schemes. 'Pan-evangelical' Bible distribution had given way to denominational or even congregational projects. Second was a matter of marketing, of the BFBS image. Duffield spoke of '*the little prominence* which the societys [*sic*] practical labours have given to them. My firm conviction is that if any large plan of operations was to proceed from this committee a great impetus would be given to the Society's labours in this town and neighbourhood.' Abandoning the proposed arrangement with Ardrey, Duffield proposed that four colporteurs be engaged to work in Birmingham and surrounding district, in order to 'revive the languishing interests of the society'. Duffield 'implore[d] the sub committee not to think that [he was] led away in presenting them with this rough statement by any mere fondness for planning'.

Two years later the Birmingham secretaries wrote to Earl Street, again requesting a grant for colportage. They pointed out their dilemma:

If we support our Depot and Agency, it will entirely exhaust our subscriptions, and this we need scarcely say would have an immediate tendency to deprive us of them altogether. Our friends here who subscribe to the Bible Society would scarcely be satisfied if their money were spent upon our local machinery. The free grants which we make to the Parent Society are popularly regarded as the test of our efficiency.[54]

This is a clear statement of the Bible transaction in the late fifties, at the local level in the expanding manufacturing centre of Birmingham. People were inspired by and contributed to the foreign project of the Society. This project, however, had traditionally depended upon sales of cheap Bibles to the domestic population, and volunteer agency to effect such sales was no longer forthcoming. Nor was it as effective as it had been half a century earlier.

Colportage replaced volunteer agency with a system that sold large numbers of books. Equally important in many ways, it generated ample amounts of rhetoric concerning the piety of the colporteurs and the desirability of contributing to their support. What colportage lacked was the personal involvement, the gift of time and trouble, the link between rich and poor, upon which the Bible transaction had traditionally been based. People at Earl Street were uneasy about the situation, but no one could see any way to change it, until Ellen Ranyard approached the Committee to support an intriguingly innovative project.

Gareth Stedman Jones has shown, in *Outcast London*, how there developed after mid-century an image in middle-class minds of the Metropolitan poor as depraved as well as deprived. The effects of urban squalor were imagined by their betters to be permeating the very heredity of working-class people, so that their physical stature diminished along with their morality. Stedman Jones contrasts the imagery with the reality of numbingly alienating environmental conditions. The London poor had to contend with a narrow employment market where much of the work available was at sweated rates such as those offered to women bookbinders, located in a city where housing was poorly constructed, insufficient and not easily replaced. But dead-end

Figure 16 Ellen Henrietta Ranyard: 'L.N.R.' (1810–79).

jobs and poor housing were perceived, in middle-class eyes, in terms of 'demoralization' and 'degeneration' on the part of a 'casual residuum'.[55]

Or as Ellen Ranyard called them, the 'submerged sixth'. Mrs Ranyard's corps of 'biblewomen' and their 'lady superintendents' undertook to cross the barriers of class, and help the London poor. To use her favourite metaphor, their mission was to forge the 'missing link' between the upper and lower classes, connecting rich and poor by bonds of gender. Ellen Ranyard, who adopted the coy pseudonym 'L.N.R.', started her philanthropic career within the Bible Society as a collector and later secretary for various Ladies' Associations.[56] She had been deeply moved by an experience at the age of sixteen, when Elizabeth Saunders, the friend who had inspired her to take up

Bible work, died of typhus contracted as a result of visiting the poor. She later moved with her family to Swanscombe, Kent and was married in 1839 to Benjamin Ranyard. As Minute Secretary of the newly formed Ladies' Association for Greenhythe and Swanscombe, Ranyard gained experience in managing a colporteur and was careful to report on the experiment to her District Agent, the Rev. T. Phillips.[57]

Ranyard's District Agent recognized her literary talents when he became Secretary of the Jubilee Committee. He asked her to write a commemorative book for the occasion. *The Book and Its Story* (1853) combines Ranyard's interests in biblical archaeology with her fervent evangelicalism. It begins with a retelling of the Bible narrative, moves into a history of the vernacular versions in the context of English Protestantism, and finishes up in a rush with the glorious achievements of the British and Foreign Bible Society. Because it fell within the category of 'note or comment', the book could not be distributed or even officially recognized by the BFBS, but the Committee voted £100 from the Jubilee Fund as a recognition of her services.[58]

Ranyard published a small pamphlet in 1854 entitled *The Bible Collectors, or Principles in Practice*. She described how the collecting process worked, in villages and also in large towns. The pamphlet was full of practical advice, such as the suggestion that the Specimens of Type (see figure 7) be glued to calico to prevent their wearing out. She promoted the revival of Ladies' Associations, but wrote frankly about their decline and the rise of colporteurs. As for the chain of command from ladies to gentlemen within the Association, to the Auxiliary, and finally to Earl Street: 'the gentlemen . . . should always be ready to assist the ladies . . . It is sometimes so difficult to get anything that is wanted, through the indifference of gentlemen's committees, that the ladies are driven to separate communications with London.'[59] Like Maria Hope thirty-five years earlier, Ranyard found the social constraints against such unladylike behaviour extremely frustrating.

In 1856 the Ranyard family moved to London, taking up residence in Hunter Street. Ranyard later told her supporters that she had been disappointed with her experience of Ladies' Associations in the Metropolis. 'She had joined one or two of their Ladies Committees and observed with regret the very fleeting and changeable character of Ladies Visitation in the courts & alleys of the city owing to their perpetual absences from home and more over [*sic*] their general difficulty in finding access further than the door.'[60] The document just cited was a draft: the grammatical weakness is not typical of Ranyard's prose. But the uncompromising criticism is typical of her approach to Bible distribution.

Ranyard may be seen as the spiritual heir of Charles Stokes Dudley, reinterpreting his appeal to women as Bible distributors in high-Victorian terms. Ranyard and the now-elderly Dudley admired each other. When in February 1858 Ranyard was involved with the Queen Square Ladies' Bible

Association in London (near her Hunter Street home in Bloomsbury), she offered to reorganize the Committee 'on Mr Dudley's plan'. The members told her they had tried it before and found it 'unnecessarily complicated'.[61] Ranyard's experience at Queen Square may have helped her to decide on a new form of service, independent of the existing association. Dudley, for his part, told Ranyard that Ladies' Associations were best, but biblewomen (he called them 'colporteuses') were acceptable in 'exceptional cases'.[62]

Ranyard told her own story of the new mission in *The Missing Link; or, Bible-Women in the Homes of the London Poor. By LNR., Author of 'The Book and Its Story'*, first published in 1859. It describes how in the winter of 1856–7, she told a physician friend of her search for 'a poor, good woman, who would venture with a bag of Bibles into every room, as a paid agent for the Bible Society, and give a faithfull [*sic*] account of her trust'. The doctor had just received a letter from a woman called Marian who had expressed a wish to help 'the lost and degraded of [her] own sex, whom, from their vicious lives, no tenderly reared female would be likely to approach'. This was just the sort of person Ranyard was seeking. Marian's visits would renew the old Bible Society project of close personal contact, and of dedicated sacrifice. But the contact would be Marian's, and the sacrifice only indirectly Ranyard's own. She knew she could be more effective if she sent an agent in her place.

It is visitation in their homes, and by those whom they will permit to enter, which is needed by the London poor. The Clergyman himself is thought by a large class too good and grand; the visits of the Scripture Reader and the City Missionary are objected to by many of the husbands in their own absence. Of the Lady Visitor they will beg, and think she has no right to come to them except she brings relief; and they say, besides, that she is seldom punctual.[63]

Marian was permitted to enter her neighbours' homes. Ranyard provided her with Bibles and Testaments at Bible Society prices, and a wage of 10s per week. This last was funded by a £5 grant from the Bible Society, one of the many payments out of the Jubilee fund to sponsor colportage.

Apparently a natural social worker, Marian expanded her services, inviting several of her clients home for tea where she overcame the fact that 'places like St Giles have their own pride and their own reserve'. She added to her repertoire recipes for soup (goes far to prevent the craving for gin), directions for making clean beds, and clothing clubs where the women gathered for community sewing of materials purchased by the biblewoman and sold to them at cost. She was careful to divide her time into the five hours a day paid for by the BFBS and the overtime during which she pursued her other activities.[64]

Ranyard's first attempt to extend the mission failed, when she asked Marian to give on-the-job training to other workers. But the biblewoman, showing an exemplary respect for the working-class culture in which she lived and worked, told Ranyard that the people she visited resented 'any perpetual introduction to strange faces, and asked if they were going to be made a puppet-show of?' Determined to expand the scope of her idea, Ranyard publicized the project in a periodical entitled *The Book and Its Missions*, and recruited other 'lady superintendents' who in turn selected biblewomen. 'Martha', recruited from amongst dust-women in Paddington, was particularly humble: 'no one would call her a naturally superior woman, like "Marian"'.[65] By June 1859 there were twenty-eight biblewomen and almost as many lady superintendents. In addition to BFBS support, a parallel philanthropy, 'Female Domestic Missions', raised funds to support the extra-biblical functions.

The lady superintendents were in charge of all money and books. When the junior members of the partnership tried to acquire clothes or bedding in advance for very needy clients, 'the *lady* element of punctuality and perfect order in the accounts' intervened. Ranyard extolled the virtues of trans-class co-operation:

The 'woman' goes where the 'lady' might not enter, and performs offices which are most fittingly rendered by persons of the working class. The floor is scrubbed by a good 'woman' better than by a pious 'lady'. Yet the lady can find the scrubbing-brush, and the soap, and materials for soup, and supplies of clothing, and the funds that are needful, and the sympathy and counsel which are indispensable, and be very blessed in her deed.[66]

The purported close relationships between women across the barriers of class portrayed in Ranyard's rhetoric are of interest to students of women's history. We want to know whether women in the past saw themselves as similar to all other women, or whether they identified with men of their social class.[67] Ellen Ranyard tried to convince her lady superintendents and her evangelical supporters that the mission crossed the boundaries of class, forging new links between women. It seems much more likely, however, that 'ladies' and 'women' lived in separate women's cultures, each with their own experience of patriarchy. Even in Ranyard's own presentation of events, her patronizing attitude to Marian Bowers and the other biblewomen is clear.[68]

Among followers of her own class, she was described as a formidable individual: 'extremely kind and extremely firm'.[69] A letter from her to a lady superintendent who had failed to get funding for her district shows how Ranyard manipulated the emotions of her followers:

I have always *hoped* that with your connections and residence at the west end of London, you would like other superintendents *aid* in obtaining funds for your own Bible-Mission ... I am sorry to hear that Mrs Burfoot should say that she 'does not wish to undertake a district with the Main object of selling Bibles' – as if selling large-*print* Bibles for easy reading by the people were not the best possible mode of access to new people. It is not a speech worthy of one of our women – therefore we shall the less regret her loss. I put it also to your own candour and second thoughts. Can you expect an individual or a Committee who have spiritual work at heart to continue contributions to work in the hands of two private individuals *year after year* who never let them know any thing about it? ... You certainly cannot be said to have worked '*under me*' – *with* me was all I ever wished, and at one time I hoped that the spiritual sympathy might have grown up between us, by *occasional* quiet interviews, such as I have with many of our workers.[70]

The letter does not convey any sense that the 'lady superintendents' experienced their work for the mission as intellectual or social emancipation, nor is it evidence that networks of friendship and sympathy were established unless they had 'L.N.R.' at their centre. And we have seen in Ranyard's conflict with Marian over access to the latter's clients that relations between women at the working-class level were equally complex and intense.

The letter to 'my dear young friend' stresses Ranyard's commitment to the Bible-distribution part of her mission. Similarly, a rare pamphlet held by the British Library exemplifies Ranyard's ideas about class, gender and bibliophilia. *The True Institution of Sisterhood; or, a Message and its Messengers* by L.N.R. was published in 1862. In it Ranyard stresses that the principles of the BFBS 'tend to keep the Agency on a broad basis'.

When from want of help and direction from her Lady Superintendent, or because she is the only female worker, she is involved too much in the secular affairs of the Mission, sells very few Bibles, and thinks *that* work is almost done in the district, we have time after time observed that the peculiar blessing departs – she is become either a sick-visitor, or vaguely, a 'female missionary'.

To preserve a coherent model of management, it was necessary to centre the mission around the distribution of printed books: 'The Mission must continue a Bible Mission, and must always be going down to the lowest.' Ranyard explained how the cultural imperialism of foreign missions could be transposed to London: 'Having observed the power of NATIVE AGENCY in Foreign Missions, it also struck her that a good poor woman, chosen from among the classes she wished explored, would probably be the most welcome visitor; while, as a paid agent, she could be kindly and firmly, though perhaps invisibly, directed as circumstances might require.' The 'decent poor', in her opinion, were well supplied after fifty years of BFBS activity. But the Mayhewian 'wandering folk' were not, and it was necessary 'to do something to place these people in a condition to profit by the book they were willing to buy' – 'it was almost impossible to sit down to read the Bible to them in the midst of their dirt'. The 'missing link' to connect with these people was the 'necessity for the re-establishment of intercourse between the higher and lower grades of Female society in our great city'.

It was further seen that the two classes of workers must be intimately connected together; that the influence of each Lady and her Bible-woman, as a twisted cord, must be let down into these depths; the SISTER IN CLASS bringing up the daughters of shame and neglect into the clean and quiet little Mission-room with hearts that will respond to the teaching of a SISTER IN CHRIST of any grade.[71]

The Ranyard project establishes the social function of bookselling in the mid-century Bible transaction. Like other BFBS supporters, Ranyard deplored the idea of giving away books: 'Our agents frequently observe ... that "lightly come, lightly go", is the fate of the *gift* Bible.'[72] She preferred the selling of books, by individuals hired for their class and gender similarity with their clients. How the project worked at the level of working-class neighbourhoods is a subject for another study.[73] But at the level of Ranyard's rhetoric, the image of the biblewomen was powerful. It presented anew, in mid-century language, the message of Dudley and his colleagues in the Ladies' Associations of thirty years earlier: difficult issues of economics, politics and class conflict could be solved. This time, significantly, a woman spoke for the idea. She claimed that a new conceptual category would translate all these problems into gender terms: man-to-man contact had notably failed, but as yet untried was the idea that women could reach out to other women across the bounds of class. But not unmediated. The quasi-commercial, quasi-spiritual transaction of the Bible sale might yet make the utopian ideal a reality.

The BFBS Committee's response to the Ranyard phenomenon was cautiously supportive. The original £5 grant was extended so that the total contribution for 1857 and 1858 was £128. When Ranyard began to publish a periodical *The Book and Its Missions* she arranged to have the *Monthly Extracts* stitched up with it.[74] In January 1859 she asked for a male colporteur who would work 'in conjunction with the Bible Women labouring in London under her superintendence' and as an instructor.[75] This arrangement was temporary. The relationship was regularized in January 1859, when rules were designed to protect the metropolitan Auxiliaries without hampering the effectiveness of the new agents. Where there was no Auxiliary, Ranyard could employ biblewomen on behalf of the BFBS, at 10s per week for five hours daily 'except Saturday, which day may be devoted to domestic purposes, and attendance on the Lady who acts as Superintendent'. But when female voluntary collectors were available, the BFBS Domestic Agent for the district had to negotiate with Ranyard, 'with a view to placing that part of the sphere of operations, which it may be least desirable for Ladies to visit, under the care of the Female Colporteur, for Bible Society purposes'. It was also desirable that the Lady Superintendents be members of the District Bible Society Committee. Voting another £100 of Jubilee-fund colportage money to the project, the Committee 'rejoice[d] to perceive the large amount of moral and social benefit which has already accompanied the work'. Despite this approval there were further 'lengthened conversations ... with a view of preventing the work of the Female Bible Colporteurs from interfering with the Association System in the Metropolis'. The Committee reported to the membership that year that while Ranyard's mission was 'the pioneer of a great social work', they felt 'the importance of drawing a clear line of distinction between Bible work and social work'.[76]

By December 1859 the system had to be simplified and dramatically modified. Colportage grants to local Auxiliaries were no longer available from the Jubilee fund, so that it would have been difficult to continue paying the wages of biblewomen. Cash grants were replaced by free grants of books, which Ranyard's agents were to sell at Society prices. Ranyard's mission used the income to pay wages. This was a departure from BFBS practice. The Society was providing indirect support to an acceptable programme of distribution. But it was also, for the first time except for extraordinary grants to charitable agencies, circulating books with no cash return. The Committee continued to keep close track of Ranyard's activities. One year after the grants of books were authorized, they set up a special Subcommittee to handle the relationship with her mission. Messrs Binns, Coles, Fordham, Forster, Gregory, Mirrielees, Norton and White saw to it that the Lady Superintendents drew scriptures from the depots of Auxiliary Societies, to be charged to the Earl Street Committee.[77]

Ranyard was interested in the format of the large-print Bibles she circulated, and innovative about promoting them. Back in Kent she had pasted Specimens of Type to calico; now she bullied the Society into providing whole pages of the various editions as samples. The Domestic Agents were asked by their local Auxiliaries for something similar, and a book was prepared 'containing a page of each Edition of the English Bible published by the Society'. The Agents suggested 'that the pages be printed on both sides of the paper, that it be stated in a foot note when a Testament and a Testament & Psalms are printed in the same type and that the book be bound in cloth with cut edges'.[78] This was a sophisticated promotional vehicle, much more appealing than the one-page 'Specimens of Type' that had dazzled the subscribers of the twenties.

Mrs Ranyard described the BFBS financial support to her staff as the 'Queen's Shilling' and insisted that it maintained the purity of her agency and its commitment to the circulation of the scriptures. Other grants were designated for different purposes. It is difficult to believe that working-class women who had taken on social work as an alternative to selling watercress, for example, differentiated clearly between one source of philanthropic funding and another. But Ranyard insisted that:

The Bible-woman may be employed for two, three, four, or five days, ONLY IN SELLING BIBLES ... She must not do any other work at the same time. If the people offer to subscribe for clothing and beds, she will say, 'I only do one thing at a time,' and 'the right thing first.' ... There would be great evil in mixing the two departments of labour; the Bible Society would never know what they paid for, and mistakes would be made in the accounts; while a particular benefit to be gained, by assembling the Women at a given hour at one place [for a clothing club meeting], would be lost likewise.[79]

Committee and donor consciences may have been soothed by this promise of the separation of spheres. Even if biblewomen distinguished between their work as booksellers and as social workers, however, it is unlikely that their clients were aware of the subtleties of the transaction in which they were engaged.

Mrs Ranyard's periodical, *The Book and Its Missions*, was retitled in 1864 in honour of her most popular book, *The Missing Link Magazine*. It circulated harrowing tales of living conditions in St Giles and other London slums, and inspiring accounts of conversions. It also continued to circulate the *Monthly Extracts* and to renew the appeal of the latter periodical to evangelicals who wished to support scripture distribution.

BFBS subscribers were no longer being asked to descend themselves 'into the depths' but to support financially, or at most superintend, the work of an alien class of people who did this kind of thing. It was clearly understood that however pious biblewomen were, like colporteurs they needed the money and were paid for what they did. Volunteers were no longer asked to enter the homes of the poor. It was not only unpleasant for them, but also ineffective. Instead, women and men of the affluent mid-Victorian middle class were asked to give generous financial donations to support the project from a comfortable distance.

Looking at women's participation in the Bible Society from the ladies of Liverpool in 1819 to the biblewomen of St Giles in 1860, we can consider to what extent the BFBS was a vehicle for women's emancipation in the nineteenth century. If emancipation is defined in terms of participation in public events, and successful experience in a transaction that was commercial and social as well as spiritual, then the Society was clearly important. At the beginning, when middle-class women like Maria Hope were restricted to a domestic role, they nevertheless tenaciously insisted upon their right to participate in the evangelical project. If male attention flagged, they seized the opportunity to carry on and were proud of their superior abilities to organize and manage. Later, when denominational and other activities claimed the time of many religious women, Ellen Ranyard and her lady superintendents recruited and organized working-class women to renew the tradition of selling Bibles to working-class people in their homes. They used the unexceptionable, beyond-criticism status of the institutionalized BFBS to establish a remarkable system. The biblewomen were the first paid social workers in the history of the profession, and their work might well have been impossible without the obscuring veil of Bible distribution.[80]

In the middle decades of the nineteenth century, then, the original BFBS plan of book distribution broke down. Sheets of the scriptures were rolling off the presses and uniformly bound copies proceeded in orderly bundles out of the bookbinding shops. Interest in missionary work and in colportage at home and abroad remained intense, but without the impetus of scarcity there was little energy for the original plan of philanthropic distribution. For Victorians of middling wealth and modest aspirations, however, the cheap

Bible of the BFBS was a desirable product for its own sake. Many of the Society's new supporters, wishing to purchase Bibles and New Testaments for their own use or for gifts to friends and family, demanded that the Society offer them for sale at a shop. Service to the individual consumer who was not a subscriber had always been troublesome. Under the Auxiliary/Association system, Bible depots had been essentially private places. Distributors had collected books from the depot to deliver, either door-to-door or at public meetings. Occasionally individual customers made their way to depots, especially in London, but for the Society to open public depots, and staff them with commissioned booksellers, was to undermine the local Auxiliaries. However when books, including Bibles, became more generally available and the Bible Society began to take its place as a national institution, this alternative had to be considered.

Early in 1857, after 'a lengthened conversation' concerning wider distribution in the Metropolis, the Committee decided to establish open depots where Bibles, New Testaments and – eventually – 'Portions' (Gospels bound separately in enamelled cloth) could be purchased.[81] The large London Auxiliaries quickly adapted to the system. The depots were under their control, except in districts where there was no BFBS local Auxiliary, in which case the central agent or individual 'friends' in the locality managed the shop. No scriptures in English were sold 'to the public generally' from Earl Street, only Bibles and Testaments 'in Foreign Living Languages'. But the depots were free to attract what customers they could. The Committee even supplied them with cabinets and with a zinc plate advising the public that Bibles and Testaments were available.

The Committee tried to maintain the strength of the old system within the new, offering books to non-subscribers at a new price 'For General Sale', and to the poor at the cost price. The difficulty was to identify who was poor. Auxiliary Collectors, or in their absence clergymen, city missionaries, colporteurs or scripture readers were permitted to certify poverty. (Within three months of the policy's institution there was a printed form.)[82] Scripture readers and 'others seeking the spiritual welfare of the poor' were asked to watch out for people interested in purchasing the Scriptures by small payments, and to give their names to the local Society. Boards were posted in Schools and public institutions advertising the existence and prices of the district depot. Each depot contained a book in which free contributions ('however small') could be entered. While it was desirable that the depot be kept by an enthusiastic Christian volunteer, provision was made to allow a remuneration of 10 per cent if necessary. The fact that the depots were institutions more commercial than benevolent is hinted at in a letter from the Secretaries of the East London Auxiliaries proposing 'a very large extension of Bible Depots, or for entering into enlarged connections with the Book Trade'.[83]

Depots controlled by BFBS members were still not sufficient to meet the demand for cheap Bibles. By 1850 the Society had entered the railway age, arranging with W. H. Smith and Son to sell foreign-language Bibles and Testaments at railway station depots. Later a shilling railway Bible in English was prepared, of which over 14,000 copies were sold by 1863. For those unable to purchase a copy, officials were supplied with 'Bible Boxes' to protect station copies on the Midland railway. In deference to visiting foreigners, the railway station book stalls in large cities and coastal towns were furnished with Bibles and Testaments in French, German, Italian and Spanish.[84] Volumes were supplied for the sitting and sleeping rooms of hotels and boarding houses in cities, towns and watering places.[85] Police stations, if they employed at least three or four men, were supplied with large-type Bibles. But there was a limit to innovative distribution: the correspondent who suggested that the Society place a copy of the scriptures in every London cab was not encouraged.[86]

Not all new distributors were favoured. Carus Wilson asked in 1856 how much aid the BFBS would give to a bookhawking society he planned to establish in Portsmouth and the Isle of Wight. The Domestic Agents were asked to advise the Committee on whether or not bookhawking societies should be encouraged. The answer was no. Although the bookhawkers' policy ('We must endeavour to drive away the Hawkers of bad books. We can only hope to succeed in our endeavour by offering for sale ... good books of every kind, at the cheapest possible rate.') was very close to that of the BFBS, the Committee believed that such societies were a threat to Auxiliaries and Associations.[87] They were also concerned that tracts, potentially controversial, were for sale alongside Bibles and Testaments. The principle of distribution 'without note or comment', when the juxtaposition of Society Bibles with other texts might be construed as a comment, was still functioning. In 1861 the newly formed Society for Reading Aloud the Word of God in the Open Air (whose objectives included the sale of the scriptures at cost price) was cautiously allowed to purchase at half price. The Society, however, abused the trust of the BFBS, selling below cost price despite repeated admonitions. By January 1863 the new organization was defunct 'owing to the want of support'.[88]

In 1864 it was finally determined that Earl Street and the London depositories were not sufficient to supply the needs of the Metropolis, and the Committee decided 'to obtain an Establishment at the West End of London for the sale of books'.[89] Cheap Bibles for the better-off, bound in roan, coloured calf or morocco, and edged in gilt, could now be had without recourse to a local voluntary Auxiliary. Although still not available in common bookshops, the price of the new books no longer incorporated a contribution to the foreign project, and their circulation could not be construed as a social transaction between rich and poor.

6 · THE TRANSACTION RENEWED, 1850s AND 1860s

At Bible meetings during the high-victorian years, subscribers enjoyed the satisfaction of hearing that the peace and prosperity their country was currently experiencing had been brought about by Bible distribution, and they responded generously to calls for a resolute continuing commitment to the cause in the face of new dangers. The apparent end of Chartism in 1848, for example, was attributed to the Society's efforts over the previous decades. And when the Roman Catholic Church began to establish British dioceses in 1851, there was an appeal for a special effort within Britain in order to halt the so-called 'papal aggression', now that 'extraordinary attempts are making to propagate among us a system known to be hostile to the unrestricted use of the Inspired Records'.[1] The Great Exhibition was the occasion for a display of 170 different versions published in 130 languages, while the Crimean War initiated a resolution to provide a New Testament to each soldier going on foreign service, and some members wondered: 'Is the ploughshare of war to break up new furrows, in which the "seed of the kingdom" may be cast?'[2] And in 1863 the combined threats of *The Origin of Species* and of *Essays and Reviews* to the literal truth of the scriptures were comfortably countered with the publication of a 2d Testament and a 6d Bible, 'as the surest safeguards against doubt and unbelief'.[3]

The sanguine claims of the fifties and sixties, however, concealed a fundamental change in the character of the British and Foreign Bible Society. In the beginning the founders had established a strong centralized organization, transposing their experience of business and commerce into the management of a voluntary society. Then foreign agents and missionaries abroad, and subscribers and supporters at home, developed a market for cheap Bibles and Testaments, indirectly stimulating the printers to record levels of production. The bookbinders of London packaged the product in a variety of appropriate covers, ready for the bookseller. Distribution was the point in the publication circuit where the BFBS departed from normal publishers' practice. In the first half-century the circuit had been closed by voluntary circulation, as members of local Auxiliaries and Associations, mostly middle-class women, sold books door-to-door to the poor, and from their town and village depots.[4] When this means of book distribution – which was not only inexpensive for the publishers at Earl Street but capable of generating an intense personal

Figure 17   Book-shaped boxes for collecting donations to the British and Foreign Bible Society.

commitment – changed in the fifties and sixties, the Bible transaction became a different sort of social relation. Increasingly, supporters – instead of collecting subscriptions for books – solicited donations for the Society, sometimes receiving the funds in book-shaped collecting boxes (see figure 17).[5] The popular concept of cheap Bibles began to focus not so much on the artifacts, as on the ideal.

The pulse of change may be taken at an 1867 meeting in Witchampton, Dorset, described by the District Secretary (since 1861 they were no longer called Agents) G. T. Edwards in the *Monthly Reporter* (no longer merely *Extracts of Correspondence*). Edwards regarded this as 'the model Bible Association of all England. Here is a village numbering not more than about 600 inhabitants, which sent last year, in Free Contributions to the Parent Society, £94 5s 10d, and, since 1830, the total amount of £1641 12s 7d.' Part of Witchampton's donation was from 'the parrot of a worthy woman, who had taught it to ask for Contributions with a tin Collecting-box attached to its cage, [which] produced £2'.[6] In London, as in the provinces, the Society seemed to be inescapable. Its influence had penetrated to the poor weavers' cottages in Spitalfields, where one woman ruefully recounted her experience: 'My husband bought "that Book" in Ireland, and it's changed him so, I've never had a bit of a dance or fun with him since. I sold it once for half a pint of whisky; but ... I was obliged to get it back.'[7] These illustrations may be multiplied by hundreds of accounts of collectors and donors in villages, towns and cities, and tested against the more substantial evidence of receipts, productivity and expenditure. Taken together, they indicate that the organization had got firmly woven into the fabric of English society: popular participation in the publication of scriptures was now accepted socially, taken for granted, even expected.

When the hero of James Anthony Froude's *Nemesis of Faith* presumed to criticize the BFBS at a 'religious tea-party', he offended the sensibilities of his neighbours, who were convinced that 'a universal millennium was very near indeed through this Bible activity', which would save a world 'grinding between the nether millstone of Popery and the upper millstone of Infidelity'. In earlier years the Society's leaders had urged circumspection and prudence upon those who shared their conviction, not the flaunting of parrots or the insulting of literary clergymen. Now Froude's character was scorned because he 'shrank from meetings where a number of people are brought together ... to give money to help others in a remote employment. There is a good deal of talking and excitement, and they go away home fancying they have done great things.'[8]

The Society's tremendous contemporary prominence may be observed in the context of its participation in the Great Exhibition of 1851. The Crystal Palace was built to house exhibits from all over Britain and the rest of the world. Prince Albert worked closely with the exhibition organizers to demonstrate human progress in the scientific and technical realms. At first glance there seemed to be no place for the celebration of religious triumphs. Edwin Hodder, Lord Shaftesbury's biographer, has described how his subject, as incoming President of the BFBS, asked Prince Albert for a BFBS display at the Great Exhibition. His Royal Highness first declined, on the grounds that the theme of the fair was scientific progress. Shaftesbury cited the existence of versions of the scriptures in 170 languages, which justified inclusion in the Exhibition 'from an intellectual point of view', and the Prince graciously told him 'you have proved your right to appear'.[9] The incident is evidence that BFBS officers had access to the Royal family and to politicians. The old BFBS policy of appointing aristocrats to its official positions continued to pay off handsomely. It also suggests a new willingness to let the Society stand on its reputation as a publisher, not to emphasize its image as a religious society. But behind the scenes, in the minute books and correspondence, the incident is more complex. It appears that some space was initially granted to the Society by the Exhibition officials, but that it was insufficient. Initially, a mere 5 square feet of wall, with a stand projecting 2 feet from it, was allowed. The Committee's representatives were thinking in terms of a bookcase 30 feet by 7, and 2 feet deep. This request was granted on 27 January 1851 by the Exhibition's Council of Appeal, but as excitement mounted, the Society became convinced that it was not enough.[10]

Plans went ahead to select foreign-language and English versions for the exhibition and to bind them uniformly in plain blue morocco with gilt edges. Realizing that large numbers of Exhibition visitors would be drawn from all over the world, the Society circulated multilingual handbills, announcing that editions of the New Testament and Psalms were supplied on loan for the use of hotels and lodging houses. These books were bound more modestly in sheep and stamped with their loan status. Someone even suggested that a man be hired to circulate in the Crystal Palace bearing a large placard on a board, but this idea was not put into practice.[11] In April the Subcommittee reported that they had secured a display in a bookcase 23 feet long by 9 feet high, containing 'a set of 170 versions in 127 languages of the Scriptures bound uniformly in purple morocco with gilt edges & ranged open on slopes, each version labelled with its own title & in English, & the number of copies printed in each language expressed'. The report continued: 'After many difficulties & much objection on the part of the Executive Committee [of the Exhibition] to the admission of so large a Case & its removal from the very unsuitable position first assigned to it, the Case is now fixed in the northern aisle of the western division immediately behind the Fine Arts Court.' The Secretaries made further concessions to the holiday spirit of the Great Exhibition, by opening accounts with local booksellers and with Religious Tract Society depots to sell scriptures in the European languages; the Earl Street depository was opened for public sale during the exhibition, and 100 copies each of French-English, French-German, and Italian Testaments for loan stock were placed in lodging-house and hotel rooms.[12]

But when the Bible Society's subscribers began to visit the Great Exhibition, they were dismayed at the modest size and obscure location of the exhibit. Strong remarks were made on the subject at a public meeting. A month after the Exhibition's doors had opened, Lord Ashley was approached to intercede with the Prince Consort. George Browne told the new President that 'very great dissatisfaction' had been expressed, and asked Ashley to use his influence to secure a better position, adding the reasoning that Ashley presumably used with Prince Albert: 'As works of art and genius, as well as of industry, learning, and Christian piety, we think these *Specimens* may well be regarded among the "curiosities" of the age; – and as well deserving a prominent place ... But I will not attempt to furnish your Lordship with arguments in support of our suit.'[13] No doubt Lord Ashley did intercede with the Prince, but the story has been simplified and strengthened, so that the degree of prominence of the display has been replaced by a threat to its very existence.

Even after royal intercession, the display still failed to satisfy some BFBS subscribers, who as usual felt they had a right to offer detailed advice to the Secretaries. James Cadbury of Banbury wrote to Browne, suggesting that 'the difficulty of the present hidden part the general Exhibition of Scriptures is placed in', might be solved if 'a copy of each translation [were placed] in connexion with every Court ... to form part of the objects of interest attached to that Country'. One can imagine the reaction of Prince Albert and of his scientific and technical advisors to this pious suggestion. Cadbury also urged the Committee to consider 'the Foreigner admiring his own productions. He may be really unconscious that a Bible exists in his country. Can you have a better mode of introducing it to him.'[14] Browne and his predecessors had expended considerable energy, for fifty years, on introducing the scriptures in foreign countries. So, most likely, had Cadbury himself, but the enthusiasm of the grand fair was infectious. The incident suggests that the Society was beginning to have to seek new justifications, intellectual and aesthetic, rather than spiritual, for its prominent position in the mainstream of society.

Despite the smugness, the established respectability and the assured rhetoric of the Victorian Bible Society, there is evidence of significant deterioration at the level of its internal economics, and of its structure as a voluntary organization. Although income soared for projects like the 'Million Testaments for China' fund, it became increasingly difficult to recruit women or men to distribute Bibles and Testaments in London. Even in villages like Witchampton, 'free contributions' to the foreign project were easier to generate than penny-a-week subscriptions. Many supporters now found themselves inspired by a more abstract vision of global conversion, a vision that required the persuasive powers of the missionary, not merely the accessibility of the printed word. The renewed Bible transaction was less dependent upon the publishing process, and it was no longer shaped by intense volunteer involvement in the production and distribution of printed books.

The Jubilee of the Society in 1853–4 may be taken as a turning point, when the subscribing members of this powerful organization began to show evidence of a changing commitment. On 7 March 1853 a small Jubilee meeting was held at the London Tavern, in the room where the Society had been founded forty-nine years before. Of the founders, only Foreign Secretary C. F. A. Steinkopf and one member of the Committee, William Alers Hankey, survived to be honoured. The next day a gala crowd gathered in Exeter Hall to celebrate the Society's Jubilee and initiate the raising of a special fund, which eventually amounted to over £70,000. Charles Stokes Dudley, however, by now the voice of the past in the councils of the Society, warned that there were disadvantages even to Royal patronage. 'I am rejoiced & thankful that our good Queen's attention was called to the Jubilee fund', he told Hitchin. '[God bless] you, & every loyal subject will say amen! but Papists & Tractarians will not respond, after such an act.'[15] Few other members of the Society were concerned. They got on with planning for the celebration. A special Jubilee Subcommittee, staffed by the Rev. Thomas Phillips, prepared publications and received deputations from local Auxiliary leaders.[16] One of these was Manchester: the local secretaries insisted that the Irish migrants now flooding into their city be included among the beneficiaries of the Jubilee fund. Eyre and Spottiswoode published four new editions for the occasion, a Crown quarto, a Small Pica, and a Diamond Bible, all with marginal references, and a Pearl foolscap octavo Bible.[17] C. S. Dudley was invited to edit the manuscript of a 'Jubilee statement' but was prevented by his failing health. Nevertheless 'an extraordinary amount of printed paper' was produced by the Subcommittee, and the reader of their minutes begins to wonder whether this group almost took over the business of the Society during the year of Jubilee.[18]

The special fund was cast in such a way that the situation of its beneficiaries appealed to the philanthropic impulses of the mid-century culture. The fund had five objectives: first the adoption of colportage throughout Great Britain during the Jubilee year, along with supplies to emigrants and other special grants. The second objective was special grants to Ireland, as recommended by Manchester; third, a campaign in 'India, Australia, and other British colonies'. Fourth was a plan for special grants to China. Finally there was a pension fund to aid the retired employees of the Society and their widows and children.[19]

News of the Taiping rebellion in China, and of the commitment of its leaders to Christianity, had raised British hopes for a massive programme of evangelism there. The notion of printing and distributing one million copies of the Chinese New Testament was particularly appealing: children contributed from their pocket-money and deprived themselves of fireworks on the fifth of November; the tea-dealers of Edinburgh, Leith and vicinity decided that the project 'had special claims on the tea-trade' and contributed generously. The amount estimated to produce a million copies at 4d each was exceeded by February 1854, when £18,382 had been raised, but contributions continued until the total was £52,368. The disbursement of this sum was much more difficult than its collection. Canton reports that 'in the broad and enthusiastic simplicity of its first conception at least, the Million Testament scheme was never realized', and by 1862 the Committee had to admit themselves to be 'in perplexity of mind, if not in dejection of soul' on the subject.[20] But the initial enthusiasm was overwhelming. Unlike the years of the Apocrypha controversy, when subscribers carefully considered the Society's distribution policy before contributing to a project abroad, people now seemed willing to give generously to support a simple and compelling idea, even though no practical strategy had been developed to realize its execution.

The Bible Society was now very wealthy. The figures in the appendix show that income increased dramatically in the fifties and sixties, mostly as a result of the Jubilee and China funds. The expenditures rose in proportion, supporting ambitious projects of translation and distribution around the world. Sales of books at home, and the parallel contributions from Auxiliary Societies, also increased although at a modest rate that did not keep pace with national increases in population or in wealth.

It is instructive to compare the Bible Society with other recipients of charitable donations. In his *English Philanthropy*, David Owen used figures for 1861 from *Low's Charities of London* to delineate 'the infinitely diverse expressions, almost aberrations, of the humanitarian impulse'. In that year Sampson Low calculated the aggregate income of 640 London agencies at nearly £2.5 million. With this in mind, we may examine the 'Abstract of the Cash Account' in the Bible Society's 1861 annual *Report*.[21]

For the general purposes of the Society:	£84,255
For Bibles and Testaments:	82,910
From Chinese New Testament fund	644
From India Fund	134
Contributions to benevolent fund	571
Sale of stocks	6,510
Sale of exchequer bills	15,016
	190,040
Balance in hand 31 March 1860 (cash and bills)	16,738
Total receipts:	£206,778

By contrast, Low calculated that funding for Metropolitan general hospitals amounted to £58,049 in donated income plus £126,809 from dividends, property or trade. Educational causes (thirty-one societies promoting and aiding schools) took in £73,443, supplemented with £14,934 from investments. Low lumped the BFBS with fifty-five other 'Bible and Home Missionary Societies', the aggregate income of which was the second-highest total, £332,679 plus £35,780. The highest-earning charities in Low's compilation were the twenty-five Foreign Missionary funds, earning more than £600,000 in all.[22] Besides indicating clearly that the BFBS rated among the wealthiest of Societies, Low's figures also demonstrate its encroaching weakness. Foreign missions, close as they were to the Society as translators of new versions and as distributors, were attracting the bulk of new donations. Tales of missionaries, like anecdotes about colporteurs and biblewomen and the text of George Borrow's *The Bible in Spain*, were now capturing the national imagination.

Its increasing resemblance to other contemporary religious causes, however, does not fully explain the mid-century transformation of the BFBS. The Society is still most accurately characterized as a consumer of printing and bookbinding services, that is, as a publisher oriented to producing large quantities of books as inexpensively as possible. The changing character of the Society's popularity must be interpreted also in the light of trends in the contemporary book trade. Readers in the mid-Victorian years had no difficulty in obtaining books. The cheap Bible was freely available thanks to stereotyping and standing type, to tough paper, to efficient printing and inexpensive binding. Cheap literature, moreover, was everywhere – both the pious and improving kind and more entertaining varieties – printed by steam in massive quantities.[23] The British 'religious public' was no longer motivated, as it had been in 1804 and up to 1840, by a scheme designed to obtain book-trade products and services in bulk and at affordable prices. The scarcity of printed Bibles had been confronted and dealt with long ago, to a large extent by the Society itself. Some working-class people, as at Manchester in 1845, could afford to buy a copy in a single purchase, while others, as in Mrs Ranyard's slums, were susceptible only to the right kind of agent. Wealthier mid-Victorians, if they considered the problem of making cheap Bibles more widely available, were more likely to question the propriety of the Queen's Printer's monopoly than to contribute to the BFBS.

The final assault on the 'bibliopolist' and his 'monopoly in the word of God' took place in 1859–60, in the context of an increased popular commitment to the idea of free trade. The Corn Laws had been repealed in 1846 and advocates of *laissez-faire* were quick to claim for their doctrine all the economic advantages that followed. A board of arbitrators had recently (1852) declared that there should be free trade in books.[24] Surely it was anathema, went the cry, that the trade in Bibles should be protected. A further Select Committee of the House of Commons looked into the Queen's Printers' and Universities' patents. The Committee included several prominent politicians: William Ewart, Lord Robert Cecil, John Bright and Lord Robert Montagu. In the end they recommended against renewing the Royal patent, but on such a slim majority that the privilege was renewed after all, in 1860. The Bible Society's interest in maintaining the monopoly has not previously been pointed out. During the presentation of evidence to the Select Committee, an officer of the Society spoke strongly, albeit unofficially, in support of the *status quo*. Although it cannot be proved that the BFBS was the reason why the privilege survived, there is clear evidence that the Society preferred that it be maintained, and a strong possibility that their formidable authority, thrown into the balance on the side of the privileged Presses, may have affected the outcome. In any case, their effect on the price of Bibles and on the dynamics of the privileged Presses had already been such that the outcome of the Select Committee made very little difference, either to the domestic market or to the fortunes of the Queen's Printer and the Universities. Until further technological improvements became available, Bibles were unlikely to be much cheaper.

This thwarted Select Committee produced a report that reads like a summary of all the anti-monopolist opinion of the previous twenty years.[25] They argued that the exclusive privilege was 'wrong in principle' and 'opposed to public interest'. In their opinion the effect of abolishing the Scottish King's Printer's monopoly had been a 50 per cent reduction of the selling price, and the same benefits could be had in England. 'Perfect freedom of competition would be likely to produce and maintain the greatest attainable cheapness, as well as the utmost beauty and attractiveness of typography and binding.' Textual accuracy would be guaranteed by the vigilance of the Christian public, the care of clergy and ministers, and by 'the special attention of religious societies established for the purpose of circulating the Bible'. Other safeguards were the criticism of the press, 'the knowledge which booksellers must acquire of the merits of different editions', the interest of printers and publishers, whose inaccurate editions would be unsaleable, and finally the efforts of Eyre and Strahan and the Universities to sustain their reputation, together with the stereotype plates and other advantages which they possessed.

Opponents of the privilege noted that prices charged by the Queen's Printer had been falling since 1840, and ascribed the situation to competition caused by the abolition of the patent in Scotland, and the subsequent incursion into England of Edinburgh Bibles produced by William Collins and other printers. But there was an alternative explanation. When the 'bibliopolist' himself, William Spottiswoode, took the stand, he attributed the change to the use of steam presses and other machinery. Robert Potts of Trinity College, Cambridge, who frequently used the services of the University Press, agreed. But other witnesses, both printers and non-printers, were quick to draw the conclusion that abolition had reduced prices in Scotland, and would do the same in England and Wales, without any loss of accuracy. Witness Frederick Warne, a publisher who knew

nothing about the Bible trade, observed that his firm objected to the monopoly on principle.

Those whose objections were practical were more vehement. Charles
Knight, politician and publisher of the Society for the Promotion of Useful
Knowledge, who had produced a very popular Pictorial Bible in 1836,[26]
argued strongly for free trade in Bibles, proposing some textual moderniz-
ations which he said would be possible when the hidebound monopolists
were out of the way. He referred to the convention of printing in italics, in the
scriptures, words not used in the original languages. Knight said the practice
confused ordinary readers and should be abolished for common editions.
Punctuation should be modernized. He instanced, as an advantage of competition, Bibles produced in Scotland with an innovative binding feature:
they were bound with initial letters of individual books impressed on the
fore-edge. Robert Besley, the stereotype printer, testified once more, arguing

that one of the effects of this monopoly was to exclude from the printing of the Bible
the mechanical skill and taste of the present time, and to perpetuate the same form of
book from generation to generation; the same uncomfortable thing to handle, and the
same uninviting page to read ... Were the duty taken off paper, and the Bible printing
monopoly done away, I would venture to predict that in 10 years the present class of
what are called cheap Bibles and Testaments will be, in booksellers' phrase "scarce
and valuable," and their places supplied by good wholesome readable books.

Referring to a modernized paragraph edition of the Gospels (edited by Dr
Henry Cotton, and printed privately at Oxford by John Henry and James
Parker in 1857) with no chapter heads, brackets instead of italics for words
not in the original, and other innovations, Besley offered the intriguing
suggestion that the printers should have a copyright on 'that mode of
arrangement in printing', that is, on the book's design. Knight and Besley
were both up-to-date printers, in tune with contemporary trends in book
publishing, sensitive to a commercial market, and anxious to take advantage
of the popular demand for cheap Bibles. The radical tone of their proposals
about book design marks the limits of the Bible Society's willingness to
innovate. The Committee and Secretaries were efficient and direct, but not
iconoclasts. They were prepared to tinker with the page format, move
references and delete tables, but not to change drastically the physical
experience of Bible-reading. They retained the traditional evangelical rever-
ence for the sacred text, which translated into a passion for accuracy.

For the first time at one of these Select Committees, a Bible Society
executive testified. James Franklin, the Depositary who had succeeded
Richard Cockle in 1851, told them he superintended the purchase and issue of
books and negotiated with printers, papermakers and bookbinders. Franklin
gave it as his 'private opinion' (he was not representing the BFBS officially)
that the present system was advantageous. In his view the number of orders
divided among three Presses induced competition, but more would not. He

noted that the Society's foreign Bibles printed by open competition cost more than did English ones. Asked about the possibility that the monopolists might combine 'to keep prices up', he answered, 'I should consider, as a man of business, that such a course would be highly injudicious and suicidal.' Suicidal because such an action would cause the privileged Presses to lose their monopoly. As we have seen, this was diplomatic: the Presses had certainly begun by agreeing upon the prices, but for many years now had submitted to having them established by the Societies.

Asked about the large increase of circulation in 1846, Franklin did not mention the extraordinary demand in Manchester that year. Instead he attributed it to the effect of contracting for the services of a single binder. John Bright, himself one of the most outspoken of freetraders, saw his chance and asked why such arrangements would not work in a free market for printing. No, Franklin said, 'the cases are not exactly parallel'. The chief advantage of a Bible-printing monopoly was accuracy. 'In every case of discovery, the Society requires all copies (even those scattered over the country at its various depots) to be made perfect, even to the minutiae of orthography and punctuation.' Franklin preferred shops where printing the Bible was the sole occupation, not secondary to other work: 'The Bible printer is constantly reading and re-reading his Bibles, one with another, and always varying the combinations, so that in the process of time almost every edition is compared with every other one, and every variation, to the minutest particular, brought to light.' For Franklin and his principals at Bible House, the limited competition among the three Presses was as close as they could possibly come to the sort of contracted monopoly they had secured at the bookbinders, and an acceptable way to keep control over the production of books without actually undertaking the operation of a printshop. The traditional argument for the Universities' privilege, that they would maintain the accuracy of the scriptures, now extended to the Queen's Printer too. To retain the Bible Society's custom, they kept each other up to a very high standard.

The Queen's Printer's patent still survives, along with the charters of the two University Presses. They control the printing of the Authorized Version of 1611 only, not the Revised Version and the myriad other English-language renderings published since then. But since the middle of the nineteenth century, the privilege has not been a great source of profit to the Presses that hold it. Printing historian P. M. Handover notes that 'since the demand for cheap Bibles, competitively produced, the profits in Bible printing have not been sufficient to attract infringement of the patent, and no prudent English book printer is likely to attempt it'. And as M. H. Black observes, 'the margins secured by the competitors in this market were now almost as thin as the paper they used'. The existence of the BFBS and its decentralized popular structure had a profound influence on the economics of the privileged Presses. The effect has been succinctly stated by a historian of printing with respect to

Oxford: 'the Bible Societies created a ready market which at first reduced prices but later depressed them'. Black, speaking of the Cambridge Press in the early eighteen-sixties, continues, 'the University presses, who could reasonably represent that they needed something like the Bible if they were to accept losses on scholarly publishing, were less able to feel that the Bible was a support they could rely on'.[27]

In the light of our knowledge of the economic and social structure of the British and Foreign Bible Society, it is possible now to sharpen this analysis. It seems that the lucrative Bibles of the privileged Presses gave way to the cheap Bibles of the Society. Before about 1840, books were costly to produce, and the BFBS could persuade the Presses to offer only modest economies of scale. In those days the Committee was satisfied with moderately high prices for the domestic market, since half the value of books sold by local Auxiliaries remained in Earl Street for the foreign project. Since 1840, however, the cost of producing Bibles and Testaments in English had been dropping. And when the Society was forced to seek alternative measures for home distribution at mid-century, the direct relationship between prices at the privileged Presses and the funds of the organization came to an end. By the late fifties, then, not only had costs declined, but the foreign project of the BFBS was no longer subsidized by book sales generated through the medium of the local voluntary Auxiliaries. Nor did the 'monopolist' dare to augment prices artificially, despite his patent. It was shared by two other privileged Presses, and all were subject to the vigilance of the Committee and Secretaries.

A further implication of the relationship between the BFBS and Oxford and Cambridge concerns the development of the two University Presses as scholarly publishers. The Society's Bibles were not examples of fine printing, such as a University Press might have been expected to produce. Around 1852, Edward Pickard Hall, one of the Oxford partners wrote:

> No one regrets more than the present managers of the privileged presses the prevalence of the cheap and nasty principle. But what are they to do? The great Bible and Prayer Book distribution societies in order to lose as little as possible by their liberal distribution of books ... screw down the price to the lowest possible ... What can be expected when a testament containing 464 pages, the paper for which alone costs a penny, is expected to be set up, machined, dried, pressed and sold for three-half-pence.[28]

Had they not been preoccupied with printing 'cheap and nasty' Bibles, the Presses might have experimented with modern book design and with fine printing. On the other hand, without the patent to sustain the physical plant and bring in technological innovations, the Presses might not have survived at all. Undoubtedly Bible-printing was very significant to both Universities. And it was not until after the privilege became unprofitable that scholarly publishing finally came into its own.

The Bible Society, not the privileged Presses, rendered Bible-printing a commercial and mass-market proposition in the nineteenth century. From the beginning, the 'commercial part of the Committee' knew how to appreciate the advantages of competition, as they had told Andrew Wilson, and learned how to manage it to produce the cheap editions they required. They did not ask the Presses to produce fine collector's editions of the scriptures. Batey notes that 'it is impossible to look back with satisfaction to the years from 1820 to 1870 when the main occupation of the Press was the printing of cheap and inferior Bibles. It is not surprising, therefore, that the Press at Oxford produced no outstanding Bible during the hundred years of our review.' But though fine quality was neglected, an outstanding quantity of plain, sturdy, useful Bibles was produced at all three Presses in that time, in a great variety of formats. The government was told that Bibles were printed 'cheaper than the cheapest newspapers of the day'.[29] The economics of Bible-publishing had been recast in mass-market terms, and it was not the privileged printers, but rather popular enthusiasm for the Society, that created the transformation.

The privilege, nevertheless, was extremely useful to a Society whose history of crisis and conflict had not been forgotten. As long as they acquired the books they circulated in Britain from the privileged Presses, the Committee and Secretaries could disclaim final accountability for the price, the quality, the format, and above all the accuracy of the books they circulated. These matters were still the responsibility of another institution. Similarly the contract with Lorina Watkins had allowed Andrew Brandram and George Browne to tell subscribers they had no right to interfere with the wages of bookbinders. The Bible Society used the rhetoric of *laissez-faire* to its own advantage, offering one monopoly to an entrepreneur on the basis of competition, and upholding another in the name of accuracy. The Bible Society needed the privilege, just as the Presses needed the Society's popular market. The Society's leaders at Bible House were well aware for many years that there was a limit to 'the cheap and nasty principle'. Joseph Tarn, Andrew Brandram and George Browne, with Richard Cockle and James Franklin, knew that in order for the Bible transaction to flourish as an international proposition, the price of books at home should not be 'screwed down' to the lowest possible point. This was not a view that could be trumpeted in promotional publications, because it was not always easy to convince local Auxiliary and Association members that prices at home should remain reasonably high to maintain funding for distribution abroad. But it was a crucial element in the economics of the Bible transaction, and one that underlies the decision in the nineteenth century not to allow 'free trade in Bibles', but rather to maintain a 'monopoly in the word of God'. The relationship between the Society and the Presses was symbiotic. Each acted to shape the other's history, so that in 1865 the Syndics of the Press at Cambridge agreed, 'to contribute £50 out of the Partnership Funds towards

Figure 18   Second Bible House, 146 Queen Victoria
Street, London.

the Building Fund of a new Bible House for the British and Foreign Bible Society'.[30]

The occasion for the Society's abandonment of Earl Street and undertaking the construction of a new Bible House was the Thames Embankment Bill, passed in 1863. Designed to improve the flow of traffic between Westminster and the City, it required the demolition of offices and warehouses, including 10 Earl Street, and the construction of a new thoroughfare from Blackfriars Bridge to the Mansion House. The Society built an elaborate establishment at number 146 in the new Queen Victoria Street, where a foundation stone was laid in June 1866 by the Prince of Wales. Special funds were raised for the purpose. Besides the donation from Cambridge University Press, Queen Victoria gave £100, and many others added their contributions. The design was by the Parisian Edward l'Anson, who also designed the Royal Exchange Buildings (see figure 18).[31] There were criticisms that the new building was wastefully opulent, and the District Secretaries warned that 'by way of meeting questions and objections ... a fuller statement should go forth from this House, as to the reasons for selecting the contemplated situation of the new House and the cost of the Site & building'. Furthermore, if donations were insufficient, they said, the expenditures should be taken from 'the large reserve fund now in possession of the Society rather than that the ordinary contributions of the Auxiliaries should be diminished by any general appeal'.[32] The Auxiliaries, it was felt, could not stand any further assaults on their finances. The new building, with its magnificent staircase and central location, was opened in 1869.[33]

The officers who presided over the move, and over this period of financial growth and voluntary decline, were mostly new to their positions. Anthony Ashley Cooper, Lord Ashley, about to become Lord Shaftesbury, took over the presidency in 1851 when Lord Bexley died. He added the BFBS to the long list of philanthropic organizations in which he held honorific positions. John Thornton served as Treasurer until his death in 1861, and John Bockett, a Clapham gentleman retired from business, held the post until 1869. On the executive staff, Andrew Brandram died in 1850.[34] G. J. Collinson was appointed to fill the office in 1851 but died and was replaced by Robert Frost (1853–7) and then successively by John Mee (1858–61) and Charles Jackson (1862–79). Samuel B. Bergne took over as Dissenting Secretary when George Browne retired in 1854. William Hitchin had been Assistant Secretary to the Society since 1837 when Joseph Tarn died. In the depository, James Franklin replaced Richard Cockle in 1851.

As we saw in chapter 1, the Committee membership in these prosperous years included a higher proportion of 'gentry', and of medical and military men. In a wealthier society, retired businessmen could afford to live as country gentlemen, or at least in suburban leisured comfort. And the contemporary trend to increasing numbers in the professions was reflected in a larger cohort of career physicians and soldiers on the Committee. There were still numerous merchants, bankers and tradesmen, but the demographic and social identity of these descriptions had changed somewhat by mid-century. As Edward Corderoy of the Southwark Auxiliary said at a Jubilee meeting, 'Forty years ago men lived over their warehouses or adjoining their counting houses: now, all seek fresh air as soon as the toils of business are over' – and escape to their homes in the suburbs.[35]

As the participation of volunteers declined, the commitment of staff became more important. Charles Stokes Dudley led a team of field workers, the Domestic Agents, until his retirement in 1857. Dudley's territory was taken over by the Rev. J. P. Hewlett. Hewlett had long been involved with the Society, having travelled as a volunteer 'deputation' to local Auxiliary meetings for twenty years.[36] An astute observer of the contemporary scene, he presented a report, later 'printed for private circulation', at a Conference of the District Secretaries in 1867. This constructive critique of the Society is a useful document that indicates the changing tone of the organization.[37]

Hewlett identified some 'circumstances which ... hinder the growth, and even the continuance, of the prosperity of our Society'. The first such circumstance was no less than the fundamental principle of distribution without note or comment, which Hewlett characterized as 'the *breadth*, the *catholicity, of its basis*'. Hewlett still valued this catholicity, but he realized that religious politics had changed since the days of the Clapham 'saints'. In the atmosphere of denominationalism and religious parties that had developed by 1867, 'few feel a deep and personal responsibility for that which avowedly belongs to no party'. He did not recommend any alteration in the Society's structure or constitution, but noted that District Secretaries and indeed the whole management of the Society should begin to recognize a new way of thinking.

Secondly, Hewlett observed, 'the Society is *no longer* invested with the charms of *novelty* ... [so that] we can scarcely reckon on winning crowds as in the days of Owen and of Dudley'.

The third point is crucial to our understanding of the way the Society was interpreted by contemporaries. Hewlett referred to the controversy over prayer at meetings discussed in chapter 1 above:

The Society is increasingly *religious*, and increasingly identified in religion with that party, whether in or out of the Established Church, which is called '*Evangelical.*' There cannot be the shadow of a doubt but that, without altering a single letter of our constitution, the all but universal practice of opening our meetings with oral prayer has virtually revolutionized the Society ... [I]t is rare indeed to find present at [meetings] either Tractarians or Broad-Churchmen, on the one hand, or violently political or rationalist Dissenters on the other. Hence also we *have* much less, and from year to year must expect still less, of the support of worldly men. The decidedly religious element will increasingly repel the drinking squire, the swearing lord, and the man who has taken the chair in the hope of increasing his votes at the next election.

Here we have an unembarrassed analysis of how the Society's recruitment policy had changed since the thirties and forties, when printed Bibles had been hard to find but the circulation of them appealed strongly to all sorts of people, including 'worldly men'. Hewlett pointed out that 'as such men drop off, the Society must suffer in regard to funds, to numbers, and to mere worldly respectability'. The transformation had already begun. Local Auxiliaries and the Committee itself had been opening meetings with prayer since 1858.

Then Hewlett turned to the fact that the BFBS was a publishing business. He noted that 'owing to changes of a comparatively recent date' (presumably the sale at the depositories of such luxurious editions as the roan gilt-edged Pearl Bible)

the Society ... has acquired the appearance and the reputation of being a *commercial* institution, and this, in some respects, greatly to its disadvantage. In earlier days the *charitable* nature of our operations was constantly kept before the public. There was an urgent necessity to be met, and it *was* met, sometimes in the way of *direct gift*, more commonly in that of handing over a plain, cheap Bible, with what has been called the 'charity brand' upon it, in return for the small cost received in weekly pence through the medium of our Ladies' Associations.

Hewlett was not denying that the Society was in fact a mercantile institution. What concerned him was the commercial image, recently acquired, which conflicted with the older popular view of the BFBS as a 'religious society'. He continued, discussing the difficulties encountered by the various efforts to improve circulation:

We had then no depots, no sales in open shops, no rivalry with 'the trade,' or with other societies, no gilt-edged or clasped Bibles. It is otherwise now. The *pressing* necessity has, very generally, disappeared. Our depots and our elegant Bibles are everywhere. Trade jealousy is aroused. Other societies are engaged in a neck and neck race with us. We allow percentages on sales. We regard the numbers sold as one test of prosperity. We have the reputation of having become commercial, and in truth, are so, in all things but one – *profit*.

Perhaps, he hinted, the BFBS should sell the highly valued slick Bibles at a profit, which could be invested in the foreign operations. 'Certainly, the odium would not be greater with the trade.' Similarly, although more discreetly, a contemporary editor and publisher observed that the Society's objective was 'never to the entire satisfaction of the great printing organisations ... For long years the words "Sold under cost price" ... excited mingled feelings among those interested in the book trade.'[38]

Hewlett's other worries were more general, concerning 'the *state and habits of Society*'. Unlike the generation of 1804 ('our more quiet and plodding fathers'), contemporary business made people greedy: 'Moderate profits, and a moderate competency, the result of many years of steady application, have ceased to attract.' Men were too busy with business and commuting to 'join in the quiet consultations of a Bible Committee'. Presumably Hewlett and his colleagues had first-hand and frustrating experience of inattention, both at local Auxiliary meetings and in the Earl Street Committee room. On the other hand 'the claims of *pleasure* are pursued with an eagerness no less absorbing'. He ruefully recognized 'that the habits of sixty years ago were much more favourable to those who *founded* the Society, than are those of today to us who seek to *maintain* it in prosperity'. The new diversions in question were archery, croquet, bazaars, rifle-shooting, oratorios and concerts, regattas, 'and every conceivable form of amusement'. Furthermore all classes, even artisans, had contracted 'luxurious and expensive habits'. Their contributions had not kept pace with their income: 'the guinea which a man gave to the Society when he was a struggling tradesman remains a guinea now that he is, or is presumed to be, a prosperous merchant. Hence the free contributions ... have not increased in proportion to the increased wealth of the country.' Nor did the fluctuations of the economy help. When the price of Cornish tin had been nearly halved by competition, the contributions of Cornwall Auxiliaries were not likely to be maintained.

Another problem was the trend to urbanization, viewed with consternation by many observers: 'The country village is, in proportion to its means, a far better friend to the Society than the great city. We all know the result if the West-end of London be compared with Dorsetshire, or Bradford with the Isle of Anglesea [*sic*]. All these things in our social state at the present time appear to bode more or less unfavourably for the future of our Society.' Echoing Ellen Ranyard, Hewlett found that the Metropolis was an unsympathetic place to recruit Bible workers.

Turning his attention to the churches, Hewlett found that denominational rivalries were weakening the old commitments to the Bible Society. By the mid-sixties, much of the energy for pan-evangelical co-operation had dissipated, and many people felt drawn instead to denominational projects. 'If the Church takes it up warmly, the Dissenters are cold. If some one Dissenting community resolutely stands by it, then other Dissenting bodies and the Church stand aloof.' He scorned the 'pernicious heresy' of Ritualism within his own Established Church and aestheticism outside it: 'Whatever weakens attachment to Protestant principles and practices tends to weaken the Bible Society.' There were increasing numbers of requests to organize Associations around a Church or Chapel, rather than a geographical District. Even more ominously, it was becoming difficult to get an English bishop to appear at the Annual Meeting at Exeter Hall.

Hewlett even dared to suggest that more churches and chapels were being built than were needed by 'those actually under the power of religion'. Novel societies and philanthropies abounded, and 'to encourage them is one of the good-natured whims of the present day'. To the detriment of the old Bible Society. Hewlett was tactful enough not to specify examples. He concluded, however, that the Christian ministry was becoming secularized, with a variety of activities 'toning down the spirituality, and marring the real religious usefulness, of great numbers'. It was increasingly difficult to find 'gentlemanly, able, catholic, and spiritually-minded men, to represent the Society'. Clearly the Clapham Sect evangelicals and their associates who had founded the Bible Society had been 'gentlemanly, able, catholic, and spiritually-minded' as well as shrewd business executives and sophisticated merchants. We have seen evidence that the new evangelicals who sat on the Committee of 1845 when Brandram threatened to resign over bookbinding prices were more grasping and less gentlemanly, if as 'able' in a limited commercial sense as their predecessors.

Finally, the Society, even in its days of respectability, was the victim of 'mistakes or calumnies ... which are still industriously circulated'. These included the 'so-called Popish version question' (accusations that the Society published translations made from the Latin Vulgate rather than from the Greek and Hebrew, for use in Roman Catholic countries). Also, 'Persons, ignorant of all languages but their own, are loud in condemnation of our incorrect translations.' From another quarter, 'The old book-binding slander has been revived since, and as a direct consequence of, the publication of our sixpenny Bibles, and twopenny New Testaments. "The books cannot be produced for the money, *therefore* the poor journeymen printers and binders ... are ground down, worse than half-starved, and, at their expense, the Society contrives to be thought generous."' Hewlett was convinced, not only that there were rocks ahead, 'but that we are in the very midst of them ... On the whole, will it be a surprising thing if, in days to come, the Society should not do more in England than hold its own?'

Hewlett's paper provides a confidential, frank internal summing-up of the Society's position in the late sixties. It is valuable evidence of significant change within the organization, both in its business and its social aspects. Underlying the content of Hewlett's report is his recognition that the BFBS had become institutionalized, that it was embedded in the everyday life of mid-nineteenth-century society. The problem he identified was that the larger society was less hospitable than earlier to the Bible Society. Victorian prosperity, he felt, was bad for voluntary and personal Bible distribution. But there was no question of terminating the domestic publishing programme. The social institution was also a book-publisher, and Hewlett's document can be interpreted in the light of difficulties experienced by the Society as publisher, in the areas of domestic marketing and distribution. The major problems of production and packaging had been solved. But the spontaneous demand created by Auxiliaries and Ladies' Associations during the 1810s and 1820s, and the eager clamour of Sunday School teachers during the thirties and forties, were finished. The Society had changed by the 1860s. The income was high, the reserve fund was ample, and the Committee was responsible for heavy expenditures at home and abroad.[39] But the Bible transaction, the delicate set of relationships both cultural and commercial that Dudley called the 'system of the Bible Society', had undergone a fundamental transformation. Other philanthropies were claiming the attention of a fickle 'religious public', and annexing voluntary labour that the BFBS had formerly taken for granted. As a result, book distribution began to be seen as the responsibility not of volunteers but of a paid staff. The fact that the staff were colporteurs and biblewomen obscures the transformation. Their work, exclusively with Bibles, was supported by charitable donation and could be described in 'the Press, the Pulpit, and the Platform' in terms of piety and benevolence. But the fragile economics of the transaction, as constructed forty years before, had been shattered.

The comfortably-off people of mid-Victorian England no longer needed the BFBS in the same way that their grandparents had. The successive political threats of Jacobinism, of working-class infidelity, and of Chartism had apparently passed. There was a new threat, from the apparent social degeneration of 'outcast London', and a new hope, in the notion that China and Africa might be evangelized. But nobody really believed that book-publishing alone would help. Ellen Ranyard's innovative attempt to renew the transaction underlines the weaknesses of the contemporary system. She created a complicated model wherein Bible distribution was linked together with social work and nursing. Clearly, the demand for Bibles at home was no longer enough to maintain the Society. From the sixties on, it was the foreign project that took centre stage, and Auxiliaries, when they existed, were fundraisers, not booksellers.

This fundamental transformation in the Bible transaction is reflected in the magniloquent conclusion to the 1864 *Report*:

Were there no lands in which the Bible is still proscribed, and no laws which rendered its circulation penal, were Papal superstition less defiant, and Abyssinian cruelty less fierce, did the antichristian confederacy of the West relax in its enmity to the Truth, and were the Eastern apostasy as tolerant in spirit as it is fair in speech, the difficulties with which your Committee have to contend would be less frequent, and the doubts by which their minds are at times disquieted would be less grave.[40]

Despite such pleas, the Committee had to contend with an institutional structure that was disintegrating, even though it could still generate substantial financial contributions.

There were other reasons too, reasons even further outside the Society's control than changes in the means of producing and distributing books. The progressive effects of education, of social legislation and of science made it more difficult to sustain the notion that what people needed most was a copy of the Bible. The Secretaries did their best, celebrating in the 1862 *Report*, for example, 'the value of an Institution which opposes every phase of error with the simple Word of God, and refutes every theory of infidelity or scepticism, or latitudinarian indifference, with a revelation from heaven'. But in the 1860s, such statements were beginning to sound philistine and narrow-minded to some. People had read Darwin and were wondering whether or not the Book of Genesis was literally true. Or they were contemplating a further round of Parliamentary reform that would widen the franchise dramatically, or they had been convinced that women's education and women's careers should not be limited to philanthropic work. In the face of all these changes – social, intellectual, political and cultural – it was difficult to convince people of the efficacy of a plan for collecting subscriptions to promote the circulation of the scriptures.

Sir James Stephen reflected at mid-century on the experience of evangelicalism:

To Lord Teignmouth, and to the other founders of the Bible Society, an amount of gratitude is due, which might, perhaps, have been more freely rendered, if it had been a little less grandiloquently claimed by the periodic eloquence of their followers. Her annual outbursts of self-applause are not quite justified by any success which this great Protestant *propaganda* has hitherto achieved over her antagonists ... [I]t is no longer doubtful that the aspect of human affairs may remain as dark as ever, though the earth be traversed by countless millions of copies of the Holy Text. The only wonder is, that such a doubt should ever have arisen – that reasonable people should have anticipated the renovation of man to the higher purposes of his being, by any single agency – without an apparatus as complex as his own nature – or without influences as vivifying as those which gave him birth.

Stephen continued, bringing into his criticism of the Bible transaction the new ideas about human nature that educated people were beginning to take for granted:

To quicken the inert mass around us ... it is necessary that the primeval or patriarchal institute of parental training should be combined with an assiduous education; with the various discipline of life; with the fellowship of domestic, civil, and ecclesiastical society; and, above all, with the re-creative power from on High devoutly implored and diligently cherished. The wicked habitations by which our globe is burdened, might, alas! be wicked still, though each of them were converted into a biblical library.[41]

Under the influence of this sort of thinking, the Bible transaction declined in the 1860s: but it did not disappear. The British and Foreign Bible Society (in England and Wales) and related Societies all over the world (under the umbrella of the United Bible Societies) are still collecting funds to pay for new translations and new editions. The rules have changed drastically, even the 'fundamental principle': the object of the Society now is to promote not only the circulation but also the use of the holy scriptures. Such an evangelical policy in the evangelical nineteenth century in Britain would have invited sectarian conflict and organizational ruin. Instead what succeeded, marvellously for a time, was a programme based upon the significance of the book as physical object. The Bible Society's Committee published books; women and men in local Auxiliaries and Associations sold books; the people they reached out to owned books, read books, gave books to their children, and valued books. BFBS subscribers were sustained by a conviction that to produce and distribute cheap Bibles would effect 'the renovation of man to the higher purposes of his being', and that conviction was the motive at the core of the Bible transaction.

EPILOGUE

THE BRITISH AND FOREIGN BIBLE SOCIETY, at the beginning of the
nineteenth century, discovered that there was a dearth of cheap Bibles.
Setting out, full of evangelical zeal, to fulfil the demand, the Committee and
membership found themselves fully engaged in the contemporary book trade,
at the very moment when the transition from hand-printing to machinery was
in progress. The correspondence and other records in the archives of the
Society demonstrate – vividly, often wittily, and sometimes tragically – how
the gentlemen of the Committee and the ladies of local Auxiliaries went about
supplying not only their own country, but the whole world, with cheap Bibles
and Testaments. The single-minded tenacity of these women and men –
dedicated as they were to the production of a single text, in durable volumes,
at low prices, in massive quantities – transformed the book trade at large,
especially the fortunes of the three Presses that printed English-language
Bibles, of the shops that competed to put them into cheap bindings, and of the
booksellers who were thus deprived of a staple product. At the same time, this
book-publisher managed a social transaction whereby its project became
institutionalized as part of Victorian culture. Beginning as it did in 1804 and
surviving the tumultuous Regency and early Victorian years to adapt itself to
the mid-century, the Society may indeed be seen as part of the transition to
Victorianism. These concluding pages discuss how a knowledge of the Bible
transaction might contribute to our understanding of nineteenth-century
culture and society. The question is formulated by examining the way the
transaction was handled, the manner in which the Society's managers presented its project to their contemporaries. And the answer seems to be that
the Secretaries and Committee obscured the publishing reality of the BFBS
while consciously working to create the image of a 'religious society'.

The tension between these two aspects manifested itself most clearly as
between Earl Street and Auxiliary views of the BFBS. In London the business
of circulating cheap Bibles was a commercial concern (albeit with an
evangelical object) whereas in the provinces it was a means of disseminating
the gospel that happened to involve the purchase and sale of books. Sometimes the tension created splits along other lines. In the Apocrypha controversy the distinction was mostly Church vs. Dissent, with Anglicans as
hard-headed publishers trying to serve a market, and Dissenters as narrowly

puritanical sectarians. When it came to organizing Associations, in places like Liverpool, the conflict was articulated in terms of gender. Women collected funds, to save souls, and men spent them – to publish books. Although the character of the BFBS as a nineteenth-century institution was shaped by these tensions, they were seldom articulated in public, where the Committee and their executive staff were reluctant to come forward in debate. The questions of free trade in Bibles and of the privilege, or 'monopoly', were argued without their formal intervention. Threats of scandal endangered the image of the Society as a religious body, and thus its human and financial resources. But even in the Channor and Watkins affairs, the publishers at Earl Street came out of their counting-house only a little way, just far enough to protect and enhance the Society's reputation. They were painfully aware of the fragility of their project, incorporating as it did so many ideas and values that were themselves under debate. For example, using working-class people as donors as well as recipients of charity was dangerous: but the alternative, to leave paupers without benefit of the scriptures, seemed foolhardy. Having 'ladies' involved was risky: appropriate roles for women were being argued in public as well as in private, with Bible collecting all too often the locus of debate. Using innovative techniques at the printing press and the bindery might fail, or be censured: but if the urgent demand of local Societies for books was not met, they would disperse in frustration and neither national nor global plans be fulfilled. Auxiliaries and Associations were wonderful proof that the BFBS idea was infectious: but they might easily create scandals that would pull down the whole edifice.

The managers of the Bible Society over its first sixty years handled this unstable situation by adopting a policy of ordinariness. They actively obscured, as much as they possibly could, what the Society was really doing, choosing instead to foster a popular image of bland do-goodery. Spokespersons for the Society were very careful to manage its rhetoric appropriately. Charles Stokes Dudley, in a discussion of how Associations should record interesting 'Facts and Observations' and pass them on to headquarters, put it this way:

It cannot be too strongly impressed on the minds of Collectors, that the *best* fact is that which is *best* authenticated; and the *best* observation, that which is the result of experience. Facts, like valuable fruit, should be attentively watched, and suffered to ripen and mature before they are gathered; and it will be generally found, that those are the most precious which have been the longest in attaining this state of maturity. Nor is an inferior degree of caution and prudence requisite in reporting these facts: – compression, simplicity of language, and a disposition to withhold rather than exaggerate the truth, will always render a fact more pleasing in itself, and excite a greater degree of interest in the auditors.[1]

Dudley was thinking of critics like H. H. Norris, ready to pounce on any report of Bible Society activity which could possibly be exposed as an untruth. But his observation may be applied also to the way that the Society used mature, well-developed facts to manipulate its own image: the constant stream of anecdotes about miraculous, but somehow unproblematic conversions that fill the annual *Reports* and *Monthly Extracts*. We may speculate that the Society's rhetoricians produced a discourse that, in effect, flattened their own story. The 'fact' that the BFBS was a hard-headed commercial publisher was of no help in raising funds.

Instead, the Bible Society's annual *Reports*, *Monthly Reporter* and other promotional materials produced a steady flow of narrative, reassuring supporters about the value of their work, and inspiring them to renew their efforts. There was plenty to sustain them: the forty-eighth annual *Report* (1852), the Secretaries announced, had swollen 'into a moderate-sized volume, and [required] to do it justice a well-defined map, and a diligent study of some days to become master of its contents'. Other publications, not directly sponsored by the Society, also increased its fame and the complacency of its subscribers. One example is George Borrow's *The Bible in Spain*, published by John Murray in 1843 and re-issued many times to become a best-seller. A more conventional example is Ellen Ranyard's *The Book and Its Story: A Narrative for the Young on Occasion of the Jubilee of the British and Foreign Bible Society*. This book was published by Bagster in 1853, with subsequent editions in each of the next four years.[2] Subscribers who read and enjoyed these popular books confirmed their belief in the Bible Society's respectability and worthiness.

Not despite but because of these and other stories about it, the BFBS has become almost invisible in conventional accounts of nineteenth-century history. Historians of religion have not noticed theologians debating the best way to distribute Bibles. Literary critics have not been troubled by the place of the local Bible Society Auxiliary in *Pride and Prejudice* or in *Middlemarch*. Economic historians have not yet taken up the matter of scripture-publishing, nor social historians the question of BFBS membership as an index of class mobility. Despite the existence of a massive archive, particularly rich in contemporary commentary, the history of the Society has until recently remained unexplored. This is not altogether the fault of historians. The BFBS Committee and Secretaries worked within a policy that promoted such invisibility. For them, publicity usually meant trouble, whether they were circulating the Apocrypha or sweating their bookbinders. Instead, they undertook to manage the Society's image. They did this negatively by suppressing scandals and damping down conflicts, and positively by publishing promotional pamphlets and periodicals. The Secretaries knew they had in their keeping a powerful institution. This institution consisted not only of the bricks-and-mortar of Bible House, or the paper-and-ink, leather-and-glue of the books, but of the Bible transaction itself, the powerful idea that this was the secret of England's greatness, the way to avoid revolution at home and to disseminate English values abroad.

The Bible Society is a subject open to further research and study. The Society's archives are full of vital material on the activities of local Auxiliaries and Associations, and rich in detailed evidence of the business methods of the Committee and their staff. Nor should studies of the Bible Society and its place in contemporary culture be limited to the rich material in Cambridge. Now is the time to return to contemporary literature, and to look for the record that Andrew Brandram and his colleagues worked so hard to obliterate. One example. When people said they went to a 'Bible meeting', they did not mean getting together in someone's parlour to read the scriptures (physical format unspecified), pray together and drink tea: they meant sitting around a committee table with their denominational rivals, and splitting up their town into districts and subdistricts, counting out currency and books, deciding who would visit whom, and reporting on the past week's successes and failures. They meant reading aloud the *Monthly Extracts of Correspondence* and discussing, perhaps evaluating, the reports of missionaries and agents circulating the scriptures abroad. And perhaps they meant other things too, things that we don't yet know because we haven't asked the right questions.[3] When we think of circulating the scriptures in concrete, physical terms, in terms of the book as artifact, we discover an image of the process quite different from the one that appears when we think of it in the abstract.

D. F. McKenzie, in his evocative remarks on 'bibliography and the sociology of texts', speaks of 'bibliography [as] the discipline that studies texts as recorded forms, and the processes of their transmission, including their production and reception'. In that very broad sense, the foregoing has been an exercise in bibliography. The physicality of BFBS Bibles, as exemplified in corrected and recorrected plates for the French Bible, or in Small Pica type to meet the demands of near-sighted readers, and again in covers stamped with a 'charity brand' signifying the poverty of recipients, has been a theme underlying this study of the publishing history of the Society. But the broad brush of the present study has meant that very little could be done in the way of detailed bibliographical analysis. The publishing records in the archives, used in conjunction with the books that the Society produced, will generate some very useful studies that should throw light on contemporary book-production methods as well as on the texts and physical format of Bibles.[4]

Not only cultural history and bibliography but also the study of the book trades in the nineteenth century look different in the light of an analysis of the Bible Society as publisher. Publishing history has tended to define its subject in terms of the literary entrepreneur, who relates both to authors and to readers in the process of selecting those texts he or she considers worthy to be put into circulation. Bible-publishing is only one of numerous situations where the text is not regarded as a literary artifact, but the process of making it public requires the people involved to concern themselves with typographers, with printers and papermakers, with bookbinders and booksellers, and with readers. Government publishing is another obvious example, but so is the business of 'charitable trading', as carried on by such institutions as the National Trust, or by groups advocating the amelioration of cultural, environmental or social-service practices. In the nineteenth century, the Religious Tract Society and the Sunday School Union were publishers. So were the English Historical Society, the Entomological Society and Exeter Hall. Sir James Stephen observed that 'Ours is the age of societies. For every redress of every oppression that is done under the sun, there is a public meeting. For the cure of every sorrow by which our land or our race can be visited, there are patrons, vice-presidents, and secretaries. For the diffusion of every blessing of which mankind can partake in common, there is a committee.'[5] And he might have added that for most of these impulses there were pamphlets printed, periodicals circulated and books published, each of which was part of the legitimate business of the contemporary publishing trades.

At the conclusion of the 1860 *Report*, the Secretaries closed their review of domestic and world activities of the Bible Society with these words: 'to indulge in any prolonged comments, would only be distracting the mental eye by engaging the listening ear'. As we have seen, the Society's rhetoric tended to engage the 'mental eye' of its supporters, with vignettes of conversion and of success in the face of great difficulty. If these stories were also tales of exotic places and adventurous activities, all the better. At the same time they sought to 'distract' the 'listening ear' of the average subscriber from the reality of the Society as a commercial publishing business. Now, though, we can hear the voices of Charles Stokes Dudley and Andrew Brandram, Maria Hope and Ellen Ranyard, Andrew Wilson and Lorina Watkins, talking about how to print, bind and distribute the cheap Bibles they published.

APPENDIX. TABLES OF RECEIPTS AND EXPENDITURES

The data displayed in the tables below is compiled from annual *Reports* of the British and Foreign Bible Society. Each year the *Report* included a 'Summary of the Cash Accounts', which laid out in considerable detail the financial position of the Society. Table 10 records average BFBS receipts for five-year periods, 1804–64. Table 11 records expenditures for the same periods. The tables were prepared with the help of a computer data base, by summarizing the amounts shown in these accounts, according to criteria determined by the author. The figures were further reduced to average amounts for five-year periods, to produce manageable tables. The averages are expressed in thousands of pounds sterling (shillings and pence are suppressed) and also as percentages of the total amounts for the five-year period. It will be noticed that the amounts in the 'Total' columns of tables 10 and 11 are not equal; this is because of the five-year averaging, and the disregarding of shillings and pence.

The summaries are organized under the following headings:

RECEIPTS

(a) Sale of Bibles and Testaments (sales of books), divided between British editions (Brit.) and all foreign-language editions (For.). British sales include the receipts from *Reports*, *Abstracts* and *Monthly Extracts*. These two figures are added to calculate total sales.

(b) Auxiliary contributions (Aux.) represent the amounts received as 'free contributions' from Auxiliary societies.

(c) Individual subscriptions. These amounts were received from private subscribers, at the basic rate of one guinea per member per year. They are included to compare receipts from traditional sources with those from book sales.

(d) Miscellaneous contributions (Misc.). These amounts include donations, life subscriptions, congregational collections and legacies.

(e) Dividends and interest (D/I). These are dividends on stocks, interest on exchequer bills and on other investments. The *Reports* specify which securities were purchased.

(f) Special projects (Spec.). This is income from special funds. In the 1830s the 'Negro Fund' supplied literate ex-slaves with New Testaments. In the 1850s the Jubilee Fund paid for colportage and other projects, including a fund to supply one million New Testaments to China.

(g) Divestment of surplus (Divest.). This is income produced by the sale of exchequer bills and other securities.

EXPENDITURES

(a) Printing and binding charges. As in the 'receipts' table, these amounts are divided into British and Foreign, and then added together.

(b) British agents (Brit.). This category includes salaries and expenses for Domestic Agents, later called District Secretaries. It is included to show the cost of managing the Auxiliary/Association system within Britain.

(c) Foreign agents (For.). These are the salaries and expenses of the Society's agents abroad.

(d) Administration (Admin.). This category includes insurance, the expenses of the depository, the poundage allowed to sales agents on subscriptions, the cost of stationery and stamps, taxes, fuel and such costs as the use of Exeter Hall for May Meetings.

(e) Promotion (Prom.). This includes the cost of producing the annual *Report*, the *Monthly Extracts*, and other printed materials for Auxiliary members. As such it was part of the cost of maintaining the Auxiliary/Association network. No figures are available under this heading for the years 1824–9 inclusive.

(f) Salaries (Sal.). The salaries are those of the Secretaries, the Accountant and the clerks. It does not include the remuneration to Agents or to the Depositary.

(g) Investment (Inv.). Amounts spent on the purchase of exchequer bills, stocks and other securities.

(h) Special funds (Spec.). This column includes expenditures from the funds collected for extraordinary purposes.

Table 10. *Average BFBS receipts for five-year periods (amounts expressed in thousands of pounds and as percentages of the total)*

	Sales of books								
	Brit.	For.	Aux.	Ind.	Misc.	D/I	Spec.	Divest.	Total
1805–9	2.0	0	0	2.0	4.3	0.3	n/a	2.3	10.9
	18%	0%	0%	18%	40%	3%	0%	21%	
1810–14	11.2	0	29.1	3.7	6.3	0.7	n/a	9.8	60.8
	18%	0%	48%	6%	10%	1%	0%	16%	
1815–19	25.1	0.1	56.4	3.0	5.2	1.9	n/a	27.4	119.1
	21%	0%	47%	3%	4%	2%	0%	23%	
1820–4	44.9	2.6	37.1	2.6	7.2	1.7	n/a	34.1	130.1
	35%	2%	29%	2%	6%	1%	0%	26%	
1825–9	33.8	3.6	35.6	2.1	7.1	2.0	n/a	23.2	107.5
	32%	3%	33%	2%	7%	2%	0%	22%	
1830–4	36.0	5.7	28.3	2.0	11.0	1.3	n/a	19.5	103.8
	35%	6%	27%	2%	11%	1%	0%	19%	
1835–9	38.2	8.4	30.5	1.9	17.5	1.8	15.0	14.9	116.1
	33%	7%	26%	2%	15%	2%	13%	13%	
1840–4	43.0	10.9	31.0	1.9	11.7	1.2	n/a	17.4	117.1
	37%	9%	27%	2%	10%	1%	0%	15%	
1845–9	36.0	15.0	31.7	1.8	14.7	1.3	n/a	14.1	114.6
	31%	13%	28%	2%	13%	1%	0%	12%	
1850–4	35.6	18.0	34.4	1.8	16.8	1.1	97.0	18.2	145.2
	25%	12%	24%	1%	12%	1%	67%	13%	
1855–9	43.0	24.8	43.9	2.5	22.1	2.7	4.5	25.7	169.2
	25%	15%	26%	2%	13%	2%	3%	15%	
1860–4	48.0	30.8	52.2	2.9	28.5	2.4	1.0	25.0	190.8
	25%	16%	27%	2%	15%	1%	1%	13%	

Table 11. *Average BFBS expenditures for five-year periods (amounts expressed in thousands of pounds and as percentages of the total*

	Printing/Binding		Agents		Admin.	Prom.	Sal.	Inv.	Spec.	Total
	Brit.	For.	Brit.	For.						
1805–9	4.3	1.6	0.0	0.0	0.7	0.1	0.2	3.9	0.0	10.8
	40%	15%	0%	0%	6%	1%	2%	36%	0%	
1810–14	28.4	12.8	0.3	0.3	2.1	2.5	0.3	13.2	0.0	59.8
	48%	21%	1%	1%	4%	4%	1%	22%	0%	
1815–19	49.6	23.6	0.7	1.6	3.2	3.5	0.7	31.8	5.6	116.9
	42%	20%	1%	1%	3%	3%	1%	27%	5%	
1820–4	56.2	26.7	1.5	2.1	3.9	1.1	1.1	36.7	0.5	129.4
	44%	21%	1%	2%	3%	1%	1%	28%	0%	
1825–9	49.3	33.0	1.4	1.9	2.4	0.0	1.9	18.1	0.9	108.1
	46%	31%	1%	2%	2%	0%	2%	17%	1%	
1830–4	49.2	24.8	1.8	2.1	2.4	2.2	1.9	19.1	0.0	103.5
	48%	24%	2%	2%	2%	2%	2%	19%	0%	
1835–9	56.5	28.5	2.8	3.5	2.8	2.4	2.1	17.8	0.0	116.3
	49%	25%	2%	3%	2%	2%	2%	15%	0%	
1840–4	52.9	35.5	2.9	3.1	2.5	2.5	2.1	22.3	0.0	123.6
	41%	29%	2%	3%	2%	2%	2%	18%	0%	
1845–9	48.7	41.8	3.0	2.8	2.0	2.5	2.0	11.9	0.0	114.7
	43%	36%	3%	3%	2%	2%	2%	10%	0%	
1850–4	48.0	40.6	3.9	2.4	2.3	2.6	1.9	38.8	11.9	142.8
	34%	28%	3%	2%	2%	2%	1%	27%	8%	
1855–9	58.5	65.0	4.6	2.5	2.8	2.4	2.4	23.4	8.4	170.0
	34%	38%	3%	2%	2%	1%	1%	14%	5%	
1860–4	64.1	63.8	5.0	12.0	2.9	2.5	2.4	32.1	5.6	190.3
	34%	34%	3%	6%	2%	1%	1%	17%	3%	

NOTES

PREFACE

1. Albert Peel, *These Hundred Years: A History of the Congregational Union of England and Wales* (London: Congregational Union of England and Wales, [1931]), 138–9. The remark comes from an 1845 editorial in the Congregationalist *Christian Witness*, of which Campbell was editor.

2. For official histories published by the Society at the appropriate anniversaries see John Owen, *The History of the Origin and First Ten Years of the British and Foreign Bible Society*, 2 vols. (London: BFBS, 1816); George Browne, *A History of the British and Foreign Bible Society, From its Institution in 1804 to the Close of Its Jubilee in 1854*, 2 vols. (London: BFBS, 1859); and William Canton, *A History of the British and Foreign Bible Society. With Portraits and Illustrations*, 5 vols. (London: John Murray, 1904).

3. John Sutherland, *Victorian Novelists and Publishers* (Chicago: University of Chicago Press, 1976), 22.

4. Thomas Laqueur and Frank Prochaska respectively have rediscovered and interpreted those institutions for a modern audience, and located them in current historiographical discourse. Thomas Laqueur, *Religion and Respectability: Sunday Schools and Working-Class Culture 1780–1850* (New Haven and London: Yale University Press, 1976) and F. K. Prochaska, *Women and Philanthropy in Nineteenth Century England* (Oxford: Clarendon Press, 1980).

5. D. F. McKenzie, *Bibliography and the Sociology of Texts* (London: British Library, 1986), 6–7.

I SAINTS IN PUBLISHING

1. R. K. Ensor, *England 1870–1914* (Oxford: Clarendon Press, 1936), 143. For a comment on Barker's painting see Leonard Bell, 'Artists and Empire: Victorian Representations of Subject People', *Art History* 5, 1 (March 1982), 73–86.

2. Roger E. Stoddard, 'Morphology and the Book from an American Perspective', *Printing History* 17 (1987), 12. Stoddard says 'the iconography of book interaction, the collecting and criticism of pictures showing people with books, has yet to be essayed in any comprehensive way'.

3. Charles Stokes Dudley, *Letters Addressed to a Friend in Wales ...*, 3rd edn (London, 1832). Dudley based his estimate on an assumed fifteen Committee members for each of 2,500 Auxiliaries and Associations. The same year Baptist Noel estimated that there were over 37,000 Committee members, while Joseph John Gurney claimed there were over 100,000 subscribers. (Cited in Roger Martin, *Evangelicals*

United: *Ecumenical Stirrings in Pre-Victorian Britain 1795-1830* (Metuchen, N.J.:
Scarecrow Press, 1983), 91–2 from B. W. Noel, *An Appeal on Behalf of the British and
Foreign Bible Society* (London: James Nisbet, 1832) and J. J. Gurney, *Terms of Union*
(Norwich, 1832).

4. [W. Ward], *A Letter on the Subject of the British and Foreign Bible Society ... by an Old
Friend of the Society for Promoting Christian Knowledge* (London: J. Hatchard, 1810),
44.

5. Martin, *Evangelicals United*, chapter 8. See also Susan Pederson, 'Hannah More
Meets Simple Simon: Tracts, Chapbooks, and Popular Culture in Late
Eighteenth-Century England', *Journal of British Studies* 25 (January 1986), 84–113.

6. For more on Mary Jones see Canton 1: appendix 1. The Bible Society's Library
holds many editions of the Mary Jones story. For comments on the formation of
the BFBS, see Roger Martin, *Evangelicals United*, 80–5 and Ernest M. Howse,
Saints in Politics: The 'Clapham Sect' and the Growth of Freedom (London: George Allen
and Unwin, 1953), 110–11.

7. For the Religious Tract Society see Martin, *Evangelicals United*, chapter 8. Martin
also provides a summary of the criticism which arose concerning the first BFBS
edition of the scriptures in Welsh.

8. See Howse, *Saints in Politics*; Geoffrey Best, 'The Evangelicals and the Established
Church in the Early Nineteenth Century', *Journal of Theological Studies* 10 (April
1959), 63 – 78; and Ian Bradley, *The Call to Seriousness* (London: Cape, 1976).

9. A. C. Zabriskie, 'The Rise and Main Characteristics of the Anglican Evangelical
Movement', *Historical Magazine of the Protestant Episcopal Church* 12 (1943), 83.

10. Boyd Hilton, *The Age of Atonement: The Influence of Evangelicalism on Social and
Economic Thought, 1795-1865* (Oxford: Clarendon Press, 1988); Donna T. Andrew,
'London Charity in the Eighteenth Century' (Ph.D. diss., University of Toronto,
1977), 290.

11. Canton 1: 9–10. See also Henry Morris, *The Founders and First Three Presidents of the
Bible Society* (London: Religious Tract Society, n.d.). For Wilberforce see Howse,
Saints in Politics, 110 who cites Robert Isaac and Samuel Wilberforce, *The Life of
William Wilberforce*, 5 vols. (London: John Murray, 1833, vol. 3, 91) and demon-
strates that (contrary to the *Life*) the Bible Society was not a Wilberforce creation;
his sons exaggerated his role.

12. Herbert Marsh, *A Reply to the Strictures of the Rev. Dr Isaac Milner* (1813) quoted in
Martin, *Evangelicals United*, 104. For the SPCK see W. O. B. Allen and Edmund
McClure, *Two Hundred Years: The History of the S.P.C.K. 1698–1898* (London:
SPCK, 1898), and William Kemp Lowther Clarke, *A History of the S.P.C.K.*
(London: SPCK, 1959).

13. Martin, *Evangelicals United*, 89, 103. Howse, *Saints in Politics*, 172.

14. Best, 'The Evangelicals', 65.

15. Howse, *Saints in Politics*, 113. For annual *Reports* see C. S. Dudley, *Analysis of the
System of the Bible Society* (London, 1821), 14–15.

16. Alexander[?] Christie to Rev. John Campbell (Leith), HCIn, 21 June 1804.

17. Martin, *Evangelicals United*, 84.

18. *Historical Catalogue*, 274.

19. Canton 2: 359.

20. A Country Clergyman, *An Address to Lord Teignmouth ...* (London: F. C. and J.

Rivington, 1805), 13; [John Owen], *A Letter to a Country Clergyman* (London: J. Hatchard, 1805), 50.

21. George T. Edwards, 'Old Friends of the Bible Society', *Bible Society Monthly Reporter* (October 1892), 168–9.
22. Bound volumes of controversial pamphlets collected by Owen are housed in the Bible Society's Archives at Cambridge University Library.
23. John Stoughton, *History of Religion in England from the Opening of the Long Parliament to 1850*, 8 vols. (London: Hodder and Stoughton, 1901), vol. 7, 190; vol. 8, 377. Borrow, *The Romany Rye* (London: John Murray, 1857), chapter 4. Josiah Pratt, secretary of the Church Missionary Society, was initially appointed the Anglican Secretary, but was replaced by Owen after a month.
24. Martin, *Evangelicals United*, 212; Stoughton, *History of Religion*, vol. 8, 378.
25. Canton 1: 43.
26. I am grateful to Kathleen Cann for this information. Roger Martin describes the Society as 'a central clearing house for a number of evangelical enterprises'.
27. Martin, *Evangelicals United*, 85–7.
28. Brandram to H. Leeves, FCOut, 28 December 1843.
29. Biographical data from Morris, *Founders of the Bible Society* and from biographies published in Martin, *Evangelicals United*, appendix. Tarn to Committee, HCIn, 3 August 1810. See also SubMin 1: 111, 3 August 1810.
30. Smith to Tarn, HCIn, 9 February 1808; 1 March; 5 March; 21 April.
31. Smith to Tarn, HCIn, 21 June 1808.
32. Minutes of Auditors, 1, 18–19, 7 May 1810. The Collector had a day-book in which subscriptions were entered, and also an alphabetical register of subscribers, with ruled columns for years and identical names numbered. The Accountant too kept a day-book in which receipts and payments were entered, and a ledger in which to post by double entry the entries from the day-book. He also had an alphabetical register of subscribers, and a book for all donations under 10 guineas. In 1820 the Society changed to single-entry accounts, keeping a cash book, a ledger, and an abstract book. Very few of these detailed financial records have survived.
33. Davies was a Dissenter; his occupation is not known. SubMin 1: 9 and 12 July 1808, 5 July 1810.
34. Wagner's occupation and denomination are unknown. He lived at 3 Grosvenor Road, Chelsea (SubMin, 27 Feb 1809).
35. SubMin (Audit), 121, 29 April 1811.
36. Canton 1: 46. Detailed financial figures are reproduced in the appendix.
37. Martin, *Evangelicals United*, 99–101. See also official histories and Percy R. Thomas, 'The Concept of an Ecumenical Bible Society Movement 1804–1832' (Ph.D. diss., University of Lancaster, 1980).
38. Martin, *Evangelicals United*, 103–5; F. K. Brown, *Fathers of the Victorians* (Cambridge: Cambridge University Press, 1961), 295–316.
39. A Country Clergyman, *A Second Letter to Lord Teignmouth* (London: F. C. and J. Rivington, 1810), 5–7.
40. I am grateful to Kathleen Cann for clarifying this matter.
41. GenMin, 7 June 1813. Martin, *Evangelicals United*, 124.
42. Martin, *Evangelicals United*, 125.

43. Browne, *A History of the British and Foreign Bible Society*, vol. 1, 186–8.
44. E. M. Forster, *Marianne Thornton 1797–1887: A Domestic Biography* (London: Arnold, 1956), 137.
45. Rev. Dr William Thorpe, of Richmond, to Teignmouth, HCIn, 14 August 1824. Bibliographers will note that while distinct gatherings and leaves can easily be commingled within one binding, it is virtually impossible that each side of a single leaf be commissioned separately.
46. [Edward Edwards], 'A Letter to the Editor of the Quarterly Review', *Quarterly Review* (June 1827), 1–28. Canton (1: 361) incorrectly attributes this article to Southey. Willam Roberts, *A Letter to the Editor of the Quarterly Review, in Answer to the Animadversions contained in an Article in the LXXIst Number of that Journal, upon the Conduct of the Committee of the British and Foreign Bible Society, by a Lay Member* (London: Printed for L. B. Seeley and Sons, 1827). William Roberts (1767–1849), a barrister and writer living in Clapham, had served on the Committee in 1813.
47. The publication at Cambridge in 1833 of a Duodecimo Greek and English New Testament, printed in parallel columns, was probably an aid to missionary translators (Archives of Cambridge University Press. Press Syndicate. Orders for the Press, 1823–43. Hereafter cited as CUP PS.OP Pr.V.5).
48. Martin, *Evangelicals United*, 133–4; Canton 1: 354–61. The quotation is from Joseph Hughes, *The Subject of Prayer at Meetings of the British and Foreign Bible Society Considered in a Letter to the Right Hon. Lord Teignmouth* (1830). For the Trinitarian Bible Society see Andrew J. Brown, *The Word of God Among All Nations* (London: TBS, 1981).
49. Canton 2: 140–1. In *Evangelicals United*, Martin recommends the following source on the 'Baptizo Controversy': E. B. Underhill, *The Baptists and the Bible Society* (London: Yates and Alexander for the Bible Translation Society, 1868).
50. Anon. to Committee, HCIn, 29 April 1831.
51. Brandram to Isaac Lowndes, FCOut, 15 May 1848. J. P. Hewlett, *A Paper*, 5–6. See Canton 2: 164–5.
52. *Monthly Extracts* (February 1842), 303.
53. Doreen M. Rosman, *Evangelicals and Culture* (London: Croom Helm, 1984), 7.
54. Harold Perkin, *The Origins of Modern English Society 1780–1880* (London: Routledge and Kegan Paul, 1969), 280.
55. Ford K. Brown, *Fathers of the Victorians*, 261.
56. E. P. Thompson, *The Making of the English Working Class*, (Harmondsworth: Penguin, 1968), 914; Elie Halévy, *History of the English People in the Nineteenth Century* vol. 1 *England in 1815* (London: Ernest Benn, 1912).
57. Roger Martin, in *Evangelicals United*, expresses dissatisfaction that the Bible Society's archives contain 'an insuperable deficiency in source materials', that is, in evidence of theological discourse. His concern exemplifies the weakness of a religious approach to the BFBS. Martin notes that 'the Society's minutes and correspondence are, for the most part, singularly monotonous, for they deal almost exclusively with business transactions including orders for Bibles, payments and receipts'. In other words, they are an unparalleled source for a project in the history of publishing.
58. In my dissertation, 'The Bible Transaction: A Publishing History of the British and Foreign Bible Society, 1804–1864' (Ph.D., York University, 1988), an appendix

provides full biographical details on all members. Post-office and other contemporary directories were used to discover occupational designations. The categories of analysis were arrived at, first, by counting members of the Committee according to occupation and denomination. With respect to their commitment to the Society, their duration of service was noted, as well as the date when each member joined (early, middle or late in the sixty-year period), and their involvement with key Subcommittees. Several other variables were noted: education, place of residence, authorship and honours. The Committee was examined also as a case study in the personnel of evangelicalism, with particular reference to the association of its leaders with Cambridge University and with the community of Clapham.

59. Lawrence Stone, 'Prosopography', *Daedalus* (Winter 1971), 48. 'The method employed is to establish a universe to be studied, and then to ask a set of uniform questions – about birth and death, marriage and family, social origins and inherited economic position, place of residence, education, amount and source of personal wealth, occupation, religion, experience of office, and so on. The various types of information about the individuals in the universe are then juxtaposed and combined, and are examined for significant variables. They are tested both for internal correlations and for correlations with other forms of behavior or action.'

60. More specific definitions were stated in the by-laws (GenMin 4: 254, 19 November 1810): 'members of the Church of England' meant 'persons who communicate with some clergyman of the Established Church ministering under Episcopal authority'; 'Foreigners' were 'natives of Foreign Countries resident in London or its vicinity', while 'Members of other Denominations of Christians, such as do not come under either of the former descriptions' were counted as Dissenters.

61. John Owen, *The History of the Origin and First Ten Years of the British and Foreign Bible Society*, 79.

62. T. Sikes, *A Humble Remonstrance to the Lord Bishop of London* (London: 1806), 50. Bishop Porteus had shocked many by becoming an ardent proponent of the Bible Society.

63. For participation in the BFBS and other evangelical organizations by members of the Society of Friends, see Elizabeth Isichei, *Victorian Quakers* (Oxford: Oxford University Press, 1970), xxi.

64. In 1816 there was a Papal Bull attacking the Society. See *Anti Biblion, or the Papal Toscin... The Present Pope's Bull Against Bible Societies* (2nd edn 1817). Cited in Martin, *Evangelicals United*, 97. In 1823 Pope Leo XII published another Encyclical attacking the Society.

65. Martin, *Evangelicals United*, 86.

66. *Dictionary of National Biography*.

67. When William Hooper Ropes was in St Petersburg he acted as an agent for the BFBS and also for the American Bible Society. See Henry O. Dwight, *The Centennial History of the American Bible Society* (New York: Macmillan, 1916).

68. GenMin 3: 32, 6 May 1807. Meyer was a merchant with E. Simeon and Co., at Salvadore House, while Sundius was variously a translator, a notary and a ship and insurance broker.

69. Dates of birth and death are known for only fifty-two Committee members (17.3 per cent). In these cases it is possible to compute the age at which they joined the

Committee. Leonore Davidoff and Catherine Hall, *Family Fortunes: Men and Women of the English Middle Class 1780–1850* (London: Hutchinson, 1987), 225–8.

70. In his will (at the Public Record Office), Thornton is identified as Edward Norton Thornton of 174 High Street, Borough, Southwark and Clapham Common in the County of Surrey, undertaker.

71. They were Thomas Allan, Thomas Pellatt and J. W. Warren (SubMin 3: 285, 16 April 1818).

72. Major C. F. Head of Clapham to [?], HCIn, 9 April 1840.

73. Standish Meacham, *Henry Thornton of Clapham* (Cambridge, Mass.: Harvard University Press, 1964).

74. Joseph Tarn to Lord Amherst, CB 4, 167, 21 October 1811.

75. In *Family Fortunes*, Davidoff and Hall have prepared statistics on 'Middle-class men and occupations'. Their mid-century sample is roughly compatible with the present one, in that trade was followed by professionals. My 50 per cent in 'commerce' is significantly larger than their 28 per cent in 'trade'. This may be accounted for partly by different methodologies (their category 'salaried' may include some I have counted as 'commercial'), and the peculiarities of the BFBS constitution, where eminently middle-class clergymen could not be members of the Committee. More significant is the fact that their sample is provincial, while mine is of Londoners, where larger concentrations of merchants and tradespeople did business, and farmers were under-represented (231–4).

76. Canton 1: 319; Rosman, *Evangelicals and Culture*, 34–7; Hilton, *Age of Atonement*, 10; John Kent, *Holding the Fort* (London: Epworth Press, 1978), 101.

77. J. P. Hewlett, *A Paper Read at the Conference of the District Secretaries of the British and Foreign Bible Society, February 5th, 1867, and at Their Request Printed for Private Circulation* (London, [1867]), 6. Some evidence of these changes appeared in the occupational structure of the Committee. As it entered the 'middle' years of the period, the number of 'gentlemen' increased from one to nine, a circumstance that may mean that Bible Society membership was becoming more desirable and respectable for those who were not committed evangelicals. More probably it indicates that some former merchants had retired to suburban respectability, where directories listed them as gentlemen. The medical contingent also increased dramatically. The changes of the third twenty years are less dramatic. Army and Naval officers began to show up in the Committee rosters. The proportions of 'gentlemen' and members of medical professions both dropped. Tradespeople increased slightly. These shifts probably reflect factors such as a network of acquaintances who invited each other to participate in this particular charitable endeavour, rather than the demographics of particular occupations.

78. Clear evidence of evangelical connections has been found for fifty-five Committee members (18 per cent). These, however, are only the most prominent. A collation of the subscription lists of major evangelical organizations would probably unearth many more.

79. Ford K. Brown, in *Fathers of the Victorians*, speaks of the BFBS and the Church Missionary Society 'creating a great new constituency of Evangelical reform' (p. 275). The other six societies were the Religious Tract Society, the London Society for Promoting Christianity Amongst the Jews, the Prayer Book and Homily Society, the British Newfoundland and North America Society for Edu-

cating the Poor, the General Society for Promoting District Visiting, and the Church Pastoral Aid Society (p. 342).

80. Hewlett, *A Paper*, 6.

81. SubMin 1: 86–7, 12 and 21 May 1807.

82. Cited by Robert Haldane, *Second Review of the Conduct of the Directors of the British and Foreign Bible Society, containing an Account of the Religious State of the Continent: in Answer to a Letter Addressed to the Author, by the Rev. Dr Steinkopf* (Edinburgh, 1826), 114. In a letter to Joseph Tarn, J. J. Gurney of the Norwich Auxiliary explained: 'I wrote to Lord Orford ... (not knowing his character) & I received a plain common answer. I believe the letter which has been circulated (& which I am inclined to think *he* circulates) was never sent to anyone' (HCIn, July 1824).

83. This perspective was qualified somewhat by J. S. Reynolds, *The Evangelicals at Oxford* (Oxford: Marcham Manor Press, 1975).

84. Twenty-two of these were churchmen, six Dissenters, one foreigner and six of unknown denomination. The only other significant group is Bloomsbury, where thirteen members lived. There are numerous addresses in the City: in the early years these were probably homes located 'above the shop' and in the later years would have been business addresses. Also in the later years members began to live in new suburbs such as Brixton, Clapton, Tottenham, Camberwell and Stamford Hill.

85. T. H. Darlow, ed., *Letters of George Borrow to the British and Foreign Bible Society* (London: BFBS, 1911), 127. Borrow was attempting to reassure a Spanish politician that his purposes as the Society's agent in Spain were harmless. The year was 1836.

2 A BIBLE TRANSACTION, 1804–1840

1. Chapter 3.

2. Davidoff and Hall, *Family Fortunes*, 95.

3. Anon. to Wilberforce, HCIn, 3 December 1808.

4. Rev. Frederick Nolan, *Objections of a Churchman to Uniting with the Bible Society...* (London: F. C. and J. Rivington, 1812), 1; Robert Forby, *A Letter to the Right Reverend the Lord Bishop of Norwich ...* (Norwich, 1815), 71–2; James Edward Jackson, *Reasons for Withdrawing from the Hibernian Bible Society* (Dublin: Richard Milliken, 1822), 4.

5. The translator was Captain John Norton. His book was the first test of the 'without note or comment' principle, since the preface it contained, addressing the Mohawk people about the value of the scriptures, had to be cancelled.

6. Canton 2: 457–60.

7. Canton 1: 46–7.

8. David Owen, *English Philanthropy* (Cambridge, Mass., Harvard University Press, 1964), chapters 4–6.

9. John Feather, *The Provincial Book Trade in Eighteenth-Century England* (Cambridge: Cambridge University Press, 1985), 51.

10. Michael Sadleir, *The Evolution of Publishers' Binding Styles* (London: Constable, 1930), 33–5.

11. SubMin 2: 178, 20 October 1809. It was not until 1903 that the system of trade

depots was discontinued and the Society began to 'follow the procedure of other publishing firms & throw its business open to the trade generally' (Archives Index, December 1903, Minutes of the Estimates and Property Subcommittee).

12. Dudley, *Analysis*, 19.

13. Dudley, *Analysis*, 136–9.

14. See CB 1, insert at p. 155 of a printed copy of the rules of this association. 'Females' were 'not to be called upon to act as collectors.'

15. Dudley, *Analysis*, 136–9.

16. Canton 1: 46.

17. GenMin 3: 116–17, 4 April 1808.

18. Canton 1: 144.

19. The 'fundamental principle' meant that the book had no official connection with the organization that was its subject. In fact Dudley used the proceeds to bale himself out of bankruptcy.

20. George T. Edwards, 'Old Friends of the Bible Society – II Charles Stokes Dudley', *Bible Society Monthly Reporter* (September and October 1892). The Bible Society's HCIn has a separate box of Dudley letters up to 1836, and more scattered through later boxes. The one about his *Analysis* is directed to Joseph Tarn and dated 22 February 1819.

21. Canton 1: 471–83.

22. GenMin 5: 18–19, 21 January 1811.

23. Dudley, *Analysis*, 141. For Phillips see *Memoir of the Life of Richard Phillips*, by his daughter (London, 1841).

24. Dudley, *Analysis*, 211–17.

25. Dudley to Tarn [?], from Birmingham, HCIn, 7 April 1827.

26. Martin, *Evangelicals United*, 111–18; Richard Lloyd, *Strictures on a Recent Publication ... and an Admonitory Address to the Female Sex* (London: F. C. and J. Rivington, 1819), 115; [Thomas Sykes], *Reasons for not Attending the British and Foreign Bible Society, in a Letter to N. Vansittart, Esq by a Country Clergyman* (Chelmsford, n.d. [1812?]), 8–9.

27. H. H. Norris, *A Practical Exposition of the Tendency and Proceedings of the BFBS* (London: F. C. and J. Rivington, 1814), 343–4; Fisher to Hughes, HCIn, 18 March 1817, including a copy of Fisher's letter to the Rev. John Nelson Goulty, Secretary of the Henley Auxiliary Bible Society. For other examples see Nolan, *Objections*, 42, where he charges the Society with associating with foreign nationals of enemy countries, and Rev. Charles James Burton, *A Short Inquiry into the Character and Designs of the British and Foreign Bible Society* (Canterbury, n.d. [1817?]):

> That from bodies thus organized, unrecognized by, and therefore not very regardful of, the laws, danger menaces the State, is a proposition needing not much proof. In a moment of time, as it were, every wheel of the machine may be set to work; the grand agitators, knowing from their various Missionaries, the exact state of popular prejudice and sentiment, well assured upon whom they may rely, will some day or other be seen in their true character, not merely of fanatical religionists, but of Revolutionary Leaders.

28. GenMin 4: 41, 4 September 1809; Canton 1: 50–62.

29. Dudley, *Analysis*, 35–6.

30. See, among others, the statement by Chevalier Ernest Bunsen that the BFBS was 'the mother and mistress of more than 8000 Bible Societies ... not as having dominion over their faith but as helpers of their joy' (*The Jubilee Memorial of the BFBS 1853–1854* (London: BFBS, 1854), 8).
31. Dudley to Tarn, HCIn, 19 April 1815; Dudley, *Analysis*, 157.
32. Dudley, *Analysis*, 215.
33. Dudley, *Analysis*, 211–13.
34. Dudley, *Analysis*, 208–9.
35. BFBS *Report* (May 1817), 317–18. The publications in question may have been copies of Paine's *Rights of Man*, then circulating widely (Thompson, *The Making*, 114–25).
36. Tarn to W. B. Briggs of Wakefield, CB 10: 177–8, 13 January 1818.
37. See also Rev. A. O'Callaghan, *Thoughts on the Tendency of Bible Societies...* (Dublin, 1816), 57: 'On men tottering into pauperism ... a considerable part of this vast sum is levied, by means of Bible Associations, penny-a-week societies, parochial contributions, "gospel preaching", artful flattery, and ceaseless importunity!'
38. Dudley, *Analysis*, 214.
39. BFBS. Minutes of inaugural meeting, 7 March 1804.
40. Richard Lawson (surgeon of Lostwithiel, Cornwall) to BFBS, GenMin 4: 31–2, 30 July 1809.
41. Dudley, *Analysis*, 255.
42. Some of the titles in the literature concerning working-class culture have been Thompson, *The Making*; Robert D. Storch, ed., *Popular Culture and Custom in Nineteenth Century England* (London: Croom Helm, 1982) and F. M. L. Thompson, 'Social Control in Victorian Britain', *Economic History Review* 2nd series 34, 2 (May 1981), 189–208.
43. Dudley, *Analysis*, 238.
44. Gurney to Tarn, HCIn, 11 May 1813.
45. Thompson, 'Social Control', 206.
46. For more on the question of women's religious participation as an aspect of their public role, see Davidoff and Hall. Another fine contribution to this discussion is an article by Alex Tyrrell, '"Woman's Mission" and Pressure Group Politics in Britain (1825–60)', *Bulletin of the John Rylands Library of Manchester* 63 (1980), 194–230.
47. Dudley, *Analysis*, 370.
48. Frank Prochaska, *Women and Philanthropy in Nineteenth Century England*. Prochaska divides women's power into that of the purse and of the cross; this approach, unfortunately, obscures the role of women in the BFBS since it was both a charitable and a religious organization, as well as a business.
49. Tyrrell, '"Woman's Mission"', 209–17.
50. There is a rich literature on women in early-nineteenth-century evangelicalism. Particularly appropriate to this subject are the following: Barbara Pope, 'Angels in the Devil's Workshop', in *Becoming Visible*, Bridenthal and Koonz, eds. (Boston: Houghton Mifflin, 1977); H. D. Rack, 'Domestic Visitation: A Chapter in Early Nineteenth-Century Evangelism', *Journal of Ecclesiastical History* 24 (1973), 357–76. See also Anne Summers, 'A Home from Home – Women's Philanthropic Work in the Nineteenth Century', in *Fit Work for Women*, Sandra Burman, ed. (London: Croom Helm, 1979).

51. Robert Steven to Tarn, HCIn, 15 October 1818.
52. Margaret B. Simey, *Charitable Effort in Liverpool in the Nineteenth Century* (Liverpool: Liverpool University Press, 1951), 16.
53. Dudley, *Analysis*, 371–4. See also Canton 1: 62.
54. Maria Hope to Tarn, HCIn, 25 February 1819; 14, 24 and 29 April. Maria Hope's correspondence with Tarn, Dudley and Robert Steven continues until 1822. She later married Edward Jones of Ruthin in Wales and the BFBS Archive has three letters from her about Bible Associations there.
55. Buddicom and S. Hope to Secretaries, HCIn, October 1819.
56. SubMin 4: 166, 5 November 1819.
57. Gurney to Tarn, HCIn, 11 April 1816; [W.?] Sundius (Cornhill) to Tarn, HCIn, 11 February 1820; Lee to Tarn, HCIn, 10 January 1821; 21 March.
58. H. H. Norris, *A Respectful Letter to the Earl of Liverpool* (London: F. C. and J. Rivington, 1822).
59. Martin, *Evangelicals United*, 115.
60. Public Record Office, ASSI 31/24, Agenda Book: Surrey Lent Assizes, 1821 at Kingston upon Thames. ASSI 35/261/3, Indictments, no. 157 Richard Channer. (The name is usually spelled Channor.)
61. John Townsend (1757–1826); educated Christ's Hospital in London and Trevecca College; 1781 ordained pastor of the Independent Church at Kingston, Surrey and moved to Bermondsey where he founded the London Asylum for the Deaf and Dumb in 1792; a director of the LMS and RTS. (Biographical information from Martin, *Evangelicals United*, 217.)
62. Henry Neave Rickman, 'Fraud on Bible Associations', *BFBS Monthly Extracts* (April 1821).
63. Bible Society's Archives. Minutes of the Southwark Auxiliary Bible Society, volume commencing 1818. Subheading Rotherhithe Upper [Bible Association], 13 December 1820.
64. In 1836 J. Glubb wrote to the Poor Law Commissioners suggesting that Boards of Guardians supply each Union workhouse with scriptures. The reply signed by Edwin Chadwick promised to consider the idea (HCIn, 1836).
65. See Canton 1: Appendix 1 for a list of local auxiliaries up to 1817, showing date established, names of patrons, and contributions.
66. GenMin 19: 29 May 1829; DepMin 2: 99, 15 June 1829.
67. An example of the kind of trouble an agent could get into is afforded by Dudley's sojourn in Nottingham in February 1822. He was accused of 'giving present advantage to the Dissenters' by such actions as attending a meeting at the Lancastrian school on a Sunday (this was a misunderstanding; he had believed the meeting to be at a private home) and 'preaching' to the labouring classes ('the object was to convey . . . a clear & practical view of the nature, plan, & effects of Bible Associations: – but nothing like "preaching" was heard. . .') (Dudley to Committee, SubMin, 21 February 1822).
68. Ruth Richardson, *Death, Dissection and the Destitute* (Harmondsworth: Penguin, 1988), 227.
69. DepMin 2: 169, 29 November 1831; Spence to Brandram and Hughes, HCIn, 12 December 1831.
70. Printed circular from Brandram and Hughes to 'Dear Sir', HCOut, 19 March 1833.

71. Phillips supplied the figures and proposed the pawnbrokers be prosecuted 'to prevent the great abuse of Christian benevolence'. It is interesting that Phillips himself was in the habit of purchasing cheap Bibles and Testaments at pawnshops for Sunday School rewards. This frugal custom was presumably not admired at Earl Street (James Phillips of Worcester to [?], HCIn, 22 January 1834; George Hulme of Reading to Brandram, HCIn, 2 April 1834).
72. Dudley to Brandram, HCIn, 21 May 1825.
73. GenMin 27: 243, 15 June 1838; 260, 29 June; 264, 2 July; 279, 13 July.
74. Thomas Laqueur, *Religion and Respectability*, 123.
75. GenMin 15: 57, 31 January 1825; 19: 129, 29 May 1829.
76. GenMin 28: 363–5, 30 December 1839.
77. Rev. M. Castledon (of Woburn) to Secretaries, HCIn, 15 January 1840.
78. Laqueur, *Religion and Respectability*, 37–40, 112.
79. W. Watson to G. Browne, HCIn, 15 February 1840.
80. Browne (writing from Toft, Lincolnshire) to Brandram, HCIn, 5 August 1840. For 'infant schools on infidel principles', (Owenite and Chartist Sunday schools) see Laqueur, *Religion and Respectability*, 179–86.
81. J. Brown, Lombard Street (member of Southwark Auxiliary) to Brandram and Browne, HCIn, 7 February 1840; Edward Corderoy to Brandram, HCIn, 6 April 1840.
82. 1840 *Report*.
83. GenMin 28: 419, 14 February 1840.
84. William Watson to G. Browne, HCIn, 15 February 1840.
85. For example they got word that a Nottingham bookseller was retailing the cheap editions at a profit of 6d on the Bibles and 2d on the Testaments (GenMin 28: 435, 24 February 1840).
86. Browne to Brandram, HCIn, 19 August 1840; Dudley to Brandram, HCIn, 15 August 1840.

3 THE BFBS AND ENGLISH PRINTERS, 1804–64

1. Lucien Febvre and Henri-Jean Martin, *The Coming of the Book: The Impact of Printing 1450–1800* (London: Verso, 1984. First published in French, 1958), chapter 5.
2. P. M. Handover, *Printing in London from 1476 to Modern Times* (London: George Allen and Unwin Ltd, 1960), 74–5.
3. For descriptions of these editions see A. S. Herbert, *Historical Catalogue of Printed Editions of the English Bible 1525–1961*. Revised and expanded from the edition of T. H. Darlow and H. F. Moule, 1903 (London and New York: BFBS and American Bible Society, 1968), numbers 444, 942–3, 309 and 319. It has been suggested that the omission of 'not' in the 'Wicked Bible' was deliberately done to discredit the printers (P. M. Handover, 'The "Wicked" Bible and the King's Printing House, Black Friars', in the *Times (London) House Journal* (December 1958), 215–18.
4. M. H. Black, 'The Printed Bible', in *The Cambridge History of The Bible*, S. L. Greenslade, ed. (Cambridge: Cambridge University Press, 1963), 461–2.
5. The history of the University Presses is better served than that of the Royal Printer. For the King's (Queen's) Printer see Handover, *Printing* and the memoir

by Richard Arthur Austen-Leigh, *The Story of a Printing House: Being a Short Account of the Strahans and Spottiswoodes* (2nd edn, London: Spottiswoode and Co., 1912). For Cambridge in the period covered in the present book see M. H. Black, *Cambridge University Press, 1584–1984* (Cambridge: Cambridge University Press, 1984), and two older books by S. C. Roberts, *A History of the Cambridge University Press, 1521–1921* (Cambridge: Cambridge University Press, 1921) and *The Evolution of Cambridge Publishing* (Cambridge: Cambridge University Press, 1956). For the earlier period see D. F. McKenzie, *The Cambridge University Press, 1696–1712: A Bibliographical Study* (Cambridge: Cambridge University Press, 1966). For Oxford in the Bible Society period see Nicolas Barker, *The Oxford University Press and the Spread of Learning, 1478–1978: An Illustrated History* (Oxford: Clarendon Press, 1978) and Peter Sutcliffe, *The Oxford University Press: An Informal History* (Oxford: Clarendon Press, 1978); Oxford's earlier years are discussed in Harry Carter, *A History of the Oxford University Press* vol. 1 *To the Year 1780* (Oxford: Clarendon Press, 1975). The importance of reading the vernacular scriptures is discussed in Susan Brigden, *London and the Reformation* (Oxford: Clarendon Press, 1989).

6. The account of the earlier history of the Bible privilege given here is based upon Carter, *History of the Oxford University Press*, 27–9; 71–2; 93–109, on Handover, *Printing*, chapter 3 and on Black, 'The Printed Bible', 455–61.

7. C. H. Timperley, *A Dictionary of Printers and Printing* (London: H. Johnson, 1839), 484.

8. Charles Batey, 'The Oxford Partners: Some Notes on the Administration of the University Press 1780–1881', *Journal of the Printing Historical Society* 3 (1967), 54–5; Sutcliffe, *Oxford*, 4.

9. Butterworth to Tarn[?], HCIn, 8 March 1804.

10. Wilson to 'The Chairman & Gentlemen of the Printing Committee', HCIn, 23 December 1806.

11. The term comes from *Historical Catalogue*, number 1485. For stereotyping see Philip Gaskell, *A New Introduction to Bibliography* (Oxford: Clarendon Press, 1972), 191–5, 207–13 and Horace Hart, *Charles Earl Stanhope and the Oxford University Press* (London: Printing Historical Society, 1966. First published 1896). For Wilson see Michael L. Turner, 'Andrew Wilson: Lord Stanhope's Stereotype Printer. A Preliminary Report', *Journal of the Printing Historical Society* 9 (1973 – 4), 22–65.

12. CUP PS.OP 1803–23, Pr.V.4.

13. SubMin 1: 12, 3 April 1805.

14. Watts to [Tarn], CB 1: 162–4, 28 Oct 1805. He wrote again in November to apologize and to explain how the mistake would be remedied: 'The second Edition of the 12mo Test[ament] (just on the finish) is however free from this error; and the Binders may be supplied with cancel leaves ... as soon as I am informed of the number required' (HCIn, 20 November 1805). This is *Historical Catalogue*, number 1490; the error comes at Gal.4:29.

15. It did not really become profitable until the 1830s when the problem of breakage of the plaster-of-paris moulds was solved by the use of flexible moulds made of laminated paper, called *flang* by their French inventors and 'flong' by English printers (Gaskell, *New Introduction*, 201–6).

16. Owen to the Syndics, CB 1: 177–9, 13 December 1805.

17. F. A. Mumby, *Publishing and Bookselling* (revised edn, London: Jonathan Cape, 1949), 149.
18. CUP PS.OP 1803–23 Pr.V.4, 20 February 1806. But at a meeting in October the title-page decision was left to the discretion of each University.
19. Tarn to William Owen (Denbigh, North Wales), CB 2: 24 October 1807.
20. However the Vice-Chancellor agreed to pass the letter on to his successor. Tarn to the Vice-Chancellor of Cambridge, CB 3: 64–5, 16 October 1806; Vice-Chancellor to Tarn, CB 3: 67, 20 October 1806. For earlier negotiations between Wilson and the Committee, see SubMin 1: 54–7, April to June 1806.
21. Wilson to 'The Chairman & Gentlemen of the Printing Committee', HCIn, 23 December 1806; Tarn to Wilson, CB 2: 45 – 6, 26 December 1806; Wilson to Tarn, HCIn, 5 January 1807; Tarn to Wilson, CB 2: 60, 12 January 1807.
22. SubMin 1: 1, 5 April 1804.
23. *Historical Catalogue*, number 6797.
24. This version was presumably number 3831 in the *Historical Catalogue*, printed in London by C. et W. Galabin and F. Wingrave in 1804.
25. The name in the Subcommittee Minutes is Whittington. There is, however, no Whittington listed in Philip A. H. Brown's *London Publishers and Printers c. 1800–1870* (London: British Library, 1982), while the Leather Lane firm of Charles Whittingham had been in operation since 1789. It should also be noted that Samuel Rousseau is not listed by Brown. He may have been a neighbour of Joseph Tarn, who lived in Spa Fields.
26. The details of this early order were as follows: Bourgeois type, twenty-seven lines wide, fifty-two long, not reckoning head line or catch word, at £3 19s 6d per sheet for 2,000. The paper was charged at 26s per ream by Key.
27. See below, chapter 5.
28. The Subcommittee minutes of 28 April 1806 record a letter from the Rev. Mr Blumhart of Basil [*sic*] concerning Mr Haas's method of stereotype printing in that city. This information was to be communicated to Lord Stanhope and Mr Wilson, requesting their opinion. No record has been found of this correspondence, and the original letter has not survived. However an extract from it was printed in the 1806 *Report*. I am grateful to Alan Jesson for clarifying this matter for me.
29. The offer continued, promising that the Society could regain control of the plates by paying him the cost of the types, offset by a reduction in consideration for 'whatever might have been worked off by him'. The casework (typesetting) would come to £13 6s 0d per sheet of thirty-six pages to a stereotype sheet, seventy-four lines by seventy-eight letters on each page, amounting to £385 14s 0d, supposing the whole to make twenty-nine sheets (SubMin 1: 41, 27 January 1806).
30. The minutes refer to an edition of 1744, which does not appear in the *Historical Catalogue*. A later minute identifies the book as the 1772 edition, printed at Basle from Martin's version, edited by Pierre Roques (*Historical Catalogue*, number 3826). Earlier Basle editions of Roques's correction of Martin appeared in 1736 and 1760.
31. SubMin 1: 74, 30 November 1806.
32. Blair to Tarn, CB 2: 64–5, 2 March 1807. See *Historical Catalogue*, number 8491.
33. The 1810 Portuguese edition is not listed in *Historical Catalogue*.
34. SubMin 1: 129–30, 21 July 1808. See *Historical Catalogue*, number 8492.

35. SubMin 1: 163, 15 May 1809; Rutt to Tarn, HCIn, 16 June 1809; 24 November 1815.
36. SubMin 1: 79, 12 January 1807. The first French New Testament is number H3835 in the Bible Society's Library Working Catalogue (an updated version of the published *Historical Catalogue*). The imprint reads: 'A Londres, Imprimé avec des planches solides par A. Wilson, Aux Frais de La Société pour l'Impression de la Bible, en Langue Angloise et en Langues Etrangères. 1807.'
   Wilson did print New Testaments from the Society's plates for his own use. See Bible Society's Library Working Catalogue number H3835a, imprinted: 'A Londres, Imprimé avec des planches solides par et pour A. Wilson, Duke Street, Lincoln's Inn Fields, et se vend chez Vernor, Hoode, et Sharpe. Poultry. 1808.'
   A minute of 1852, authorizing the destruction of old plates, noted that the plates for the 12mo French Testament had generated twelve editions, consisting of 93,000 copies. 'They were last used in 1838 & are completely worn out' (DepMin 4: 222, 8 March 1852).
37. SubMin 1: 145, 12 December 1808; 164, 12 June 1809.
38. SubMin 1: 190, 8 January 1810. Rutt's terms were for pages seventy-three lines long by eighty letters wide; composition 8s 6d; plates to the standard of Nonpareil metal would cost 5s each, with no reduction for duplicate plates, and he undertook to do the work in fifteen months.
39. Brightley to Tarn, HCIn, letters of August to December, 1808.
40. SubMin 2: 73, 30 September 1811; 76, 21 October; 78, 28 October; 80, 4 November; 164, 2 November 1812; 171, 7 December; 184, 8 February 1813; 227, 1 November; 241–2, 22 December; SubMin 3: 47, 1 July 1816; 48, 8 July; 54, 27 July; 57, 2 September; 59, 4 September. See *Historical Catalogue*, numbers 8492–4.
41. Marjorie Plant, *The English Book Trade: An Economic History of the Making and Sale of Books* (London: George Allen and Unwin, 1974. First published 1939), 273.
42. SubMin 2: 240–2, 20–2 December 1813.
43. SubMin 2: 245, 24 December 1813.
44. SubMin 2: 257, 7 March 1814; Bacon to Tarn, HCIn, 25 July 1814; Wilson to Tarn, HCIn, 28 July. Advised by Des Carriers, the Subcommittee decided that the imprint should read as follows. 'A Norwich: Imprimé Sur les Planches Stéréotypes d'A. Wilson, par R. M. Bacon, avec une nouvelle machine de son invention, Aux frais de la Société pour l'Impression de la Bible en Langue Anglaise, & en Langues Etrangères' (SubMin 2: 273, 1 August 1814).
45. Bacon to Tarn, HCIn, 30 July 1814; 15 December. At about this time John Smith at Cambridge was promising Tarn that he would use the Donkin and Bacon machine for Brevier Bibles if it arrived in time. According to Plant, the machine was set up at Cambridge but was 'found too complicated for general use' (Smith to Tarn, HCIn, 18 November 1814; Plant, *English Book Trade*, 273).
46. SubMin 3: 6, 2 October 1815; 73, 28 October 1816; 4: 105, 28 January 1819. See, however, *Historical Catalogue*, number 3857 for a copy dated 1820.
47. GenMin 3: 220, 20 March 1809; 228, 3 April.
48. Barker, *Oxford*, 42. GenMin 4: 43, 4 September 1809; 106, 5 February 1810. Dawson to Tarn, HCin, 14 February 1810. The 'beautiful pocket edition' was in either Pearl or Nonpareil type. 'Finishing' refers not to manufacturing paper, which did not begin at Oxford until 1855, but to preparing it for printing.

49. GenMin 3: 228, 3 April 1809; Tarn to the Chairman of the Printing Subcommittee, HCIn, 12 February 1810; Eyre and Strahan to Tarn, HCin, 14 February 1810; SubMin 1: 211, 19 March 1810. Emphasis in original.

50. The Subcommittee also considered acquiring Bibles from the King's Printer for Scotland, in Edinburgh. A letter from Messrs Oliphant and Balfour, who held the patent, explained the terms on which they would supply pocket Bibles, and Butterworth, Pellat and Phillips were detailed 'to consider if the Society can legally distribute or sell the Scots editions of the Bible, and to report thereon'. The legal advisers, however, decided that the Society was not free to sell the Scottish editions in England, although they could be circulated in Ireland as well as in Scotland (SubMin 2: 2–3, 2 July 1810; Oliphant and Balfour to Committee, HCIn, 7 July 1810; SubMin 2: 94, 6 January 1812).

51. SubMin 2: 61–2, 29 April 1811; 13 January 1812.

52. SubMin 2: 239, 6 December 1813; Tarn to Smith, CB 4: 103 – 4, 3 May 1811.

53. GenMin 5: 160; SubMin 2: 239, 6 December 1813; SubMin 1: 139, 13 July 1812; Tarn to Strahan, CB 6, 145, 20 April 1814.

54. Precise figures are not available for the early years. See table 5, 'Privileged Presses' Shares of BFBS Orders, 1826–30'.

55. CB 9: 453–6, 23 December 1817. Tarn's advice has not made its way into the Press records. An undated memorandum about this time considers the problem of diminishing sales of Bibles and Testaments. The writer made no mention of the Bible Society, believing the reason was that Longmans, as partners of the King's Printer, were underselling the Cambridge agents in London. The solution proposed was to recruit more agents at more competitive terms, particularly for London, and to reduce the prices of the most profitable books (CUP Press Accounts 1811–24, Pr.P.1.).

56. SubMin 2: 241–2, 22 December 1813; 3: 76, 5 November 1816.

57. Austen-Leigh, *Story of a Printing House*, 28. Oxford acquired its first steam presses in 1834 (Barker, *Oxford*, 40) and Cambridge in 1838 (Black, *Cambridge*, 136). The evidence presented in this chapter makes it possible to correct the assertion of M. H. Black, in his history of the Press, that even in 1838 when Cambridge decided 'that it appears expedient to introduce machinery into the Pitt Press', the Bible Society 'resolutely set their faces against books so printed'. Black's evidence is an obituary memorial of John William Parker (published in the June 1870 *Bookseller*) which implied that the Society and its servants were backward (Black, *Cambridge*, 136). See also S. C. Roberts, *A History of the Cambridge University Press*: 'for many years … the Bible Society stoutly refused to purchase books printed by steam presses' (137).

58. GenMin 11: 239, 5 February 1821.

59. Gaskell, *New Introduction*, 214–21.

60. Smith to Tarn, CB 8: 59–60, 18 December 1815; Eyre and Strahan to Tarn, HCIn, 20 December 1815.

61. Tarn to Eyre and Strahan, CB 8: 39–41, 27 January 1816.

62. Joel Munsell, *Chronology of the Origin and Progress of Paper and Paper-Making* (5th edn, New York: Garland, 1980. Originally published 1876), 70.

63. Maidstone Auxiliary to Committee, HCIn, 17 January 1817; SubMin 3: 101, 24 February 1817. Maidstone, in Kent, was a papermaking town, and the protest was probably motivated by economic concerns.

64. Letters dated January 1817 from T. Edmonds, B. Arnold, Francis Bryant, W. Venables, and circular letter dated 21 July from Tarn to Arnold, Bryant, Emery, Venables and Smith and Allnutt (CB 9: 322–30).

65. SubMin 3: 188–9, 29 October 1817.

66. Tarn to privileged presses, CB 10: 62, 23 May 1818.

67. Tarn to Collingwood and to Smith, CB 10: 85–9, 13 June 1818; Tarn to Smith, SubMin 4: 9, 18 June 1818. Francis Bryant of Barford was a frequent correspondent. He and Tarn exchanged friendly letters and even family visits, and the BFBS records show a steady increase in the papermaker's prosperity as a result of his connection with the Bible Society.

68. A history of the company states that Dickinson came to depend heavily on BFBS custom. When he installed a steam engine in 1824 a fortunate order from the Society permitted him to begin making a profit from the investment. And Mrs Dickinson's diary for 19 January 1826 records that 'Dearest seems better today owing to the Sec[retar]y to Bible Soc[iet]y telling him that he had sent an order to Cambridge for bibles on condition of their using his Machine paper. This is good news just now' (Joan Evans, *The Endless Web: John Dickinson & Co. Ltd. 1804–1954* (London: Jonathan Cape, 1955), 45, 49).

69. SubMin 4: 47–54, 23 September 1818. Subcommittee members at the time were William Blair (bibliophile surgeon), Robert Steven, P. J. Heisch and Joseph Reyner, all merchants, and Howard himself. The method involved using a device called a steelyard to measure how much weight a piece of paper could support.

70. See D. C. Coleman, *The British Paper Industry* (Oxford: Clarendon Press, 1958).

71. SubMin 4: 105, 28 January 1819; 114, 17 February. The test was entrusted to Smith of Watford. The minutes do not specify how he carried it out.

72. SubMin 4: 99–100, 15 January 1819; Smith to Tarn, HCIn, 29 January 1819 and 10 November 1820.

73. DepMin 1: 22, 28 November 1820; 27, 10 March 1821.

74. Beatrice Warde, *The Crystal Goblet. Sixteen Essays on Typography* (Cleveland and New York: World Publishing Co., 1956).

75. M. H. Black, 'The Evolution of a Book-form: The Octavo Bible from manuscript to the Geneva Version', *The Library* 5th Series 16, 1 (March 1961), 15–28.

76. The old names are no longer accurate enough for modern bibliography, and they are now usually replaced by accurate measurements in millimetres. In this chapter the old names serve as *de facto* titles for the various editions of the same text that were produced by the Society, while measurements are used to distinguish between one page-format and another.

77. N. Elliot of Exeter to [Seeley?], HCIn, 21 February 1810.

78. The initial pages were produced at Cambridge (Smith to Tarn, HCIn, 12 February 1810); SubMin 3: 248, 13 February 1818; 4: 109, 8 February 1819; GenMin 10: 305, 21 February 1820.

79. SubMin 3: 243, 9 February 1818. Forty years later, a parson suggested that chapters should be numbered in arabic, not roman, numerals, for the convenience of readers not familiar with the old convention (DepMin 6: 44, 21 February 1859).

80. Sharp to [?], CB 1: 24, 8 August 1804; SubMin 2: 100–1, 20 January 1812; 3 February.

81. Warde, *The Crystal Goblet*, 151; 'Size of Print', *Penrose Annual* 40 (1938), 76; Black,

'Evolution', 16; Kurt Weidemann, 'Biblica: Designing a New Typeface for the Bible', *Visible Language* 16, 1 (Winter 1982), 53.

82. The multiplicity of editions does not appear in the *Historical Catalogue*. A bibliographer who has worked closely with seventeenth- and eighteenth-century Bibles in the Bible Society's collection writes that 'it must be conceded that DMH [Darlow, Moule and Herbert's *Historical Catalogue*] is in need of fundamental revision – at least for the period I have consulted it for … in order to set its descriptions on a proper bibliographical footing' (B. J. McMullin, 'The Bible and Continuous Reprinting in the Early Seventeenth Century', *The Library* 6th Series 5, 3 (September 1983), 263). Similarly, not all of the nineteenth-century books are differentiated clearly.

83. Caleb Stower, *The Printer's Grammar* (London: B. Crosby and Co., 1808), 43.

84. For working-class difficulties with light and eyesight, see David Vincent, *Bread, Knowledge and Freedom* (London: Methuen, 1981), 120–5.

85. Tarn to Eyre and Strahan, CB 6: 156–7, 25 May 1814.

86. GenMin 3: 43, 15 June 1807; 125, 2 May 1808; Tarn to Watts, CB 2: 85–6, 15 June 1807.

87. CUP PS.OP 1803–23 Pr.V.4, 13 July 1807.

88. Tarn to Watts, CB 2: 177, 22 March 1808; Watts to Tarn, HCIn, 14 April 1808; SubMin 1: 114, 18 April 1808; Owen to Syndics of the Cambridge University Press, CB 2: 202, 11 May 1808.

89. CUP PS.OP 1803–23 Pr.V.4, 13 June 1808.

90. The descriptions of books are based upon copies examined at the Bible Society's Library, Cambridge University Library. See *Historical Catalogue*, numbers 1528 and 1604.

91. Eyre and Strahan to Tarn, HCIn, 26 April 1814. The books may be found in the Bible Society's Library Working Catalogue numbers 1603 i, ii and iii and 1685a. The 56-line Oxford Bible of this period (Catalogue number 1638) is not directly comparable, as it has marginal references.

92. Bible Society's Library Working Catalogue number 1635ii.

93. Bible Society's Library Working Catalogue number 1958c.

94. *Historical Catalogue*, number 1558, printed from stereotype by Oxford University Press in 1812. This book is listed as Nonpareil, but a measurement of the type reveals that it was one of the early Pearl Bibles.

95. DepMin 2: 4–5, 10 July 1826; 235, 3 March 1834; 271, 6 April 1835. CUP PS.OP 1823–43 Pr.V.5, 6 July 1836.

96. CUP PS.OP 1823–43, Pr.V.5, 29 August 1831. SubMin 2: 160, 4 July 1831; 165, 24 October.

97. GenMin 26: 247, 29 May 1837; 354, 4 September; *Report*, 1839. Samples were requested from Oxford, but the Queen's Printer's specimen was found superior, and 5,000 were ordered at 5s 4d each (DepMin 3: 56, 3 July 1837).

98. See BFBS Library Working Catalogue number 1908a(i) for an Oxford Pearl Octavo Bible with references, dated 1857. This may, however, have succeeded an earlier version of the same format which has not survived.

99. DepMin 3: 103, 4 October 1841; 31 March; 2 April; 3 October; 28 November 1842; CUP PS Printing Order Book 1824–58, Pr.V.7,

100. CUP PS.OP 1823–43 Pr.V.5, 16 February 1830 and 13 October 1835; DepMin

3: 66, 1 January 1838; DepMin 4: 18–21, 11 October 1847. See also Browne, *History of the BFBS*, 22.

101. GenMin 29: 253–4, 23 November 1840.

102. GenMin 19: 436, 2 April 1830. In 1811 Wilson Birkbeck had proofread and collated the first stereotype Testament, comparing it with Blayney's and other editions. But even then the Syndics of Cambridge Press were asked to make the final decision (Browne, 31).

103. Curtis to Secretaries, 27 January 1832, enclosed in Brandram and Hughes to Cambridge University Press, CUP PS.OP 1823–43 Pr.V.5, 14 February 1832.

104. Alfred W. Pollard, ed., *Records of the English Bible* (London: Dawsons of Pall Mall, 1974. First published 1911), 65–76.

105. CB 12: 236–45, 27 January to 21 July 1832. CUP PS.OP 1823–43, Pr.V.5. Cambridge formed a Sub-Syndicate to answer the Secretaries' letter on the Curtis affair (28 February 1832). Eyre and Spottiswoode to Brandram and Hughes, HCIn, 25 February 1832.

106. Parliament. *Report from the Select Committee on King's Printers' Patents with the Minutes of Evidence, and Appendix* Sess. 1831–2 (713) vol. 8, 1.

107. The Society did, however, apparently ask the Presses to comment on the question (Parker to Tarn, HCIn, 29 April 1833; Spottiswoode to Tarn, 30 April). Both printers assured the Society that their profits were very moderate.

108. Parliament. *Report from the Select Committee Appointed to Inquire into the Nature and Extent of the King's Printers' Patent in Scotland*, Sess. 1837 (511) vol. 13, 1.

109. Adam Thomson, *Charges against the British and Foreign Bible Society* (London, 1843).

110. Gray *et. al.*, of Hexham Auxiliary to Committee, HCIn, 9 November 1840; Brandram to Gray, HCOut, 24 November; other examples in 1840 correspondence are Browne to Hitchin, HCIn, 11 September; W. Douglas (Newcastle-on-Tyne) to Committee, 29 October; Hitchin to Rev. R. Frost, HCOut, 18 November; Bexley to Brandram, HCIn, 15 December; Rev. G. Wardlaw (Blackburn) to Secretaries, HCIn, 28 December.

111. Brandram to Brackenbury, HCOut, 28 December 1840; Brandram to Bourne, HCOut, 20 November; T. Phillips to Hitchin, HCIn, 17 December.

112. GenMin 29: 256–7, 27 November 1840. See also CUP PS.OP Pr.V.5, 14 November 1840.

113. GenMin 29: 336–7, 5 February 1841.

114. Hitchin to Dudley, HCOut, 6 November 1840.

115. Parker to [?], HCIn, 19 December 1840.

116. Parker to [?], HCIn, 31 December 1840.

117. Adam Clarke to Tarn, HCIn, 1 November 1813. The printer was James Powell of the Deaf and Dumb Institution and the job was a New Testament in Spanish.

118. John Smith, one of the Cambridge printers, published in 1829 *Observations Relating to the Affairs of the Press*. (See CUP Press Guard Book: Printers 1586–1886 (CUR 33.1).) S. C. Roberts quotes Smith as blaming the BFBS for dampness problems: '"Send up the books in gatherings" (*i.e.* divisions) was the repeated order of the Bible Society – "and we will spare you the trouble of booking off etc., etc." Many thousand copies were thus supplied which were never properly dried' (135–6). It must be noted that I have found no such

communication in the records either of Cambridge University Press or of the Bible Society.

119. Dudley to [?], HCIn, 15 May 1845.

4 THE BFBS AND LONDON BOOKBINDERS, 1811–1864

1. Robert Darnton, *The Business of Enlightenment* (Cambridge, Mass., Harvard University Press, 1979), 2.
2. Lionel S. Darley, *Bookbinding Then and Now: A Survey of the First Hundred and Seventy-Eight Years of James Burn & Company* (London: Faber and Faber, 1959), 12.
3. Gaskell, *New Introduction*, 231. See also Bernard C. Middleton, *A History of English Craft Bookbinding Technique* (London: The Holland Press, 1978) and Eleanore Jamieson, *English Embossed Bindings 1825–1850* (Cambridge: Cambridge Bibliographical Society, 1972). For illustrations see Ruari McLean, *Victorian Publishers' Book-Bindings in Cloth and Leather* (London: Gordon Fraser, 1974).
4. John Adams, *The House of Kitcat: A Story of Bookbinding 1798–1948* (London, 1948), 17. Kitcat was one binder used by the Bible Society.
5. Darley, *Bookbinding*, 25.
6. Darley, *Bookbinding*, 15–16, quoted from the diary of Sarah Bain.
7. CB 1: 133, 18 August 1805.
8. SubMin 2: 24, 4 November 1805.
9. SubMin 1: 132, 1 August; 134, 15 August 1808.
10. Thomas Smith to Tarn, HCIn, 28 March and 4 April 1808. The stars were replaced in 1812 by a letter incorporated in the design of the BFBS stamp. Bird to Tarn, HCIn and SubMin 2: 2, 2 July 1810.
11. SubMin 2: 87, 25 November 1811.
12. SubMin 2: 128–32, 29 June 1812.
13. H. G. Pollard, 'Changes in the Style of Bookbinding, 1550 – 1830', *The Library* 5th Series 11, 2 (1956), 87.
14. Most of these names appear in Ellic Howe, *A List of London Bookbinders, 1648–1815* (London: Bibliographical Society, 1950): Thomas Burn, Samuel August Bielefeld (probably a German binder), George Collier, George Buss, Thomas Birch, John Polwarth (not Polworth), John Hayes, George Kitcat. The following binders mentioned above are all listed: John Bird, David Nelson, Thomas Payne (not the brother of Roger Payne the famous eighteenth-century binder) and George Lister. There is no mention of Seear, Watkins, Pettitt or Bewsey. The Philanthropic Society is not listed directly, but Howe refers to Kitcat having bound at the Bridge Street Bridewell 'an institution similar to the Philanthropic where boys were taught trades'. Howe lists George Ford, but the BFBS later corresponded with William Ford.
15. Jones to [?], HCIn, 1808.
16. Tarn to [?], CB 10: 289–91, 24 December 1819.
17. Auxiliaries were very seldom permitted to arrange for binding locally. Cambridge was one exception, since there was an active Auxiliary in the University town. And the society in Edinburgh was granted permission to purchase books in sheets, from the King's Printer for Scotland, in 1810 (SubMin 2: 96, 13 January 1812; GenMin 4: 179, 20 May 1810).

18. At first only one binder could be found who used canvas, a Mr Pounsford, who was given a contract for 500 Nonpareil Bibles in black canvas, with thicker boards than usual and the backs lined and including headbands. Five hundred Brevier Testaments were to be similarly bound, without headbands (SubMin 1: 132–5, 1 August 1808).

19. Douglas Leighton, 'Canvas and Bookcloth: An Essay on Beginnings', *The Library* 3rd Series (1948–9), 39–49. See also Michael Sadleir, *The Evolution of Publishers' Binding Styles 1770–1900* (London: Constable, 1930). DepMin 1: 121–9, 5–18 July 1824.

20. Darley, *Bookbinding*, 16. See also SubMin 2: 186, 8 February 1813.

21. DepMin 1: 63–4, 11 February 1823; 2: 127–8, 10 September 1824.

22. Gurney to Tarn, HCIn, 3 July 1813; SubMin 2: 85, 18 November 1811; DepMin 1: 144, 20 December 1824. Only one book was available unbound, in boards: the very expensive 'Quarto [really octavo pages on large paper] Small Pica Bible with wide-margins for writing upon', was published in boards for the owner to have bound to order.

23. DepMin 3: 44, 18 November 1836. The period was January 1834 to November 1836. The grants were mostly for Sunday Schools and for Ireland.

24. The circular letter has not survived. DepMin 2: 40–1, 2 June 1827; GenMin 18: 9, 4 February 1828. Neither Cross nor Hickson appears in Howe's *List*.

25. Ellic Howe and John Child, *The Society of London Bookbinders, 1780–1951* (London: Sylvan Press, 1952), 146. John Stuart Mill recommended Dunning's pamphlet on *Trade Unions and Strikes*, and Dunning admired Mill's *Principles of Political Economy* (*Bookbinders' Trade Circular*, 27 March 1862).

26. Darley, *Bookbinding*, 29.

27. Howe and Child, *Society*, 101–2.

28. Howe and Child, *Society*, 105; Darley, *Bookbinding*, 31–2. See also Middleton, *History*, 228–30 and Gaskell, *New Introduction*, 235.

29. Journeymen Bookbinders to Committee, HCIn, 1 January and 7 February 1831.

30. GenMin 20: 318, 3 January 1831; DepMin 2: 147, 5 January

31. Howe and Child, *Society*, 103–4; Ramsay MacDonald, *Women in the Printing Trades* (London, P. S. King and Son, 1904), 32. The General Committee minute books for March 1831 to November 1836 have not survived.

32. MacDonald, *Women*, 32–3; Journeymen Bookbinders to Committee, HCIn, 20 and 28 December 1833.

33. Howe and Child, *Society*, 103–4.

34. GenMin 31: 232, 2 January; 262–5, 6 February 1843.

35. S. Ranyard (Kingston) to W. Sanger, HCIn, 3 February 1843.

36. GenMin 31: 269, 14 February 1843; 271–5, 17 February.

37. *Bookbinders' Trade Circular* 3, 13 (January 1862), 66; Howe and Child, *Society*, 148.

38. Andrew Brandram, *Letter to the Committee of the British and Foreign Bible Society* (privately printed, 10 January 1845).

39. Sidney Pollard, *The Genesis of Modern Management: A Study of the Industrial Revolution in Great Britain* (Cambridge, Mass.: Harvard University Press, 1965), 38–47.

40. Brandram to J. Bacon, HCOut, 9 October 1849; *Patriot* (9 October 1849).

41. Brandram to Corderoy (Southwark Auxiliary), HCOut, 5 September 1849.

42. I am grateful to Kathleen Cann for providing this information. See DepMin 2: 70, 10 March 1823.

43. DepMin 3: 205, 19 May 1845; 206–7, 26 May; 222–3, 14 July. Watkins offered specific discounts on each of the prices and 2.5 per cent further discount for the whole contract.

44. Dudley to Tarn, HCIn, 5 December 1845. See chapter 5 for the 'Manchester movement'.

45. DepMin 3: 233–5, 13 November 1845; 17 November; 27 March 1848. The renewal was repeated in July 1851 (DepMin 3: 21 July 1851).

46. Darley, *Bookbinding*, 37. Darley erroneously dates the call for tenders as 1843.

47. Lorina Watkins's brother Farrell acted as manager and supervised the staff, but she was clearly in control.

48. DepMin 5: 56, 12 February 1855; 58, 12 March; 61–2, 19 March.

49. DepMin 6: 77, 14 November 1859.

50. Obituary, *Bookbinders' Trade Circular* 3, 13 (January 1862); she died at thirty-three of pulmonary disease, presumably a result of leather-dust in her lungs.

51. See, for example, *The Democrat* (November 1886). This was a paper favouring free education, an eight-hour day, tax reform, home rule, adult suffrage and paid MPs. A Cardiff correspondent asked them to inquire about 'a complaint frequently made', that binders of penny Bibles were underpaid and overworked. A visit to the Bible Society's shop, then at Walworth, convinced the editors that wages and working conditions were acceptable. But why, they asked, use people for jobs that machines could do?

52. T. J. Dunning, *An Address to the Donors, Subscribers and Friends of the British and Foreign Bible Society, and the Religious Public in General, by the Journeymen Bookbinders of London and Westminster, in reply to a Statement of the Contractress of the above Society Contradictory of Certain Portions of their 'Appeal' on the Subject of 'Cheap' Bibles* (London, 1849).

53. Dunning to Committee (with enclosure), HCIn, 24 August 1849; Brandram to Dunning, HCOut, 3 September 1849. The BFBS correspondence after 1836 is not indexed, but the letters and clippings about this affair are gathered together in the 1849 box in a bundle marked 'In Re Binders' Appeal'.

54. George Cartwright (Lyme Regis) to Brandram, HCIn, 1 September 1849; Rev. David Wheeler (Worcester) to Andrew Brandram, HCIn, 14 December 1849; Bunsen to Brandram, HCIn, 5 December 1849; Marsh to Brandram, 5 December; Minton to Committee, 14 September.

55. Marsh to Brandram, 5 December 1849; Dudley to Brandram, 27 November.

56. Dunning, *Address*, 1, 8.

57. Dunning to Committee, HCIn, 3 November 1849.

58. 'Our Little Bird', *Punch, or the London Charivari* (3 November 1849), 183; *Weekly Times* (11 November 1849), 799.

59. Corderoy to Brandram, HCIn, 13 December 1849; *Monthly Extracts* (28 February 1850), 557.

60. Westminster Auxiliary Bible Society, Minute Book, 15 October 1849 to 18 April 1850. Cribb to Coode, Westminster Auxiliary Bible Society Records, 9 February 1850.

61. T. J. Dunning, *Reply to a Letter from the Committee of the Southwark Auxiliary Bible*

Society, to the Committee of the British & Foreign Bible Society, embodying the 'Report of a Sub-Committee appointed by them' . . . To investigate certain Statements respecting the Binder for the British and Foreign Bible Society, and the Female Workers in her Employ (London, 1850).

62. Dunning, *Address*, 1.
63. Dunning, *Reply to a Letter*, 10.
64. After the crisis, bookbinding continued under the same arrangements. When Lorina Watkins died on 3 September 1852, the contract was continued by her brother Farrell Watkins, who had managed the shop for her during the conflict with Dunning. Watkins renewed the contract in 1857, and extended it for seven years in 1860. At that time his plant in Southwark was torn down to permit the construction of the Chatham and Dover Railway. He argued that the longer period would justify his building new shops and introducing new machinery. When Watkins died in 1863 his wife took over, thus returning the business to female hands.

5 THE BFBS AND BOOKSELLING, 1804–1864

1. Terry Belanger, 'From Bookseller to Publisher: Changes in the London Book Trade, 1750–1850', in *Book Selling and Book Buying: Aspects of the Nineteenth Century British and North American Book Trade*, Richard G. Landon, ed. (Chicago: American Library Association, 1978), 8–9.
2. John Feather, *The Provincial Book Trade in Eighteenth-Century England* (Cambridge: Cambridge University Press, 1985), 75.
3. *Historical Catalogue*, numbers 1409, 1413, 1405.
4. Henry Curwen, *A History of Booksellers, The Old and the New* (London: Chatto and Windus, [1873]), 303. See also Frank Mumby, *Publishing and Bookselling* (London: Jonathan Cape, 1949), 197 – 8.
5. Mumby, *Publishing and Bookselling*, 237–9; Anthony Wagner to Tarn, HCIn, 21 March 1812.
6. Black, *Cambridge University Press*, 136, 156, 160.
7. Books for the BFBS were ordered directly from Oxford, but delivered to Gardner in London for collection (Gardner to Tarn, HCIn, 5 March 1814).
8. Clarke, *History of the S.P.C.K.*, 141–5, 188–9, 192.
9. HCIn, Watts to Tarn, 12 August 1806; 29 July 1808.
10. SubMin 3: 104, 10 March 1817. About the same time (15 February 1817), Cambridge University Press began to allow its agents 20 per cent, instead of the cumbersome 'seventh book' arrangement (CUP PS.OP 1803–23 Pr.V.4).
11. SubMin 2: 29, 10 December 1810; 32, 17 December. Seeley had been a bookseller in Ave Maria Lane since about 1784 (*DNB* entry on his son, bookseller Leonard Benton Seeley). There was a competition for the post; Seeley's competitors were Messrs Black and Co. and Messrs Darton and Co. (SubMin 1: 110, 4 April 1808).
12. Seeley to Tarn, HCIn, 20 June 1808; 9 July; Tarn to Seeley [copy], HCIn, 14 December 1809.
13. Watts To Tarn, HCIn, 14 April 1806; GenMin 6: 215, 7 February 1814.
14. GenMin 4: 24, 19 June 1809; Letter dated 30 September 1809, 1810 *Report*, GenMin 5: 17, 21 January 1811.

15. SubMin 3: 21, 8 December 1815; Seeley to Committee, HCIn, 8 July 1816.
16. GenMin 8: 28, 8 June 1816; 64, 2 September; 167–8, 20 January 1817; 412, 19 January 1818. Anthony Wagner, originally a Committee member, was engaged as 'collector' of subscriptions in August 1810. His correspondence with Tarn dealt with lists of names for the annual *Report*, subscribers in arrears, and deposits to the Society's bankers, Down and Co.
17. Bagster to Tarn, HCIn, 5 April 1824.
18. SubMin 3: 248, 12 February 1818.
19. The Society's eloquent adversary, the Rev. H. H. Norris, claimed that since the formation of the BFBS, 'Bibles are prophaned to the basest purposes, being hawked about by Jew Boys amongst their contemptible merchandize, being in use at Cheesemongers to wrap up their articles of traffic, and being bartered in the Gin Shop for the means of intoxication' (*Practical Exposition*, 46–7).
20. Steven to Tarn, HCIn, 21 June 1820; Rev. E. T. M. Phillips (of Hathern) to Brandram, HCIn, 25 September 1833.
21. SubMin 2: 3, 2 July 1810.
22. 1805 *Report*.
23. Canton 1: 143–62.
24. Canton 1: 128, 135, 138.
25. Canton 1: 119–42.
26. Canton 1: 163–83.
27. Canton 1: 184–210. A list of all the Bible Societies founded in Europe, showing the amounts sent to them from London can be found in Canton 1: Appendix 4.
28. Canton 1: 389.
29. Canton 1: 399. See also Margaret Fison, *Colportage: Its History and Relation to Home and Foreign Evangelism* (London: Wertheim, Macintosh and Hunt, 1859). For colportage in France see Henri-Jean Martin and Roger Chartier, eds., *Histoire de l'édition française* tome 1 *Le livre conquérant* (Paris: Promodis, 1982), 405–7 and tome 3 *Le temps des éditeurs* (Paris: Promodis, 1985), 243–6, 251–3.
30. Canton 1: 399–400.
31. Canton 2: 192–200.
32. Michael Collie, *George Borrow Eccentric* (Cambridge: Cambridge University Press, 1982), 178, 183; See also Leslie Howsam, 'The Readers in George Borrow's Text: The Committee of the British and Foreign Bible Society and Borrow's *The Bible in Spain*', in *Proceedings of the 1987 George Borrow Conference*, Gillian Fenwick, ed. (Toronto, 1988), 43–55.
33. 1845 *Report*.
34. Asa Briggs, *Victorian Cities* (Harmondsworth: Penguin, 1968. First published 1963), 56, 96.
35. James Dilworth to Brandram, HCIn, 18 October 1845.
36. Dilworth to Brandram, HCIn, 24 October 1845.
37. Dudley to [?], HCIn, 5 November 1845; to Hitchin, 6 November; to Brandram, 7 November.
38. Dilworth to Brandram, HCIn, 7 and 16 November 1845.
39. Dudley to Brandram, HCIn, 22 and 25 November 1845; 26 December.
40. Dudley to Browne, HCIn, 16 December 1845; DepMin 3: 240, 24 December 1845.
41. Dudley to Brandram, HCIn, 19 February 1846.

42. Dudley to Brandram, HCIn, 18 April 1846; GenMin 34: 223, 24 April 1846; Dilworth to Dudley (copy in Dilworth to Brandram), 15 May; Dudley to Brandram, 16 May; Dudley to Brandram, 6 June.
43. Canton 2: 163–4.
44. Richard D. Altick, *The English Common Reader: A Social History of the Mass Reading Public 1800–1900* (Chicago: University of Chicago Press, 1957), 74–5.
45. Fison, 192, 44; SubMin (Jubilee) 88, 17 June 1853; 1854 *Report*.
46. 1856 *Report*.
47. DepMin 4: 203, 24 October 1851.
48. [Draft of] The Memorial of the Committee of the British and Foreign Bible Society to the Rt. Hon. W. E. Gladstone, Chancellor of Her Majesty's Exchequer. Inserted in SubMin (Jubilee) between ff. 176 and 177.
49. Dudley to Brandram, HCIn, 9 November 1846.
50. Marten, Thomas and Hollams to Hitchin, HCIn, 5 July 1850. The opinion was that of Sir J. Thesinger.
51. GenMin 38: 228, 8 July 1850; 239, 15 July; 370, 21 October. Trevelyan was himself a BFBS supporter. The 1839 *Report* includes a copy of a letter from him ('late a Member of the Committee of the Calcutta Auxiliary Bible Society') to the Agent in Calcutta, on the benefit of producing the Bengali Testament in Roman type: 'the greatest advantage . . . is, that it will cut up the existing native literature by the roots, and give rise to a new and purified literature, unconnected with the abominations of idolatry'.
52. W. E. Gladstone to Shaftesbury, HCIn, 15 June 1853.
53. Canton 3: 11–12; 1848 *Report*; 1854 *Report*.
54. Bible Society's Archives. Birmingham Auxiliary Bible Society Minute Book, February 1838–March 1858: (i) copy of a letter, Bergne to James, 20 December 1854, at pp. 288–90, read at a Committee Meeting on 8 January 1855; (ii) Duffield statement at pp. 295–8, n.d.; (iii) copy of letter requesting colportage, J. B. Marsden, J. A. James, W. Chance and W. R. Lloyd to BFBS Committee, 10 January 1857, pp. 343–6.
55. Gareth Stedman Jones, *Outcast London: A Study in the Relationship between Classes in Victorian Society* (Oxford: Oxford University Press, 1971). See also his *Languages of Class: Studies in English Working Class History 1832–1982* (Cambridge: Cambridge University Press, 1983).
56. Born London, 1810, daughter of John Bazley White, a cement manufacturer, and raised a nonconformist. Her son Arthur Cowper Ranyard (1845–94) was an astronomer. She also had two daughters, each of whom died at the age of eighteen. Ellen Ranyard died 11 February 1879, of bronchitis. The Greater London Record Office holds a collection of books and manuscripts associated with Ranyard and her mission. See also Frank Prochaska, 'Body and Soul: Bible Nurses and the Poor in Victorian London', *Historical Research* 60, 143 (October 1987), 336–48.
57. She requested that the BFBS pay a grant for the colporteur's salary. Ranyard to Rev. T. Phillips, HCIn, 21 November 1853; 25 November; 1854 *Report*,
58. SubMin (Jubilee) 14, 3 December 1852; GenMin 46: 129, 20 September 1857.
59. Ranyard, *The Bible Collectors, or Principles in Practice* (London: Samuel Bagster and Sons, 1854), 120–1.

60. Greater London Record Office, A RNY 231/2. [Notes for an address] 'To the Members of the Committee', 20 November 1869.
61. BFBS archives. London. Queen Square Ladies Bible Association, 1826–73: vol. 2.
62. *The Book and Its Missions* 3 (1858), 189–90.
63. Ellen Ranyard, *The Missing Link* (Fredericton, N.B.: C. W. Wetmore, 1861. First published London: James Nisbet and Co., 1859), 17, 20, 221. Marian's surname was Bowers. In an attempt to convey some of the flavour of the book, I have chosen to adopt Ellen Ranyard's usage and refer to Bowers by her given name.
64. Ranyard, *The Missing Link*, 46, 302.
65. Ranyard, *The Missing Link*, 58–9, 72.
66. Ranyard, *The Missing Link*, 247, 275.
67. See *Sex and Class in Women's History*, Judith L. Newton *et. al.*, eds. (London: Routledge and Kegan Paul, 1983).
68. For another point of view see Françoise Ducrocq, 'The London Biblewomen and Nurses Mission, 1857–1880: Class Relations/Women's Relations', in Barbara J. Harris and JoAnn K. McNamara, eds., *Women and the Structure of Society* (Durham, N.C.: Duke University Press, 1984).
69. Lizzie Aldridge, *Florence Nightingale. Frances Ridley Havergal. Catherine Marsh. Mrs Ranyard ('L.N.R.')* (London: Cassell and Co., 1885), 101.
70. Greater London Record Office. Ranyard to 'my dear young friend', 29 November 1878.
71. Ranyard, *The True Institution of Sisterhood; or, a Message and Its Messengers* (London: James Nisbet and Co., [1862]), 18–19; 4; 6–9.
72. *Monthly Reporter*, 2 December 1861.
73. In the Ranyard collection at the Greater London Record Office there are some fragmentary records of biblewomen's names, addresses, and journals that might be used as part of a community study to put the project in its social context. There is also an interesting report (A RNY 87) on late nineteenth-century women's work and exploitation in London.
74. *The Missing Link*, 271; GenMin 44: 168, 21 January 1856.
75. GenMin 47: 238, 31 January 1859; 251, 7 February; 383, 9 May.
76. GenMin 47: 216–17, 10 January 1859; 310, 28 March; 1859 *Report*.
77. GenMin 48: 179–80, 5 December 1859; 49: 204, 19 December 1860.
78. GenMin 54: 168–70, 20 February 1865. I have not found a copy in the BFBS archives.
79. Ranyard, *The Missing Link*, 300.
80. Kathleen Heasman, *Evangelicals in Action: An Appraisal of their Social Work in the Victorian Era* (London: Geoffrey Bles, 1962), 37.
81. GenMin 45: 287, 4 February 1857; 366, 30 March; DepMin 6: 166, 9 September 1861.
82. GenMin 47: 20–2, 5 July 1858; 119–20, 18 October; DepMin 4: 33, 12 December 1858; DepMin 6: 38, 10 January 1859.
83. GenMin 46: 269, 18 January 1858.
84. DepMin 4: 132, 22 November 1850; 6: 37–8, 10 January 1859; 40, 14 February; GenMin 48: 150, 7 November 1859; DepMin 7: 49, 12 February 1863; GenMin 51: 380, 2 March 1863. For W. H. Smith and railway station depots, see Charles Wilson, *First With the News: The History of W. H. Smith 1792–1972* (London:

Jonathan Cape, 1985), chapters 5 and 6. Wilson does not mention the trade in Bibles.

85. GenMin 43: 392, 13 August 1855. Over-generosity on the part of local Auxiliaries was checked by asking them to urge the managers of such establishments to pay at least half the cost price to have their rooms stocked (GenMin 44: 316, 14 April 1856). This policy anticipated that of the Gideon Society, founded in the United States in the early twentieth century. Like the BFBS it was the project of Christian businessmen.

86. GenMin 44: 12, 15 October 1855; G. Browne to W. J. Smith, HCOut, 6 September 1853; the Committee had decided Smith's suggestion was 'not expedient'.

87. For bookhawkers see 'Henry George de Bunsen: The Hawker: His Work and his Day', the text of a paper read at the Conference of the Church of England Bookhawking Union held at Derby, 21 September 1859 in 'Document: The Hawker', *Publishing History* 12 (1982), 87–96. GenMin 45: 221, 22 December 1856; 233, 5 January 1857; 290, 9 February 1857.

88. GenMin 49: 446, 17 June 1861; 50: 107, 16 August; 117, 23 September; 145, 7 October; 51: 290, 5 January 1863.

89. DepMin 7: 107, 15 February 1864.

6 THE TRANSACTION RENEWED, 1850S AND 1860S

1. Canton 2: 152; 1851 *Report*.

2. 1854 *Report*. This sort of thinking echoes the contemporary development of Christian militarism, a 'changing attitude to the soldiery' which Olive Anderson has related to the war in the Crimea ('The Growth of Christian Militarism in Mid-Victorian England', *English Historical Review* 86 (1971), 46–72.) Kathleen Cann has given a full account of the BFBS participation in the Crimea in her unpublished paper, 'A Bible Society Agent in the Crimean War', dated 1980.

3. Canton 3: 10.

4. For the concept of a 'publication circuit' see Robert Darnton, 'What is the History of Books?', *Daedalus* (Summer 1982), 65–84.

5. SubMin 5: 76, 31 May 1855; the supplier was H. Houghton, who offered to supply two gross of the boxes at 3s 2d each for Melbourne and Sydney.

6. *Monthly Reporter* (March 1867), 472–3.

7. Ranyard, *The Missing Link*, 119.

8. James Anthony Froude, *The Nemesis of Faith* (London: John Chapman, 1849), Letter IX, 60–2. I am grateful to J. M. Robson for this reference.

9. Edwin Hodder, *The Life and Work of the Seventh Earl of Shaftesbury, K.G.* (London: Cassell and Co., 1886), vol. 2, 342 – 3; Hodder cites Shaftesbury's speech to an Auxiliary Bible Society in 1877, including his regret that the Commissioners had 'thrust [the Bibles] into a remote corner'. See also Geoffrey B. A. M. Finlayson, *The Seventh Earl of Shaftesbury, 1801–1885* (London: Eyre Methuen, 1981), 368–9; John Pollock, *Shaftesbury: The Poor Man's Earl* (London: Hodder and Stoughton, 1985), 100; Canton 2: 169.

10. The Committee was represented by Henry Roberts, an architect, and Thomas

Farmer, who manufactured oil of vitriol. DepMin 4: 122–3, 13 May and 10 June, 1850; 148–51, 13–27 January 1851.

11. DepMin 4: 151, 27 January 1851; 169, 21 April.

12. DepMin 4: 172–4, 28 April 1851.

13. Ashley to Browne, HCIn, 14 May 1851; Browne to Ashley, HCOut, 16 May; GenMin 39: 243, 2 June.

14. James Cadbury (Banbury) to Browne, HCIn, 15 June 1851.

15. Dudley to Hitchin, HCIn, 28 December 1853.

16. Phillips was Domestic Agent for Wales. The Subcommittee's members were C. A. Barlow, John Bockett, R. C. Bowden, T. M. Coombs, Thomas Farmer, Josiah Forster, James Foster, John Radley and W. Taylor. Later Henry Gregory, Richard Matthews and H. H. White were added. The volume of minutes of the Jubilee Subcommittee is dated from 1 March 1852 to 21 April 1854.

17. DepMin 4: 265, 21 February 1853.

18. SubMin (Jubilee), 34–5, 28 June 1853; 135, 127–46, 18 November.

19. Canton 2: 445.

20. Canton 2: 447–9; 3: 434; 1862 *Report*.

21. David Owen, *English Philanthropy 1660–1960* (Cambridge, Mass.: Harvard University Press, 1964), 169–73. Figures have been rounded to the nearest pound. By 1861 the 'Abstract' filled twelve pages of the *Report*, with both receipts and expenditures shown in considerable detail. To bring them into line with the tables in the appendix, the following amounts taken together count as 'general purpose' receipts: Auxiliary contributions, individual subscriptions, miscellaneous contributions, dividends and interest. The special projects are those for China, India and the 'benevolent fund' for employee pensions, while the items described in the tables as 'divestment of surplus' represent the proceeds from selling stocks and exchequer bills.

22. Sampson Low, *The Charities of London in 1861* (London: Sampson Low, Son and Co., 1862), vii–xi.

23. Altick, *English Common Reader*, 277–93.

24. James J. Barnes, *Free Trade in Books. A Study of the London Book Trade since 1800* (Oxford: Clarendon Press, 1964).

25. Parliament. *Report from the Select Committee on the Queen's Printer's Patent*, Sess. 1859 (144.Sess.2) v.395 and Sess. 1860 (162) xxii.577.

26. *Historical Catalogue*, number 1827; illustrated in Greenslade, ed., *Cambridge History of the Bible*, plate 45. It sold 350,000 copies in six years (Altick, *English Common Reader*, 303).

27. Handover, *Printing in London*, 94. Black, *Cambridge*, 137. Black attributes the decline in profits to the incursions of various Scottish printers into the English market, particularly William Collins, who began in 1858 to sell Bibles in London. For a report from Cambridge on the situation, which blamed the Scottish printers, see CUP Press Guard Book: Miscellaneous, 1744-1890 (CUR 33.7), 79, 25 May 1849. This factor did not directly affect the Bible Society, whose policy of using only the privileged Presses remained inviolate. Charles Batey, 'The Oxford Partners. Some Notes on the Administration of the University Press 1780–1881', *Journal of the Printing Historical Society* 3 (1967), 59.

28. Quoted in Batey, 'The Oxford Partners', 60.

29. CUP Memorandum Book 1854–73 (Pr.V.9), letter of 9 July 1859, C. J. Clay to Spencer Walpole MP (Secretary of State), recommending the Queen's Printer's patent be renewed.
30. CUP PS.OP 1843–74 (Pr.V.8), 29 March 1865.
31. Canton 3: 3.
32. GenMin 54: 168–70, 20 February 1865.
33. It closed in 1985, when the Society opened a new Bible House at Swindon, Wiltshire and deposited its Library and archives at Cambridge University Library. The original façade and the staircase are preserved, but the building has been renovated extensively.
34. Brandram had been in office twenty-seven years. According to Canton (2: 166) he was 'worn out with many labours, with much travelling, with pastoral and domestic duties'. It seems very possible that the stress of the Watkins/Dunning affair of 1849 – 50 hastened Brandram's death. George Browne wrote his Jubilee *History of the British and Foreign Bible Society* in retirement.
35. *The Jubilee Memorial of the British and Foreign Bible Society, 1853–54* (London: BFBS, 1854), 186.
36. Canton 3: 39. Even after Hewlett took over his territory Dudley continued to correspond on behalf of the Society. He died on 4 November 1862 at the age of 82.
37. J. P. Hewlett, *A Paper Read at the Conference of the District Secretaries of the British and Foreign Bible Society, February 5th, 1867, and at Their Request Printed for Private Circulation* (London, [1867]).
38. Clement Shorter, *George Borrow and his Circle* (Boston: Houghton Mifflin, 1913), 155.
39. Receipts from Auxiliaries remained very nearly constant between 1860 and 1884. Canton (3: 21) reports average annual Auxiliary contributions as follows: 1860–4, £47,040; 1865–9, £49,367; 1870–4, £50,719; 1875–9, £54,789; 1880–4, £52,895.
40. 1864 *Report*.
41 James Stephen, *Essays in Ecclesiastical Biography*, vol. 2 (London: Longman, Brown, Green and Longmans, 1853), 358–9.

EPILOGUE

1. Dudley, *Analysis*, 441.
2. Michael Collie and Angus Fraser, *George Borrow: A Bibliographical Study* (Winchester: St Paul's Bibliographies, 1984), 38–50. As for Ranyard's book, 23,000 copies were sold in the first nine months, and 60,000 had been printed by 1859 (Canton 2: 452).
3. See Alfred Lord Tennyson, 'Sea Dreams', in *Enoch Arden and Other Poems*, describing a hypocrite:
   > And oft at Bible meetings, o'er the rest
   > Arising, did his holy oily best,
   > Dropping the too rough H in Hell and Heaven,
   > To spread the Word by which himself had thriven.
4. For an example see Joyce M. Banks, 'The Printing of the Cree Bible', *Papers of the Bibliographical Society of Canada* 22 (1983), 12–24.
5. Stephen, *Essays*, vol. 2, 384. I am indebted to Michael Black for the idea that this kind of publishing can be seen as 'charitable trading'.

SELECT BIBLIOGRAPHY

Altick, Richard D. *The English Common Reader: A Social History of the Mass Reading Public 1800–1900*. Chicago: University of Chicago Press, 1957.

Black, M. H. *Cambridge University Press 1584–1984*. Cambridge: Cambridge University Press, 1984.

Bradley, Ian. *The Call to Seriousness: The Evangelical Impact on the Victorians*. London: Cape, 1976.

Brown, Ford K. *Fathers of the Victorians: The Age of Wilberforce*. Cambridge: Cambridge University Press, 1961.

Canton, William. *A History of the British and Foreign Bible Society. With Portraits and Illustrations*. 5 vols. London: John Murray, 1904–10.

Chadwick, Owen. *The Victorian Church*. 2nd edn, 2 vols. London: Adam and Charles Black, 1966–72.

Darnton, Robert. 'What is the History of Books?', *Daedalus* (Summer 1982), 65–84. Reprinted in *Books and Society in History*, Kenneth E. Carpenter, ed. New York: R.R. Bowker, 1983.

Davidoff, Leonore and Catherine Hall. *Family Fortunes: Men and Women of the English Middle Class 1780–1850*. London: Hutchinson, 1987.

Feather, John. *A History of British Publishing*. London: Croom Helm, 1988.

Handover, P. M. *Printing in London from 1476 to Modern Times*. London: George Allen and Unwin Ltd, 1960.

Howse, Ernest M. *Saints in Politics: The 'Clapham Sect' and the Growth of Freedom*. London: George Allen and Unwin, 1953.

Martin, Roger H. *Evangelicals United: Ecumenical Stirrings in Pre-Victorian Britain 1795–1830*. Metuchen, N.J.: Scarecrow Press, 1983.

McKenzie, Donald Francis. *Bibliography and the Sociology of Texts. The Panizzi Lectures 1985*. London: British Library, 1986.

Mumby, Frank A. and Ian Norrie. *Publishing and Bookselling*. London: Cape, 1974.

Myers, Robin and Michael Harris, eds. *Development of the English Book Trade, 1700–1899*. Oxford: Oxford Polytechnic Press, 1981.

Plant, Marjorie. *The English Book Trade: An Economic History of the Making and Sale of Books*. 3rd edn, London: George Allen and Unwin, 1974.

Sutcliffe, Peter. *The Oxford University Press: An Informal History*. Oxford; Clarendon Press, 1978.

Webb, Robert K. *The British Working Class Reader, 1790–1848: Literacy and Social Tension*. New York: Kelley, 1971. First published 1955.

INDEX